THE OTHER HALF OF GENDER

THE OTHER HALF OF GENDER

Men's Issues in Development

Edited by
Ian Bannon
Maria C. Correia

THE WORLD BANK

ISBN-10: 0-8213-6505-3
ISBN-13: 978-0-8213-6505-2
eISBN: 0-8213-6506-1
DOI: 10.1596/978-0-8213-6505-2

Library of Congress Cataloging-in-Publication Data

The other half of gender : men's issues in development / edited by Ian Bannon and Maria
C. Correia
      p. cm
     Includes bibliographic references and index.
     ISBN-13: 978-0-8213-6505-2
     ISBN-10: 0-8213-6505-3
  1. Men—Developing countries. 2. Community development—Developing countries.
3. Economic development projects—Developing countries. I. Bannon, Ian. II. Correia,
Maria.

HQ1090.7.D44O84 2006
305.3109172'4—dc22

2006045195

Contents

Foreword

For years, poverty was viewed primarily as an economic phenomenon—people lacking sufficient resources to meet their most basic needs. But in recent years, the concept of poverty has broadened to encompass multiple dimensions, ranging from empowerment, voice, and inclusion to accountability of institutions and lack of security. Gender, however, has stubbornly remained a one-sided topic, with the focus firmly on women as the discriminated, disenfranchised group. Men are seen as the guilty party, lurking ominously in the background. Little effort has been devoted to understanding men's possible motivations, let alone their own gendered conditions.

As with other development agencies, the World Bank took an early interest in the situation of women. In 1977, it appointed a women in development adviser and in 1986, it established the Women in Development Unit, which, as the term implies, squarely focused on women. In 1994, however, the Bank adopted a new operational policy acknowledging that, to reduce poverty effectively and sustainably, development assistance needed to address the differential impact of development interventions on women and men. The new policy marked a shift from an approach focused exclusively on women and girls to a broader integration of gender issues into Bank assistance to increase women's participation in development. Despite the policy change, as with other development agencies and institutions, gender has in practice continued to focus on the plight of women. Masculinity, as a gendered construct, has been largely absent from the development and gender literature and discourse.

However, a more balanced approach is beginning to emerge that also seeks to shed light on the male side of the equation. This is a positive development for women and the gender community to the degree that men are seen as responsible for the negative conditions that affect women and the obstacles they face. But it is more than this. There is also an undeniable reality that men merit understanding in their own right. In recent years, scholars and the media have begun to raise awareness of the development issues faced by boys and men in developed countries. As discussed throughout this volume, there is an increasing, though still tentative, interest in developing countries in the need to involve men and in exploring issues of masculinity as they interact with the development process.

This volume contributes to the small, albeit growing, literature on men and gender in the context of development. It is in no way an exhaustive look; rather, it provides a collection of research and think pieces that examine the way development affects men. It aims to expand the debate and discourse on gender and development to encompass men and to identify the critical knowledge and data gaps that can help us better understand men and concepts of masculinity. With a more complete understanding of development as a gendered process that impacts both men and women, we hope ultimately to influence policy design and implementation that can move us closer to the goal of gender equity.

The social development community—with its focus on inclusion and social cohesion—is committed to this broad-based view of gender. We believe that the time has come to better understand men from a gender perspective, for the benefit of men, women (from whom and with whom men gain so much of their identity), future generations, and society as a whole.

Steen Lau Jorgensen
Director
Social Development Department
World Bank

Acknowledgments

We are grateful to many colleagues and friends who encouraged us to put together this volume. We particularly appreciate the continuous support we received from Guillermo Perry, chief economist of the World Bank's Latin America and the Caribbean Region, who was convinced that a more balanced approach to gender would lead to improved lives for both men and women, and who encouraged this work from its outset. We also thank Wendy Cunningham, Navtej Dhillon, Caroline Kende-Robb, Michael Kimmel, William Maloney, Peter Morgan, Dan Owen, Pia Peeters, Lawrence Salmen, and Benjamin Weil, all of whom contributed in different ways and at different stages to the production of this book. A special thanks to our production editor, Dana Vorisek, for invaluable assistance in shaping the different contributions into a cohesive volume. Finally, we gratefully acknowledge the financial support of the Norwegian and Finnish governments, which funded different chapters of this book and have, over the years, generously supported innovative work in the World Bank through the Trust Fund for Environmentally and Socially Sustainable Development and the Trust Fund for Gender Mainstreaming.

Contributors

Mary Amuyunzu-Nyamongo holds a Ph.D. in Social Anthropology (University of Cambridge, 1994). She is currently the Executive Director of the African Institute for Health and Development (AIHD), based in Nairobi, Kenya. She has been involved in a range of research and program activities in Burkina Faso, Ethiopia, Ghana, Kenya, Malawi, Tanzania, and Uganda. She has published on a range of health and development areas, including child health, HIV/AIDS, urban poverty, adolescents and youth, gender, and health in general.

Ian Bannon is the Manager of the Conflict Prevention and Reconstruction Unit in the World Bank's Social Development Department. He is an economist with an extensive career in the World Bank, having worked in Africa, Latin America and the Caribbean, and South Asia. He has researched and written on gender, education, private investment, child health, natural resources, mental health, and the links between conflict and development. His recent publications include *Natural Resources and Violent Conflict: Options and Actions* (coedited with Paul Collier, World Bank 2003) and *Gender, Conflict, and Development* (cowritten with Tsjeard Bouta and Georg Frerks, World Bank 2005).

Gary Barker is Chief Executive of Instituto Promundo—an NGO based in Rio de Janeiro, Brazil, that works in gender equality, violence prevention, HIV/AIDS, and youth development. He has coordinated research and program development on the socialization of young men in Africa, Asia, Latin America and the Caribbean, and North America, in collaboration with international and national organizations. His most recent publication is *Dying to be Men: Youth, Masculinity and Social Exclusion* (Routledge 2005).

Barry Chevannes is a Professor of Social Anthropology at the University of the West Indies, Mona, Jamaica. He is a leading expert on the Rastafari movement in

Jamaica and has also published on Caribbean culture and masculinity. His work includes the 1999 Grace Kennedy Foundation Lecture, "What We Sow and What We Reap: Problems in the Cultivation of Male Identity in Jamaica," and the book *Learning to be a Man: Culture, Socialization and Gender Identity in Five Caribbean Communities* (University of the West Indies 2001).

Maria C. Correia is Manager of the Multi-Country Demobilization and Reintegration (of ex-combatants) Program in the Africa Region of the World Bank. For almost a decade, she led the World Bank's efforts to address gender issues in Latin America and the Caribbean. Over her career, she has researched and written on gender across a range of sectors, including agriculture and rural development, education, health, and labor markets, as well as youth and social development. Her recent publications include *The Economics of Gender in Mexico: Work, Family, State and Market* (coedited with Elizabeth Katz) and *Caribbean Youth Development* (cowritten with Wendy Cunningham).

Paul Francis is Senior Social Development Officer in the Africa Department of the International Monetary Fund. He has worked on the integration of social development and conflict perspectives into policy and operations in a variety of institutional environments, including the World Bank, the United Kingdom's Department for International Development, and United Nations agencies. He has published on a range of development issues, including social capital, decentralization, rural poverty, and common property management.

Carlos Iván García Suárez is a Colombian writer and communications-education specialist. He is an international gender consultant and founder and member of the Men and Masculinities Collective in Bogotá. His publications include "Edugénero," a pedagogical series on research for changes in gender relations in educational institutions. He has also coauthored publications on masculinity, gender and domestic violence, children's sexual abuse, prostitution, and gender and sexuality. He is currently a Ph.D. candidate in social sciences, children, and youth.

Fredy Hernán Gómez Alcaraz is a Colombian sociologist. He works as a researcher, consultant, and trainer in the areas of gender and masculinity, reproductive and sexual health, violence prevention, and human rights. He is associated with the School of Gender Studies at the National University of Colombia and has worked in the capacity of advisor to numerous organizations, including the United Nations Population Fund (UNFPA) and the Programa de Promoción de Derechos y Redes Constructoras de Paz de la Consejería Presidencial de Programas Especiales. He has authored and coauthored numerous publications on themes such as gender and social change, male sexual and reproductive health rights, masculinities in Colombia, and masculinities and domestic violence.

Joyce P. Jacobsen is Andrews Professor of Economics at Wesleyan University in Middletown, Connecticut. Her research lies mainly in the area of labor economics, including migration, sex segregation, and the effects of intermittent labor market attachment on women's earnings. She is author of *The Economics of Gender* (Blackwell, second edition, 1998) and coauthor (with Gil Skillman) of *Labor Markets and Employment Relationships* (Blackwell 2004). She received a Ph.D. in Economics from Stanford University, an M.Sc. in Economics from the London School of Economics, and an A.B. from Harvard University.

José Olavarría is a Professor and Researcher at the Facultad Latinoamericana de Ciencias Sociales (FLACSO) in Chile, where within the area of gender he is responsible for research on men and masculinities. He has worked and published widely on a range of issues, including gender, men and masculinity, labor and paternity, reproductive and sexual health, youth and education, and gender mainstreaming in public health. He is a Ph.D. candidate in social sciences at the University of Buenos Aires.

Christine Ricardo is Senior Officer for the Gender and Health Program of Instituto Promundo, a Brazilian NGO. She coordinates an international initiative for the promotion of young women's empowerment and sexual and reproductive health, and she supports the development and dissemination of programs to engage young men in the promotion of gender equity and health. She holds an Sc.M. in Population and International Health from the Harvard School of Public Health and has extensive experience as a volunteer for organizations providing mentoring and other support services for women and children. Prior to joining Promundo, she worked for a non-profit organization in Boston, Massachusetts, that promotes equal access to educational opportunities for youth in low-income communities.

Paul Richards holds the Chair in Technology and Agrarian Development at the Wageningen University in the Netherlands and is Professor of Anthropology at University College London. He recently led teams carrying out social assessments of postwar Liberia and Sierra Leone for the World Bank. His publications include the edited collection *No Peace, No War: An Anthropology of Contemporary Armed Conflict* (Currey & Ohio University Press 2004).

Marc Sommers is an Associate Research Professor of Humanitarian Studies at the Fletcher School, Tufts University. He is also a Research Fellow at Boston University's African Studies Center. He has researched and written on at-risk children and youth, education, conflict negotiation, child soldier, urbanization, human rights, coordination, and security issues in war and postwar contexts. His work has taken him to 20 war-affected countries. His recent publications include *Islands of Education: Schooling, Civil War and the Southern Sudanese* (UNESCO 2005). An earlier book, *Fear in Bongoland: Burundi Refugees in Urban Tanzania* (Berghahn 2001), received the Margaret Mead Award for 2003.

Introduction

IAN BANNON AND MARIA C. CORREIA

Why Men and Development?

"With a few notable exceptions, men are rarely explicitly mentioned in gender policy documents. Where men do appear, they are generally seen as obstacles to women's development: men must surrender their positions of dominance for women to become empowered. The superiority of women as hard working, reliable, trustworthy, socially responsible, caring and co-operative is often asserted; whilst men on the other hand are frequently portrayed as lazy, violent, promiscuous and irresponsible drunkards" (Cleaver 2000, p. 1).

Conceptual Shifts from Women to Gender

In the 1970s, feminist activists, writers, and scholars made gender a visible social construct in development. Prompted by the 1970 release of Esther Boserup's then seminal book *Women's Role in Economic Development*, academics and the development community began to see women in a new light. As a result, the earlier focus on women's role in family welfare, characteristic of the 1950s and 1960s, shifted to women's economic role and their active participation in development. The term "women in development" (WID) came to encompass this new model (Moser 1993).

By the 1980s, the limitations of the WID approach had become evident, and "gender and development" (GAD) replaced WID as the dominant paradigm. GAD offered a new way of tackling women's subordination by examining socially and historically constructed gender relations between women and men, rather than treating women in isolation from men (Moser 1993). Conceptually, GAD

xvii

distinguished sex (a biological construct) from gender (a social construct), thereby demonstrating the dynamic nature of women's and men's roles and relations. But while the theoretical underpinnings of WID and GAD were clearly different, and GAD brought a more sophisticated view of the situation of women, development practice on gender remained virtually unchanged (Cornwall 1997). In operational terms, the change implied only a simple shift in vocabulary.

Why Men and Development?

Since the 1990s, a new impetus has emerged to understand the male side of gender and the concept of masculinity. Originally raised in intellectual circles and by the media in countries such as the United Kingdom and the United States, the interest has been spawned by concerns over rising male unemployment, the declining proportion of men in higher education, and boys' underperformance in primary and secondary schools. Research and writings on men and masculinity in the developing world have also begun to appear, particularly in relation to reproductive and sexual health programming and HIV/AIDS. The literature reflects a belated recognition that men are also gendered beings and have gender identities.

Over the last decade, men and gender have also become more visible in international development forums. In the Beijing Declaration, adopted by the Fourth World Conference on Women in 1995, governments expressed their resolve to encourage men's full participation in promoting gender equality. The role of men and boys has also been addressed by other intergovernmental forums, including the World Summit on Social Development (1995) and its review session (2000), as well as the special session of the General Assembly on HIV/AIDS of 2001 (Flood 2004). More recently, in March 2004, the 48th session of the Commission on the Status of Women (in New York) adopted as one of its themes the role of men and boys in contributing to gender equality (Flood 2004).

Despite these trends and new interest on men, gender work continues to focus almost solely on women. Among developing country governments, development agencies, and civil society organizations alike, when we talk of gender, we mean women. If men are discussed at all, it is usually in relation to their role in advancing women's equality, rather than men's gender issues in and of themselves.

Gender advocates will argue that the continued priority of women makes sense. They assert that until the disadvantages faced by girls and women are substantially redressed, the needs of boys and men are of secondary importance. Indeed, although the last part of the 20th century saw considerable improvement in the status of women and gender equality in developed countries and, to a lesser extent, in developing countries, women and girls remain disadvantaged relative to men and boys in a myriad of ways.

But this misses the point. The inclusion of men in gender work is not about transferring benefits or attention from women and girls to boys and men, but rather making interventions more meaningful. Women's well-being often cannot improve without including men because gender is relational; it concerns relationships between men and women that are subject to negotiations (Cleaver 2003). Addressing gender issues, including those that disadvantage women, thus requires understanding the perceptions and positions of both women and men. With respect to men, this means understanding masculinities, i.e., what it takes to be a man or ways of being a man. Lack of comprehension of the social constructs that govern men's (and women's) behavior and gender relations can undermine actions directed at women or render them ineffective.

There are other reasons for including men in gender work. First, women are not always the losers and men are not always the winners in gender systems. Generalizing about men and women, therefore, risks overlooking gender-specific inequities and vulnerabilities, for example, the power that elite older women exert over younger or poorer women or the influence that elders might have over young men (Cornwall 2000). Second, globalization, economic change, poverty, and social change have eroded men's traditional role as providers, causing men to seek affirmation of their masculinity in other ways (for example, unsafe sexual practices and domestic and social violence), which affects not only men but also their partners, families, and society at large.

Objectives and Origin

This volume provides a contribution to the nascent but growing interest in male gender and masculinity issues as it relates to development policy and practice. While in no way comprehensive, it attempts to add insights into questions such as: How do gender constructs negatively affect men and how do these issues vary across countries and cultures? In the context of developing countries, what are the central gender issues that affect men? Are men's issues important only to the extent that they advance women's equality, or are they important in and of themselves? If so—and given the extent of gender disadvantages still faced by women— what is the relative importance of men's issues and what should be done about them?

This book had its origins in an overview paper on gender and men's issues prepared for the World Bank in 2002 that generated considerable interest within the organization. Following the overview paper, the Bank commissioned a series of papers on men in Latin America and the Caribbean to better understand how gender issues played out in the region. The research focus then shifted to Sub-Saharan Africa to learn how gender issues vary across continents and cultures.

The chapters that follow attempt to bring the gender and development debate full circle. From a focus on empowering women during the late 20th century, the first years of the new millennium are witnessing a wider examination of the entire spectrum of gender and development, with the goal, as Joyce Jacobsen notes, of moving "closer to a more holistic gender framework that addresses gender as it pertains to both women and men and examines gender as a system." The inclusion of male gender issues in the gender framework is likely to be the third major evolution in the gender paradigm, following on WID and GAD.

Organization of the Book

Men and gender issues are analyzed in this collection from a variety of approaches and perspectives. The book starts with an overview chapter that examines gender issues across countries and then moves into specific topics, first in Latin America and the Caribbean and then in Sub-Saharan Africa. A final chapter summarizes some of the common messages emerging from the chapters and suggests policy directions. Here we briefly summarize the main findings of each chapter.

In chapter 1, "Men's Issues in Development," Joyce Jacobsen examines available country-level data from developed and developing countries and identifies three issues in development worthy of concern for men, namely, the destruction of human capital through communicable disease, violence, substance abuse, and institutionalization; the disadvantages in human capital accumulation (formal schooling); and new strains on men's work and family life as a result of changing gender roles. She finds that cumulatively, men's "human capital"—defined as anything increasing a person's potential to be a capable, productive member of society—is already endangered by higher (vis-à-vis women) rates of infant mortality, violence (of which men account for the vast majority of victims and perpetrators), substance abuse, and addiction. Men also have lower life expectancies than women. Men's marginalization in the workplace—due to women's increasingly strong standing—threatens traditional notions of masculinity, which further undermines men's human capital. Women face both increasing hostility from their male partners and the burden of new pressure as they attempt to retain their status in the workplace and provide most of the care within their households with little additional help from men.

Chapter 2, "Men's Gender Relations, Identity, and Work-Family Balance in Latin America," by José Olavarría, discusses how economic systems affect and infringe on couples, family, and gender relations in Latin America. It begins with a historical summary of the social order at the turn of the 20th century, explaining how a patriarchic system was inspired by Napoleonic principles that segregated the domestic (private) and the productive (public) spheres. Under this system, gender roles were segregated, and men and women had clearly prescribed roles. This paradigm no longer works in the 21st century. The chapter shows how the structure of the modern economy, with its emphasis on multitasking and outsourcing, pose a risk to men's security by undermining the traditional patriarchal nuclear family and men's traditional identity as sole figure of power and authority within a family. Countries—particularly in Latin America—therefore need to address the new imperatives of the modern economy and the resulting changes in the nuclear family. If work is the coordinating axis of people's lives, the issue at stake is how to reconcile work and private life so that different types of families (biparental; monoparental; or including grandparents, uncles/aunts, grandchildren, nephews/nieces, etc.) can remain a central presence in the organization of people's lives. Olavarría points to the need to open a public debate on work and family, with the goal of shedding more light on the process of economic globalization, the impact of globalization on people and families, trends of future families, and the role of the state.

In chapter 3, "Men's Participation as Fathers in Latin America and the Caribbean," Gary Barker analyzes the axis of masculine identity expressed through fatherhood. Based on a review of the theoretical and empirical research on the role of men in families and children's development and well-being, he affirms that men's participation as fathers matters. Fathers' presence, for example, is generally positive for children and household income; men's greater participation in child care and domestic chores is also generally good for women. Moreover, men derive benefits from positive engagement as caregivers and fathers. The paper presents program, policy, and research considerations for governments in Latin America and the Caribbean as well as for development agencies. While evaluations of such programs are limited, Barker cautions us to avoid generalizations about what men (or women) want for themselves as members of a couple or of a family. He also notes that to provide the maximum benefit for families and individuals, we must listen to the voices of fathers, recognize their own needs and interests, and make clear how men will benefit when they are actively engaged as fathers.

Chapter 4, "The Role of Men in Families in the Caribbean," by Barry Chevannes, examines male marginalization in the Caribbean, with a focus on the family. By reviewing sociological and anthropological studies on the matrilineal structure of Caribbean families, Chevannes argues that the perception that men are morally dysfunctional is far from normative and that structural and cultural factors affecting men and women are critical in defining men as fathers. The chapter includes theories about the origins of the structure of the Caribbean family and describes various types of fathers based on their presence and absence in the household and their relationship with the mother of their children. A cross-cutting theme is that regardless of the type of family they belong to, all men see their role primarily as provider and often as disciplinarian, similar to the role of men in patriarchal families. The chapter also presents brief case studies to demonstrate the scope of possibilities in men's role as providers and to underline the important role men play as fathers regardless of whether they are "visiting" fathers or reside with their offspring. Fatherhood is important to men's sense of their own identity and for the well being of their children.

In chapter 5, "Masculinity and Violence in Colombia," Fredy Hernán Gómez Alcaraz and Carlos Iván García Suárez examine with a gender lens the complex scenario of violence in Colombia, a country plagued by chronic violence, arguing that masculinity is linked to the exertion of multiple forms of violence. The authors interpret and comment on masculine participation in social and private types of violence, focusing particularly on the intricate interrelation of being a criminal and a victim. They argue that peer pressure among men, the destabilization experienced by men in the face of social change, and the ancestral masculine exertion of power are factors that play a role in men's violent behaviors. The authors establish three complex and dynamic relational models between masculinity and the exertion of all types of violence. The chapter ends with a presentation of some of the recent actions taken in Colombia on the issue of masculine identities, which confirm that violence is an issue that concerns and affects all Colombian men. It proposes actions and interventions that could address and prevent violence. These recommendations could contribute to peace negotiations and postconflict policies aimed at deactivating certain aspects of masculinity addressed in this chapter. The hypothesis is applicable to other regions experiencing turmoil, ongoing conflict, and chronic violence, such as Sub-Saharan Africa and the Middle East.

Chapter 6, "Growing Up Poor and Male in the Americas," Gary Barker's second chapter in this volume, paints a vivid portrait of the attraction of low-income young men living in Rio de Janeiro, Brazil, to gangs and how this appeal is linked to gender constructs of manhood. Gangs in Rio meet the needs of this population that are ignored by the formal sectors of society. They provide income, a sense of belonging, and connection, needs that are often unfulfilled at home and in the community, as well as a sense of meaningful identity for young men with bleak futures. Sadly, education does not provide the same financial rewards for low-income youth as it does for youth in middle-income groups. Motivating young men in such low-income urban settings is difficult because class, race, and gender barriers, combined with limited social capital, hinder their employment opportunities. However, Barker provides us with several imperatives for addressing the masculine identity of these young men. He argues for policy and program development to encourage boys and young men to embrace nontraditional, alternative masculine identities that encourage reflection on gender relations and care for the self and others; he also advocates for discussions about gender masculinities in the classroom, the workplace, and in workforce training. Barker notes the importance of changing peer group and community norms. Finally, he finds reason to believe that these imperatives are attainable—gang involvement, violence, and callous attitudes toward women are not inevitable male destinies. The plurality of male identities, even in low-income settings, holds the key to understanding and promoting change.

In chapter 7, "Fearing Sub-Saharan Africa's Young Men," Marc Sommers sets the case of Rwanda within the larger context of Sub-Saharan Africa's urbanization and growing male youth population. He offers a critique of the youth bulge thesis, which paints Sub-Saharan Africa's male urban youth as a menace to the continent's development and a primary source of instability. He points out that contrary to the dire predictions that emerge from the urban youth bulge approach, Sub-Saharan Africa's conflicts have been rural-based. In his analysis of Rwanda's youth before the genocide, he focuses on land scarcity, lack of opportunities, and the entrapment of young men in grinding rural poverty as contributing factors to the mobilization of youth to carry out the genocide and perpetrate unspeakable acts of violence. The chapter also notes that while the government recognizes the importance of addressing the needs of young men, current approaches are underfunded and do not address the underlying factors that contributed to the mobilization of youth during the genocide. Sommers argues that urbanization and migration to cities represents an outlet for difficult conditions in rural Rwanda, especially the scarcity of land, but notes a prevailing bias in government and donors that assumes that youth must be integrated in rural areas. Programs instead need to work where youth are (increasingly, in cities) rather than where donors and the government think they should be (rural areas). Coupled with better targeted youth programs in urban areas, Sommers argues for the need to include young women in youth groups and programming in Rwanda today.

Chapter 8, "Young Men and the Construction of Masculinity in Sub-Saharan Africa," by Gary Barker and Christine Ricardo, applies a gender perspective to young men in Sub-Saharan Africa in examining two of the most salient issues in the region today: conflict and HIV/AIDS. Their analysis finds that a key requirement to attaining manhood in the region is achieving some level of financial independence, employment or income, and subsequently starting a family. Moreover, achieving manhood in the Sub-Saharan African context often depends on an older man—one who holds more power—deciding when a young man is able to achieve socially recognized manhood. Initiation practices, or rites of passage, are important factors in the socialization of boys and men throughout the region because sexual experience is frequently associated with achieving a socially recognized manhood. In some settings in the region, young men's participation in conflict and use of violence become ways to obtain empowerment, or essentially a means to achieving and wielding power for young men who perceive no other way to achieve it. Other forms of violence prevalent in Sub-Saharan Africa are clearly linked to masculinity, including gang activity, vigilante groups, and ethnic-based conflicts. Throughout the study, the authors make references to alternative, nonviolent versions of manhood, to elements of traditional socialization in Sub-Saharan Africa that promote nonviolence and more gender equitable attitudes on the part of young men, and to forms of socialization that reduce the vulnerabilities and violence of young men. They argue that the challenge in promoting changes in gender norms is to tap into voices of change and pathways to change that exist in Sub-Saharan Africa.

In chapter 9, "Young Men and Gender in War and Postwar Reconstruction," Paul Richards traces the historical and social roots of the marginalization of youth in West Africa's Upper Guinean forest. He discusses the region's history of slavery, which continues to shape social relations and traditional customs to this day, especially the role of traditional chiefs and customary law in the exploitation of youth labor and the role of "big men" and polygamy in trapping young men in a perpetual state of youth—unable to marry (and hence to be recognized as an adult) and subject to fines for adultery, which they must pay through a form of indentured labor. The traditional sharecropping system (*metayage*) further trapped young men in a world of circular migration between alluvial mining and subsistence farming in the fringes of the Guinean forest. Richards argues that the roots of conflict in West Africa represented a struggle between the chiefly classes and the young men whose labor they exploited as farmers and diamond laborers. This division of labor is deeply embedded in the history of postslavery social institutions, underpinned by systems for access to land, skill formation, marriage, and justice. It leads to the formation of a large underclass in which young men (and women) have no stakes or commitment to society at large. The violence that erupts, its "dramatur-gical expression" in Richards' terminology, is particularly fierce, taking on the char-acter of a crusade against society itself. Richards ends the chapter by suggesting the need to focus on the jobs and skills of marginalized youth, reform of the *metayage* system and land-leasing arrangements, improvements in the quality and coverage of education (especially in rural areas), reform of marriage and property rights, and a call for governments and donors alike to take youth and gender policies and programs seriously.

Chapter 10, "Collapsing Livelihoods and the Crisis of Masculinity in Rural Kenya," by Mary Amuyunzu-Nyamongo and Paul Francis, explores the gender-related impacts of social and economic changes in parts of rural Kenya. The authors find that the decline of the livestock economy, reduced opportunities for migrant labor, the collapse of agricultural industries, and the poor performance of the coop-erative movement in the last two decades have led to high levels of poverty, which in turn have resulted in a decline in men's ability to fulfill the role of provider. Drawing on both quantitative and qualitative data collected in 2005 in six districts of Kenya, Amuyunzu-Nyamongo and Francis find that as livelihood systems have become increasingly strained, women have responded by becoming more involved in income-generating activities and petty trading, and they have organized into groups to pool resources for investment. Men's loss of livelihood, in contrast, has undermined their central role as provider, led to their loss in power, negatively affected their self esteem and identity, and led to their marginalization and disen-franchisement. These shifting gender roles within the households and communities and the corollary frustrations faced by men have increased the incidence and sever-ity of conflict and domestic violence, alcoholism, and family instability, as well as growing levels of crime in rural areas. Important intergenerational effects were also observed from the loss of positive male role models, learned aggression from wit-nessing violence and increased tensions, and conflict between adults and children. One interesting finding is that initiatives by government and development agencies to emancipate women have contributed to men's marginalization, and in the process, inadvertently increased women's work burden and violence against them.

Lastly, chapter 11, "Gender and Its Discontents," by Maria C. Correia and Ian Bannon, draws some general recommendations from the volume and presents emerging approaches that offer potential for addressing male gender issues and applying a more inclusive gender perspective—"men-streaming" development. Although in recent years there has been increasing academic and policy interest in the need to involve men in gender work and in exploring issues of masculinity, especially in some developed countries, there is far less clarity on how this should be done. The last chapter thus explores possible points of entry for work on men and development issues.

Abbreviations

ABC approach	Abstinence, partner reduction, and condom use
ANC	African National Congress (South Africa)
CDF	Civil Defense Forces (Sierra Leone)
CEDE	Center for Economic Development Studies
CERAI	Centres d'Enseignement Rural et Artisanal Intégrés (Rwanda) [Integrated Centers for Rural and Artisanal Education]
CIA	Central Intelligence Agency (United States)
DABS	Administrative Department of Social Welfare (Colombia)
DALY	Disability-adjusted life year
ELN	National Liberation Army (Colombia)
EPL	People's Liberation Army (Colombia)
FARC	Colombian Revolutionary Armed Forces (Colombia)
FGD	Focus group discussion
GAD	Gender and development
HALE	Healthy life expectancy
IDB	Inter-American Development Bank
IDP	Internally displaced person
ILO	International Labour Organization
INML y CF	National Institute of Legal Medicine and Forensic Sciences (Colombia)

IPPF	International Planned Parenthood Federation
LRA	Lord's Resistance Army (Uganda)
MAP	Men as Partners (South Africa)
MIJESPOC	Ministry of Youth, Sports, and Culture (Rwanda)
NCO	Noncommissioned officer
NGO	Nongovernmental organization
RPF	Rwandan Patriotic Front
RUF	Revolutionary United Front (Sierra Leone)
STI	Sexually transmitted infection
UNAIDS	Joint United Nations Programme on AIDS
UNDP	United Nations Development Programme
UNFPA	United Nations Population Fund
UNICEF	United Nations Children's Fund
WDI	*World Development Indicators*
WHO	World Health Organization
WID	Women in development

Men's Issues in Development

JOYCE P. JACOBSEN

Why Are Men's Issues in Development Important?

This chapter introduces readers to men's issues in development. It considers what these issues are, substantiates their existence, and considers how particular policy interventions within the broader gender and development agenda might address them. The issues are treated in a global context to emphasize their consistency across developed and developing regions of the world. This is not meant to deemphasize their importance in developing countries, but rather to emphasize the unmet needs of men throughout the world.

Due to its objective, this chapter is primarily descriptive. It attempts to summarize available gender-disaggregated data to illustrate men's issues and references, selected research, and country studies. As such, it could be considered an annotated outline and a starting point for further research and potential policy interventions to address men's issues in development. The remainder of this section seeks to address the question of why we should study men's issues. The central part of the chapter surveys relevant data and studies regarding men's issues in development. The concluding section offers a set of recommendations on future research and policy directions.

The Undertreatment of Men's Issues

Two important intellectual trends involving men have come about in the development community over the last decade. One is increased attention within the development community to the link between gender and development policy. Gender activists may reasonably believe that not enough resources are devoted to implementation of the policies and practices they advocate, and that there is still a long way to go in effectively mainstreaming gender across development activities. However, an extensive body of literature from inside and outside the large development institutions is devoted to exploring the role of gender in policy implementation and distributional outcomes. A number of relatively noncontroversial

themes have emerged from this literature and the development community, including the problem of domestic violence, the need for equal schooling and literacy
for girls and boys, and the assertion of female control over reproductive decisions.
The gender and development community has been able to rally behind these and
other themes.

In addition, there is a body of focused research to support this agenda. In recent
years, the World Bank has consistently highlighted gender issues in its annual *World
Development Report*. The Bank also recently published a thorough discussion of gender issues in development (World Bank 2001a), a strategy to mainstream gender in
its work (World Bank 2002a), and an evaluation of Bank gender policy (World Bank
2005d). Through its annual *Human Development Report*, the United Nations
Development Programme (UNDP) has done much to develop and publicize the statistical measurement of gender inequality, including with tools such as its gender-
related development index and its gender-empowerment measure.

The second trend is increasing popular and scholarly interest in men's issues and
the concept of masculinity in a number of developed countries, particularly
Australia, the United Kingdom, and the United States. This interest has included
economic concerns regarding increased male unemployment, particularly long-
term or structural unemployment, concerns regarding the reduced proportion of
men in higher education, and concerns regarding how boys fare in primary and
secondary education. It has also included social concerns regarding high rates of
male violence, for men commit acts of violence in far greater numbers than
women, but has also called attention to the fact that violence disproportionately
claims men as victims (except for domestic violence). Interest in the role of men
has also encouraged efforts to address issues related to fatherhood and men's reproductive health; Australia's Department of Health and Family Services has taken the
lead on efforts involving the latter.

Many of the writers and researchers on men's issues are academic social scientists whose writings display familiarity with feminist approaches to social science
issues. This vein of work is not antifeminist, but rather it seeks to extend the insights
developed regarding female roles into a complementary discussion of male roles.
Work on men and masculinity includes writings by psychologists such as Pollack
(1998, and other works) and Connell (1995, and other works). Sociologists (including Kimmel [1996] and several other single-author works and edited volumes) and
organizational behaviorists (Hearn 1992) have also weighed in, along with political scientists, anthropologists, and literary criticism scholars. Numerous other
recent works have appeared in a popularizing vein, including Faludi (1999). Work
by non-English-speaking authors is less common, but Welzer-Lang (2000) has
made recent contributions in French; Ghoussoub and Sinclair-Webb (2000) have
written about male issues in a Middle Eastern context; and a number of anthropological studies on masculinity have focused on cultural contexts (Gutmann
1996, regarding Mexican men).

These writings are generally of a qualitative nature, often based on case studies
and with no particular focus on ensuring representative sampling. This approach is

appropriate given the particular aims of these works, namely to illustrate in an exploratory way the issues men face in conforming to—or attempting to conform to—particular normative versions of masculinity. Indeed, case studies served to give voice to men and illuminate their lives in ways that were missing from the stylized picture of a man and maleness in early gender studies.

What has been generally missing is work that expands the substantial intersection between these literatures. Works combining these two intellectual trends are few and relatively recent, which is not surprising. Early gender-in-development approaches were in some cases openly hostile to men and were directed at correcting and offsetting male biases in development, although this approach has reversed in current work.[1] For instance, Moser (1993) states that gender planning allows one "to recognize that because women and men have different positions within the household and different control over resources, they not only play different and changing roles in society, but also often have different needs" (p. 15).

Yet a reading of the relevant literature and Web sites produced by the gender groups in major international development agencies and nongovernmental organizations reveals little focus on male issues. Oxfam (in the United Kingdom) is a notable exception; it has several publications and projects focusing on male issues among its publications (Sweetman 1997, 2001b). At UNDP, the Gender in Development group recently wrote a "manifesto" for considering masculine roles in development contexts (Greig, Kimmel, and Lang 2000). As discussed later in this chapter, the Joint United Nations Programme on AIDS (UNAIDS) and the World Health Organization (WHO) are attempting to integrate men's issues into HIV/AIDS programs and policies.

There are obvious reasons why, in practice, gender in development continues to be largely about women in development. There is no question that women are disadvantaged in numerous ways throughout the developing world, both in absolute terms and relative to men. This chapter in no way argues otherwise. However, there are specific areas of concern, some new and some very old, that relate to men.

Although the focus of this chapter is on issues that have a direct impact on the well-being of men, it is also true that many of these issues are inseparable from the question of how they affect the well-being of women. While recognizing this second factor, the chapter nonetheless argues that the direct effects of men's issues should be considered. Any formal and comprehensive analysis of the benefits and costs of particular policies, however, should also take into account indirect effects on the well-being of women, and sometimes children. For instance, a decrease in violence in a society will undoubtedly provide gains to all demographic groups. In addition, policies to aid males are not advocated as either/or alternatives. For example, arguments that boys are underrepresented in subsets of an education system are not arguments for raising boys' participation by reducing the representation of girls, but rather that boys' representation should be increased relative to their age cohort. Programs that reduce male unemployment at the expense of female employment would be similarly inappropriate. Paying attention to both male and female issues need not be inconsistent to the extent that development means expanding the pie so that everyone can have a bigger absolute part of a society's resources.

The Symmetries and Diversities of Men's Issues

There is remarkable symmetry in the way that women's issues have been discussed in developed and developing country contexts. To give just one example, the problem of poor female-headed households has been approached using similar arguments and policies in different organizations and in different parts of the world. In contrast, men's issues have not been approached in the same way in developed and developing countries.

While developed countries—particularly Australia, the United Kingdom and the United States—appear to be the main source of recent interest in male issues and masculinity, a number of men's issues have remarkable consistency across countries, whether they are developed or developing. This is particularly true of health and violence, where researchers in developing countries—in particular Brazil, Chile, and Mexico—have been on the leading edge.

Stating that there is consistency across developed and developing contexts in men's issues is not the same as arguing that there is an essentialist nature to male patterns. Indeed, while biological differences appear to contribute to these patterns, the very lack of constancy in statistical measurements related to men's issues across societies makes clear that social context is critical. Since attention paid to men's issues is disproportionately based in developed country experiences, these issues appear almost as luxuries if taken up in a developing country context.

But this could also be argued for women's issues.

Why is it the case that men's issues are more likely to appear in the context of developed countries?

One possibility is that men's issues, to the extent that their impact is felt disproportionately among low-status men (whether measured by income, caste, race, ethnicity, social class, or other identity markers), are more likely to be invisible in societies where low-status persons are relatively more disenfranchised (even when low-status persons are more numerous). Indeed, it may be that low-status males are less enfranchised than low-status women within social and political structures. This is a controversial point that is not easily proven by available research. Indeed, many people have argued the opposite. For instance, in the introduction to a recent volume on poverty in developing countries, García (2000) focuses on how women's poverty is different from men's and in general makes the case that poor women are systematically worse off than poor men. Çagatay (1998) also argues that women are poorer than men and that poor women are poorer than poor men. Poverty is generally measured on a household basis, a point Çagatay emphasizes to argue that female-headed households are generally the poorest of the poor. However, this may mean that single persons, i.e., men unattached to any type of family structure, might be disproportionately overlooked in aggregate household data. Indeed, the presence of a large number of female-headed households in a society implies that a large number of men have migrated in search of work or who are imprisoned, single, or deceased. These outcomes are not necessarily favorable to the male side of the equation.

The concept of alpha and beta males has come to social science from animal biology, particularly the study of primates. Consider the notion that beta males may be systematically overlooked within their social structures (or within the social structures on whose sidelines they lurk). These may include men who are homeless, alcoholic, imprisoned, mentally ill, disabled, or just plain socially inept. The image conveyed by a range of derogatory terms in English—geek, loser, nerd—is clearly that of a male.

Indeed, much of the focus on gender inequality in contemporary societies comes from comparing the alpha, or "winner" males, with the situation of women. While it is true that the overall gender earnings ratio is skewed in favor of men in all societies, some of that skewing is the result of disproportionately high earnings among the highest-earning males. In the United States, for example, there is greater earnings inequality among men than among women (Jacobsen 1991). In turn, many of the male-dominated jobs women aspire to tend to be society's high-earning jobs. For instance, much of the media discussion regarding women's progress in the United States is about how women can get around the "glass ceiling" in business management. Other male-dominated occupations get little attention. Women (and men) aspire to be lawyers, doctors, scientists, business executives—i.e., high-paying, prestigious occupations—not garbage collectors, miners, or butchers.

This potentially systematic invisibility of marginalized men is worrisome because it can lead to systematic omission of these men from published statistics (statistics that are often not disaggregated by various demographic subgroups). While disaggregating these statistics may reveal that there is less of a problem than we think, without such knowledge the potential problem remains unaddressed.

This focus on winning and losing men in a social structure leads one to question whether there is a single concept of maleness or masculinity. Perhaps there is one normative masculinity, or male model, to which all men attempt to conform, but only those who reach or approximate this model can become the winning males. This model would include, most critically for the current context, the notion that men do and should have power relative to women, and that they generally control the allocation and distributional functions of society.

The concern with defining but then breaking away from normative or hegemonic notions of masculinity is a major theme in the literature on men's issues. A focus on hegemonic masculine identity, to the extent it is understood to coexist with patriarchy, has led researchers to ignore "the social importance of critical but subtle variations within 'masculinity', many of which work against men" (Sampath 1997, p. 48). However, as Connell points out, "To recognize diversity in masculinities is not enough. We must also recognize the relations between the different kinds of masculinity: relations of alliance, dominance and subordination" (1995, p. 37). Separating the role of hegemonic masculinity from men allows one to critique masculinity but not necessarily men, so that it becomes clear that "it is not men per se, but certain ways of being and behaving, that are associated with dominance and power" (Cornwall 1997, p. 11). Indeed, studying men rather than masculinity brings attention to status, and to the connections between gender, age, race, and class (White 1997). As Sampath notes, "Research into the effects of patriarchy on women has been relatively thorough, but this may have deflected attention away from the fact that men are dominated by other men, and are denied alternative expressions that could be more benign to women. It is only with a recognition of the potential for a range of identities that the effect by men on men as well as women can be appreciated" (1997, p. 53).

Appreciating the non-monolithic nature of the male experience leads one naturally to concern for those men who suffer less favorable outcomes in any society, whether in a developed or a developing country. The next section identifies aggregate data in an attempt to highlight the men who are particularly disadvantaged within and across societies. This is difficult to do due to the highly aggregated nature of much of the internationally comparable data. However, by organizing statistics in a way that draws attention to cases where men apparently suffer disproportionately unfavorable outcomes relative to women, we may begin to shed some light on men's issues in development.

What Are Men's Issues in Development?

"The human male is, on most measures, more vulnerable than the female" (Kraemer 2000, p. 1609).

Erosion and Accumulation of Men's Human Capital

This chapter identifies two main types of issues related to men. One is ongoing strains in the process of accumulation and destruction or erosion of men's human capital, where human capital is broadly defined as any factor that increases a person's potential to be a capable, productive member of society. This includes health, general education, job-specific training, and even additional years of life. The second issue is the changes in roles and identities—within families, within the workforce, and within societies—that men currently face. These changes are taking place in both developing countries, as they transition from preindustrial to industrial economies, and in developed countries, as they transition to postindustrial economies. Development policies could conceivably affect one area with little effect on the other, although interrelationships are important to consider in the implementation of specific policies and programs.

A range of international data sources is used to illustrate the various issues in developed and developing countries, with reference to particular illustrative country cases when it is not possible to present a broadly available data source. While there are many shortcomings with using available data, it can still be useful in illustrating aggregate trends.

Erosion of Human Capital

Erosion of both men's and women's human capital occurs at an enormous pace in developing countries, and comes from numerous sources: disease, risk-taking, violence, and addictive/compulsive behavior, among others. Arguably, men's human capital is destroyed at a greater rate than women's. This section discusses accumulation, mainly in the context of the formal education sector, where it appears that the rate at which men are developing human capital is slowing relative to that of women. This difference in rate is not necessarily a bad thing if it is the result of greater accumulation by women, but in some cases it appears that men's rate of accumulation is slowing significantly. The accumulation and preservation of human capital is viewed here as a way of expanding human capabilities, although there are other approaches that do not view human capital as the most important aspect or measure of human capabilities (see, for example, Sen 1989).

There is increasing evidence from the medical and scientific communities that men are disadvantaged relative to women in terms of physical robustness. For this reason, the development community has taken an interest in health and mortality-related issues among men within a general context of gendered patterns and outcomes.[2] The data suggests that men face serious problems in the broad area of human capital erosion, often by their own hands. It is also clear that biological differences between men/boys and women/girls cannot account for the broad range of outcomes by sex across and within societies (see WHO 2000b). Hence there is clearly room for policy interventions to attempt to reduce the erosion of men's (and women's) human capital on numerous fronts.

LIFE EXPECTANCY AND MORTALITY RATES. Men generally have lower life expectancy at birth than women. Table 1.1, drawn from the World Bank's 2005 *World Development Indicators* (WDI), lists selected countries in decreasing order of the male-female differential in life expectancy. Countries from the former Soviet Union lead the list, with the highest negative differential between male and female life expectancy (12 years). Remarkably, women have greater or equal life expectancy in all but four of the 161 countries underlying table 1.1 (Maldives, Namibia, Qatar, and Zimbabwe). Perhaps more notably, the range of values for the male-female differential (a 14-year range, from −12 years to +2 years, with a median of −4), emphasizes how life expectancy by gender is not entirely biologically determined. Rather, life expectancy is affected by particular societal contexts.

Most countries have experienced a decline in male and female adult mortality rates since the mid-1960s. Female mortality rates, however, have dropped more rapidly than male mortality rates, in large part due to enormous reductions in maternal mortality. This has caused the male-female differential in mortality rate to be positive for the majority of countries. Notable exceptions to this pattern include a number of Eastern European countries, where male mortality has increased sharply (and in several cases the female mortality rate has also risen). And in Sub-Saharan Africa, the male rate has generally dropped but the female rate has risen.

Table 1.1 **Male and Female Life Expectancy, Selected Countries, 2003**

Country	Male	Female	Male-female
Highest male-female			
Russia	60	72	−12
Belarus	62	74	−12
Estonia	65	77	−12
Lithuania	66	78	−12
Kazakhstan	56	67	−11
Lowest male-female			
Nepal	60	60	0
Qatar	75	74	1
Namibia	41	40	1
Zimbabwe	39	38	1
Maldives	66	64	2
Median male-female			**−4**

Source: World Bank 2005b; WHO database.

INFANT MORTALITY RATES. Large declines in infant mortality since the mid-1960s have benefited both sexes. However, as table 1.2 indicates, there are still large differences in infant mortality rates by sex in most countries, with male children almost invariably affected by much higher mortality (the median male-female differential is seven deaths per thousand). The gender difference in mortality rates tends to shrink substantially in countries that succeed in decreasing average infant mortality rates, although a detailed examination of infant deaths in the United States shows a higher number of male than female deaths from a wide variety of causes, many of which are generally preventable (U.S. Department of Health and Human Services 2001).

CAN GENDER DIFFERENCES BE REDUCED? These data emphasize a point that is debated in the scientific literature as to degree but is largely ceded in substance: much of the male life expectancy gap is due to environmental factors, another large part due to lifestyle factors, and a smaller part can be attributed to heredity (Lang, Arnold, and Kupfer 1994). Nonetheless, a number of hereditary factors related to being male apparently affect not only death rates, but also more broadly defined robustness. There are numerous possible medical explanations for this intrinsic robustness differential: females have two cell lines (i.e., two X chromosomes; Christensen et al. 2000), differential constituency of lipids in the body (Hazzard 1985), higher resistance to cancer invasion (Micheli et al. 1998), a lower iron load and slower metabolism (Perls and Fretts 1998), and greater immune activity (Holden 1987). Males have too much Y-chromosome and too much testosterone (Ibid.). In almost all animal species observed in the wild, females live longer than males (Perls and Fretts 1998).

Table 1.2 Infant Mortality Rates, Male and Female, 2002

Country	Male	Female	Male-female
Highest male-female			
Côte d'Ivoire	130	93	37
Liberia	169	135	34
Gabon	74	49	25
Ethiopia	124	101	23
Burundi	97	74	23
Lowest male-female			
Egypt, Arab Rep. of	55	55	0
Sweden	4	3	1
Israel	6	6	0
Luxembourg	3	4	−1
Trinidad and Tobago	28	33	−4
Median male-female			7

Source: Demographic Health Services; WHO database.

The relatively lower robustness shows up in other ways as well. Males have a greater risk of death between conception and birth, with a higher rate of miscarriage than females. Boys exhibit a higher rate of developmental and behavioral disorders, including reading delay, hyperactivity, autism, clumsiness, stammering, and Tourette's Syndrome, all of which occur three to four times as often in boys as in girls (Kraemer 2000). Kraemer points out that rather than attempting to compensate for these disorders by treating boys more tenderly, parents typically adopt the attitude that boys are, or must be made, more resilient than girls. This adds social insult to biological injury, causing a boy's inborn disadvantage to be amplified. Indeed, society appears to treat men as more resilient throughout their lifespan, subjecting them to a wider range of perils, as discussed below.

EROSION MEASURED BY QUALITY-ADJUSTED LIFE EXPECTANCY. A number of attempts have been made to adjust the raw measure of life expectancy to take into account quality of life and time spent in poor health. One concern is that while females generally live longer, their quality of life may be lower due to poorer health than men. The Global Burden of Disease project popularized one such measure, namely disability-adjusted life expectancy (Murray and López 1996). In essence, years of additional life, if lived with relative incapacity or suffering due to nonfatal conditions, are weighted at less than one year. The World Health Organization (WHO) measures healthy life expectancy (HALE) based on life expectancy at birth adjusted for time spent in poor health (WHO 2004).[3] Table 1.3 displays healthy life expectancy at birth for males and females and the male-female differential. The male-female differential in healthy life expectancy remains substantial and similar to the unadjusted life expectancies shown in table 1.1 (with

Table 1.3 **Male and Female Disability-Adjusted Life Expectancy at Birth, 2002**

Country	Male	Female	Male-female
Highest male-female			
Russia	53	64	−11
Latvia	58	68	−10
Estonia	60	69	−9
Lithuania	60	68	−9
Ukraine	55	64	−9
Lowest male-female			
Zimbabwe	34	33	1
Botswana	36	35	1
Kuwait	67	67	0
Maldives	59	57	2
Qatar	67	64	3
Median male-female			**−3**

Source: WHO database.

the same range of 14 years for the male-female differential in unadjusted life expectancy). The differential ranges widely across countries, although it has a lower median than in table 1.1 (−3 years median male-female difference in the adjusted life expectancies versus a median of −4 years in unadjusted life expectancies). Hence, whether we examine life expectancy or healthy life expectancy, men are at greater disadvantage than women in the vast majority of countries. Exceptions to this pattern are found in many Middle Eastern countries, while a number of Sub-Saharan African countries have very similar rates by sex.

CAUSES OF LOWER QUALITY-ADJUSTED LIFE EXPECTANCY. A related way of thinking about quality adjustment is to consider disability-adjusted life years (DALYs) estimated by WHO.[4] Global DALY estimates reveal some important gender differences. Men are more susceptible to perinatal conditions and there are twice as many male cases of tuberculosis as there are female cases (Holmes, Hausler, and Nunn 1998). Men are much more likely to die of injuries. A number of non-communicable conditions are much more prevalent among men, including digestive diseases, congenital abnormalities, and respiratory diseases. Many of these causes of death appear preventable by changes in adult lifestyle, while a number of others are related to higher male infant mortality. Notably, men appear less likely to participate in the health care delivery system if it is noncompulsory. For instance, in the United States, men visit a doctor and a dentist less often than do women (U.S. Department of Health and Human Services 2000). Men are also disproportionately affected by injuries. Men have close to two times the number of DALYs of women, although they have DALYs three times higher than women in the case of violence and seven times higher in the case of DALYs lost due to war (WHO 2004).

A number of diseases and disabilities severely impact men relative to women and, depending on the country context, could potentially be addressed through policy interventions targeted at men. Such interventions include HIV/AIDS prevention and treatment, violence prevention (including warfare and suicide), and substance abuse prevention and treatment.

HIV/AIDS. Of particular interest among communicable diseases is HIV/AIDS, a major epidemic in many parts of the world. HIV/AIDS is of particular concern in part because it is a major cause of death among middle-aged persons and therefore a major force in the erosion of human capital for many societies, particularly in Sub-Saharan Africa. Young men aged 15–24 in developing countries are particularly affected by HIV, especially in Sub-Saharan Africa, where the disease had a prevalence rate of 9.2 percent for young males compared with 4.5 percent for young females as of 1999 (World Bank 2001b). Worldwide, males accounted for almost 70 percent of HIV cases in 2003 (World Bank 2005c). This pattern, however, is substantially different in Sub-Saharan Africa, where men account for 43 percent of those infected. In recent years, efforts have been made to target men and develop a male perspective in combating and treating the disease (Carovano 1995), partly because men are seen as the vector of infection even in cases where the male-female case ratio is less than one (Engle 1995). The Joint United Nations Programme on HIV/AIDS (UNAIDS) has studied the gendered aspects of HIV/AIDS (1999a), with a focus on men's vulnerability due to their high rates of rural–urban migration and correlation of unsafe sex practices with substance abuse. More recently, WHO argued for the need to integrate gender into HIV/AIDS programs, pointing out that for males, "...gender norms create social pressure to take risks, be self-reliant, and prove their manhood by having sex with multiple partners...[which] expose men and boys to the risk of infection and create barriers to their use of HIV/AIDS prevention, care, or support services" (2003, p. 5).

VIOLENCE. Disease and work-related injuries have an impact beyond the affected individual, mainly that person's immediate family. Violence, however, often affects entire communities and even countries. Of all the forces aimed at destroying humans and human capabilities, violence is probably the most male-gendered (although unsafe driving behavior also looms large). In a recent comprehensive overview of the gendered aspects of violence, Breines, Connell, and Eide (2000) point out that in Australia, Europe, and the United States, men stand charged for 80–90 percent of all violent crimes. Indeed, a look at 62 countries that report data to the International Criminal Police Organization shows that in 2001, the percentage of males among criminal offenders for a wide range of crimes (including homicide, serious assault, theft, fraud, and drug offenses) is almost always greater than 70 percent, with a median percentage of males across countries ranging from 81 percent for fraud to 90 percent for serious assault.

This higher prevalence of criminal behavior among men translates into higher incarceration rates for men. As reported by the International Center for Prison Studies (2001), men vastly outnumber women in all countries reporting the gender breakdown of their prison populations (ranging from 4 to 1 in Mozambique to 142 to 1 in Malawi, with a median ratio of 22 to 1). Both perpetrators and victims of violence are predominantly male. For instance, the majority of homicide victims are men, particularly throughout the Americas (Shrader 2001). Male-on-male violence takes a particularly large toll on young men.

While violence appears to be predominantly associated with men, particularly young men, this does not mean it is an essential feature of males. As Nisbett and Cohen (1999) argue, the variation in homicide rates within and among countries points to the critical role of culture. Their research shows that in small cities in the southern and southwestern United States, the homicide rate for white males is about double the level in the rest of the country. They argue provocatively that high homicide levels are related to a culture of male honor, and trace this back further to argue that cultures in which animal husbandry is practiced have higher homicide rates because in such cultures, it is important for a man to be seen as someone who does not take animal theft lightly. However, homicide rates were high in Central America and in the northern part of South America (especially Colombia and República Bolivariana de Venezuela) before the recent Central American civil wars and the upsurge in cocaine trafficking. Conversely, in Argentina and Uruguay, homicide rates were and continue to be much lower (Buvinic, Morrison, and Shifter 1999). This trend is contrary to Nisbett and Cohen's pastoral argument, and although the time frame is shorter, it nonetheless suggests that closer examination of violence-related differentials within Latin America are more justified rather than blanket assumptions by researchers that all of Latin America operates under a culture of honor and machismo.

A variety of male responses occur in situations of warfare, including aggression, resistance, pacifism, and cowardice. As Large points out, "If we analyse men's experience and identity in current war and disintegration, we find a complex identity issue which undermines any simplistic assumption that violence and war-making is inherently characteristic of male human beings" (1997, p. 25). Interestingly, this gendered nature of war and the multiple roles that people play within war and within postconflict societal reconfiguration has generated little discussion. Topics such as how to demobilize soldiers effectively and how to reintegrate conflict participants (the majority of whom are men) into society until very recently did not include gender dimensions. Much of the gender-related literature on postconflict issues has focused on women's roles, or on children *qua* children, without gender differentiations.

Violence resulting from warfare has the greatest impact on a society, but other forms of violence, also gendered, can affect significant subsectors of society. Extrafamilial violence exists for a substantial proportion of adolescents, and again disproportionately affects males. For instance, in a study of Slovenian high school students, 29 percent of boys and 17 percent of girls reported having "been the victim of blackmail, intimidation or physical aggression from [their] peers" (Tomori, Zalar, and Plesnicar 2000, p. 434). The victims and the perpetrators are typically male; the suspected perpetrator is male in four out of five cases in United States juvenile courts (Mulrine 2001).

Family and domestic violence has been widely discussed and studied from a gender perspective. Men are disproportionately the perpetrators and women disproportionately the victims of such violence. Many perpetrators of domestic violence (and also many victims) have themselves witnessed or been the victims of domestic or extrafamilial violence. Holter describes a 1988 survey in Norway that found that "the main predictor of men's acceptance of male domestic violence against women...was not men's background relations to women, nor their type of masculine identity, but instead their background relations to other men. Two items were significant: having experienced bullying in childhood or youth ... and having experienced violence in the family of origin" (2000, p. 63).

The most intensely personal type of violence is violence against oneself, which in the extreme becomes suicide. A WHO database shows that as of 2004, of the 93 countries reporting gender disaggregated suicide rates, in all but two countries (China and São Tomé and Principe), male rates exceed female rates. In more than half of the countries listed, male suicide rates are three times or higher than female rates. In the case of China, this reversal appears to be related to the high "success" rate of rural women who attempt suicide, which they often accomplish by drinking pesticide (Rosenthal 1999).

SUBSTANCE ABUSE AND ADDICTION. It can be argued that various forms of addictive or compulsive behavior also constitute violence against oneself. However, addictions also carry a high cost for society. For example, a study using Canadian data showed that alcohol, tobacco, and illicit drug use cause 21 percent of deaths, 23 percent of lost years of potential life, and 8 percent of hospitalizations (Single, Robson, and Rehm 1999). While substance abuse is a bigger problem in developed countries, the burden of addictions, measured by decreased health, may increase substantially in developing countries as more people survive to middle age. Much of the gender differential in mortality in Russia has been attributed to heavy male rates of alcohol and tobacco use (Shkolnikov, Field, and Andreev 2001).

Death and disability rates related to alcohol and substance abuse are substantially higher for men than for women (WHO 2004). As of 2002, death and disability rates due to alcohol abuse were close to six times higher for men than for women, and alcohol abuse itself was close to four times higher for men than for women. The male-female ratio for alcohol abuse has a particularly noteworthy gender differential in terms of usage, abuse, and rates of related diseases. In Latin America, there is a much higher prevalence of alcohol dependency for men among every age group and nationality that has been studied (Pyne, Claeson, and Correia 2002). Males account for nine out of ten alcohol and drug violations among juveniles in the United States (Mulrine 2001). In Japan, alcohol consumption per capita has increased fourfold since the mid-1960s and has led to increased male mortality rates from cirrhosis, while female cirrhosis mortality rates have decreased (Makimoto, Oda, and Higuchi 2000).

Substance (narcotic) abuse rates are more similar by gender, although men still exceed rates for women, and they also suffer more severe consequences from substance abuse, at least in developed countries. In the United States, among persons treated at university medical centers for drug and alcohol abuse, women had lower rates of life-time admissions treatment days and total cost of substance abuse treatment than men (Westermeyer and Boedicker 2000). Other U.S. studies show that women are more likely to remain abstinent after treatment for cocaine dependence (Weiss et al. 1997) and are more likely to complete drug abuse treatment programs (Kingree 1995; Hser, Anglin, and Liu 1991).

Notably, female and male drug users have different psychosocial profiles. Female users tend to have lower self esteem and more family and social problems, while men have higher rates of antisocial personality disorders and higher rates of prior home-lessness (Kingree 1995; Weiss et al. 1997). Male drug abusers report more antisocial behavior, including vandalism, use of weapons, and setting fires (Goldstein et al. 1996). Addicts who are the least successful in overcoming drug dependency are dis-proportionately young, unemployed single men (Hser, Anglin, and Liu 1991).

One area in developed countries in which men appear to be making real progress, particularly relative to women, is in reducing tobacco dependency. Men appear to have higher sustained quit rates after treatment programs, particularly those using nicotine gum as a withdrawal aid (Bjornson, Rand, and Connett 1995). However, smoking remains a major cause of lower male life expectancy in devel-oped countries. One five-country study attributed 2.4 years, or more than 40 per-cent of the total sex difference in life expectancy in 1970–74, to smoking; by 1985–89 this figure had dropped to 1.8 years, or 30 percent of the difference—unfortunately in large part because of the increase in the loss of female life expectancy (Valkonen and VanPoppel 1997).

Smoking rates appear to be rising in developing countries, particularly among young people. While the rates among women are rising, the rates among men are still much higher. For instance, in Bulgaria, men are more than twice as likely to smoke as are women (Balabanovaa, Bobak, and McKeea 1998). In Indonesia, there is a very low rate of women smokers even though they are relatively active in the tobacco growing and processing sectors (Barraclough 1999). Apparently cultural prohibitions against women's smoking but neutrality toward or acceptance of men's smoking continue to work in favor of women's health.

A number of narcotics indigenous to and widely used in developing regions are almost unknown in developed countries, except among immigrant groups. Two such narcotics are betel and qat, both mild stimulants. Men are the primary con-sumers of qat, which plays a central role in Yemeni culture and is also widely used in Djibouti, Eritrea, Kenya, and Somalia (Murphy 1992; Rushby 1995). Betel is widely used over much of Southeast Asia and New Guinea, with an esti-mated 10–25 percent of the world's population chewing betel quid regularly (Pickwell, Schimelpfening, and Palinkas 1994). It is not clear if there is a strong difference in usage by sex in all regions, although one study in Kaohsiung, Taiwan (China) found that 94 percent of betel users are male and all daily users are male (Chen and Shaw 1996). Several studies of junior high school students in a variety of countries found a much higher prevalence of betel chewing among boys than girls (Yang et al. 1996). Although betel use is associated with oral cancer, the main trouble with both betel and qat is the time and money users spend on the drugs (Cooper 2000; Chang 1997).

A different type of addiction is gambling. This is a hard topic on which to find reliable figures, partly due to the illegal nature of the practice in many settings. In the United States, women and men are relatively equally represented among casino customers, with a slight skewing toward women (52 percent of customers are women; Hoffman et al. 1999). However, it is clear that men are heavier gamblers. Men have a one-and-a-half to two times higher prevalence of at-risk, problematic, and pathological gambling (Gerstein et al. 1999). While many anecdotal reports from developing countries note a higher rate of gambling behavior among men, there are no comparative statistics to ascertain whether male prevalence among heavy gamblers is universal.

Accumulation of Human Capital

Men fare better than women in terms of human capital accumulation. However, a number of trends have emerged suggesting that men in some countries have experienced slowing rates of accumulation of human capital, one main form of which is formal schooling. This is not to imply that informal types of human capital accumulation are not important, but they are generally harder to measure in developing countries. While we know that in developed countries measures of employment tenure and work experience are critical determinants of earnings, these types of studies are not yet available for developing countries, at least not for representative samples of workers. However, extrapolation from developed country studies, coupled with the knowledge that men have higher labor force participation rates, can lead one to infer that men in developing countries likely have a substantial edge over women in the accumulation of human capital. Whether these rates of accumulation are rising or falling is hard to determine. In settings where workers in their prime are particularly hard hit by HIV/AIDS, it is likely that these accumulation rates are falling.

PRIMARY EDUCATION. Data from *The State of the World's Children*, published by the United Nations Children's Fund (UNICEF 2004) show that in 2002 (or the most recent year available), the female primary gross enrollment ratio exceeded the male gross enrollment ratio in only 17 of the 195 countries listed, and was equal to the male ratio in 28 countries). Countries with higher female participation tend to have high gross enrollment ratios, often over 100. Of the 17 countries with high female enrollment, only four had enrollment ratios below 100 (The Bahamas, Jordan, Nauru, and the United States). Although more boys than girls enroll in primary education, girls are somewhat more likely to progress to grade 5. Of the 82 countries in the WDI that as of 2001/02 reported the share of grade 1 students who reach grade 5, 43 have a higher rate for females (World Bank 2005c). Table 1.4 presents countries with the highest male-female differentials; Lesotho and South Africa lead the list.

SECONDARY EDUCATION. At the secondary level, a much larger number of countries (69 out of 135 that report gender disaggregated data) display higher enrollment ratios for girls than for boys as of 2001/02, while only nine (with widely varying enrollment ratios) achieve equality (UNESCO 2004). A wide geographic range of countries is represented among the 69 countries with higher female enrollment. These countries, however, tend to have higher enrollments on average than countries at the other end of the scale, implying that this gender imbalance is more likely to emerge when educational attendance is relatively high.

These aggregate numbers have not escaped notice in developed countries, where there has been renewed interest in gendered educational outcomes. In the United States, boys earn 70 percent of D and F (i.e., below average) grades, comprise two-thirds of students considered learning disabled, represent a majority of high school dropouts, and make up 80 percent of students diagnosed with attention deficit disorder. Girls outnumber boys in student government, honor societies, school newspapers, and debating clubs (Mulrine 2001). Even in sports, where boys are still substantially overrepresented in the United States, the participation of girls has increased rapidly, due in large measure to Title IX. In the United Kingdom, results from the General Certificate of Secondary Education examination, taken at age 16, show "a considerable gap between the sexes in scholastic achievement: 42.8 percent of boys compared with 53.4 percent of girls get grade C or above...and in lower social classes the gap is even greater" (Kraemer

Table 1.4 **Percentage of Grade 1 Students Reaching Grade 5, Male and Female, 2001/02**

Country	Male	Female	Male-female
Lesotho	66	81	−15
South Africa	80	94	−14
Bangladesh	49	59	−10
Dominican Republic	65	74	−9
Colombia	66	73	−7
Philippines	76	83	−7
Sudan	81	88	−7
Venezuela, R.B. de	81	87	−6
Botswana	85	90	−5
Jamaica	88	93	−5
Nicaragua	62	67	−5

Source: World Bank 2005b.

2000, p. 1610). This pattern of girls outperforming boys on secondary school standardized tests is common across most of Western Europe (WHO 2000b). In the United States, the dropout rate, which is higher for males than for females (11.9 percent of males and 10.5 percent of females age 16–24), is five times as high for students from families in the lowest income quartile relative to the highest income quartile. Boys are more likely to repeat at least one grade; in the United States, 16.9 percent of males age 16–24 and 9.6 percent of females report having been retained for at least one grade (U.S. Department of Education 2000).

These phenomena are not confined to developed countries. For instance, higher grade repetition rates have also been reported for boys in Mexico (Parker and Pederzini 1999). While the focus of educational interventions over the last few years has been on women, the development community is beginning to take note of these statistics. In stating its concern over the gender differences that appear to disadvantage boys in a number of countries (e.g., several Latin American and Caribbean nations), the World Bank has called for potential "education interventions or other social policies that target males rather than females" (2001a, p. 265).

Research into these differences has identified a number of factors that may work against boys' academic achievements, including prevalence of learning disabilities among boys, differences in the socialization of boys and girls, differences in the way school environments affect boys and girls, and higher rates of work outside the home for boys than for girls (WHO 2000b). Again, there appears to be substantial room for program intervention to improve academic outcomes for boys.

HIGHER EDUCATION. The majority of countries that report gender disaggregated data at the tertiary of higher education level show higher gross enrollment ratios for women (49 out of 92 countries in 2001/02; UNESCO 2004). Higher female enrollment ratios are common in developed countries, including Australia, Canada, most European countries, and the United States, where gross female enrollment ratios are generally 25–50 percent higher than male enrollment ratios. Countries with similar enrollment ratios by sex tend also to have relatively low tertiary enrollment ratios, and numerous developing countries have ratios that favor men.

In part, higher enrollment ratios for women in developed countries reflect increasing numbers of women returning to school to obtain or complete a degree after previously dropping out. However, this is not the whole story, and the numbers still imply that in a steady state, more women than men will receive higher education. Indeed, the pattern shows up already among new potential entrants to the tertiary sector. In the United States, 51 percent of recent high school graduates are men, but 61 percent of the male graduates and 64 percent of the women enroll in college or other degree-granting institution after high school. This is not a matter of men temporarily delaying entry: 34 percent of all 18–24 year-old males and 37 percent of all females in the same age group enroll in tertiary education. The net result is that 44 percent of students in degree-granting institutions are men (U.S. Department of Education 2000). Although in some cases men may have good earning prospects without the need to attend higher education, tertiary education is an important form of human capital accumulation and a source of higher life-time earnings for both sexes.

VARIANCE IN GENDER OUTCOMES. Men are generally subject to a higher variance of education outcomes. They are disproportionately represented among both high achievers and low achievers. This is true whether measured by achieve-ment test scores, grades obtained, or incomes earned. This variation in outcomes, however, is not predominantly due to genetic factors, otherwise we would expect greater consistency across societies. The influence of nongenetic factors suggests there is considerable scope for interventions to reduce variation in men's (and women's) outcomes, both within and between societies. To the extent that the aim of human and social development is to pull up the most disadvantaged, low-achiev-ing men would justify a special focus.

Men's Changing Roles and Identities

"... in terms of cultural evolution men may well have done their job: they have pretty much set up modern civilisations and technologies; they may not be needed to keep them going" (The Economist 1996a).

Although The Economist's statement of a decade ago was clearly meant to be provocative, many of the trends noted in this editorial and the accompanying arti-cle "Tomorrow's Second Sex" (1996b), remain relevant. These include the appar-ent reduced participation of men, at least relative to women, in formal economic work, the corresponding lack of increased male participation in household tasks (e.g., child care) leading to a net increase in the work performed by women, and strains on social and family structures caused by the apparent obsolescence of tra-ditional male roles not replaced by alternative positive roles.

THE CHANGING STRUCTURE OF WORK. Major changes in the occupa-tional and economic structures of most developed countries began in the 1970s and reached full force in the 1980s and 1990s. These changes are leading to a dynamic reconfiguration of work and labor markets which, although felt more strongly in developed countries, are also starting to ripple out to developing coun-tries. Unionized sectors, which were heavily male-dominated, lost ground in employment and wage setting. In the United States, the female-male wage ratio, after a fairly stable period, began to rise steadily in the 1980s, mainly because male wages were falling. This trend was not uniform across other developed countries, due in part to more centralized wage-setting systems and differences in the timing and coverage of anti-discrimination laws. Women in developed countries moved into the labor force in increasing numbers beginning in the late 1970s, particularly the more dynamic economic sectors, while men were disproportionately repre-sented in the declining sectors, including manufacturing, mining, and agriculture

(Jacobsen 1991).The Economist article (1996b) asserted that the increase in knowl-
edge-based employment exacerbated the rising unemployment of men relative to
women. While women's participation in formal labor markets is still lower than
men's participation, the indicators reviewed below suggest that there are important gender dynamics at play that may have important implications for socially-
determined gender norms and patterns.

LABOR FORCE PARTICIPATION. The female labor force participation rate has
increased steadily over the past three decades (1980–2003) in developed and developing countries and across all regions (table 1.5). Of the 151 countries listed in the
2005 WDI, 109 experienced an increase in female labor force participation rates over
the period 1990–2003. In the majority of cases, this is because the female rate has risen
substantially while the male rate has fallen. Of the 109 countries recording an increase
in female participation, 84 countries also experienced a fall in male participation rates.

UNEMPLOYMENT. The majority of countries that report disaggregated unemployment data by gender have a relatively higher female rate. Of the 83 countries
with gender-disaggregated data in the 2005 WDI, 51 report higher female unemployment. Long-term or structural unemployment, however, has a somewhat greater
impact on men. Of the 34 countries that report gender disaggregated long-term
unemployment, 18 have higher male rates (World Bank 2005c). Although there has
been increasing interest in developed countries, especially in European countries, in
determining which groups are most affected and vulnerable to structural unemployment (especially men), there is little comparable research for developing countries.[5] Arias analyzed household survey data for urban areas in Argentina, Brazil, and
Costa Rica and found the greatest increases in unemployment incidence and duration among the "typical vulnerable 'young, informal, and less educated' group,"

Table 1.5 **Female Labor Force Participation Rate, 1980–2003**

Country	1980	2003	1980–2003
World	39.1	60.9	21.8
Low-income countries	37.9	54.6	16.7
Middle-income countries	40.2	65.1	24.9
East Asia and Pacific	42.5	75.0	32.5
Europe and Central Asia	46.7	66.8	20.1
Latin America and the Caribbean	27.8	46.3	18.5
Middle East and North Africa	23.8	34.5	10.8
South Asia	33.8	47.3	13.5
Sub-Saharan Africa	42.3	62.3	20.0
High income	38.4	63.7	25.3

Source: World Bank 2001b and 2005b.

although he also finds increased duration of unemployment among older and more educated men (2000, p. 1). Even in countries that were part of the former Soviet Union, where unemployment has affected women as much as or more than men, there is concern that men's roles in transition and post-transition societies are weakening in both the public and private spheres (Ashwin 2000).

REVERSE DISCRIMINATION. Do male workers suffer any type of gender discrimination in the labor market? Since pay differentials tend to overwhelmingly favor men relative to women, discrimination would likely affect hiring rather than pay. While a number of studies have established that in some sectors employers in developing countries have a strong preference for female labor (e.g., *maquiladoras*) there appears to be no systematic analysis of the impact on overall labor markets or male employment patterns (Ward 1990; Deyo 1989; Joekes 1987).

A related question is the degree to which the increase in women's formal labor supply may have led to the crowding out of men. Research on the U.S. labor market appears to show that women, particularly African American and Hispanic women, are a substitute for recent immigrants and minorities (Hamermesh 1986). To the extent that these are the relatively disadvantaged male members of the labor force, the increase in women's participation may disproportionately affect worse-off men.

MIGRATION. There has been little systematic research on the gendered nature of internal and external migration. Men tend to migrate farther and are more likely to be external migrants (Momsen 1991). Examples of gender-differentiated migration include the flow of female domestics from Asian countries to the Middle East, the rush of male miners to mining operations in Africa, and the general flow in Africa of men to urban centers, which leaves women behind to maintain household and community structures (Lovgren 2001; Wilkinson 1987). Urban-rural gender patterns appear to be different in different regions; for example, there are more women than men in Latin American cities and more men than women in African cities (Momsen 1991). While much of the feminist literature has tended to focus on issues relating to female migrants or the women left behind, little attention has been given to the needs of male migrants or of the men who stay in rural areas.

CHANGING SOCIAL STRUCTURES. A number of social changes are occurring simultaneously with changes in the structure of labor markets and work. Disruptions in the social order may be empowering for some individuals or specific groups, including women, but they may be highly disruptive for others, particularly those who are least able to adapt or who stand to lose the most from new norms and social patterns. The latter may well include men. Much of the reaction from feminist researchers and activists is that disruption in the patriarchal social system will be hard on men. A different approach would call attention to those people who have the most trouble adapting to rapidly evolving social structures, especially if they have indirect and negative effects on women. If men are disconnected from or alienated by changes in society, it is difficult to see how this would benefit women. The next section highlights some concerns regarding men's participation in broadly defined areas of social interaction (marriage, parenthood, and family and community involvement).

MARRIAGE. Many social trends that negatively affect women may have corresponding adverse effects on men, although the latter are rarely discussed. For example, a serious issue in some countries in Asia has been the skewing of sex ratios due to a variety of antifemale practices, including selective abortion (Johansson and Nygren 1991; Coale 1991). Although these practices are unambiguously and justifiably condemned, there is comparatively less attention placed on the fact that as a result of these changes, many men now face a high probability of never marrying or marrying relatively late in life.

There is increasing evidence that marriage is "good" for men, good in terms of its apparent link to better physical and psychological health and higher income (Nock 1998; Waite and Gallagher 2000). Nock argues that normative marriage—by which he means "the institution of expectations, laws, beliefs, customs, and assumptions that are a part of every marital relationship" (1998, p. 41)—is "the only way by which most males can become 'men'" (p. 6). However, for a variety of socioeconomic reasons, not all men will have the opportunity to marry, and some men will be forced to delay marriage, thus delaying successful transition to adulthood.

Data on world marriage patterns for 2000, collected by the UN Population Division, show remarkable consistency across countries. Among 20–24-year-old adults, with one country exception, women are more likely to be married than men (UN Population Division 2000). For most countries, the difference in male-female marriage rates at this age is substantial. In 112 of the 191 countries listed, the percentage of women ever married in the 20–24 age group was more than 20 percentage points higher than for men (with a 24.4 median percentage point difference between the marriage rates). To the extent that marriage is a desirable social state, at least for men, the data suggest that fewer men are able to marry at an early age. Interestingly, most Caribbean countries tend to have low gender differentials in marriage rates for the 20–24 age cohort, but marriage rates for both sexes are also extremely low.

Perhaps more tellingly, for most countries the gender differences in relative marriage rates continue later in life. By the time men reach their late forties, their marriage rate has increased substantially, although in a majority of countries they are still less likely to be married than women. The percentage of women ever married among 45–49-year-olds is higher than for men in the same age group in 125 of the 191 countries included in the UN Population Division's 2000 data set, although the gap has narrowed considerably, with a median difference of 0.7 percentage points in marriage rates.

As other authors explore in this book, there are many complex reasons that help to explain the apparent difficulties in establishing and maintaining stable marriages, but most researchers view these difficulties as clear indicators of social stress and point to the inability of young people, men in particular, to afford marriage. Wilson (1996) argued that the low rates of marriage among African Americans were due in large part to the weak labor market for African American men. He appears to be supported in this argument by the recent increase in the marriage rate for the U.S. African American community during a period of rising employment in the late 1990s.

PARENTHOOD.   Changes in marriage patterns both reflect and give rise to changing roles for men in the family structure. The role of the family itself has changed over time in a myriad of ways but still serves multiple essential functions in both developing and developed societies. In developed countries, men find themselves simultaneously called upon to do more childcare-related tasks, albeit for fewer children per family, while at the same time they find their ties and claims on the family weakened, particularly in cases in which they have been separated by divorce or partially disenfranchised by never having married the mother of their children. Fathers' degree of involvement with their children appears to be strongly influenced by the state of their relationship with the children's mother (Engle and Leonard 1995). Even in intact families, there is ongoing discussion over the redefinition of the role of the household head (moving toward a dual-head model), where control over household finances and decision making is continually negotiated rather than settled by the man early in the marriage. Similarly, division of labor, whether between market and nonmarket or regarding the division of household chores, is subject to implicit or explicit negotiation in many contemporary households. As women's paid work has increased, men have decreased their paid work hours (particularly in a life cycle context rather than during prime working age) but they have not correspondingly increased the hours they devote to household work.

     Popular and scholarly literature on changing roles within marriages and families is more substantial for the developed countries than for developing countries. Researchers tend to treat marriages and families in a dispassionate demographic context, focusing more on women and their fertility histories than on men. Although demographic researchers have shown some interest in men's issues, Newby and Biddlecom (1997) argue that these studies, particularly those focused on fertility, tend to treat men from a problem-oriented perspective, or as women's partners, rather than as individuals with distinct reproductive histories.

     To arrive at a potential redefinition of fatherhood that will carry men through the 21st century, there has been a growing realization since the mid-1990s that men and fatherhood must be treated as integral to children's lives. For instance, in a report on men and children, UNICEF (1997) argued that it was imperative to consider the role of men in the lives of children, although it took an instrumental approach by analyzing how the altered socialization of male children would improve women's lives in the long run.[6] There has also been growing interest in the United States in increasing understanding of the difficulty low-income men have in maintaining connections with their children. As a result of this growing interest, researchers have investigated the roles that men, particularly as fathers, play in children's lives, including how they may facilitate children's intellectual and social development and, more broadly, the different ways in which men can be fathers (Bruce et al. 1995; Bernard van Leer Foundation 1996). Sweetman (1997) describes three distinct roles for men as fathers: biological, economic providers for the family, and "social fathers." It appears that the role of social father requires the most redefinition, although in developing countries the provider aspect is also critical.

FAMILY AND COMMUNITY INVOLVEMENT. Men are important as social fathers within extended families and as social persons within communities. Men's roles in extended families and communities have been changing as well, but not in ways that are thoroughly researched and well understood. While Putnam's (2000) work on reduced community ties within the United States at the end of the 20th century is provocative, little comparable work exists in either a developed or developing country context. More work is needed to understand the web of ties within families and communities, the gendered nature of those ties, and their importance to men's and women's well being. The development and urbanization process affects formal and informal community involvement, including relations with peer groups, in ways that are little understood. For example, systematic study of the role of formal and informal mentors in children's lives is only beginning.[7]

The treatment of troubled men and elderly men by families and society is little understood in both developed and developing countries. In developed countries, troubled men tend to be largely removed and isolated from the community and society. Greater numbers of men than women reside in a variety of institutional settings, including mental hospitals, correctional institutions, chronic disease hospitals (including those for patients with tuberculosis), and homes for the mentally handicapped (Schmittroth 1995). In the United States, men outnumber women in these settings in every age group except the most elderly, and the total number of women in these settings outnumbers the total number of men by over 1 million (U.S. Department of Commerce 2001).

Men are also disproportionately represented among the homeless. In urban settings in the United States, single men comprise some 44 percent of the homeless population, while families with children account for 36 percent, single women make up 13 percent, and unaccompanied minors (many of whom are male) represent 7 percent. Some 22 percent of homeless people are mentally ill; 37 percent are substance abusers; 15 percent are veterans (U.S. Conference of Mayors 2000). In Latin America, most street children—children who live, work, and sleep in the streets, and who generally lack regular contact with their families—are boys (Takahashi and Cederlof 2000). To some degree, care for elderly men has not been considered a problem because in many countries there are not large numbers of people who survive to old age.

Conclusions: What Can We Do?

This chapter argues that it is important to consider men's issues in human and social development as part of a gender and development agenda. While much of the evidence presented here does not exclusively focus on developing countries, the aim is to underline the argument that a substantial proportion of men are disadvantaged even in developed countries. We must put aside arguments regarding essentialism or the naturalness of existing patterns, just as we have put them aside in the past to argue against the notion that it is natural for women to have inferior status in societies. Rather, compassion and the desire to raise living standards in all areas should be the guiding principle of development efforts. Many men in developing (and developed) countries lead lives that could be measurably improved by targeted programs and policies.

An important concern in arguing for more attention to men's issues is that this could come at the expense of resources for programs that focus exclusively on women. The argument in this chapter, and throughout this book, is not that resources for men's programs should be carved out of gender programs that focus on women, but that men's issues should be integrated into more holistic gender programs on the grounds that they are more likely to be effective in improving gender equity. More comprehensive gender programs may also attract additional resources for gender work, including by reallocating resources from other programs that, while not presented as gender-focused, tend to favor men.

There appears to be growing, if still somewhat muted, support in the gender and development community for involving men in women-focused programs. Chant and Gutmann (1999) report on their interviews with 41 specialists (33 women and 8 men) on development and gender questions, specialists who represent nearly 30 organizations, agencies, foundations, and consultancies with broad involvement in women in development and gender and development (GAD) projects. According to Chant and Gutmann, "All but three or four individuals expressed a strong desire for involving men in GAD work. That said, less than ten individuals were able to describe actual work done with men by their organizations. Further, nearly all people consulted conveyed serious concerns regarding how men should and should not be brought on board" (1999, p. 57).

While there may be growing interest in the need to involve men, it is less clear how this should be done. Six recommendations are offered here. The first two advocate additional data collection, dissemination, and research to make more concrete many of the topics touched in this chapter. The next four address programmatic changes within the development community. The recommendations aim to encourage the development community to adopt a more holistic approach toward gender issues, an approach that takes explicit account of how men and women contribute to, participate in, and perpetuate gender relations.

Foster Additional Data Collection and Disaggregation

In recent years there has been considerable progress in improving data on women, though greater efforts are needed to disaggregate data by gender including differences for men and women. A number of countries, including Canada, the Philippines, and Sweden, have made gender-disaggregated official government statistics routinely available to the public (Caiazza and Hartmann 2001). In addition to better gender-disaggregated data, there is also a need for new types of gender-disaggregated data. Shrader (2001) makes interesting suggestions about how it may be possible to collect crime and violence statistics to better understand their gendered dimensions.

There is also a need for more gender-disaggregated data when analyzing ethnic or other marginalized groups and communities within countries. Too often, concern for marginalized groups obscures complex gender relations within the groups; much detail is lost by collecting only country-level data on these groups. Good examples of countries attempting to fill this need include Canada, which is producing disaggregated analysis of its native peoples, and the United States, where there is growing interest in understanding social patterns within Hispanic groups, including regional differences and differences between Hispanic subgroups.

Sponsor Research in Areas Potentially Relevant to Male Issues

As discussed in this chapter and throughout this book, changes in social structure are impacting the roles of men in complex ways that are not yet clearly understood in terms of direct effects on men and in terms of gender relations and effects on women. Areas that would benefit from additional research include, but are not limited to: the roles of men in the socialization of children, interhousehold dynamics as new labor patterns emerge, the lives of single men, and gender roles within ethnic and marginalized communities.

Although there are a number of new initiatives to include men in gender-based programs, little is known about how to include men effectively. While many projects have laudable objectives, they may fail or experience high dropout rates if they require too much time or a level of emotional involvement that men are not prepared to commit. Islas (1999) describes a Mexico City organization's sessions with men involved in domestic violence as very confrontational and with a high dropout rate. A program by the International Planned Parenthood Foundation (IPPF) in Jamaica faced similar challenges for both the men and the facilitators involved (2001a). Another IPPF program that used a CD-ROM to engage young men, however, met with high approval by users, perhaps in part because they could use the material in a relatively private setting and at their own pace (2001b).

Continue to Incorporate Men into Gender Planning Initiatives

Incorporating men in gender planning initiatives can occur at the higher (leadership) level and at the local level. Bhasin (2001) discusses experiences with gender workshops, male-only and mixed, in South Asia. Joshua (2001) provides a shorter but informative analysis of similar workshops in East Africa. Such workshops may work better with male trainers as active participants (Joshua 2001; Smith 2001) and may be organized around specific issues or services such as family planning (AVSC and IPPF 1999a; Helzner 1996).

Fund Initiatives Related to Male Issues

A case can be made to support innovative approaches that target issues faced by men, which in many cases can be linked to existing service delivery and policy interventions. Some promising examples in developing countries are described below.

DISCUSSION OF MASCULINITY. Salud y Género, a Mexican group that runs workshops for men, implements a "participatory methodology" to help men "reflect about masculinity and male involvement and to find new ways of expressing themselves" (Barker 1998a). Workshops focus on secondary school youth, men in prisons, and staff and volunteers with various health, education, community development, and rural development organizations. Alsop (2001) describes a number of other Mexican programs for men.

DOMESTIC VIOLENCE. Many programs work with men involved in domestic violence in an attempt to modify behavior (UNICEF 2000; Men as Partners for Ending Violence Against Women and Children).

HEALTH ISSUES. UNICEF (1997) describes various initiatives targeting men, including HIV/AIDS and syphilis awareness programs, and discusses family roles in a Vietnamese program.

FAMILY PLANNING. The Population Council (1998) sponsored a program in Bangladesh to involve men in family planning. EngenderHealth (2001a) has several examples on its Web site of how men have been involved in its family planning programs. There appears to be increasing awareness of the need to involve men in discussions on reproduction and reproductive health. Sternberg (2001) describes work with Nicaraguan men to identify their issues of concern and to understand the stereotypes in their culture. AVSC and IPPF (1999b) describe programs in Bolivia, Brazil, Colombia, and Mexico that promote male involvement in family planning, including opening male-only clinics in some cases.

PARENTING. The Bernard van Leer Foundation (2001) has funded and documented a number of projects that examine the roles of the father in various societies (including in the Caribbean and in Arab-Israeli communities) and consider how to involve fathers more with their children.

SUBSTANCE ABUSE. The World Bank has funded alcohol abuse-related health projects in Argentina and Eastern Europe (Pyne, Claeson, and Correia 2002).

Although there are some important new male-focused initiatives, it appears that these efforts are marginal and underfunded within gender programs. The same could probably be said of programs targeting women, so the point is not to argue for more funding for male-centered programs, but instead to integrate these programs within gender initiatives focused on women and argue the case for stronger funding and support for more comprehensive and integrated programs.

Modify Existing Programs to Reduce Negative and Amplify Positive Effects for Men

Programs should explicitly consider how various development interventions impact men, whether or not they are labeled as gender programs. As argued by Moser (1993), this would naturally occur along with a parallel exercise regarding women. In cases where clear tradeoffs exist between making women better off and making men worse off, programs should consider other factors, such as the disadvantaged (low-class) status in society of the gendered groupings, before making decisions about who to favor.

Modification of existing programs may initially take the form of identifying and prioritizing needs for specific groups of men. For instance, WHO (2000a) coordinated a set of regional surveys around the world in which health promotion programs that worked with adolescent boys were asked to identify needs and consider effective settings and strategies for working with this age group. In the World Bank's own work, a number of projects—Chile Municipal Development II, Panama Health, and Ecuador Modernization and Reform of the Health Sector—have explicit targets for male participation or specific subprograms targeted at men.

Support "Alliance Politics" to Incorporate Men

Several writers suggest mobilizing men toward a goal that at first glance is not gender-related, but that turns out unavoidably to involve discussion of gender relations. Connell advocates alliance politics, where "the project of social justice depends on the overlapping of interests between different groups (rather than mobilization of one group around its common interest)" (1995, p. 238). He cites as an example the environmental movement, which has forced activists to understand and come to terms with the gendered nature of human interactions with the environment. This approach generally requires men to reject explicitly notions of masculinity that would lead, say, to exploitation of the environment. Thus, while the concept of masculinity is related to environmental problems, it is not based on the need for male unity and solidarity to achieve a common goal. This is in sharp contrast with the general assumption that gender advocacy and political action need to be based on unity and solidarity among women.

Notes

1. See, for example, Chant and Gutmann (1999, pp. 11–29) for a capsule history of different approaches to gender in development.
2. See WHO (1998) for a statement on gender and health.
3. The 2004 WHO World Health Report defines HALE as the equivalent number of years in full health that a newborn child can expect to live based on the current mortality rates and prevalence distribution of health states in the population.

4. One DALY can be thought of as one lost year of "healthy" life and the burden of disease as a measurement of the gap between the current health of a population and an ideal situation where everyone in the population lives into old age in full health (WHO 2004).
5. For some pioneering work in this area, see Smith (2001) on disadvantaged men in the United Kingdom.
6. See also the earlier UNICEF consultation report (Engle 1995).
7. See Tierney and Grossman (2000) for a generally positive evaluation of long-term effects of the U.S. Big Brother/Big Sister Program.

Men's Gender Relations, Identity, and Work–Family Balance in Latin America

2

JOSÉ OLAVARRÍA

Changes that began during the last decades of the 20th century and are continuing into the 21st century are bringing about deep transformations in Latin American societies. Perhaps the most apparent changes are related to economic globalization, the role of national governments, demographic processes, and technological innovations. Less visible but just as profound are the transformations in people's daily lives.

Both men and women have seen their private and public lives affected by these dynamic processes. There has been a considerable increase in all types of public demands. Men and women increasingly acknowledge themselves as users, beneficiaries, consumers, clients, officers, workers, or citizens, depending on their activities and the settings in which they carry out these activities. Expectations and demands in each of these interactions require men and women to play different and complex roles. Significant changes have taken place in private lives and within family relations, especially related to intimacy, the meaning of bodies, family life and expectations, and attitudes toward work and leisure, among others.

Overall, these macro- and microsocial processes are having major consequences on aspects of social life. These include gender relations and identities, social reproduction processes, and especially, challenges in balancing family and work.

Social Order During the 20th Century: Work and Families

It is important to remember that the separation between work and home— between the space where one lives and the space where production occurs—took place only after the industrial revolution, particularly in urban areas (Jelin 1994). Due to this separation, a specific type of family began to emerge, namely the nuclear patriarchal family. This type of family arrangement responded to emerging economic requirements by replicating the structure of the new industrial labor force and to the need to ensure a stable labor force in this economic structure by controlling and disciplining family life in poor urban areas (beginning in Europe in the 17th century and in North America in the 18th century; Donzelot 1979). Under the nuclear patriarchal family, the father was the breadwinner and household head, while the mother was in charge of domestic tasks and child care. In urban areas of Latin America, this process began during the final decade of the 19th century. The nuclear patriarchal family arrangement was first consolidated among middle-income groups and began to expand to low-income groups in cities and areas with large industrial and mining concentrations. Current gender identities, roles, and relations in the region arose from this context (Fuller 1997, 2001; Gutmann 2000; Olavarría 2001a, 2001b; Viveros 2002; Viveros, Olavarría, and Fuller 2001).

"Patriarchal nuclear family," "sexual division of labor," "dichotomy of public and private realms," and corresponding gender identities and relations are expressions of sociocultural, economic, and psychological processes. These processes determined the identities and socialization of men and women, but they were also affected by legislative arrangements and public policies that promoted and imposed this particular mode of gender relations and identities and the way in which the demands from work and from family could be balanced. Over time, and especially in the second half of the 20th century, the patriarchal nuclear family became the prevailing paradigm, supported by the legislative framework and inspired by the end of 19th century Napoleonic principles and codes. This legal framework advanced and implemented family-related public policies—among them the relationship between spouses and between fathers and their children—which only began to be modified at the end of the 20th century through amendments to the civil code and new family codes that acknowledge diversity in private and family relations. In some countries, these relationships are still ruled mostly by civil codes and marriage laws that have been in place since the second half of the 19th century.

As urban middle-income groups expanded in the beginning of the 20th century, various state policies aimed to strengthen nuclear families and ensure an acceptable quality of life. These policies reaffirmed the structure of relationships within the family and imposed increasingly specific responsibilities on the father/male as the breadwinner, protector, and authority over his spouse/wife and children. This mainly urban, nuclear family was based on the conception of the household as father, mother, and children, which distanced itself functionally from other relatives (grandparents, uncles, aunts, nieces, nephews, married sons and daughters, and grandchildren, among others). This concept of nuclear family was in sharp contrast to the (typically rural) extended family. The stability and permanence of the nuclear family was dependent on the father's paid work, his authority over other family members, the exclusive devotion of the mother to household tasks (childcare and domestic chores), and the wife's obedience to the husband. If any of these actors were unable to fulfill their roles or obligations, the family would be in crisis, since there was little immediate support from other relatives (which would have been present with the extended family).

Promotion of the nuclear family also occurred in response to the need to settle and integrate the increasing population of men, mainly farmers, who began to migrate to large urban centers during the last decades of the 19th century. Some viewed this as a social issue that required attention in the name of social justice and humanitarian concerns. Others considered these migrants dangerous due to the poor health and sanitary conditions in which they lived, conditions which in some cases were believed to lead migrants to crime or subversion against the state in order to satisfy their basic subsistence needs (Halperin 1997; Rosenblatt 1995).

In addition to efforts made to settle migrant men in a specific place and to create conditions for them to establish and become responsible for their own nuclear families, there was increasing demand for a stable and skilled labor force and for public servants to support the expanding role of the state. Population growth and colonization policies were also promoted. This period saw the consolidation of a labor structure substantially different from that based primarily on the rural *hacienda*. This new labor structure was established according to the prevailing demands of capitalism, especially those associated with large urban factories, mining operations, commercial and export agriculture, and the growing requirements of governments as they·extended their reach within their territory (Hutchison 1995).

These demands fueled the consolidation of a new social order and an enabling labor structure. It called for ensuring a stable and responsible salaried workforce, stable in its occupation and social position and able to procreate and perpetuate the family structure. These conditions required men to identify with their workplace and employers and to commit to a family that depended directly on them. At the same time, these men's wives were devoted to reproductive tasks, childcare, and upkeep of the household. Thus, the labor structure and the type of family promoted were mutually reinforcing. They served to enforce a social order that supported the production and the reproduction of the labor force and a social life that revolved around the nuclear family (Klubock 1995).

Most of the demands and struggles of middle-income groups and organized labor movements of the 20th century—originally based mainly in large, urban mining and agricultural export centers and later in rural areas (*campesinos*)—focused on increasing access to public resources from which they were excluded or partially excluded until the first decades of the 20th century. These groups aimed to improve their quality of life and gain recognition as social actors with legally established rights and duties. These advances were generally attained after long bargaining processes and struggles with governments and entrepreneurs. As a result, public policies were implemented that provided low- and middle-income groups with more or less effective labor laws that established terms and conditions for work contracts and salaries, minimum conditions for job security, limits on working hours, minimum wage and salary conditions to ensure family livelihoods, and unionization and negotiation mechanisms to resolve disputes between workers and employers. In some cases, these policies also included pension and health plans and expanded access to housing and education. For the productive sector, this meant a labor supply of more socially integrated, educated, better fed, and healthier workers who were better equipped to participate in the labor force and in the responsibilities involved in being part of a factory, mining operation, or agricultural enterprise. In turn, the government had access to a supply of civil servants better qualified to perform public administration functions and provide public services such as education, health, and internal and external security.

The meaning of work and the establishment of a family, gender relations, and male and female identities were directly related to the type of family unit that shaped spousal relationships and to the prevailing labor structure, which to a large extent ruled all social life. In this framework, the family unit is not an undifferentiated set of individuals who share activities linked to their livelihood. Rather, the family unit is a social organization and a microcosm of production relationships with a power structure and strong ideological and affective components that provide the foundation for its development and that support its preservation and reproduction. However, this organization also has conflicts and struggles, and while there are common tasks and shared goals, each member has his or her own interests anchored in his or her position within the production and reproduction processes, both internal and external to the household (Jelin 1994).

By the mid-20th century, these family and gender identities and relations were idealized as the standard model and accepted as normal and natural. The prevailing theory of sexual roles further cemented the ideology behind this model despite the fact that the nuclear patriarchal family most frequently was, and still is, more of an intention or ideal than a reality. As such, research on women and men in Latin America demonstrates that separation between the private (domestic) and public worlds as universal constants of social organization—with men in charge of public issues and women in charge of private or domestic tasks—does not match historical reality (Jelin 1994). At the same time, labor coalesced around what was later called the welfare state, or at least this expectation was asserted in political and ideological discourse.

Changes and Crises in the Past Thirty Years

Since the mid-1970s, this type of family and the gender relations on which it was (and still is) based began to experience a severe crisis as a result of several interrelated social processes, including economic changes and the forces of globalization. These processes had a deep impact on the predominant labor structure of prior decades, demographic trends, the demands of women's movements and the rapidly increasing access of women to the labor market, and technological innovations. For nearly a century, the most influential sectors of society supported actions consolidating a social order and implementing it through a defined agenda and state-allocated resources. This order began to weaken as new tensions, conflicts, and processes with truly unpredictable consequences began to take shape.

The State, Economic Globalization, and Labor Structure

In the mid-1970s, Latin America began a reformulation process—initially under the military dictatorship in Chile—focused on the role of the state, the economy, and the use of public resources. Reform policies launched in the 1980s reinforced this dramatic shift in the public policy agenda and led to reallocation of spending priorities and resources.

The development model prevailing prior to the mid-1970s was based on a relative consensus that conciliated work and family. As the foundations of social order began to change, however, the development model and the roles of various economic stakeholders were questioned. Hence, open-market economies began to predominate in Latin America, which considerably modified the economic role of the state that had prevailed for decades. The state increasingly gave up its leading role, reduced its size and ability to intervene directly in the economy, and focused on macroeconomic policies and issues concerning the extremely poor. Markets were liberalized and labor markets were deregulated. Sweeping legal and policy reforms were implemented, allowing the private sector to respond more flexibly to the demands of globalization.

Macroeconomic policies as defined by this new order had a major impact on labor structures and prevailing salary schemes. These policies forced a crisis of those basic social agreements that made stability, continuity, and subsistence of the patriarchal nuclear family possible and led to deep questioning of gender relations and identities.

Since the mid-1970s, there has been an extensive transformation of the state, expressed in the shifting of public policy priorities and the changing use of public resources. Previously, the state protected low- and middle-income groups, or at least this was, and to a large extent continues to be, asserted in public political and ideological discourse. This role was fulfilled through more or less effective redistributive policies that focused, among other things, on conciliating production demands with family reproduction. In the same vein, the state was to some extent an active and direct agent in the generation of employment and wealth through the development of productive capacity such as energy sources, basic industries, public works, and transportation.

This new policy led to the modification of not only the state's use of public resources, but also of the rules of coexistence that had prevailed in former decades. The redefinition of the public agenda—the way in which public resources are used—and structural adjustment policies have impacted the foundation of the prevailing labor structure and salary structure that was previously consolidated into an order that favored the nuclear family throughout most of the previous century. The impact on the labor market became apparent with the privatization of state enterprises and the associated dramatic reduction of formal employment, including the reduction of employment in central administration and in state-owned firms (Katz 2000). At the same time, labor laws underwent continual amendment to adapt to the new demands of globalization. The private sector started to play an increasingly important role in education and health. Additionally, pension systems were reformed, food subsidies were curtailed, and the state withdrew from many public utilities. State resources were increasingly directed to support safety nets and other targeted programs for the extreme poor and other disadvantaged groups, with varying degrees of effectiveness.

The new development paradigm has restructured the economy, opening and adapting it to the requirements of globalization and the need for private sector competitiveness. The emergence of a new social order based on the globalized market economy and the subsidiary state has given rise to a labor structure designed to support highly flexible production. To survive in this environment, companies must not only be very competitive but also highly adaptable to the changing demands of external markets. Two important aspects of this quest for increased flexibility are the growing importance of subcontracting and outsourcing and the adoption of more flexible labor arrangements and working hours. Companies increasingly subcontract parts of the production process to smaller contractors who in turn hire labor under very flexible contracts or working conditions. Large companies also need a more flexible labor force, one that can work continuous shifts, can be easily retrained as production processes are reengineered, and can be quickly reduced or expanded as market conditions change (Díaz and Medel 2002).

One of the consequences of the new model and the need for more flexible production systems is labor instability. Subcontracting and outsourcing has enabled companies to reduce their payroll and fixed costs but it also brings periods of temporary or prolonged unemployment and increased uncertainty to affected workers. Greater employment instability has impacted pension and retirement systems, health benefits, and housing access for a large number of people.

These new economic structures and the more flexible labor arrangements they require to be sustainable are diminishing the underlying need for a stable, nuclear family. Family livelihood, stability, and continuity are now private issues in which the state does not intervene except in situations of extreme poverty or marginalization. In a certain sense, the family has also been privatized.

Women, Paid Work, Empowerment, and Gender Equity

During the last decades of the 20th century, two important societal changes involving women occurred, with important implications for gender relations and the way work and family are reconciled. The first change was women's increased access to the labor market, often for jobs requiring higher education and skill levels. The second was the movement advocating greater gender equality across all spheres and the acknowledgement of women's rights.

WOMEN, THE LABOR MARKET, AND AUTONOMY. By the 1980s, women's participation in the labor market had grown considerably throughout Latin

America. This trend accelerated with structural reforms implemented across the region, new labor regimes, and greater emphasis on more flexible production systems. It is likely that this trend will continue as economic structures become further integrated with global production systems. For many households, the ability of women to enter the labor market becomes critical to their survival and their prospects for improving their livelihood and income. In most instances, however, women are forced to accept unstable jobs outside the home while they face restrictive gender relations within the households (Valdés 1995).

As discussed throughout this volume, a key constraint on women's access to labor markets is the unequal distribution of housework and child care within the household, which restricts their time availability. Men rarely share responsibility for domestic work or other domestic tasks within the household. As a result, balancing work and family demands has been mainly the responsibility of women, and maintaining this balance remains an important barrier to accessing labor markets and the types of jobs women are able to pursue.

When women work outside the home, their families seldom change the previous distribution of family and household responsibilities. Women have little choice but to take on what is known as a woman's double shift, or where income levels allow it, to seek domestic support. Often, therefore, one woman replaces another. Women's increasing access to the labor market has been based on the implicit premise that women's time is flexible, which may ultimately result in women working over 16 hours a day when the time they devote to productive and reproductive work is factored in (Díaz and Medel 2002).

Women are thus often persuaded or encouraged to seek flexible employment that allows them to reconcile their private lives (and domestic responsibilities) with work. However, flexible employment often entails a lack of social protection and little recognition of their condition as workers, which for many women may result in temporary, poorly-paid jobs with little security. The work schedule for many of these working women includes weekends, holidays, and nights, which prevents them from being at home when the family is most likely to assemble. It is an invasive type of work that pervades all spaces of personal and family life. Without the option of seeking full-time employment, in many instances women gravitate to lower-paying jobs and sectors that are also less stable and have poor working conditions. Hence, for many women, part-time jobs that appear as opportunities can turn out to be traps (Díaz and Medel 2002).

As a result of their participation in the labor market, however, women have gained access to additional resources, mainly income resources, over which they can exert some measure of control. Women allocate a higher share of their income to improve the well being of the household, which can have important welfare effects for children in the household. Thus, on the positive side, the welfare of the household is likely to improve as women's access to labor markets increases and the independent incomes that women generate represent some measure of autonomy and empowerment.

WOMEN, VISIBILITY, AND THE PUBLIC AGENDA. Concurrently with the processes described above, the public agenda in each society is slowly but progressively questioning the appropriateness of the prevailing gender system and the ensuing gender relations. This public discussion is the result of advocacy by feminist and women's movements, a growing body of academic and policy research, and increasing support by international actors, particularly the United Nations (Valdés and Olavarría 1998).

In the context of the strengthened Universal Declaration of Human Rights (1948) and the consolidation of democracy as a system of government, the privileged position occupied by men has been increasingly questioned. Considering equity as a goal leads to a critical assessment of prevailing male-female relations and their consequences for the lives of people and societies. Gender inequities and the way they are manifested in societies have been under discussion since the 1975 First World Conference on Women in Mexico. Shortly thereafter, the United Nations Convention for the Elimination of all Forms of Discrimination Against Women (1979) enshrined governments' commitment to gender equality and established measures to achieve equality given prevailing sociocultural, political, and economic barriers. Later conferences (held in Copenhagen and Nairobi) provided new commitments and measures.

The 1994 International Conference on Population and Development and the 1995 World Conference on Women addressed a number of issues that, although they pertained to the private sphere, have increasingly become matters of public policy due to their social impact. Exercise of sexuality, reproductive health, and violence (particularly domestic and sexual violence) are issues in which women's movements have been active in terms of advocacy and reporting. Women's movements have also been active in proposing new approaches to address these issues. Women's conferences have explicitly pointed to the need for including men both as targets of social policies and programs and as agents of change. Both conferences highlighted the responsibilities of men in reproduction and in preventing violence against women, while reasserting that gender equality with the participation of men is crucial to achieve the goals related to sustainable development.

The Inter-American Convention to Prevent, Punish, and Eradicate Violence against Women, which has been ratified by almost all countries in Latin America and the Caribbean, is an expression of governments' political will. Further political will is represented by legislation identifying and punishing domestic and sexual violence and an increase in the number of programs to protect female victims— shelters, police stations especially designed to deal with domestic violence, governmental and nongovernmental networks, and programs involving male batterers. Likewise, the Third American Ministerial Meeting on Childhood and Social Policies in Santiago in 1996, which produced the Santiago Agreement, set goals on incorporating men into several social programs, particularly in sexual and reproductive health. However, in most instances, governments need to act more decisively to enforce these commitments.

Modernization of Customs: Daily Life and Family

Modernization and globalization processes impact economies and business sectors in Latin America but they extend to other spheres of social life, particularly in urban areas, where such processes influence culture and relations in institutions and in people's personal lives. The communication and information revolution is allowing greater interaction among cultures throughout the region and across the world. These interactions are gradually weakening deep-seated cultural patterns, traditional institutions, and personal attitudes, often causing people to modify or discard practices and habits firmly established for generations.

As a result of modernization and globalization, family, marital (and other cohabiting arrangements), and paternal units increasingly accept and acknowledge greater diversity and equality between their members and increasingly recognize links that tend toward more equitable relationships. The need for more intimate and affectionate spaces has intensified, and as such people value a greater physical presence at home and more opportunity for leisure activities. Concern for and time devoted to one's own body has also increased (Fuller 2000; Olavarría 2001b; Viveros 2000). Private life has been democratized to some extent due to new laws on families and domestic violence, so that a man's resources and power over his children or wife have been weakened. These changes have helped to establish spaces that increasingly protect children and women from the formerly all-embracing male power. Many formerly socially tolerated and accepted practices are now penalized crimes.

The pattern of transformation emerging, especially in urban areas, represents a step forward from a traditional hierarchical and authoritarian structure (in terms of the most immediate and relevant individual relationships) to other more egalitarian and democratic structures that stress the commitment, emotional intensity, and autonomy of the parties (Gysling and Benavente 1996; Valdés, Benavente, and Gysling 2000). Hence, globalization and changes in domestic economies and labor structures have driven the demands of modernity in households by forcing people to question gender roles and by launching a process that reverses established patterns of male-female relations, both in terms of their people's identities and their relationships as couples and as members of their gender.

By generating uncertainty regarding men's role as breadwinners and by weakening men's authority within the household, these changes are having an impact on the paradigmatic family and the marital institution as originally conceived by civil norms enshrined in Napoleonic codes. Women are increasingly becoming providers and are gaining autonomy and empowerment. For many men, the household has become one of the few, if not the only, realms of power, sometimes with regretful consequences such as domestic violence. Simultaneously, women are becoming more autonomous as they access labor markets, obtain higher levels of education, benefit from laws that expand the protection of women and children, and are able to articulate demands for greater equality with their partners.

Thus, the separation between the public and private domains is vanishing rather quickly. Men do not necessarily provide all the economic support for a household. On the contrary, a large percentage of women are also providers, and many women have become the sole breadwinner of the household they head (Arriagada 2001). Women are also raising questions about the sexual division of labor, claiming that men should share domestic and childcare tasks.

The concept of romantic love has also been questioned over the past few decades, although it was the main factor encouraging the construction of a family nucleus and marriage, especially during the 20th century (Giddens 1992). To a large extent, romantic love is still the basis of family and marriage: the freedom to choose a partner, mutual affection and care, procreation, and the basis of a lifelong bond. The Chilean civil code, for example, refers to marriage as a solemn contract by which a man and a woman are perpetually bound for life, in order to live together, procreate, and provide each other with mutual assistance. The indissoluble nature of this bond as the factor that cements and perpetuates marriage and the nuclear family is currently undergoing a crisis. For a growing number of people, the disintegration of the love relationship, the presence of domestic violence, or the inability of men to support a family are reason enough to dissolve the bond. This has given rise to historically unprecedented rates of separation and divorce.

Population statistics reveal the tensions and conflicts of the demographic changes accompanying new social realities. Changes are apparent in rates of fertility, marriage, divorce, matrimonial annulment, and children born out of wedlock. The past few decades show significant decreases in the gross birth rate, fertility per age, and the maternal replacement rate. The marriage rate has also declined and the percentage of children born out of wedlock has increased, especially those born to adolescent females.

Simultaneously, major changes have taken place in the size of families within each phase of the family life cycle, a phenomenon that may be attributed to profound demographic changes, especially to declining birth rates since the 1970s. Likewise, life expectancy at birth has increased substantially and living conditions between men and women are increasingly diverse (Arriagada 2001).

Men, Changes, and Issues of Identity and Gender

Economic transformations, increased presence of women in labor markets, and increased demands for equity and the acknowledgement of women's rights, as well as cultural changes, have affected men. In this new setting, men's condition as household authority and main breadwinner is in question; men's jobs and salaries are unstable; and men face constant anxiety about potential salary cuts and unemployment, either due to outsourcing or the need for greater labor flexibility in a globalizing environment. Men's paid work—the axis of family life—which frequently allowed and still allows for the conciliation between work and family, is undergoing a crisis. Gender relations and identities within the family are being questioned, and for men, the concept of masculinity that prevailed for most of the 20th century is also in crisis.

The dominant male identity model imposes mandates that let men and women know what is expected from them. This model also acts as a reference against which they compare and are compared. Under such a model of masculinity, being an adult male involves working (for pay), forming a family, having children, and becoming the household authority and breadwinner, among other things. This is in contrast to women, who stay at home, take care of children, and receive the protection and economic support of their husbands (Fuller 1997, 2000; Viveros 2000; Valdés and Olavarría 1998; Olavarría, Benavente, and Mellado 1998; Olavarría 2001b).

Under this reference model of masculinity, with its standards and measures of manhood, being a man is something to be achieved, conquered, and deserved. Hence, to become a man, the male must meet certain requirements, including working, forming a family, being a breadwinner, and having children, in order for other men who have already achieved this condition to accept him as a man, and for women to acknowledge him as a man.

One of the most defining elements in men's lives is the idea of owing themselves to work, because working means being responsible, meritorious, and capable, attributes that characterize manhood in its full adult phase. Work gives men autonomy and allows them to form a family, become breadwinners, fulfill their duties toward the family, protect the family, and be the household head and authority. Men feel this mandate as an enormous pressure, especially those who have precarious jobs and few resources. Overall, men experience the loss of a job and unemployment as a profound degradation, with a resulting crisis in self esteem that engulfs their lives.

Another equally important defining element requires adult males to adhere to a preestablished paternity model, one that entails much more than merely begetting offspring. Adult men are and must be fathers. Wedlock, or the cornerstone of life with a female partner, is procreation. Being a father is to take part in nature: this is the established model and no questioning is permitted, for fear of transgressing the natural order.[1] Paternity is one of the major steps in the progression from youth to adulthood and one of the challenges to be surmounted. Paternity is also the culmination of the great initiation rite of becoming a man. If a man has offspring, he will acknowledge himself as and be acknowledged as a full man, and he will feel "more manly" (Valdés and Olavarría 1998; Olavarría and Parrini 1999).

Work and paternity are fundamental steps in the life of any adult man. From this moment on, a man is important not only in general terms, but in relation to specific persons such as his wife and children. He is the household head and has authority over the family group, with legal support. He becomes responsible, as he must confront the reality of his family, support and protect it. He must be rational and guide his behavior according to a logic that is typical for the rationality of economics (as per Weber). He cannot afford to be controlled by emotions; he needs to fight for his family, as that is what is expected from him. He cannot be weak, emotional, or afraid, and he must not display any of these qualities before his wife and children. He must work to provide for his family and go outside the home in search of a job, because it is in the space outside the home where men find employment. The wife or female partner, on the other hand, is expected to obey the man. She is responsible for reproduction and for what goes on within the home; she must take care of the household and children. Her husband or male partner must protect her. She is emotional and expresses her feelings, to both her spouse and her children.

Thus the father is an important person; he is the household head and authority. His work allows him to support his family and children, he proves and exercises his heterosexuality through the offspring he begets, and he shows his power through his fertility. The man/father has a specific destiny: to establish a family built on clear relations of authority and affection with his woman and children, which allows him to support, protect, and guide them within a definite space, the household. This form of family establishes a clear distinction between public and private spheres, as well as a clear sexual division of labor between men and women. A woman's role is to complement the man, take care of children, manage the house, and collaborate with her father/husband.

Thus understood, work and paternity determine the main axis of the prevailing model of masculinity. Given the permanence in time of this way of being a man, it has become the natural way of defining who men are, in turn implicitly justifying men's power over women and other men, and thus reproducing power relations. This masculinity, which is incorporated into the construction of identities from childhood among both men and women, is the current version of patriarchy.

When faced with intimacy, men point out that these expected roles are often at odds with their personal experiences, even when they assert that these experiences are, among others, the features that distinguish men from women. Although some men try to differentiate themselves from this reference model, it is not easy. While many men recognize the model as a burden, it also gives them access to power and to dominant positions with respect to women and other inferior men in the social hierarchy (Fuller 2001; Olavarría 2001b; Viveros 2002).

Work, Gender Equity, and Public Policy

In this new social order, as never before, work is the organizer of people's lives. Work is the means through which society distributes its resources. Those who lack a job face risk and precariousness, have no steady income and no access to social security, housing, or health (Díaz and Medel 2002). Men living without a salary are also deprived of the historical foundations that allowed them to become the main— and often only—family protector, authority, and breadwinner. Employment uncertainty has become a daily reality for both men and women. A laborer arriving at his worksite one morning can find a discharge notice for reasons which he can do nothing about. By the same token, the chief executive officer of a large firm can arrive at his office to find that the firm has been taken over by another group and that he has lost his job. The main difference between these two men is that the former usually lacks savings and resources to cope with unemployment and is therefore highly vulnerable, while the latter often relies on savings or other sources of income, although his self esteem and status among his peers will be similarly affected.

The sense of belonging to the public sphere, as an identifying trait for men during the 20th century, has also been impaired. In the workplace, staff turnover between and among companies has led men to lose their sense of identity and institutional solidarity. Given the rapid increase in women's access to labor markets, men have had to increasingly compete with women for the same jobs and to accept the presence of female supervisors. The labor market, which was dominated by men in most institutions and industries, is now accessible by women with equivalent skills and qualifications. The separation between public and private spheres for men and women is quickly blurring and the public sphere is increasingly shared, although men who find this uncomfortable and incomprehensible attempt to prevent it. Many women believe this to be uniquely due to their personal qualities. But just as women are now accessing the public sphere, men are increasingly entering the private and family spheres.

Women's increasing participation in the economy and politics, increasing positions of responsibility, and higher levels of education, combined with new models of empowered women, are promoting changes in images of what is feminine and what is masculine. Women are finding their own identities in the public sphere, where work is seen as a value, a right, and a legitimate aspiration, particularly among young women. Men are beginning to look at the private family sphere as a desirable space where they would like to be and that they enjoy with different and greater intensity. Growing numbers of such men require greater intimacy and affection with their partners and children, especially during early childhood and adolescent stages. Increasing numbers of men now share household support tasks with their female partners, although for many men these tasks are still uncomfortable, and relations between male and female partners are becoming more horizontal and democratic. Several writings lend credence to changes in gender images, at least at the level of discourse and perception (Fuller 2001; Olavarría 2001b; Viveros 2002).

Conclusions

If work is the coordinating axis of people's lives, the issue at stake is how to reconcile work and private life in a globalizing environment that increasingly demands more flexible labor markets. The old model of the male-dominated nuclear family, linked to stable employment and production systems, is increasingly challenged by the new economic systems and the emergence of new family structures based on different gender relations and roles.

Although in many parts of Latin America, especially countries that are further down the path of globalization and modernization, new family structures and gender norms are emerging, a more systematic discussion and analysis of the impact of economic changes on people and their families has been missing. The lack of public discussion is in fact a failure to acknowledge the impacts these changes have had and are having on family life, formation and stability of households, and relationships between spouses and between parents with their children. This lack of public discussion is apparent in the lack of legal frameworks and regulations to protect people and families who have been harmed—impoverished and left them with little or no access to education, health, housing, retirement, and other benefits—by these processes. Because the freedom and intimacy in which people make family decisions are restricted, there are therefore no clear rights and obligations to allow for respectful, autonomous, and equitable relations between men and women and their children.

A public debate needs to be opened regarding work and family, with the goal of increased understanding of the process of economic globalization and its impact on people and families and future family trends. Key in this debate should be the role of the state. As discussed in this chapter, the state played a critical role in supporting and reinforcing the stability of the nuclear family, but as the state has withdrawn from a large number of economic spheres, there has been little discussion of its role in supporting more diverse family structures which also have to cope with more fluid economic and production environments. How can we deal with equity, diversity, and recognition of different people and families? What types of families are being created? We must answer these questions to ensure the formation and stability of families and the rights and obligations of their members. At the same time, we urgently need to establish the type of guarantees that states must provide to their citizens to secure the stability of nuclear families and the acknowledgment of diversity, gender equity, conciliation between family and work, legislation to stipulate rights and obligations in each of these spheres, and a judicial system to enforce the rights.

Note

1. Priests—men who have taken a vow of chastity—are also considered "fathers" of their flock.

Men's Participation as Fathers in Latin America and the Caribbean

Critical Literature Review and Policy Options

3

GARY BARKER[*]

his chapter provides an overview of men's participation as fathers in Latin America and the Caribbean. It covers theoretical and empirical considerations on the role of men in families and in child development and well-being; policy and program experiences; and data and implications on men's participation as fathers in the region. The chapter concludes with program, policy, and research considerations for governments and development agencies.

Increasing rates of marital dissolution, the growing participation of women in labor markets in the region (compared to men's stagnating or stable participation), and increased attention to men's roles in sexual and reproductive health have all contributed to a mounting interest in men's roles in families and their participation as fathers. At the international level, the 1994 International Conference on Population and Development and the 1995 International Conference on Women served to call attention to the roles of men in families and established international platforms for engaging men in the promotion of gender equity, including more involvement by men in their roles as fathers. In Western Europe, North America and Australia, policy initiatives and programs have been working since the mid-1980s to promote or influence men's participation as fathers. These policies and programs have been informed by a growing body of research on men's roles as

The author would like to acknowledge the contribution to this paper by the following individuals: Jorge Lyra and Benedito Medrado, PAPAI, Recife, Brazil; José Olavarría, FLACSO, Santiago, Chile; Javier Alatorre, UNAM, Mexico; and Janet Brown, University of West Indies, Kingston, Jamaica.

fathers, the impact of fathers' participation on families, and child development and well-being. This chapter summarizes some of the salient findings from this research, although the focus is on research emerging from the region.

Although the issue of men's roles as fathers has gained attention in recent years in developed countries, the amount of research and the number of program and policy initiatives in developing regions has been relatively scant. In some cases, men's roles and participation in the lives of their children has been excluded or ignored, sometimes deliberately, in the international development literature. The implications of this are that gender inequities in child care and domestic tasks endure and the roles of men in children's health, development, and well-being are largely ignored. As a recent Population Council document cogently states:

> "Though development may alter the classic portrait of marketplace gen-
> der inequality, such as wage discrimination and occupational segregation,
> a powerful form of discrimination persists when women must carry the
> major, and sometimes exclusive, social and economic costs of dependents,
> especially children" (2001).

Data suggest that worldwide, fathers contribute far less time than women to direct child care, although there is tremendous variation across regions and among men. Studies from diverse settings find that fathers contribute about one-fourth to one-third of the time that mothers do to direct child care (Population Council 2001). However, even if they are less involved in child care, fathers make decisions about the use of household income for children's well-being, education, and health care. For example, a study in Guatemala found that men were responsible for making decisions about health care in 55 percent of families when women do not earn income but only 11 percent of families where women earn more than 50 percent of the household income (Bruce et al. 1995).

There has been growing, albeit limited, attention to men's roles as fathers in the region and a slowly emerging research base, but this pales in comparison to the amount of research on men's roles in sexual and reproductive health in the region. Most of this recent research on fathers and fatherhood, as will be seen, provides ethnographic and qualitative descriptions of men, offering useful insights on men's identity formation and socialization and men's reactions to changes in labor markets and family formation. These studies provide a tremendous base on which to draw program and policy implications. Some of this research includes studies on pathways to change or on factors that seem to be leading to change in terms of how men view their roles as fathers. It offers powerful insights on how some men have changed and can change or react in positive ways to modifications in household and gender roles.

It is important to confirm at the outset that there are varied social imaginations and definitions attached to fatherhood and normative ideas of what it means to be a father. These social constructions and the symbolism attached to them restrict our notions and filter our views of the issue. Many of the policy and program initiatives that have emerged in the region have been framed around idealized, normative, or moralistic views of what being a father means—notions that may not be conducive to promoting family or child well-being or gender equity. For example, fathers' rights groups, which are often comprised of men with valid personal arguments and personal dilemmas (such groups are generally composed of divorced or separated fathers seeking greater visitation or cohabitation rights), sometimes seek to return to a traditional notion of an "intact" biological family or traditional, patriarchal notions of fatherhood. Other groups in the region have emerged out of men's genuine and laudable desire for closer relationships with their children. Only a handful of these initiatives have grown out of a concern for gender equity, that is, of engaging men in child care, child support, and domestic chores. Initiatives that seek to promote cooperation between coparents, regardless of their marital or relationship status, are even less common.

Indeed, engaging men in such programs and discussing men's roles as fathers has been hindered by numerous assumptions. Program staff and policy makers often assume that fathers are not interested in their children, or that they are less interested than mothers in their children, and that they are incompetent as caregivers, although research has confirmed that fathers are able to interpret and be sensitive to children's needs as well as mothers (Davis and Perkins 1995). Researchers have sometimes assumed that men as fathers are hard to reach, or that women's reports of men's behaviors are sufficient to understand what men believe and do.

These assumptions about men make it difficult to study and understand what men really do and believe as fathers and to design feasible programs and policies to encourage fathers' participation. Partly as a result of these challenges, in recent years many researchers and program staff have begun to separate the function of social father from the function of biological father. Social father refers to the ways men take on caregiving and other roles, regardless of their biological connection to the child. Traditionally, much of the research on fatherhood in Latin America and elsewhere focused on intact families with present biological fathers, sometimes casting in an unfavorable light on those men and families who did not follow these norms. By using the term social fathers, we are beginning to realize that some men take on important roles in the family regardless of their biological or legal connections to children. Other researchers have used the term "fatherwork" instead of fatherhood to focus on what men actually do in their roles as caregivers, rather than on the normative, idealized notions of what being a father means (NCOFF 2002).

This chapter frames the analysis of men's roles as fathers within the field and concept of masculinities—that is, understanding and studying the way men are socialized, how men's roles are socially constructed, and how these roles change over the life cycle and in different social contexts. By using the plural concept of masculinities, this theoretical framework argues that there are multiple ways of being socially recognized as men, often with hegemonic, subaltern and competing versions of what it means to be a man in the same setting (Connell 1994). Within the concept of multiple masculinities, numerous researchers in the region have described the mandates or gender scripts that many men feel obliged to live up to or are socialized into, and the implications of these scripts on the behavior, health, and well-being of the men and their families (Olavarría 2000). This construct of multiple masculinities also enjoins us to examine the diversity of men and the pressure they sometimes feel to adhere to specific norms and to understand how men's roles change in time and context.

Although there is not yet a consensus on the issue, there is growing affirmation in the field of gender studies and gender programming that studying and targeting women is not enough to redress gender inequities, and that traditional gender programming, whether in the area of income generation or sexual and reproductive health, is limited if it does not also include men (Chant and Gutmann 2002). Furthermore, much of the research on men's and women's roles in families, including their roles as parents, has been characterized by simplistic comparisons of men's and women's time or resource use. As Cornwall points out, "This crude and simplistic form of analysis offers little in the way of understanding the dynamics of difference in communities. It tells us nothing of relationships among women and among men, nor of the interaction of gender with other differences such as age, status and wealth" (1997, p. 8). Similarly, as White suggests, "In the gender and development literature, men appear very little, often as hazy background figures. 'Good girl/bad boy' stereotypes present women as resourceful and caring mothers, with men as relatively autonomous individualists, putting their own desires for drink or cigarettes before the family's needs" (1997, p. 16).

In short, men are frequently portrayed incompletely or as deficient in family life. Increasingly, though, researchers from North America and Latin America and the Caribbean are affirming that men participate in caregiving in their own ways, and that they participate more than is commonly believed (NCOFF 2002; Brown and Chevannes 1998). It is possible, of course, to make a list of men's deficiencies in the household, ranging from not providing child support to limited involvement in domestic chores to the use of violence against women and children. Nonetheless, as the research included here will attest, these deficiencies are only one part of the story. And in recent years, researchers have begun to include men's own perspectives of their roles in families.

The question that has driven much of the research on men's roles in families is whether men as fathers matter. Specifically, many advocates have asked why they should devote resources, research, and programs to men's roles as fathers when it is women who provide most of the child care. In the area of child development, many researchers have asked whether children need fathers to develop well. Taken as a whole, the research discussed here and the emerging consensus in the fields of child development and health affirm that men's participation as fathers, as coparents, and as partners with women in domestic chores and child care do matter, for the following reasons:

- Father presence, depending on the quality of that presence, is generally positive for children. The consensus in Western European and North American research is that when men (social or biological fathers) are involved in the lives of children, children benefit in terms of social and emotional development, often perform better in school, and have healthier relationships as adults. However, this research also affirms that having multiple caregivers, or having a second caregiver to support a primary caregiver, appears to be more important than the sex of the caregiver. Research from the United States and other countries about child development outcomes suggests that in stressed, resource-poor communities, having a supportive parent or caregiver is one of the most important, if not the most important, protective factor(s), and that this supportive caregiver can be either male or female (NCOFF 2002).

- Father or male presence, other things being equal, is positive for household income. In diverse settings throughout the region, research confirms that when a man or father is present in a household or a man provides child support even when he does not reside with his children, family incomes are generally higher, even if men on aggregate provide a smaller percentage of their wages to the household than women.

- Men's greater participation in child care and domestic tasks is generally good for women. Men's participation in domestic chores, including child care, and their positive participation in child and maternal health is generally positive for women, freeing women to work outside the home, to study, or to pursue activities that are generally positive for themselves and their households. While probably still a minority, some men in the region are beginning to provide additional care and carry out additional tasks in the home.

- Positive engagement as caregivers and fathers is generally good for men themselves. Some research suggests that engaged fatherhood is good for men. Men who are involved in meaningful ways with their children report this relationship to be one of their most important sources of well-being and happiness.

If men's involvement as fathers is generally positive—for children, women, and men themselves—can it be promoted through policies and programs? Although a number of programs have emerged in the last 10–15 years in the region, they are mostly small in scale and generally have limited funding, and there is almost no research on impact and relatively few in-depth descriptions of these programs. Can project interventions lead to measurable changes in men's participation in families and in the lives of their children? Are they cost effective? Is it financially worth investing in men as fathers? These questions have not been adequately answered. The most prudent answer is that we think so, but we need more research. This chapter presents some qualitative findings from programs in the region suggesting their potential impact, but the question as to whether such programs work remains largely unanswered. Finally, if we do not yet know the impact of program and policy initiatives in the lives of men, we can affirm that these issues are likely to become even more salient as more women enter the workplace, more children are born outside stable unions, and fewer households conform to traditional notions of a family unit.

Men in Families: Trends, Factors and Impact

Trends in Family Formation and Employment

Since the mid-1980s, tremendous changes in family formation and employment have occurred in the region, with widespread implications for men's and women's roles in families, including declining fertility rates and women's increasing participation in formal and informal workplaces outside the home. This section highlights the implications of these trends for men's roles in families and their roles as fathers.

In nearly all countries in Latin America and the Caribbean, the proportion of female-headed households and women's participation in the formal labor market have increased, while men's participation has either declined or remained about the same. Women's labor force participation rate in the region increased from 27.8 percent in 1980 to 46.3 percent in 2003, while men's participation rate declined somewhat (World Bank 2001b, 2005a). These trends in turn have led to shifts in the arrangement of child care and have called into question men's limited involvement in domestic tasks, including child care. In much of the region, researchers report that men and women in low-income groups face economic instability, declining wages (in some sectors, but clearly not in all), and that some men and women are working longer hours when they can find work.

One of the responses of families to economic uncertainty and the search for employment is labor migration. Particularly in Central America, Mexico, and the Caribbean, men's migration partly explains high rates of female-headed households. In Honduras in 2001, for example, an estimated 600,000 persons had left the country for work, 75 percent of whom were men. Their remittances reportedly represent up to one quarter of Honduras' gross national product (Rodríguez 2001, in Alatorre 2002).

To these trends must be added the fact that throughout the region more marriages or unions are ending in divorce or separation, marriage age has increased, and more children are born outside of stable unions. This in turn means that there is a larger proportion of children who spend time away from or live apart from their fathers.

As a result of these trends, some men are devoting more time to domestic tasks and child care, responding to the new demands on women's time and providing more child care. To a lesser extent, some men in the region are also beginning to question the trends that pull them away from their families and are reflecting about their roles as fathers. In both cases, this is a minority of men, but the social trend is nonetheless significant.

WOMEN-HEADED HOUSEHOLDS AND MARITAL DISSOLUTION. Currently, 10–30 percent of households in developing countries are defined in official data as female-headed. This rate may approach 50 percent in regions with significant internal or external male migration. According to official data, women head between one in five and one in four households in the region (Bruce et al. 1995).

In Mexico, for example, 25 percent of households are headed by a single adult, the vast majority women (Cunningham 2001). Similarly, as of 1998, about one-fourth of households in Central America were headed by women: 31 percent in Nicaragua, 23 percent in Guatemala and Costa Rica, 27 percent in Honduras, and 28 percent in El Salvador (Alatorre 2002). In the Caribbean, which is character-ized by high rates of men's migration by historical, cultural, matrifocal family struc-tures, the proportion of female-headed households is even higher, ranging from 37–49 percent (Alatorre 2002).

In addition to men's migration for work, most of the region has experienced increasing rates of marital dissolution. Data from the mid-1980s show that divorce rates of women aged 40–49 ranged from 25 percent in Mexico to 49.5 percent in the Dominican Republic, up significantly from previous years (Bruce et al. 1995). To give another example, in Panama, divorce rates increased by more than 60 per-cent, from 3.8 per 1,000 in 1986 to 6.2 per 1,000 in 1996 (Alatorre 2002).Various studies have found that in the case of separation or divorce, men are more likely than women to remarry or form new relationships.They are thus more likely to have children with more than one partner, and hence to live apart from at least some of their children for a large part of these children's lives. In a sample survey in Nicaragua, 49 percent of men aged 15–40 had separated or divorced and formed new relationships compared to 32 percent of women (Montoya 2001, in Alatorre 2002).As a result of both greater marital dissolution and later average age at first marriage, a higher proportion of children are being born outside formal unions. For example, in Chile, 45.8 percent of children were born outside of formal unions in 1998, compared to 18.6 percent in 1970 (Olavarría and Moletto 2002).

These data alone suggest tremendous changes in family and household struc-ture but they do not give the whole picture. For example, research consistently finds that female-headed households are poorer than two-parent homes. Data from the mid-1980s in Latin America found that women-headed households are over-represented in low-income groups (Bruce et al. 1995). But such findings are also limited; household data often does not tell us about connections that families have beyond the household, nor do the categories of female-headed and male-headed tell us much about the networks of social support that households may have or about individual differences in households. For example, having a man in the household (or being a male-headed household) can increase a woman's burden rather than decrease it.A study in Nicaragua of mothers of children aged 12–18 months found that women spent more time in household production when a father was present than when he was absent (Bruce et al. 1995).Men's use of alcohol or violence may mean that women effectively head households even when men are present, or that the benefit of the additional income men bring in may be offset by the social costs of men's presence.

The Caribbean offers yet another caveat related to household headship trends. In Jamaica, only 16 percent of women in their childbearing years are married.The majority of first children are born into visiting unions of young, unmarried partners. Later in life, many women and men move to common-law unions and may eventually marry. Women and men may have multiple unions and children who do not live with them. On aggregate, men give more income to the children they live with, but diverse patterns make generalizations difficult (Brown and Chevannes 1998). Qualitative data on household formation in the Caribbean describes a common pattern in which young mothers and their children live with the extended family, or pass children to other members of the extended family for care, while fathers typically maintain a visiting or nonresident relationship with their children. The man may also migrate for work. He may in some cases spend a larger portion of his resources on his own needs and with his male peers, but may subsequently form a more stable union and devote considerable resources to his "inside children," those with whom he lives. While the literature has often described such family formation in deficient or dysfunctional terms, many Caribbean researchers argue that this pattern is a functional and historically based response to promote family survival in the face of postslavery poverty and lingering social exclusion (Brown and Chevannes 1998).

FEWER FATHERS LIVING WITH THEIR CHILDREN. If merely counting female-headed households is insufficient for understanding men's and women's roles in households, one undisputable result of the higher proportion of female-headed households is that a growing proportion of children spend more years living away from their fathers than in the past. However, as previously mentioned, being a nonresident father does not mean that a father is absent. Furthermore, as various studies have found, the quality of a man's relationships with his children is generally more important than time spent with children, and even when fathers are not present, in many cases there are other men in the family setting who take on some of the roles traditionally associated with fathers. Various studies from the Caribbean suggest that many families with nonresident fathers make arrangements for visits or informal encounters between fathers and their children. However, these arrangements and interactions are seldom covered by research on fatherhood.

MEN'S WORK AND THEIR FINANCIAL CONTRIBUTIONS TO THE HOUSEHOLD. One of the major themes in gender analyses of household dynamics in Latin America and elsewhere is the lower proportion of income that men dedicate to their families compared to women, and that investing in women's income generation generally offers better returns for family well-being. For example, a study in Guatemala found that a relatively small increase in the mother's income was necessary to improve child nutrition, while an increase nearly 15 times as large was required in the father's income to produce the same results (Bruce et al. 1995). Similarly, a study in Jamaica found that households without men devote a higher percentage of their income to child-specific goods (Wyss 1995). Other researchers have countered that in some cases, men's use of their income with male peers may be a valid effort to construct and maintain instrumental social networks, which may serve as sources of contacts and information about potential employment.

In addition, if it is true that on aggregate, men contribute a lower percentage of their income than women to the household and to children, this finding may create its own reality and reinforce gender stereotypes. By focusing on women's income, some programs and policies may also reinforce the stereotype that women should and will provide for their households (and not necessarily for themselves) and that men are presumed derelict or at best self-centered when it comes to supporting the household. Data from Costa Rica and the United States suggest that social policies that focus on women as heads of households may actually drive men away from assuming family responsibilities, serving in effect to create self-fulfilling prophecies (Chant and Gutmann 2002; NCOFF 2002).

When considering men's financial contributions to the household, existing research suggests caution when making broad conclusions or generalizations. In addition, if men's economic participation has decreased somewhat in Latin America, there are unanswered questions about what this means. Some authors find no evidence of a general trend of male economic marginalization, but rather report increased bouts and duration of unemployment for some of the most marginalized men—including younger men, less educated men, and men working in the informal sector. An analysis of employment and income trends among men in Argentina, Brazil, and Costa Rica during 1988–97 found that some groups (not only men in the lowest-income groups) faced declining income. This analysis highlights the uneven nature of men's economic marginalization and questions whether such marginalization truly exists (Arias 2001). It also suggests the need to target specific groups of low-income men with employment- and income-generation initiatives, for example low-income and unemployed fathers, as some programs in North America and Western Europe have done.

Although the evidence is unclear or mixed regarding men's economic marginalization, research throughout the region (and most of the world) makes it clear that work is a central component of men's identity and social recognition. While considerations of men and their work has often been instrumental—focusing on the impact of their income on family well-being—employment and income are much more than instrumental for men. Work gives men their main social identities and provides them with a socially recognized function. For many men, having stable employment is often a requisite for marriage, or family formation. As a Chilean working class man told one researcher, "Yo era lo que era mi trabajo" [I was what my work was] (Mauro et al. 2001, p. 57). Similarly, a low-income young man interviewed in Rio de Janeiro said, "Work isn't everything, but it's almost everything" (Barker 2001). Women and children generally view fathers in these ways as well. In a sample of rural children in Peru, 50 percent said that their father's principal role was to work, followed by 20 percent who said their principal role was to buy them things, and 13 percent who said it was to help in the home. Wilson (1996), in examining the impact of changes in the employment structure (specifically the decline in industrial or factory-based work that gave men a stable income and an identity) in the United States, has documented the impact on social capital and social structures when large numbers of men are without work and pro-social identities.

The conclusion that emerges is that unemployment and underemployment for men must be understood and examined beyond economic implications. However, such considerations are rarely taken into account in social policy. For example, while child-support enforcement is fundamental for women's rights and children's well-being, it often takes a punitive view that men are derelict in paying child support, while in many cases men are unable to pay because they are out of work.

MEN AS FATHERS AND VIOLENCE AGAINST WOMEN. Although it is not the focus of this chapter, a brief analysis of men's use of violence in the home, precisely because this violence is so pervasive, is important. There is no evidence to suggest that men's use of physical violence against women in the region has increased in recent years, but there has clearly been more data produced on the issue in the last 15 years. More than 30 well-designed studies from around the world, including several from Latin America, show that between one-fifth and one-half of women interviewed have been subject to physical violence by a male partner (Heise 1994).

The causes and factors associated with men's use of violence against women are multiple, complex, and interwoven; in many cases, the underlying causes are uncertain. Clearly, the underlying factors related to male violence against women are deeply rooted in the social construction of masculinity. De Keijzer (1995) suggests that male violence against women is an attempt to reestablish "normal" or traditional gender relations, or an attempt to keep a woman in her traditional role. Kaufman (1993) and Nolasco (1993) suggest that men's violence against women is frequently seen as a valid form of expression for men, who may not be socially allowed or encouraged to express emotions in other ways. Qualitative research from the Caribbean and Brazil has found that domestic violence is often seen as part of the social contract. If the man sustains the household, the woman is expected to take care of the house and be sexually faithful to him. Violation of this contract on the part of the woman is seen by many men and women as grounds or justification for male violence.

Research confirms that men's use of violence against women is learned, and is passed from one generation to the next. Various studies have found that having witnessed or been a victim of violence in the home is associated with using violence against an intimate partner. It is also clear that children are frequently present when men use violence against women and are victims of men's violence. Although there is limited data on the issue in Latin America, one study in the United States compared the fathering traits of men who had used violence against women with those who had not. In terms of time spent with children, there were few differences, but men who were violent against women were more likely to report arguments with their children, more frequent yelling, and more negative perceptions of their children (Fox and Benson 2001).

The Benefits of Father Involvement

As previously mentioned, there are several reasons for focusing on men's participation as fathers. One is the issue of gender equity. Women continue to provide a disproportionate amount of child care, even as they work outside the home at rates approaching those of men. Furthermore, there is an emerging literature, mainly from North America and Western Europe, that men's positive involvement as fathers is good for children and for men themselves. Numerous studies in Europe and North America confirm that father's involvement, or the involvement of other men, in the lives of children is positive. This conclusion is based on several indicators of child well-being, including health, social, and emotional development; school completion rates; and flexibility of gender roles (see, for example, NCOFF [2002], Johnson [1995], Day [1998], and Bernard Van Leer Foundation [2000]). Little research of this sort has been carried out in Latin America and the Caribbean, but there are several qualitative studies and a handful of quantitative studies that suggest similar benefits from positive father involvement as those found in North America and Western Europe. This section briefly reviews those studies.

INCOME GENERATION AND INCOME SUPPORT. It is important to consider the income that men and fathers provide to their households and the proportion of income they devote to households. A study of two-parent households in Guatemala found a significant positive association between child nutritional status and the percentage of a father's income contributed to the household. The authors suggest that the percentage of income fathers contribute to the household may be a proxy for measuring commitment to his family (Bruce et al. 1995). Studies in the United States have found that the father's income has significant positive effects on children's verbal abilities, education, and future wages (NCOFF 2002). While the role of men and fathers should not be reduced to merely provider, the income men contribute to their families is an important positive outcome of their involvement. Nonetheless, there has been relatively little research in the region on men's decision-making related to income allocation, and little policy and program development to promote men's contributions to household income, with the exception of enforcement of child support.

GENDER SOCIALIZATION AND THE GENERATIONAL POWER OF INVOLVED FATHERING. While relatively little studied in Latin America, there is some empirical evidence from North America and Western Europe that positive father involvement increases the chance that sons will be more gender-equitable and more nurturing as fathers, and that daughters will have more flexible views about gender (Levine 1993; Russell and Radojevic 1992). Various researchers in North America have concluded that the warmth or proximity of a child's relationship with his or her father is correlated with nontraditional (more gender-equitable) definitions of masculinity in sons and in more progressive versions of femininity in daughters. Furstenberg (1991) found that urban African-American men who had a positive father or father figure who cared for and sacrificed for them were more likely to be involved in positive ways as fathers (Bruce et al. 1995). Qualitative studies in Latin America have suggested similar associations (Almeras 1997; Barker 2001). A qualitative study of low-income young men in Brazil found that young men who are gender-equitable had a father or other male figure who demonstrated these roles while they were children themselves.

FATHER CONTRIBUTIONS TO CHILD DEVELOPMENT AND SCHOOL ACHIEVEMENT. While research is lacking on the role and impact of fathers on child development in Latin America, there are some studies from the Caribbean that echo findings from North America and Western Europe. Various studies from the United States have found that having an involved father or a father present is related to enhanced cognitive development and school achievement, particularly for boys. Studies have also found that when fathers are more involved with children in early childhood, their children cope better with stressful situations in school (Parke 1981, in Pruett 1993). Similarly, in Barbados one study revealed that those children (a cohort of eight-year-olds) who performed better in school had more involved fathers than their lower-achieving peers (Bruce et al. 1995). Another study from Jamaica found that when fathers resided with children, boys fared better in school, although the same was not true for girls (Ramikisson 2000).

MEN IN OTHER ROLES IN THE FAMILIES. Much of the research on men in families stresses the role and participation of biological, or surrogate, fathers. Despite numerous rejoinders about the need to consider new family arrangements, research from the region and much of the world tends to focus on men in nuclear families. While the positive impact of men as social fathers is clear, it is important not to ignore the other care-giving and role-modeling that men do in families, however it is defined. Some research outside the region has examined, for example, gay or homosexual men and their care-giving for partners in their families, including for partners living with HIV/AIDS. From qualitative research, we know that men play many important roles with children, including teacher, coach, friend, and peer. While it is useful to focus on men in households or men's contributions to households, too often the other men who influence and socialize children are ignored. Qualitative research in Brazil showed that low-income young men found important role models in uncles, fathers of friends, grandfathers, and brothers who, regardless of whether a biological or social father was present in the home, sent powerful signals about gender roles (Barker 2001).

Defining and Measuring Father Participation

A recent review of literature on father involvement in the United States suggests several definitions of father participation: (a) father presence, referring to whether the father is present and available to interact with the child; (b) caregiving, referring to the amount and quality of time that fathers offer in caring for children; (c) material and financial contributions; (d) cooperative parenting indicators, referring to the degree to which the father and mother cooperate to provide care and support for children; and (e) achievement and social competence indicators, referring to actively engaging with children to promote social competence and school performance (NCOFF 2002).

FATHERS AS PROVIDERS, CHILD SUPPORT, AND LEGAL DEFINITIONS OF FATHER INVOLVEMENT. The amount and percentage of a father's income dedicated to children or the household is one indicator of father involvement that has been used in some studies. In addition to studies already mentioned, a study in Honduras found that when men were heads of households, 70 percent of their income went to the family, whereas if women headed households, 86 percent of income went to the family. This and other studies have consistently found that while men on average earn more, women dedicate a higher proportion of their earnings to the household (Rodríguez 2001, in Alatorre 2002).

Some authors have suggested (although there is relatively little empirical data to support it) that the inability of men to earn adequate income has led to an increase in family abandonment in some low-income areas and a decline in the authority of working-class or low-income fathers. There is considerable research on this issue in parts of North America and Western Europe, but little in Latin America and the Caribbean.

One important indicator of father involvement in the region is the legal registration of children. In some countries, a relatively large proportion of children are not legally recognized by their fathers. In Central America, for example, about one-quarter of children are not legally recognized by their fathers. In Costa Rica in 1990, 21.1 percent of births did not have a declared father, which increased to 30.4 percent in 2000. In Honduras and El Salvador, about 25 percent of births have no registered father (Olavarría 2000). Apart from the symbolic importance and legal bond that the establishment of paternity implies, it also has concrete ramifications in some countries. In Honduras, for example, only those children who are legally recognized by the father can receive pension benefits and request child support.

Another legal-oriented indicator of father involvement is the percentage of households headed by a single father or by separated or divorced fathers who have custody of their children. Throughout the region, this percentage of households headed by single fathers and of fathers who have custody of their children is minimal. Even in countries where child custody laws have become relatively gender-neutral, such as Norway, children stay with mothers in 88 percent of cases of divorce or separation (Cohen 2000).

MEN'S TIME DEVOTED TO CARING FOR CHILDREN. As mentioned in the introduction, various studies confirm that worldwide, men provide for only a relatively small proportion of child-care time. In Guatemala, for example, men spend about one-third of the time that women do on child care. In Nicaragua, men are said to provide such care mainly in exceptional cases, such as when the mother is ill (Alatorre 2002). In addition, various studies in Latin America confirm that fathers are more likely to be involved with recreation and play activities than in care giving or education of children (Rendon 2000). Other studies, including one from Chile, find that men are more likely to provide care for younger children when women are unable to provide this care. (Olavarría 2000). Another study in Chile found that low-income men spent less time with children than middle-income men, and that the difference between men and women in terms of hours dedicated to child care was greater among lowest-income men. Low-income women dedicated six to seven times more time to child care than low-income men, while middle-income women spent about four times more time in child care (Sernam 1998).

Even when men participate in child care, they typically define this care as helping, not as part of their normal role, and they often continue to see themselves as being able to opt out of certain aspects of domestic tasks or chores (Vivas 1993; Hernández 1996). Some researchers have suggested the amount of time men in Latin America and the Caribbean devote to child care has increased, but data is insufficient to support this claim. Data in the United States suggest that fathers' availability for their children has increased from about one-half that of mothers in the 1980s to nearly two-thirds that of mothers in the 1990s (NCOFF 2002).

With the possible exception of the Caribbean, research in Latin America has tended to focus on fathers who live with their children; relatively little is known about nonresidential fathers and their patterns of providing child care. A study on visiting fathers in Jamaica, for example, found that contrary to previous studies, which suggested limited involvement, nonresident fathers visited their children (which may or may not imply some time spent in caring for them) 3.5 times per week and often discussed the child's needs with the mothers (Barrow 2001).

There are relatively few men in the region in professions in which they provide care for younger children, such as in day-care centers or primary schools. The vast majority of child care outside the home in the region (and elsewhere) is provided by women, and the vast majority of primary teachers are women. One study from the Caribbean argued that boys rarely see a man in a teaching or caring profession until the secondary level. In some settings, there is a widespread belief that men do not know how to care for children, or that if men have more contact with children, there will be a higher potential for physical and sexual abuse.

MEN AND DOMESTIC CHORES IN GENERAL. As in the case of child care, various studies in the region have confirmed that men's participation in domestic chores in general is far less than women's, although their participation seems to have increased slightly in the last few years in some settings. For example, in Nicaragua, one study found that women devote 85 percent of the time required for domestic chores, while men provide the remaining 15 percent (Alatorre 2002). Other authors suggest that women carry out up to 90 percent of domestic work. A sample survey in Chile with 400 men and women in low- and middle-income settings found that women dedicated about twice as much time to domestic tasks per day as men. Looking at specific tasks, women on average dedicated five times more time per day to food preparation than men, eight times more time to house-cleaning and five times more to child care (Sernam 1998). Low-income women dedicated more time overall to these tasks than middle-income women.

As in the case of child care, various studies confirm that men gain little or no identity or social recognition from carrying out such chores. Some men, as one study in Chile pointed out, try to carry out domestic work in clandestine ways so they do not "ruin their reputation" (Sernam 1998). Men may see their domestic work as a type of gift to women, or as something to do on special occasions (if a spouse is ill or tired), but seldom as a question of rights. Some men may take on significant portions of domestic labor, including child care, when they are out of work, and may even report this to be positive. However, as soon as they return to work, they cease this activity (Sernam 1998).

Nonetheless, extensive qualitative and quantitative research in the Caribbean suggests that some men may contribute in more ways than are commonly assumed in domestic tasks, particularly when children are too young to help out. As in the case of the research from Chile, many men offer ambivalent messages about this work, and generally only when women cannot do it. As Brown and Chevannes state, "Such participation is rarely celebrated by men and not always by women, some of whom see a very domesticated man as 'soft' or as [someone] who watched or criticised everything the woman does in the home, thus intruding on her domain" (1998, p. 30).

FATHERS IN COOPERATIVE PARENTING. What might be the benefits of greater cooperation between men and women? For the most part, existing research measures what women do (women's roles as mothers) and men do (men's roles as fathers) separately. There is relatively little research in the region on the things that men and women do together or the ways they cooperate. While it is necessary to point out gender inequities and differences, this research tends to obscure or glide over cooperation between men and women.

Nonetheless, a few studies have examined these issues. Some programs in North America and Western Europe have also begun to use terms such as cooperative parenting, parenting alliance, or team parenting to emphasize cooperation between couples. While the issue may seem obvious, there is in fact little research on how families or couples negotiate roles, how families succeed in cooperating, and how families overcome obstacles to greater cooperation. It is surmised, however, that cooperation is positive. For example, U.S. data suggests that children benefit when their parents are mutually and positively engaged in their well-being (NCOFF 2002). Some research from the reproductive health field has found that communication between couples is associated with higher satisfaction by the couple (and men and women individually) about their contraceptive choice (Drennan 1998).

Although male-female relationships are often characterized as being fraught with mistrust and conflict (and too often with violence), there are exceptions. Data from the Caribbean suggest a variety of styles of interactions among couples. Brown and Chevannes (1998) conclude that while male-female relationships among low-income couples are often characterized by mistrust, others include sharing, equity, mutual respect, and healthy doses of humor. Similarly, a qualitative study of 20–65-year-old couples in Mexico found that many urban, middle-class, young fathers discussed contraceptive use and family size with their partners and negotiated such issues, while older fathers and rural fathers generally did not (Rojas 1999).

CHILDREN'S ASSESSMENTS OF THEIR FATHERS' INVOLVEMENT. In addition to other measures or definitions of father involvement, it is also important to consider the voices and opinions of children. Most research on father involvement in Latin America and the Caribbean, North America, and Western Europe has focused on fathers of young children, whose ability to express their opinions about their fathers is likely limited. The few studies available in Latin America and the Caribbean offer some insights into what children, including adolescents, think about their fathers and their fathers' participation in their lives. In Jamaica, Ramkisson (2001) found that a majority of children stated that they have generally good relationships with their fathers. Many children's fathers are psychologically present in their lives, whether or not they live with them. Other studies, however, have found that children and youth have negative feelings or assessments of their fathers. A representative sample of adolescents in public schools in Mexico City found that 24 percent of youth who live with their fathers reported a problematic relationship. Of those, 25 percent said that communication with their fathers was poor or limited, and 21 percent of girls and 35 percent of boys who reported a problematic relationship said that their fathers had struck them. Nearly 70 percent of all youth interviewed said they did not trust their fathers (Sánchez-Sosa and Hernández-Guzmán 1992).

Engle and Breaux (1998), in an international review of anthropological research on fatherhood, suggest three common markers of involved fatherhood in developing regions of the world: (a) interaction with the child; (b) being available for the child; and (c) assuming responsibility for the child. Indeed, these seem reasonable measures to apply in the region, particularly because they combine gender equity and the role of fathers in promoting child development. As additional research is carried out, it will be useful to define the concept of involved and positive fatherhood, particularly to evaluate the impact of program and policy initiatives seeking to promote father involvement.

Factors Influencing Father Participation

Men's participation as fathers is associated with numerous factors, including income, educational attainment, relationship with the mother, the father's own experience as being parented or fathered, age of the child, the father's age or developmental stage, and the father's attitudes or beliefs about gender roles.

SOCIAL EXPECTATIONS OF FATHERS. Qualitative research and common sense suggest that men's involvement in caregiving of children (and others) is limited because societies—mothers, family members, social institutions, policy makers, and others—do not expect it. Gender norms in much of the world define caregiving as a largely female task. Indeed, fathers' involvement as caregivers of children is still a relatively new phenomenon in many other parts of the world. A review of ethnographic reports from 156 cultures concluded that men have close relationships with infants and young children in only 20 percent and 5 percent of cases, respectively. In the vast majority of cultures, fathers are seen as providing discipline and passing on skills to children, but not as caregivers. Among the cultures studied, the authors note three universal contributions of men to children: building a caring relationship, providing economic support, and decreasing the chance of fathering outside the partnership with the child's mother (Engle and Breaux 1998).

INCOME, EDUCATIONAL ATTAINMENT, AND EMPLOYMENT. Income levels, employment status, and educational attainment are associated to varying degrees with men's participation as fathers and with their participation in other domestic activities. Research from Chile and the United States finds that low-income and unemployed fathers are less likely to support their children than fathers with high income and stable employment (Bruce et al. 1995). In addition to these associations, men's employment, household income, and women's employment interact to influence men's participation in child care and other domestic tasks. Various studies have found that men react to temporary and long-term changes in households. For example, research on two-parent households in the United States found that the father's participation in caregiving was related to the number of hours the mother works outside the home and the number of children per household. When women worked and the family had more than one child, fathers were more likely to provide care for children (NCOFF 2002; Davis and Perkins 1995).

Finally, the quality of a father's employment is also important. Longitudinal data in the United States found that a father's satisfaction with his work was a factor in the type of interaction he had with his children. Fathers who work at mundane tasks, work in sites where they have little autonomy, or work for long hours were more irritable and more likely to be authoritarian and conflictive in their relationships with their children (Bronfenbrenner 1986).

RELATIONSHIP WITH THE MOTHER. Research consistently confirms that the father's relationship with the mother, particularly if he is separated, divorced, or resides away from her, is highly associated with the father's relationship with his child. Various studies confirm that after fathers are separated from their child's mother, their payment of child support decreases and their involvement with the child is limited. In Argentina, for example, 1993 data found that only 36 percent of divorced fathers pay child support. In Chile, a 1992 study found that 42 percent of fathers of children born to adolescent mothers (the majority of whom were not residing with the mothers) provide no child support six years after their child's birth (Bruce et al. 1995).

Other studies have found, however, that there are other ways fathers remain involved after divorce or separation. A study in low-income areas in Argentina found that even after divorce, mothers continue to turn to biological fathers for decision making related to the child, particularly when discipline was necessary (de Keijzer 1998). Research on Mexican fathers who migrate to the United States while their families remain in Mexico finds similar patterns. These fathers have contact with their children for brief periods but retain ties with the child's mother and participate indirectly in child-rearing and discipline.

Nonetheless, it is clear that separation and divorce frequently change a father's involvement with his children. This overwhelming reality in the region raises an important policy and program question. With increasing rates of separation and divorce, how can nonresident fathers (and the mothers of their children) be encouraged to support their children? This issue is made even more complex by the tension that often surrounds divorce and separation, not to mention relatively high incidence of physical violence by men against women that may have precipitated the divorce or separation in the first place.

AGE OF THE CHILDREN. Various studies suggest that the age of the child is also an important factor associated with father involvement, and that fathers may be more involved and more likely to be physically present in the first years of a child's life. A study by Atkin and Alatorre (1991) found that among adolescent parents in Mexico, 90 percent of fathers live with the mother at the time of the birth of the child but only 75 percent of fathers are with the child four years later. Research from Chile also suggests that resident fathers are more likely to provide care for their children when they are younger (Olavarría and Parrini 2000). Another multicountry study, one that included Mexico, found differences in father participation based on the age and sex of the child. Mexican fathers are more likely to provide care for daughters when they are young (under age four), and more likely to care for boys when they are older (Mackey and Day 1979).

AGE AND DEVELOPMENTAL STAGE OF THE FATHER. The age of the father and his developmental stage when his children are born are also important factors in explaining father participation. For example, limited research suggests that in the region, as in some other parts of the world, adolescent fathers, like adolescent mothers, may face social pressure to drop out of school to support their children and are therefore less likely to complete secondary school than their nonparenting peers (Barker 2001). Research in Mexico suggests that an adolescent father's employment and financial situation are important factors in determining how he reacts to pregnancy and fatherhood (Atkin and Alatorre 1991).

Adolescent fathers frequently face numerous deep-rooted stereotypes by their parents, the parents of the child's mother, the mother of the child, and service providers. There is a widespread belief that an adolescent father who does not marry the mother of his child is being irresponsible, when in fact his motivations may be complex. In some cases, young fathers want to be involved with their child but are not allowed by the child's mother to be involved. In other cases, young fathers feel constrained because they are unemployed and do not feel they have the right to interact with the child if they are not financially providing for the child. Indeed, public perceptions in much of the region hold that young fathers are self-centered, uncaring, and only want sex, although literature from Brazil, the United States, and other countries is counter to this image (Lyra 1998; Jordan 1995).

Various studies from the region confirm that many young fathers, especially when they are unmarried, are involved with their children initially, but that involvement often declines over time, particularly if the relationship with the mother ends. A study in Barbados found that only 23 percent of children of unions between adolescent parents resided with their fathers by age four (Bruce et al. 1995). In Chile, 40 percent of children born to adolescent mothers are abandoned and unacknowledged by their fathers by age six (Bruce et al. 1995). Participation by young, unmarried fathers in most of the region is often affected by the relationship with the mother—whether the father has a new partner and children with this new partner, whether he is legally registered as the child's father, and his income or employment status.

Much of the literature describes fatherhood as a role transition; in various studies in Latin America and the Caribbean, fatherhood is seen as a requisite for defining oneself as a man (Olavarría and Moletto 2002; Brown and Chevannes 1998). Most fathers (and mothers), describe the birth of a child as stressful, and that it brings increased tension in relationships. Several researchers in Latin America and the Caribbean, and in North America suggest that fathers often feel ill-prepared and receive little support for this transition. Whereas women may have experience in caring for younger children as part of their socialization, boys often do not (Jordan 1995; Lyra 1998).

The nature of the transition to fatherhood is also influenced by whether the child or pregnancy was planned. For many low-income men and women in Latin America and the Caribbean, reproduction and parenthood are not planned (which does not necessarily mean unwanted), as confirmed in qualitative research with low-income populations in Mexico and Brazil (Rojas 1999; Promundo and NOOS 2003). Some men react in positive ways to an unplanned child, but for others, the role transition is more complicated, and the pregnancy may be blamed on the woman and seen as a financial burden.

FATHERING CHILDREN WITH SPECIAL NEEDS. Whether children are born healthy or have special needs is also a factor that influences father involvement. Anecdotal evidence from the United States and parts of Latin America and the Caribbean suggest that some fathers are able to be flexible and react to these special needs in positive ways, while others may be unable or unwilling to cope with extra demands.

VIEWS ABOUT GENDER ROLES. It may seem obvious to state that men's views about gender roles and sexuality are related to how they view and participate as fathers, but it is important to affirm the connection. Qualitative research on young men (aged 16–30) in the United States suggests limited awareness of themselves as procreative. In fact, in their desire for sex, some young men even seem to repress notions or concepts of themselves as procreative (Marsiglio, Hutchinson, and Cohan 1999). Extensive research in the region has affirmed that young men frequently disassociate sexuality from reproduction and see their own sexual desire as spontaneous and uncontrollable (Barker 2001).

How men and women treat extramarital relationships, which may result in pregnancy, is also related to whether men deny or accept their paternity. Research suggests that in many countries in Latin America and the Caribbean, men have more extramarital relationships than women, and thus a greater likelihood of having a child with a partner other than their wife. Research in Mexico confirms that men who have children as result of these outside relationships are likely not to provide any support to the mother or the child (Atkin and Alatorre 1991).

Men's Participation in Reproductive Health and Maternal-Child Health

While the focus of this chapter is on men's participation as fathers, various authors in Latin America and the Caribbean affirm the connection between men's attitudes about sexuality and reproductive health and their attitudes as fathers. Indeed, it is reasonable to assume that when men do not bear the cost of children, they may be more casual about their reproduction and sexual activity. Research suggests increasing participation of men in sexual and reproductive health in the region, including higher rates of male condom use, increased couple communication about contraceptive use, higher awareness and knowledge about sexual and reproductive health issues, and more favorable attitudes toward family planning and contraceptive use (Drennan 1998). Fertility rates have declined throughout the region, which means that families have more time and resources to devote to each child. While largely unproven and unstudied, decreased fertility rates may bode well for men's participation as fathers and create positive pressure on men to be more involved in the lives of children.

Although men in the region seem to be becoming more involved in sexual and reproductive health issues, their involvement in maternal health and in childbirth still seems rather limited. For example, a study in Honduras found that in 95 percent of prenatal visits, women were alone or unaccompanied by a male partner (Alatorre 2001). The implication of such a finding is that, given prevailing gender norms, pregnancy is still largely seen as a woman's issue. Research in Western Europe and the United States has confirmed that father participation in childbirth is now routine and socially expected. A qualitative study of low-income men in Brazil found that although the Brazilian Ministry of Health and WHO have affirmed the right of women to have the person of their choice accompany them in childbirth, women who give birth in public hospitals (predominantly low-income women) face tremendous barriers to having their partners present at birth. The main obstacle was hospital staff, who said that men's presence is disruptive, that men complain too much, that the presence of men makes other women uncomfortable, and that men's presence reduces privacy (Carvalho 2001). For the most part, policies and public health programs in the region have not made a concerted effort to engage men in prenatal care or childbirth, which is yet another barrier to men's later involvement with their children.

Men's Well-Being and Men's Subjective Experiences of Fatherhood

Past discussion of the effects of greater involvement by men as fathers has focused on the benefits related to children's well-being and development and to women's well-being (in the name of gender equity). Only recently have researchers begun to look at men's subjective experiences of fatherhood, their own desires regarding fatherhood, and the possible well-being that men achieve through involved father-hood. In listening to men's voices, research from Latin America and the Caribbean and other parts of the world has confirmed that involved fathers report that father-hood and their relationships with their children give their lives meaning, give them a sense of purpose, and are among the most meaningful social roles and relation-ships they experience in their lives.

There are other benefits as well. For young men in low-income settings in Brazil and the United States, various qualitative studies find that some young men describe having a child and being meaningfully engaged with their children as a motive for leaving gangs or ceasing involvement in various forms of delinquency. For other low-income young men interviewed in the United States, having a child represents a life-organizing or positive developmental experience, as it often does for young mothers in the same settings (Achatz and MacCallum 1994; Barker 1998b). A qualitative study found that for many men in Mexico, fatherhood was a "marvelous experience" that allowed them to mature and experience a sense of transcendence and which provided a powerful emotional bond that brought responsibility and pleasure (Guzmán 2001). Other studies in Mexico found that fatherhood was a factor in some men deciding to end or reduce their outside or extramarital relationships, or accept and invest in relationships (with their partners) that they may consider less than ideal, all attributes that suggest maturity.

Of course, not all men experience or seek this sense of connection or maturity upon having children. For example, a qualitative study with 55 middle-class men in Mexico found that 16 men said that fatherhood had given their lives more meaning, while 17 said that having children had not changed their lives, with the rest undefined (Nava 1995). Fatherhood is not a panacea, nor does it automatically bring with it the sense of connection or meaning described in some studies. Nonetheless, these few important examples suggest the untapped potential mean-ing of fatherhood in the lives of men and the mental health benefits that men receive. These issues need to be better understood and researched, precisely because men's self-interest in being connected fathers may be a potential hook to engage more men in their roles as fathers.

Pathways to Gender Equity: Learning from Changing Men

Whether starting from a perspective of gender equity, child well-being, or men's self-interest in involved fatherhood, more engaged fatherhood and more participation by men in household tasks is likely to be positive. Some men in the region have taken on these roles. For example, studies in Mexico find that middle-class and younger men have changed how they view gender roles, including domestic tasks (Nava 1995). Other men said their interactions with their children have changed. In one study in Mexico, 45 percent of men interviewed considered themselves to be less authoritarian and closer to their children than their fathers were with them (Nava 1995).

New social ideals of fatherhood have emerged in North America and parts of Western Europe, spurred by women's increasing participation in the labor force and the women's movement, and secondarily by some men questioning their relatively limited roles in the lives of their families. In short, change has occurred at both the societal and individual levels in terms of men's involvement as fathers in some regions of the world. What makes change possible at both these levels, and how might positive change be promoted?

We should not expect revolutionary or drastic change in seeking to understand pathways or change processes among men. Changes in gender norms and individual attitudes are often gradual, with old and new paradigms existing simultaneously. Leero (1994) suggests that in Mexico, a form of "neomachismo" or "machismo lite" now exists in which men negotiate more with partners and accept some degree of equality with women while still maintaining some traditional references of machismo (for example, believing that men have the right to outside sexual partners while women do not).

In reviewing the literature, various common factors seem to produce or lead to changes in men's attitudes and behaviors. Almeras (1997), in an in-depth qualitative study of Chilean couples and their negotiation of domestic activities, found that changes in men's attitudes and behavior are often short-term or situational (for example, living temporarily in another country where alternative gender norms existed). In a few cases, family factors are important. A few men who show more gender-equitable patterns reported having fathers or mothers who carried out nontraditional gender roles or tasks. For some men, knowledge mattered; early experience in caring for children or carrying out other domestic tasks was useful. Generally, for change to be lasting, more than one factor must be present.

Studies on men who have sought vasectomies in Latin America offer additional insights. Given the low rate of vasectomies in the region, these men can be considered different and more gender-equitable than the norm. A review of data on men who sought vasectomies in Brazil, Colombia, and Mexico found that these men are generally aged 32–35 and have a higher-than-average level of education for the country in which they live. When asked why they decided to have a vasectomy, the men cited their recognition of male responsibility for family planning, health problems of their spouses, and the concern that men feel for their wives (Vernon 1995). The woman's support was found to be extremely important in validating the male's decision to involve himself in family planning or contraceptive use in general.

All these studies suggest that a combination of factors leads to attitude and behavior change among some men: (a) individual characteristics, such as reflection about gender issues in meaningful ways or higher educational attainment; (b) situational factors, such as a change in the relationship, starting a new relationship, becoming fathers for the first time, or a temporary change in the household (for example, a spouse's illness); (c) broader contextual factors, such as perceiving changes in social norms; and (d) relationships and role models, including having nontraditional role models belonging to an alternative peer group or having a spouse or partner who encourages and enables this change.

In writing about men, various authors have suggested taking a life cycle approach to promoting change, recognizing that there are various moments in men's lives when they may be more open to changing their attitudes and behaviors, such as the birth of a child or the end or beginning of an intimate relationship. De Keijzer (1998) points out that some men who were emotionally distant from their own children are often affectionate in the lives of their grandchildren. This suggests that research should avoid simplistic notions that change among men is only possible when men are young, and that it should recognize that change is possible across the life cycle.

The resounding affirmation from research on men in the areas of HIV/AIDS and sexual and reproductive health is that individual attitude and behavior change is difficult to achieve unless changes in social norms also take place. Other researchers have suggested that individual men may face barriers to change or be resistant to change if people around them do not also change their expectations of men and manhood. In some settings, as de Keijzer (1998) reminds us, men who participate in domestic tasks may be seen as dominated by their spouses, which may have a negative connotation among their peers. In some settings, men's participation in domestic chores may imply loss of social status. In such settings, individual change will be difficult if social norms do not change.

Policy and Program Interventions: What Do We Know? What Was Tried?

Program Interventions in the Region: A Framework and Description

As attention to the issue of men's roles as fathers and men and masculinities in general in Latin America and the Caribbean has grown, a small but growing program and policy response to the issue has developed. Many of these programs started in the late 1980s and early 1990s. These programs reach only a small number of men, with relatively limited public sector involvement and little evaluation data. The programs described below are by no means exhaustive, but they are illustrative of the types of programs that have emerged in the region.

HEALTH-CENTER OR HOSPITAL-BASED EFFORTS TO ENGAGE MEN AS FATHERS. Many of the sexual and reproductive health programs that have sought to engage men have also included discussions about men's roles as fathers. Affiliates of the International Planned Parenthood Federation, for example, have longstanding initiatives to encourage men to accompany their partners for sexual and reproductive health appointments, including those related to contraception; men's sexual health needs can then be addressed at the same time as their partners' needs. Some of these initiatives have also engaged men in discussions or provided educational materials related to childbirth and child and maternal health. Few initiatives within the health care sector, however, have focused specifically on engaging men as fathers. In Brazil and elsewhere, though, a few public health facilities have started initiatives to encourage men to participate in childbirth (Carvalho 2001).

SCHOOL-BASED AND YOUTH-SPECIFIC PROGRAMS. A handful of organizations have begun to pay more attention to the socialization of younger and adolescent boys, implementing initiatives to expose boys to domestic tasks, including child care, or helping boys question traditional or prevailing gender norms. A 1998 WHO review of programs working with young men in the promotion of health and gender equity identified a number of interesting models from the region for engaging young men in reflections about gender issues (WHO 2000c). Approaches to reaching boys ranged from health centers with special hours for boys to mentoring programs that connect boys with alternative male role models. Many of the programs focus on sexual health, recognizing boys' unmet needs, but they also work in general health promotion, vocational training, counseling, educational support, and violence and substance use prevention. The programs reached boys in schools, communities, workplaces, bars, taxi stands, military facilities, and juvenile justice centers. Lessons include: the need to address homophobia; the need for high-energy activities that involve multiple themes; and the need to work with boys on self-care and prevention, something that boys often do not attend to. The majority of programs are twofold, working in boys-only groups for some themes and bringing boys and girls together to discuss gender inequality. A few Caribbean countries have promoted father-son days at school, during which girls stay at home and fathers are encouraged to connect with their sons in the school setting.

A few programs have focused specifically on the issue of fatherhood and child care. In Trinidad and Tobago, the NGO Servol provides vocational training for young people. As part of the training, all youth—young men and young women— are required to spend some time in day care centers, getting used to caring for young children. Servol staff report that for young men, this is often their first experience in caring for young children, or providing caregiving of any kind.

A coalition of four NGOs in Brazil and Mexico has developed a field-tested curriculum with group educational activities for young men designed to promote changes in attitudes related to gender, including a set of activities on fatherhood and caregiving (PROMUNDO/ECOS/PAPAI 2002).

GROUP EDUCATION AND SUPPORT FOR FATHERS. A handful of NGOs in the region (in Brazil, Chile, and Jamaica, among others) have started educational sessions, group discussions, or support groups for both adult and adolescent fathers. In Chile, the Fundación Rodelillo has carried out workshops called "Sólo para hombres" (only for men), offering group spaces for men to reflect on their experiences as fathers. These workshops parallel work with women in personal development. Fundación Rodelillo has learned that if it excludes or does not make men visible in interventions with families, not only is the intervention process slower, but in some cases men boycott the activities.

In various parts of the Caribbean, parent-training activities have included fathers in both male-only and mixed-sex sessions. Fathers Inc. is one of the oldest such programs; it has worked for more than a decade to question negative views about fathers. It carries out awareness-raising events to promote positive images of fathers and promote fatherhood development and has produced a training module that focuses on parenting skills for low-income men.

Apart from anecdotal and a few qualitative reports, these group sessions with fathers have not been rigorously evaluated. Limited evaluation of father education and father support groups in the United States suggest some positive effects in the short term. For example, evaluation of a 10-week intervention program showed improvements in child-father relationships using self-reporting by fathers (Engle 1997). Other researchers, however, have questioned whether such programs actually help fathers with their new roles (Jordan 1995; Furstenberg 1991).

MASS MEDIA AND COMMUNITY-BASED EDUCATION STRATEGIES. A few organizations in Latin America and the Caribbean, mainly NGOs, have started media-based or community education campaigns to promote more involved fatherhood. In Mexico, Salud y Género and CORIAC, for example, sponsor essay contests and have produced educational materials to promote reflections about men's roles as fathers. Costa Rica is one of the few examples where such efforts have received strong support from the government. National campaigns include messages about the need for fathers to participate in child care and other domestic chores (Alatorre 2002).

PROGRAMS FOR FATHERS WITH SPECIAL NEEDS. Many fathers in Latin America and the Caribbean (and around the world) have special needs or have children with special needs; conditions creating special needs include adolescent fatherhood, homosexuality, substance abuse, and incarceration. These special needs have been the focus of program development in North America and Western Europe, and to a limited extent in Latin America and the Caribbean. Often, special needs of fathers affect their ability to care for their children or their involvement in the lives of their children. Limited data from youth in juvenile detention facilities in Brazil suggest that a large number of the young men are fathers. Research from the United States has found that men who use substances or alcohol are less likely to participate in meaningful ways as fathers and are more likely to report the use of violence against their children (NCOFF 2002). Researchers report that there may be as many as 6 million homosexual husbands and fathers in the United States who are involved in some kind of care for their children (Davis and Perkins 1995). Davis and Perkins, however, confirm that sexual orientation has no bearing on ability to care for or nurture a child. With the exception of a few programs that work with young fathers and some prison-based discussion groups for fathers in parts of the Caribbean, programs give very little attention to fathers with special needs.

INCOME-SUPPORT AND EMPLOYMENT-GENERATION PROJECTS. Many of the challenges and obstacles to men's greater participation as fathers are related to their ability to provide financially for their children. In Western Europe and the United States, a few programs provide job-skills training or vocational counseling to low-income and unemployed or underemployed men. Some of these programs aim to assist (or force) fathers to pay child support rather than encouraging increased father-child interaction. Other programs for low-income fathers offer a mix of job training with counseling and fatherhood development. Limited evaluation of these programs in the United States found some positive impact on men's income and employment after participating in such programs and some increase in paternity establishment (Watson 1992).

In sum, despite a range of interventions with fathers in the region, there is virtually no systematic evaluation of these efforts, with the exception of program reports. This does not prove that such programs are ineffective, but rather that they have seldom if ever had sufficient resources to carry out evaluations. Programs to engage fathers in Latin America and the Caribbean are still in a nascent phases that include small programs reaching a relatively small number of fathers (many of whom probably already desire more involvement with their children). Other NGOs are generally well intentioned but often do not have a strong theory-based approach, or have not based their interventions on in-depth research into the needs and realities of fathers.

Policy Initiatives Related to Fatherhood in the Region

Along with some interesting program developments to engage fathers in the region, some initial policy related to fatherhood has been developed, but much remains to be done. All countries in Latin America and the Caribbean currently offer some type of maternity leave, and recently 16 countries increased this maternity leave in keeping with conventions supported by the International Labour Organization (ILO). However, few countries offer any paternity leave, and even in such cases it is generally short.[1] In addition, nearly all countries have passed or strengthened laws that offer women recourse to establish paternity and seek child support from fathers, although in most countries the burden of proof (and many times the costs associated with DNA testing to confirm paternity) continues to fall on women.

Chile stands out as one of the few countries in Latin America and the Caribbean where government agencies have carried out policy analyses and research on the different roles of mothers and fathers and sought to incorporate findings in public policy. For example, the national drug control agency has carried out research on the different roles of mothers and fathers in reducing substance use among youth, particularly on the role of male and female parenting styles. They concluded that the passive reactions of parents in the face of youth substance use was a risk factor and that in many cases mothers were left to deal with parenting issues, and thus fathers needed to be more engaged in direct (but nonauthoritarian) ways as active partners of mothers. These implications have been included in program efforts supported by the agency.

With a few exceptions, men's roles as fathers are largely missing from the public sector throughout the region. Clearly, such issues are complex and deserve focused review and analysis. For example, the mere establishment of maternity or paternity leave is inadequate in many countries given that such legislation generally applies only to men and women who have stable formal employment, and thus is meaningless for millions of families in the informal sector. Similarly, custody laws in the region have long favored mothers in cases of divorce or separation, generally with good reason. In recent years, some middle-class men in several countries have formed fathers' rights groups to question this trend. Understandably, women's rights groups have often countered that in most cases, mothers are more intimately involved in the care and raising of children. Some fathers, clearly, are as fit and committed to caring for and raising their children as mothers, but for numerous historical and cultural reasons, few men have been interested and willing to take custody of children in cases of divorce or separation.

Conclusions: Policy, Program, and Research Recommendations

While research in North America and Western Europe has shed some light on the issue of fatherhood, there is still a great deal to learn about fathers in Latin America and the Caribbean. When undertaking research and studying lessons learned, we must recognize that personal values about fatherhood and the roles of fathers often ignore the developmental and personal needs of fathers themselves. We often see fathers as an instrumental end—we must encourage fathers to become more responsible, caring figures within the family with the end goal of helping children. This goal is important but insufficient. To provide the maximum benefit for families and individuals, we must listen to the voices of fathers, recognize their own needs and interests, and make clear how men themselves will benefit when they are actively engaged as fathers. Programs should not ignore the rights and needs of women; they should focus on fathers as subjects with rights, needs, and realities of their own. Following are some recommendations to address fatherhood in programming, policy making, and research:

Program Recommendations

- One way to focus on men as fathers is to promote media campaigns and evaluate existing campaigns. National HIV/AIDS initiatives and safe motherhood programs can offer valuable insights on how to run effective media campaigns. Successful programs will need to overcome the idea that including men and fathers in media campaigns represents hostile competition to women's programs.
- Programs should focus generally on fathers as part of efforts to promote children's rights. This has been a key approach for UNICEF and some initiatives in the region, including CEPAL in Central America. In the United States and parts of Western Europe, focusing on fatherhood within the framework of children's rights is one strategy used to avoid creating dissension with women's rights groups.
- There is a wide gap between sexual and reproductive health and the issue of fatherhood. In recent years, there have been major advances in research, program experiences, and government involvement regarding men's roles in sexual and reproductive health. Yet these programs seldom take into account men's roles as fathers. The time is ripe for such efforts to begin.
- By the same token, programs can focus on men and fathers as part of efforts to engage men in preventing violence against women. One approach would be to provide spaces for young men to reflect about violence they have witnessed in an effort to break the cycle of intergenerational transmission.
- The question of where to work with men on issues of fatherhood is also important. One strategy is to engage men in the spaces where they spend time, including workplaces, schools, and sports groups. Offering income support and job training that includes fatherhood development for low-income fathers is one example of an activity that links men's daily lives and needs with the issue of fatherhood.
- Training is generally an important focus in fatherhood programs. There is a need to evaluate existing training materials (for example, courses in North America and Western Europe) and their effectiveness in engaging men in discussing their feelings about fatherhood. There is also a need to explore what is possible and what is desirable for training groups.
- Preparation for fatherhood should start early and should seriously consider the socialization of boys. Some programs in Brazil, the Caribbean, and Mexico have a theory-based or theory-driven approach that includes group educational activities with young men and behavior-modification communication

strategies to promote changes in young men. Impact evaluations of these programs should help draw lessons learned to inform future work.

Policy Recommendations

- New policies should include men in early child development initiatives and include a focus on recruiting men as caregivers.
- Ministries of health should begin to include men in maternal-child health initiatives.
- Policies should address the issue of children in informal unions. Some countries still do not provide for equal rights and responsibilities within these unions.
- The issue of child support requires greater attention by policy makers. While the need to legally force some men to provide support exists, this need can be served by providing free or government-supported DNA testing services.
- There is a need to review paternal leave legislation in the region and to consider which new laws and arrangements are relevant and possible.

Research Recommendations

- There is a need for policy-oriented research on men as fathers that goes beyond an aggregate analysis of gender differences to explore the complexities of gender, including gender roles, how roles evolve over a person's lifespan, and how men's behavior relates to the specific contexts in which they interact.
- Research must take the form of longitudinal studies of men's participation in families, including more research on the intergenerational transmission of ideas and patterns of fatherhood. Research on conditions that encourage or are associated with men's participation in families is equally important.
- Carrying out research in collaboration with governments and policymaking agencies increases the possibility that research results will be included in policy and program efforts.
- There is a need to undertake more research on the positive outcomes for men when they are meaningfully engaged as fathers. The idea is not just to increase knowledge of men as fathers, but to provide incentives for them to embrace fatherhood, including emotional responsibility within a family. Men need to know what they stand to gain.
- Research should focus not only on traditional, married fathers but also on alternative situations. Research areas should include families in which men serve as surrogate fathers or stepfathers, families in which fathers live apart from their children, families in which fathers and children maintain contact after marital separation, and the dynamics of relationships between men and women after separation.

- Research should review the impact of policies and legislation related to divorce and child support.
- Finally, there is need for more research on men's views, desires, and realities. Understanding how men think and feel is key to engaging them as fathers for their children.

Notes

1. There is substantial experience with paternity leave in Scandinavian countries. Sweden has had progressive parental leave policies for nearly 20 years. Working parents have a right to 12 months of paid parental leave (at 80 percent of their salary) to share between them. Prior to 1995, fathers used only 9 percent of total leave. The law was changed in 1995 to make one month nontransferable for each parent. Currently, 70 percent of fathers in Sweden use this month and 12 percent of fathers use leave beyond one month. Use of parental leave is higher among fathers with a high level of education and high income; low-income fathers say they cannot afford to lose 20 percent of their salary (Cohen 2000). While Sweden's policies would not be financially viable in Latin America and the Caribbean, these experiences may nonetheless offer some lessons on better design of maternity and paternity leave policies in the region.

The Role of Men in Families in the Caribbean

A Historical Perspective

BARRY CHEVANNES

T
he study of the attitudes, values, and behavior of males is an offshoot of feminist research and progress. To break through the glass ceiling, or even to gain equal rights and encourage men to be more involved in the home requires an understanding of that millennia-old institution found in every known society—patriarchy. The assumption often guiding the approach to gender studies and activism is that male behavior is an issue of morality. When it steps outside the bounds of socially approved norms, as in the case of incest, carnal abuse, and battering, that is clear enough. If the law does not punish offenders, social ostracism or other forms of registering displeasure signal the community's defense of the moral order. However, little distinction is usually made between such deviance and the culturally accepted aversion to domestic work, for example.

Research on the Caribbean generally concedes that slave society, by not encouraging stable family relations, was the probable cause of the chaos in family forms, although men are nevertheless blamed for the various pathologies affecting women and children—multiple relations, denial of paternity, aversion to domestic stability, neglect of financial responsibility for their children (especially "outside" children), high incidence of female-headed households, and the poor socialization of the male child. The moral argument has been heightened with the debate on male marginalization, that men had the same opportunities as women but they have squandered them and therefore have no one to blame but themselves for the fact that they are being outperformed at all levels of education.

Slowly, however, new research coupled with a rereading of the traditional literature on the African-Caribbean family, is throwing a different light on the role of men in the family and the community and on their achievement and maintenance of masculinity. This chapter discusses this research and argues that the perception of moral dysfunction is far from normative—in fact, there are structural and cultural factors affecting men and women that play critical roles in determining the behavior of males.

Family Structure and Gender in the Caribbean

One of the most striking features of the African-Caribbean families is the overall dominant position of women, both in relation to the children and in relation to the structure of families, and conversely the marginal presence or occasional complete absence of men. In the Caribbean, more than 30 percent of households are female-headed. Taken together with a similarly high frequency of female-headed families among African-Americans in the United States, it was easy to hypothesize a similarity of causes. These hypotheses became the main focus of the research first of Herskovits (1976) and then of Frazier (1951).

Herskovits's approach to the African-American family was informed by his general approach, which ran against the prevailing social attitudes, to the culture of Africans dispersed throughout the Western Hemisphere. The generally-held view was that Africans were stripped of their culture by European slavery and that the patterns of behavior, values, and beliefs they currently manifested were the result of either imitation or of habits developed under slavery. Counter to this view, Herskovits found in his research of Africans throughout the hemisphere evidence of cultural forms of expression brought from the African continent, which are still part of the existing cultural and social life of these people. Thus, Herskovits determined that many patterns of behavior among African-Americans were explained by various forms of adherence to original patterns: retention, syncretism with other (particularly European) cultures, and reinterpretation of values.

Within this general approach, Herskovits presents the female-headed family by reinterpreting the African traditions of matrilineality, in which the mother is the pivot around whom social identity is forged, polygamy is an accepted institution, and the residential unit is that of mother and children, with the father visiting. The dominance of the mother is a function of the absent father circulating among his wives.

The only English-speaking Caribbean country studied by Herskovits was Trinidad and Tobago, where he collected ethnographic data in the village of Toco. Herskovits argued that it is important to recognize not so much that many fathers do not assume responsibility for their children, but that in this system each child was socialized and prepared for his or her future place in society. This was done "whether with grandmother, with grandfather, or with mother" (Herskovits 1976, p. 110).

In addressing the African-American family, Frazier disagreed with the Africanist explanation of Herskovits, arguing instead that slavery shaped the traditions of matriarchal dominance in the African-American family, first by stripping the Africans of their culture and then by exposing them to the economic interests of their masters. Under slavery, the only enduring bond was that which existed between mother and children. Emancipation increased this pattern by introducing unemployment, which forced men to cut themselves loose from family ties in search of work. As in slavery, women were the mainstay of the African-American family. Since marriage was never a norm, men were thus afforded an institutional loophole through which to escape their responsibility.

The first to pick up the Frazerian argument in the Caribbean was Simey (1946), who was swayed by what he considered its forcefulness:"The contemporary looseness of family structure in the British West Indies required no further explanation..." (1946, p. 51). Simey thus drew five conclusions about the role of the male in the family structure.

First, Simey observed that as in the case of their African-American cousins, West Indian men in their roles as husbands and fathers were the sociological cause of the looseness of the family structure in the islands. Simey also recognized that women shared the same attitudes. Thus slavery and economic conditions at emancipation had in fact shaped the cultural practices of the present.

Second, Simey recognized that the situation may be different when the economic prospects of a peasant were favorable.

"Although it is the woman who keeps the family together, it is the man who rules; if a man establishes himself as a householder, he becomes as a matter of course the possessor of arbitrary authority. ... From the point of view of the children, the mother is dependable; the father is not. The father is feared; the mother is loved" (1946, p. 81).

In this case, the man assumed the role of head of the household but his primary relationship to his children was authoritarian control.

Third, this authoritarianism was more pronounced when such a stable family was closely connected with the church for it was through Church-sanctioned marriage that social respectability was achieved. Thus, the "close association between father and child" that was the norm in the United Kingdom and North America was an exception in the West Indies.

Fourth, owing to the social norm of illegitimacy, children grew up without fathers or effective father substitutes, a circumstance that has an important bearing on the development of personality (Simey 1946).

Finally, Simey pointed out that a natural feature of West Indian society was the "deep love for children" shared by men and women. Simey wrote that men will, as a matter of course "care for all the children of a woman with whom they may be living, to the best of their ability; settle down in a stable relationship, if their circumstances allow; or send home remittances for the upkeep of their children if they are forced to find work away from them" (1946, p. 86).

In short, persuaded that slavery and its aftermath were critical in giving the African-Caribbean family its loose structure, Simey argued that the role played by the husband-father was the greatest evidence of the effect of slavery. He went on to note, however, that where monogamy existed, the structure was patriarchal and the father's relationship to his children was authoritarian. One positive feature

Simey did not develop was men's love for children, which was such a deeply entrenched value that it caused men to become father-substitutes to their spouses' children by other men. Later writers made the same observation, although without impact on the stereotype about men not wanting children. As Higman (1975) observed, father-substitutes also existed under slavery.

Researchers of the family who came after Simey generally followed his approach. They found that the type of family pattern determined the type of relationship between father and child. For Henriques:

> "... the father ... plays a minor role in the life of the children. In many cases he is entirely absent from the household. When he is present he is not very much concerned with them, though one does occasionally meet a proud father. The children are the concern of the mother, and she in turn relies on her mother for information and instruction. In one case cited by a social worker the father did not even know the names of his twelve children" (1953, p. 131).

Family Structure and Fatherhood

Henriques distinguishes four types of families—the monogamous, the faithful concubinage, the grandmother or maternal, and the keeper—and observed that the father in a typical monogamous family is the "final authority in all disputes in the home, although as far as day to day household management is concerned the mother is the authority" (1953, p. 111). The grandmother or maternal family is referred as such "because the grandmother or some female relative, perhaps a sister, usurps the function of the father and at times that of the mother" (Ibid.). In this type of family, which originates when a daughter becomes pregnant while still living at home, the daughter's father, if he is also living in the house, "will act towards his grandchild as if it were his own child" (1953, p. 113). As for the father of the baby, the girl's family may pressure him for support, but this, observes Henriques, is usually ineffective. The father is often not known at all in such families.

Edith Clarke's *My Mother Who Fathered Me* (1966) is the most famous of all the early works on the Jamaican family, not least because of its title. Yet, in none of the three communities that Clarke studied did the number of households headed by mothers alone exceed those in which children lived with both their parents. Indeed, the proportion of households with two parents never fell below 50 percent, and altogether the average percentage of households with a father figure (father or stepfather) was over 80 percent. Still, the idea that the norm is the absent father has persisted.

Clarke's main thrust was to link the different types of mating and family composition to economic circumstances. In this respect, slavery was not the main determinant but the economic condition surrounding the formation and maintenance of households. The most well-to-do of the three communities studied by Clarke was characterized by a high rate of marriage and pronounced patriarchal relations, while the least well-off was characterized by a low incidence of marriage, a high rate of mother-headed households, and low intensity of male involvement in the home. At the same time, there were regularities that cut across class: children's most intimate relationships were with their mothers, "even in those cases where the father is present and associates himself with the upbringing of the child" (Clarke 1966, p. 158); fathers were "always more strict, more exacting and infinitely less well-known" (p, 159); and fathers entertained great hopes for their children, but only among the most well-to-do were these realizable.

With the work of Smith (1956), the anthropology of the Caribbean family reached an entirely new stage. Adopting the diachronic perspective of Fortes (1949), Smith established that the various types of families were a function of the family's own life cycle: family or household that is nuclear will become an extended three-generation female-headed family, from which a nuclear unit will fission to start a new cycle. In this perspective, the family yields the various types of mating. Visiting relationships are the norm in the early years, when couples, particularly the female, are resident in their natal home, common-law in later years when they take up common residence, and married late in life if the economic status of the husband is secure. A man's role within the family therefore changes over time, diminishing in intensity of association as it matures. His authority will derive from his status as husband and father, as his main function is provider. Naturally, when he is unable to fulfill his role as provider, he is unable to assert himself over his wife and children. If he does not live with his children, he in effect relinquishes his right over them.

From the point of view of function, Smith's approach yields an important conclusion also reached by Herskovits, namely that the family accomplishes its socializing function. First, Smith notes that "there is the general social acceptance that every individual has both a mother and a father" (1956, p. 134). As an ideal, this means that even if he is not present, the father is identified and recognized. The child's contact with him is maintained by visits if he lives in the same village, or by gifts from him. It is therefore not normal for a child to be without a father. Second, Smith believes that children are never without father-substitutes, for every woman will have some semipermanent liaisons with one or several men. And third, fathers are mainly providers who seldom act as enforcers of discipline, and, though heads of their households, are "on the fringe of the effective ties which bind the group together" (1956, p. 223). Activities in the household are centered on the woman as mother, so that in this respect the family is "matrifocal."

From the early research on the African-Caribbean family, a number of factors are prevalent in the parenting role of males. First, mothers, not fathers, are the main socializing agents for both male and female children, regardless of the structure of the family or the type of marital union. Second, fathers or father figures tend to be marginal in the day-to-day relationships of the household but are not entirely absent. Indeed, most families have a father figure, for many men will act as substitute fathers to their spouses' children from other relationships. Third, the main content of the fathering role comprises two functions: final enforcers of discipline and economic providers. Men will socialize with and entertain the children they live with, but this is not an expected role. Fourth, the economic factor is so central to the concept of fatherhood that the status of males as husbands and fathers is ultimately determined by it. The poorer and more materially deprived men are, the greater their marginality and the greater also the role of women. Conversely, when men are better off, they are more active as sources of patriarchal authority over spouse and children.

While some of these studies emanated from or were consumed by theoretical issues, others were more oriented to social policy. Or, more appropriately, the studies were in large part driven by both concerns. More recent research and writing on the Caribbean family has continued in the same vein.

As early as the 1950s, when Edith Clarke was consolidating the results of her study, concern with population growth led demographers and other sociologists to study family and mating dynamics in the Caribbean. The first to appear was the work of Blake (1961). Eliciting the views of women through the use of a questionnaire, Blake focused for first time in the history of the study of the family in Jamaica (and drawing on the earlier studies) on the disorganization and instability of the family in Jamaica, which she blamed for early pregnancy and illegitimate childbirth, and, implicitly, for added population pressure. If she did not rush to condemn the male outright, it was because her quantitative data revealed that "... far from being an expendable figure whose frequent absence causes little concern, the father is considered to play a unique and highly important role in child-rearing, a role for which women do not feel suited" (1961, p. 73). That role was to provide the discipline needed to bring up boys, which the women thought themselves incapable of. Thus, Blake's statement derives not from observed practice but from what her respondents said should be the ideal.

Where Blake's total sample was based on a mere 94 women, that of Stycos and Back (1964) was a sample of over 1,300 Jamaican lower-class women who were randomly selected using a sample frame developed by the Central Bureau of Statistics. Stycos and Back found that "... even the visiting relationship entails serious responsibilities for the male, and in eight out of ten such relationships, the female reports receiving economic support from her boyfriend. Moreover, fathers evidently feel a responsibility for their children by other women. About half the males aged 40 and over are reported (by their current spouses) to be helping to support outside children" (p. 85). Clearly, the picture of the Jamaican or the African-Caribbean father as absent and therefore delinquent was a gross oversimplification. One half of fathers were supporting their children, although it should be noted that this half was taken from among the older men, suggesting that the proportion of younger men supporting their children may be lower, the difference being accounted for by higher rates of unemployment among younger men.

While this finding by Stycos and Back was based on valid sampling procedures and therefore is generally valid, the same cannot be said of Brody (1981), whose fieldwork was carried out on 150 women and 283 men who visited family planning clinics in 1972. One therefore cannot generalize from Brody's findings that "in keeping with their low ambitions" women from broken homes "tended to have had more visiting mates according to age and impregnators per pregnancy than women benefiting from direct parental guidance;" lacked poise, affectivity and interpersonal competence; and were more tolerant of male irresponsibility (1981, p. 132). While Brody reports that more than one-third of the first children of male respondents did not live with them and that "this proportion diminishes sharply with successive children" (1981, p. 176)—the obvious converse being that nearly two-thirds of first children live with their fathers—we have no way of knowing how characteristic this is of the general population.

Roberts and Sinclair also used a small sample, but this was to provide "information of an attitudinal and qualitative nature" in order to "explore further many issues relating to reproduction and mating in the society" (1978, p. 21). This type of qualitative data would help to better interpret quantitatively derived material which was already "sufficient to give a satisfactory picture of mating habits" in Jamaica (Roberts and Sinclair 1978, p. 21).

To better appreciate his enormous contribution to studies of mating behavior in the Caribbean, it should be pointed out that while other scholars concluded that the Caribbean family structure was essentially pathological, George Roberts, calmly poring over Jamaica's 1943 census returns, was the first to advance the thesis that an illegitimacy rate reaching close to 70 percent could only point to the existence of family forms that were *sui generis* (Roberts 1955). Dispensing with the value-loaded descriptions of family and mating types, Roberts substituted the designation "visiting" to describe the initial type of union between spouses, and gave statistical validity to the conclusions reached by Smith.

After examining statistical data available for Jamaica since 1878, Roberts contended that family forms, defined on the basis of the mating type, had not changed since slavery, even though economic conditions had changed and demographic movements had occurred. Roberts therefore gives credence to the argument that the family forms are culturally determined, as people first enter visiting arrangements and thereafter tend to move through common-law unions to marriage late in their reproductive life.

Since coresidential unions by definition involve the male, Roberts and Sinclair in their 1978 study of 626 women examined the content of visiting relationships. Estimating the total amount of time the members of a visiting family spend together (43 percent of their sample were in visiting unions), the authors found that "the average time that the father spends with the children under all forms of contact is 14.5 hours per week" out of a weekly average total of 22.8 hours he spends with his family (1978). Most of these contacts take the form of visits to the home of the mother, but in a substantial proportion of cases (26 percent), contact with the children takes place when they visit the father's home. This further supports the idea that the "absent" father is not entirely absent. A study by Brown, Anderson, and Chevannes (1993) confirmed the importance of children to men's sense of identity and found that men played a far greater role in children's upbringing than previously thought.

Two other studies on the role of fathers, inspired by fertility and family planning concerns were those by Chevannes (1985) and Dann (1987). The Chevannes study, conducted for the Jamaica National Family Planning Board, was based on a national random sample of men, although a smaller sample than that of Stycos and Back. Chevannes had two pertinent findings. The first concerned the domestic marginality of men in the definition of what they ought and ought not to do within the household. Each respondent was asked to state his level of participation in five recurrent activities in domestic life: cooking, washing, tidying the house, tidying children, and shopping. Thirty percent reported that they cooked regularly, where "regularly" was defined as not less than two to three times per week. This represented the highest frequency of responses to any activity. The least popular was tidying children. The second finding had to do with the men's definition of a good father. There was total unanimity that being a good father meant providing economic support for one's children and seeing to their moral upbringing.

Dann's study, conducted in Barbados for the International Planned Parenthood Federation/Western Hemisphere Region and based on a random sample of 185 men drawn from the electoral list, produced the same finding, that men viewed themselves in the roles of breadwinner and instructor of male children (Dann 1987).

Two policy-oriented conclusions may be drawn from studies on the family with a policy orientation. One is the positive picture they paint of the position of the male as father, even in cases where the man does not live with his children. The other is the reaffirmation of the father's responsibility for the economic well-being and moral upbringing of his children, the two terms of reference of fatherhood, so to speak.

Turning to more theoretical approaches means reverting to anthropological studies carried out at community level over extended periods of time. From his study of Enterprise Hall in Barbados, Greenfield (1966) found that apart from providing a dwelling and financial support for his wife and children, a man's responsibilities to his children entailed maintaining discipline and providing for their education. Greenfield reported, "The paternal duty generally is restricted to seeing that money is available for clothing, books, lunches, bus fare and school fees if the child has the opportunity to attend secondary school" (1966, p. 104). Upon his son's graduation, a father's obligation continued by arranging for him to learn a trade. He extended support to his daughter, however, for as long as she remained a member of his household.

The role of the African-Caribbean father is captured by Rodman in his study of Coconut Village in Trinidad, "To Mind the Child." To "mind" is to "provide the money needed to bring up the child—money for food, clothing, school, etc." (Rodman 1971). More specifically, Rodman notes:

This duty of *minding* the children falls upon the father regardless of where he is living or what marital relationship he is in. An *outside child* counts as much as a child born within a *living* or married relationship and is ideally expected to receive the same amount of support. In actual fact, however, where the father is living away from the mother and child, he usually provides financial assistance in a very irregular fashion, and contributes only a portion of what is needed to support the child (1971, p. 76).

As Rodman shows, a father's separation from his children is linked to his diminished support. It is clear that Rodman is referring to permanent separation and not to the kind associated with visiting unions. While the role of father is to mind his children, the role of mother is to care, that is, to nurture and extend affection to children. Rodaman says, "The core of the father's role is to support the child financially and not to be close to him emotionally" (1971, p. 88).

Wilson's study of the island of Providencia parallels the findings of Rodman and others. A father is expected not only to contribute to the economic well-being of his children but also to ensure that his sons receive support regardless of where they are living. As for his relationship with his children, Wilson claims that a father retains a certain detachment, seeing them mainly as assets in his claim for reputation:

Though children always take the father's title, fathers have comparatively less intimate relations with their children, but rather relate to them as objects contributing to their pride. The father frequently shows off his children, and he indulges them rather more than he disciplines them. True, a mother may threaten a child that "when you pappy come back he gwan' flog you"; but this "bogeyman" role indicates the detachment of the father (1973, p. 126).

Wilson also finds that the intensity of this father-child relationship fades with separation, although he refers to:

... a number of instances in which a man, upon learning of the unhappiness of his child in his mother's household (usually with a stepfather), made arrangements to look after the child. Fathers try to contribute to the upbringing and education of their children, particularly sons, even if they have severed all relationship with the mother (1973, p. 197).

In sum, the best description of the role of the African-Caribbean father is, in Rodman's words, "to mind" his children. At the University of the West Indies Women in the Caribbean Project carried out in Antigua, Barbados, and St. Vincent, Powell (1985) corroborates this description. This sex-role differentiation takes on meaning when it is further understood that by cultural definition, the public sphere of life is the man's and the domestic sphere is the woman's. This leads to the man's detachment from the home, or as earlier anthropologists put it, his marginality.

In truth, much may be grasped about the nature of the father by appreciating the nature of God to African-Caribbean people. God is acknowledged as the creator and sustainer of life but is distant and removed from the day-to-day operations of the world, which are entrusted to the lesser but still powerful spirits. Though omnipresent, God is invisible. This analogue may be extended only so far, for man, unlike God, is subject to external forces, of which the economic is by far the most important, since it is primarily through economic force that a man's status is measured. The lower a man's economic achievement, the lower is his authority in the public eye and the lower is his authority in the domestic domain.

Portrayals of Fatherhood

Portrayals of fatherhood lead us to the more recent debate on male marginalization. As such, the reader may find useful the various portrayals of fatherhood in the autobiographical sketches of Jamaican women from the Sistren Theatre Collective.[1] The sketches are not about fathers, but for that reason they were compiled in order to "illustrate ways in which women can move from the apparent powerlessness of exploitation to the creative power of rebel consciousness" (Ford-Smith 1986, p. 1). The information that can be garnered about the interplay between men and women and their children may be a useful supplement to more formal literature. In two of the stories, a father takes his daughter Cammy to live with him because the mother is unable to maintain her. Cammy speaks favorably of her father, who no longer lives with her mother, and accepts his version of why she stopped supporting her. Cammy was in the care of her mother and was living in the household of her grandaunt when her father paid her a visit:

> One day, me faada bring two lickle dresses fi me. His girlfriend sew it fi me with her hand. Me grand-aunt tek dem and fling dem down. "Yu fi bring money!" she say. ... Me faada get vex and him stop look after me.

> When ah was four Papa come to di yard and talk to Mama and Icilda. Mama decide to give me up. Me member di day me stepmadda and me faada come fi me. ... All me can remember is dat me mada say, "Is not yuh ah giving Cammy to. Is yu girlfriend. Yuh cyaan tek care a galpickney" (Ford-Smith 1986, p. 12).

> [*One day, my father brought me two little dresses. His girlfriend had sewn them. My grandaunt took them and flung them down. "You are to bring money!" she said. My father got vexed and stopped looking after me.*

> *When I was four years old, Papa came to the home and talked to Mama and Icilda. Mama decided to give me up. I remember the day my stepmother and my father came for me. ... All I can remember is that my mother said, "I am giving up Cammy to your girlfriend, not to you. You can't take care of a girlchild."*]

According to Cammy, her mother wanted to be free to dispose of the money as she saw fit, to use it to buy and sell rather than spend it directly on her daughter. Her grandaunt understood this also, and signaled her displeasure with an insulting gesture. Here we see what child support means. It means cash, not kind, and the failure to provide it means the failure of a man to mind his child. A man does not mind his child by providing kind. Cammy does not say whether her father had intended the dresses as a substitute for money, but we do know from ongoing research that from the father's point of view, child support should be used solely and specifically for the upkeep of the particular child or children and not for any other purpose, not even in support of any of the child's half siblings. Some men risk being taken to court rather than providing cash if they have good reasons to believe that their child's mother's motive is in laying hands on the money rather than in taking care of the child.[2]

Men's concern for their children sometimes leads them to take over custody, and although there is evidence of an increase in single father-headed households, the prevailing view is that fathers are not able to provide the kind of care that mothers can. This is what Cammy's mother meant when insisting that she was giving up Cammy not to Cammy's father, but to his spouse. In Doreen's case, her father took custody of her because her mother was failing in her role as caregiver:

> Me faada tell me sah me madda was a bad woman. When me lickle she used to go a bar and drink, and lef me deh a bawl. A disadvantage mek him tek me from her and give me to me stepmadda. She send me to her madda in Benbow at St Catherine. Her name was Ruth but me call her Granny (Ford-Smith 1986, p. 97).
> [*According to my father, my mother was a bad woman. When I was a little child she used to visit the bars and drink, leaving me at home crying. Because of such disadvantage he took me from her and gave me to my stepmother. She in turn sent me to her mother in Benbow, St Catherine. Her name was Ruth but I called her Granny.*]

In a reversal of roles, Granny was strict and protective, while Doreen's grandfather:

> ... sing wid me, dance wid me and treat me like me and him is friend. If him a tink bout anyting, him always ask, "Gal, what yuh haffi say bout dat?" Him tell Ananse story and whole heap a odder story. Him even mek a lickle swing under di house bottom fi me (Ford-Smith 1986, p. 98).
> [*... sang with me, danced with me and treated me as though we were friends. Anything he was thinking about he would always ask my opinion, "Girl, what do you have to say about that?" He told Ananse stories and lots of others. He even made me a little swing under the house.*]

In this case, Doreen's grandfather played the caring role, though he did mind her by cultivating the land, while Granny pursued her occupation as a higgler.

In Prudence's autobiographical sketch, it was Papa T who balanced the stern-
ness of her godmother with his own gentleness and quietness (Ford-Smith 1986).
Prudence's life story also highlights a point made by Ford-Smith, namely that the
biological relationship guarantees that every child has a father, even if he does not
play the role:

> My father was Luke Kennedy, so I was really Prudence Kennedy, but my
> mother didn't live with my father. So when she died I took Goddy's name. He
> never used to take care of me. Around three times dem show me, "See yuh
> father passing deh!" Him never come to look for me but as he passed dem say,
> "See yuh father deh!" We never talk. Nothing like, "Come here, gal. I am your
> father." Nothing like that. No relationship (Ford-Smith 1986, p. 111).

Luke played no role in the life of his child, but it was important that his daughter know who her natural father was. The immutability and permanence of that
biological relationship ensures that a door is always open for reconciliation or help.
That's what happened to Didi, another Sistren member, whose mother became
frustrated and humiliated by her husband's philandering, and fled with the children to her parents' home in Montego Bay. There she went to work because "Papa
no sen no money (not even a one cent) fi mind we" [*Papa sent no money, not even a
cent, to mind us.*] (Ford-Smith 1986, p. 202). Nonetheless, contact was never lost.
Somehow, Didi knew where her father was, so after she grew big enough to leave
home and travel to Kingston, she went to her father:

> When me did just go deh, Papa gimme money mek me get fi buy weh me
> want. Him never turn him back pon me. Him give me all weh him can give
> me. And we reason good (Ford-Smith 1986, p. 206).
> [*When I reached there, Papa gave me money and that's how I got to buy what I wanted.
> He never turned his back on me. He gave me all he could. And we got on well.*]

Despite the fact that Didi's father was not good by folk standards, the biological relationship between father and daughter allowed her to turn to him for help
and encouraged him to assume responsibility for introducing her to the city and
to provide for her for a while.

The provider role of father is pervasive throughout all the autobiographies of
the women, particularly in the childhood years of the women. As a result, many
portraits of fathers are from a childhood perspective. In the following sketch, which
is from the perspective of a spouse, we get a glimpse of a man wayward in his
parental responsibility and abusive in his conjugal relationship, but by the end of
the story shows signs of a turnaround.

In 1968, just after graduating from primary school, Ava became intimate with
Bertie, a postman. By 1969, they were already in a visiting relationship when she
became pregnant and gave birth to Julie. By 1970, she was forced to find work because
Bertie's help was not enough. That same year Bertie began to assert himself by beating

her. In 1971, Ava became pregnant a second time and gave birth to a second daughter, Suzette, in January 1972. From a seven-year-old visiting relationship, their union grew into a common-law one when Bertie moved out of his mother's house and invited Ava to live with him. That was in 1975. But it was at that stage that things began to change. Bertie was an incorrigible gambler, so in order to be sure to get money to run the house, Ava sometimes intercepted him at his gambling den:

> Me go up deh go stand up and long out me mouth. If me no long out me mouth, me tell him friend dem me deh bout and him fi come to me. Lickle later, hear him, "Weh yuh a come up hay fah? Yuh cyaan wait till me come home?" All dem something deh. Him no like embarrassment, het him never act like him a father (Ford-Smith 1986, p. 269).
> [*I would go up there and stand with a vexed expression. Or if I didn't put on a vexed look, I would ask his friends to tell him that I was around and he was to come to me. Soon, listen to him: "Why do you come here? Can't you wait till I come home?" And things like that. He did not like embarrassment, yet he never acted as if he were a father.*]

On top of this, Bertie began sleeping out with a domestic worker, so that between his gambling and this outside woman, Ava was unable to care for the children financially. The following year they moved to a different house, but as Bertie was unable to pay his rent on account of the gambling, which he was then doing more regularly, Ava decided to leave him and live in quarters leased by her mother. Yet again, she tried to hold Bertie to his responsibility to mind his children, but without success. In desperation, she took him to the family court in 1977, but he talked her into dropping the case, leading her to believe that if the children's names were to appear in court they would be denied the chance of going to the United States. They resumed a visiting relationship.

In 1978, Ava joined with a group of women and formed Sistren, a theater collective. In 1979, Bertie entered into another outside relationship and his support for Ava and their children began to dwindle. A turning point came in 1981. With the fame of Sistren now well established at home and abroad, Bertie's attitude changed from one of a provider to that of a predator. He beat Ava cruelly for refusing to lend him money that belonged to Sistren. As the members of Sistren became stronger and more knowledgeable about domestic violence and women's right not to be beaten, the group supported Ava in having Bertie arrested. Bertie's family was outraged. She had to lock herself in from his father and later from his nephew. Ava lodged a complaint against Bertie, but the police failed to make a case against him. A lawyer dissuaded her from pursuing the matter "since Bertie is my children's father and I would still need maintenance from him," said Ava. The story concludes in November 1984 with Ava's tantalizing comment: "Bertie is living in America now. He sends things for the children more regularly and we hear from him often" (Ford-Smith 1986, p. 281).

In November 1984, Julie was nearly 14 years old. It would be revealing to know what she remembers about Bertie. Does she think of him as a good or bad father? Does his apparently newfound sense of responsibility cancel out his earlier delinquency? As for Bertie, how much was the manifest "creative power of rebel consciousness" of the Sistren Collective a challenge to him? With Ava's growing independence and her heightening consciousness of her role and status as a woman, Bertie, it is not difficult to conjecture, must have seen the new Ava as a challenge to his masculinity. In this respect, he shared a common experience with many men who look on helplessly as their traditional roles and relationships undergo change. The extent to which control over females enters into men's conceptualization of their masculinity is a theme to which we will return.

The Marginalization of Caribbean Man

The concept of male marginalization first entered the discourse in the Caribbean in 1987 in an insightful essay by Miller (1986). Prior to that, Smith (1956) established that men were marginal in the day-to-day relations and operations within the household, which he described as centered around the mother; hence the term matrifocal. Miller elevated the argument onto the political platform. Starting in postemancipation times, he argued, black Jamaicans sought to challenge the power of the white colonial elite by using the teaching profession as a ladder. Throughout the latter half of the 19th century, black Jamaicans availed themselves of the teacher training opportunities, which prepared them for leadership not only of the classroom but also of the community, and from there into the wider arena of church and political participation and representation. The colonial elite responded by blocking their ascendancy. They changed the curriculum of the training colleges, eliminating the classics and liberal arts, and making it more oriented to vocational subjects. Crucially, they recruited women to become teachers, either alongside men in the older institutions or in new colleges specifically for women. The result was a gradual shift of the demographic profile of the teaching profession from all male, to male and female, to mainly female by 1931 (Miller 1991, p. 77). Black males were marginalized from the power structure by white males, using black females.

Although his thesis was somewhat coolly received by feminists, Miller (1991) generalized his argument into the thesis that the history of conflicts between tribes, ethnic groups, and nations may be read as the history of men challenging the power of other men, or of men blocking other men from power. To wipe out future threats, the victors historically used techniques such as slaying the entire tribe, slaying the men and marrying the women, castration, enslaving the group, breaking the economic and military power of the group. With the rise of modern class society, the struggle for power has not abated, although the struggle does not necessarily take a violent form, unless it is between nations. This is where those in control of power use women as buffers. Miller posits that available data in the United States, the Caribbean, and the former Soviet Union show clearly the ascendancy and dominance of women in education and higher learning, but they also show that women are only able to staff the avenues to power, not access power. Marginalized, the vanquished express their defeat in the many manifestations of social pathology, such as crime and what Miller calls religious escapism. Miller sees the future in terms of women and marginalized men sharing a common interest in the struggle for a more democratic society.

Miller's focus on education has led to the widespread use of female enrollment and educational achievement, which are significantly better than those of males in many subject areas, to argue that males are being marginalized. Such an argument, however, ignores the question of power, or implies that educational qualification automatically translates into power, which they do not. As Lindsay shows, although women "outnumber men in the professional, executive, technical and managerial fields" in Jamaica by 28.5 to 41.8 percent, this predominance is mainly in traditionally female occupations such as teaching and nursing" (2002). To wit, only 10 percent of chief executive officers are women. In other words, women may be participating in education in greater proportion than men and they may be achieving more in terms of education, but they are still excluded from the loci of power.

Nonetheless, education has become a major area of study for understanding why males are not doing as well as females. Parry (2000), Leo-Rhynie (1987), Evans (2001), Bailey (1997), and Figueroa (1997b) are some of an expanding list of scholars seeking to clarify the issues and offer plausible explanations. Figueroa and Evans are in agreement that the traditional methods of teaching tend to favor girls; although as Bailey (2002) shows, there is evidence of gender stereotyping by male teachers in the classroom setting, which works to the disadvantage of girls in subjects such as physics and mathematics because it is generally believed that girls are not supposed to do as well as boys. The decline in male enrollment at the University of the West Indies has been so steep and dramatic, from a 50 to 50 female-male ratio in the 1976–77 academic year to 75 to 25 female-male ratio in 1999, that a study was commissioned. Some observers point out that when the ratio was reversed it was not considered a crisis, but the present underrepresentation of males is critical enough to warrant concern.

Men in Crisis: Revisiting How Boys Are Socialized

When dysfunctional behaviors are placed alongside education, describing the situation of males as bordering on a crisis is not an exaggeration. With the rise in international drug trafficking, homicide rates have been of great concern to the governments of the anglophone Caribbean.

In Jamaica, where violent crime is widely considered to be the single greatest deterrent to capital investment and economic growth, homicide has been increasing. From 33 homicides in 1998, it reached a high of 41 (per 100,000 people), in 2000 which gives Jamaica the third-highest rate of homicide in the world. In the Bahamas, homicides reached a high of 54 in 1991 but homicides declined dramatically to 19 in (per 100,000 people) 1996. Similar trends have been registered for St. Kitts and Nevis and Trinidad and Tobago. Men are the main victims and the main perpetrators. Crimes against the person, generally, and excessively high rates of homicide, in particular, affect an entire society, changing patterns of social relations and mobility, impacting the social structure through new occupations in armed personal security and putting a drain on the economy and encouraging migration. The fact that males are at the center of the homicide trend, and that the trend represents a relatively new phenomenon, ought to be enough to make men the focus of attention for policy makers. Hence the question, what is happening to our males? They are not attending school and they have taken to deviant behavior, adding to the earlier-perceived problems of sexual promiscuity, abuse of women, and paternal delinquency.

This concern has thus far resulted in two studies on male socialization. Using 20 focus groups of prepubescent and postpubescent children in Barbados, Dominica, and Jamaica, Bailey et al. (1996) found that the model of father to which boys are being socialized is that of a man who is "the boss of the family" by virtue of provider role and physical strength and who is emotionally marginal to his children even when he is present in the household. Physical strength seems to be the main difference between boys and girls, and this is used to justify the gender division of labor, which keeps girls inside the household and boys outside. As Bailey et al. suggest, "The boys' attitude to work and the expectation that girls were more suited to inside work, were taken into the schools and classrooms, with the boys reporting difficulty in disciplining themselves and in doing what was required of them in the classroom" (1996). These traits, the authors explained, are the source of the underperformance of boys in the education system, a conclusion also reached by Parry (2000), whose research was conducted around the same time. Research by Bailey et al. "suggests that the masculine identity is in conflict with the educational interests of Caribbean boys and the under-achievement of boys is likely to be the source of increasing male/female conflict" (1996).

The second study, conducted in Dominica, Guyana, and Jamaica, was commissioned by UNICEF. It was justified by the uniqueness of the Caribbean, which runs against the well-documented trend of female neglect and disadvantage that prevails throughout the rest of the world in the area of education. Combining ethnographic and drama-in-education methods, the study (Chevannes 2001b) confirmed the cultural foundations of masculinity, reinforcing many of the findings of the Bailey et al. study. Throughout the anglophone Caribbean, children are socialized into a gender-based division of labor that roughly parallels the dichotomy of work inside the house (house cleaning, tidying, washing, and cooking) and work outside (gardening, garbage disposal, tending animals, and washing the car). In rural areas, however, both girls and boys fetch water. Furthermore, the concept of the male as a provider is so consistent and strong that from childhood, boys understand it as imperative to position themselves to be in control of disposable income. They are taught or encouraged to be enterprising and pressured to orient themselves in school toward subject areas that are considered practical and able to deliver quick and substantial financial returns. Control of resources as a male imperative is directed not only toward children but also toward females. A man must provide not only for his children, but also for his spouse, regardless of her own economic status and independence. Without resources, young men are silenced before women, whose sexual favors or courtship they desire.

Another salient finding is the division of the public and private domains along traditional gender norms that determine expectations, and the socialization and behaviors of young men and women. Moral sanctions are imposed on males who hang around and involve themselves in the day-to-day running of the household, and on females who make the street corner or the village square their places of leisure. The study found other interconnected factors, such as the strong reins applied in controlling girls and the relative freedom allowed boys. Once a boy's chores are done, he is free to leave the yard in pursuit of his friends; once a girl's chores are done, she must either find other work or conduct her leisure activities at home. Such laxity in the case of boys and control in the case of girls peaks in the years following puberty and is informed by the belief that girls are soft and in need of protection, whereas boys should be tough. Hence the adage, "Tie yu heiffer, loose yu bull" [*Tie your heifer, untie your bull*]. Nonetheless, it is recognized that precisely because boys are given greater latitude, they need the strong hands of a father to guide them. In one community, men described men whose only role was in siring children as "pa;" only those who by contrast exercised a strong guiding hand merited the name "faada." Male sexuality is understood as being essentially heterosexual, allowing very little space for homosexual orientation. Homophobia appears stronger in Jamaica than in other islands, and in Jamaica stronger in urban than in rural areas. Homophobia propels boys into early initiation to prove their heterosexual orientation.

Ideals of Masculinity: Current Trends

The focus on culture does not imply that the ideals of masculinity are fixed and immutable, but it does confirm that the ideals contribute to a fuller understanding of the behaviors of men and what society expects of them. Throughout the literature is a strong and clear signal that among African-Caribbean people, being a provider is perhaps the most important aspect of what it means to be a man, even prior to having dependents.[3] Indeed, these ideals assume that one cannot be a man without having dependents, or creating dependents if need be.

Given this cultural imperative, why should it be surprising that being a provider supersedes the requirement to get an education? Historically, education has been the route of upward social mobility for the African-Caribbean people. Through education, they enter the ranks of the professions and gain access to a standard of living denied their forebears. Since the 1970s (but starting a decade or two earlier), other routes are possible. The first is the music and entertainment industry, based on a market of local producers and international consumers. Virtually overnight, with the production of a hit song, a young man may achieve stardom and wealth. For that composition, there is nothing he needs that his native wit alone cannot provide. He does not need to have studied and passed English language and literature, mathematics, history, or geography. He does not even have to know how to read and write music. Since about the 1970s, so many young men have been propelled to national and international fame and its attendant conspicuous wealth that there is no dearth of role models for young boys.

The second route is sports. From an activity undertaken for personal development and fun, sports have become big business. Long before a boy graduates from high school, there are scouts seeking to recruit him into playing for a club for a salary. Indeed, the process starts even earlier, at the primary level, as outstanding talent is recruited for high school. From there, national prominence brings him money from sponsorship by large firms and advertising contracts. While his cricket or football skills develop and his reservoir of potential is still untapped, he dreams of being traded into a club in Europe or the United States, at which point he would have plenty of money.

The third route is the informal economy, which includes the underworld traffic in narcotics. The risks are great but for many young men the lucre is too compelling to resist. Around the illegal drug trade springs a trade in arms to defend, threaten, and destroy. The drug trafficker is thus simultaneously a gunman and a killer because wherever illegal drugs are trafficked illegal weapons are also present. The rise in rates of homicide in the Caribbean is drug-related, just as the decline in these rates is related to suppression of the drug trade (Harriott 2000).

The overwhelming majority of travelers along these seemingly lucrative routes are young males. But even if only a relatively few succeed, by creating in the minds of boys models of success, they produce the effect of devaluing education as a goal. And to make it worse, the pedagogical methods do not entice them to regard school as an exciting learning experience.

Conclusions

In the Caribbean, sociological and anthropological studies have shed new light on the different roles of men in the family and the community and on concepts of masculinity. Originally motivated by feminist study and the desire to better understand patriarchy as it relates to women, new research has challenged conventional thinking that men's morally dysfunctional behavior is responsible for problems such as the denial of paternity, lack of domestic stability, neglect of men's financial responsibilities toward children, high levels of female-headed households, and the poor socialization of male children. Rather, structural and cultural factors that affect women's and men's roles play a critical part in determining the behavior of males. Studies have focused on the origins of the structure of the Caribbean family and examined typologies of fathers based on their presence or absence in the household and their relationship with the mother of their children.

Early research examined the influence of slavery and its aftermath on the structure of the household, suggesting that the slave society was probably a cause of unstable family relations and men's loose connection with their families. But regardless of the reason for the resulting family structure, Caribbean men see their role primarily as providers and often as disciplinarians independent of the type of families to which they belong. While the scope of men's involvement as providers varies, men do play an important role as fathers regardless of whether they are visiting fathers or reside with their offspring. Being a father, combined with providing economic support for one's family, is perhaps the most important factor defining manhood in the Caribbean.

The underachievement of males in education is another salient topic of study, which has led some researchers to argue that the Caribbean man is being marginalized. Poor performance in education has been attributed to male socialization, which is counter to the educational interests of boys. Boys tend to undervalue education and opt for quick financial returns in the labor market due to the social value placed on males to provide for children and spouses. Boys are socialized to operate in the public sphere, and girls in the private sphere, with moral sanctions imposed on those who do not adhere to these norms of behavior.

This new research is providing important insights into the behaviors of men and what society expects of them, thereby contributing to greater awareness of how to improve the conditions of men and women in the Caribbean. Much more needs to be done, however, to understand the policy and programming implications of these findings and insights, including evaluating the impact of current programs.

Notes

1. The group of women that formed Sistren were employed by a government emergency work program in the late 1970s that targeted unskilled, uneducated, and in some cases illiterate men and women. In order to organize themselves to present a skit on Labor Day, employees approached the staff of the School of Drama and met Honor Ford-Smith, who honed them into an extraordinary group of dramatists who quickly established a reputation for using their newly acquired craft to expose the often tragic position of women in family and society and to challenge traditional behavior.

2. According to one informant in my research on men taken before the Family Court, the court awarded him custody of his daughter but granted the child's mother visiting rights. When, after the summer holidays, the child had not returned from her mother, he discovered that his daughter was already attending school and he was being sued for maintenance support. He concluded that his child's mother was not so much interested in their daughter as in getting money. He was not prepared to fight her again over custody. A second informant says he asked his child's mother for a full list of all the child's needs—books, clothes, supplies, and toys—which he would personally buy and give to the child. He would not provide cash.

3. A television advertisement for an ATM machine depicts a female student slipping a male student engrossed in his study a note as she passes by. In the next frame, we deduce that she had invited him to the movies along with one of her friends. Although she invited him, he takes out his wallet to pay, only to find it empty. Quickly cueing in to his embarrassment, she rushes over to the ATM machine, returns and surreptitiously slips him cash, with which he then pays the cashier. The message is clear: "Use the ATM," but the language, which is so well understood by the Jamaican viewers, is that the man is controller of financial resources.

Masculinity and Violence in Colombia

Deconstructing the Conventional Way of Becoming a Man

5

FREDY HERNÁN GÓMEZ ALCARAZ AND
CARLOS IVÁN GARCÍA SUÁREZ

This chapter discusses the complex scenario of violence in Colombia and, from a gender perspective, links masculinity to the exertion of multiple forms of violence. Section one outlines some socioeconomic and gender issues relevant to Colombia. Section two interprets and comments on masculine participation in social and private forms of violence. It focuses on the complex position in which men are simultaneously criminal and victim, peer pressure among men, and the destabilization men experience in the face of social changes and the traditional masculine exertion of power. Section three presents a brief account of Colombia's internal armed conflict and men's participation in the conflict. Section four establishes three complex and dynamic relational axes between masculinity and the exertion of violence. Section five discusses existing efforts in Colombia to address masculine identities. While such efforts are not necessarily part of an integral treatment of violence, they illustrate the range of efforts used to better understand the connections between masculinity and violence in the country. Section six suggests a few possible broad approaches for addressing violence, all of which could contribute to peace negotiations and postconflict policies aimed at defusing certain aspects of masculinity addressed in this chapter.

Colombia: Social and Gender Inequality

Colombia, a country of 45 million people, has gained notoriety for numerous, dramatic acts of violence and the efforts it has made to achieve peace and social equity. Whether viewed as a developing country or one with medium human development (as it is classified by UNDP), Colombia is a nation of marked social and economic contrasts. Socioeconomic conditions have varying impacts on the country's population, depending on social class, ethnic group, generation, culture, region, and gender. This section focuses on gender, presenting a partial, although illustrative, picture of major socioeconomic features in which gender relationships are embedded.

3

Human development indicators illustrate Colombia's paradox. UNDP's 2002 Human Development Index ranks Colombia 73rd out of 177 countries. With a per capita income of $6,370, Colombia is toward the upper range of countries with medium human development (UNDP 2004). Income distribution, however, is among the most unequal in the world. The annual *World Development Indicators* (World Bank 2005a) reports a Gini index of 57.6 as of 1999. The poorest 10 percent of Colombians receive only 0.8 percent of income, compared with 46.6 percent of income for the top 10 percent.

Colombia has made significant progress in improving the well-being of women. Women's labor force participation has increased; the male-female earnings gap, while still considerable, has decreased; girls a have higher school enrollment rate than boys; and women's fertility and maternal mortality have dropped (Correia 2003). In contrast, male human capital has eroded. In terms of education, boys' completion and attainment rates have decreased and dropout and repetition rates have increased. Males are more affected by HIV/AIDS, by diseases related to alcohol and drug consumption, and by violence, both conflict and crime related. UNDP's Gender-related Development Index ranks Colombia 59th out of 144 countries (UNDP 2004).

Women in Colombia are rapidly gaining access to the labor market. The female labor force participation rate increased from 45.2 in 1990 to 52.6 percent in 2003, while the male participation rate was largely unchanged (World Bank 2005a). Women, however, have experienced a worrisome increase in unemployment. In 2000–2002, female unemployment was 19.1 percent, almost double male unemployment. Despite women's increased participation in the labor force, men continue to dominate economic activity, except in the services sector, where women's participation is almost 60 percent higher than for men.

Colombia also has made enormous progress in terms of the political empowerment of women. In 2001, Colombian women held 47.4 percent of government positions in ministries, making Colombia one of the highest-ranking countries in this area (UNDP 2004).[1] Although the 2005 World Economic Forum report *Women's Empowerment* ranked Colombia 30th out of 58 countries in terms of the overall gender gap, it ranked Colombia 15th in terms of the political empowerment of women,[2] ahead of Australia, Belgium, Denmark, Israel, and the United States (World Economic Forum 2005).

Colombia's mortality indicators also reveal important gender differences. Life expectancy for women is six years higher than for men—only slightly higher than the five years for all middle-income countries—but the gender gap in mortality rates is far higher. In 2003, the mortality rate for men was a disturbing 238 per 1,000, 13 percent higher than the average for middle-income countries. Female adult mortality, at 115 per 1,000, was ten percent lower than the average for middle-income countries (World Bank 2005b). A World Bank report on gender in Colombia indicates that even though violence impacts men and women differently, most victims of homicide tied to political, social, or drug-trafficking causes are men (World Bank 2002b).

Women have higher death rates due to nontransmittable diseases, including malignant tumors in digestive, genital, or urinary organs; ailments related to hypertension; heart problems; lung and other respiratory problems; and brain- and blood-vessel-related illnesses. However, men are by far the most common victims of traffic-related deaths (5.1 percent for men versus 2.1 percent for women), deaths due to other kinds of accidents (4.7 percent for men versus 2.3 percent for women), and deaths due to homicide and intentional injuries (24.4 percent for men versus 3.2 percent for women; World Bank 2002b).

Although Colombia has made considerable progress in terms of human development, it faces some important challenges, including the need for more equitable income and wealth distribution, improved access to health and basic sanitation services, especially in isolated rural areas, better access to and efficiency of the judicial system, and above all, sustainable peace. The latter is essential not only for sustaining Colombia's economic and social progress but also for allowing the country to gain control over the multiple expressions of violence that affect many Colombians on a daily basis and, in turn, are directly linked to several of the cultural and symbolic constructs of being and becoming a man. Only recently have a few gender studies begun to shed light on the complex factors affecting male participation in various types of violence.

Men and Expressions of Social Violence in Colombia

Internationally, Colombia is seen as a violent country, a perception generally based on the persistence of internal armed conflict, drug trafficking, terrorist actions, and a high homicide rate. In fact, this characterization of violence has been one of the country's most emblematic images, particularly during the last two decades. In reality, however, not all the violence, death, and injuries that persist in Colombia are the result of current political and military conflicts.

Homicides and Men: Turning Their Backs on Themselves and Their Environment

Colombia's violence worsened since the mid-1970s and is among the highest in the world. Using the homicide rate as a proxy for violence, official figures show an increase from 15 to 70–90 per 100,000 inhabitants between 1974 and the second half of the 1990s (Garfield and Arboleda 2003; Llorente et al. 2001). The homicide rate in the 1990s was more than three times higher than the average rate for Latin America and the Caribbean, the region with the world's highest homicide rates (Shaw, van Dijk, and Rhomberg 2003). In some cities, murder took on almost epidemic proportions. In the early 1990s, Medellín (the second largest city in the country) recorded a rate of over 400 per 100,000 inhabitants (Garfield and Arboleda 2003).

A report of the Center for Economic Development Studies (CEDE) of the University of the Andes (Llorente et al. 2001) shows that 16 percent of the districts surveyed by the census in Bogotá had rates higher than 100 homicides per 100,000 inhabitants in 2000, which CEDE points out is a level usually associated with war. At a national level, there is one homicide every 20 minutes, a figure that has not changed since 1996. For 2001, the National Institute of Legal Medicine and Forensic Sciences (INML y CF 2002) reported 289,717 cases of violence nationally. The same report pointed to 42,081 cases of deadly injuries under categories including homicides, road accidents, suicide, other kinds of accidents, and other violent deaths. The extent of violence has major adverse effects on the health, security, and development prospects of Colombians. In 2001, homicides accounted for more than 1 million potential years of life lost in Colombia.[3] It is thus not surprising that much of Colombian public opinion considers the country to be in a constant state of war. Regardless of whether the war is conceived as a political war, a social war, or simple criminality, violence is perceived as an element that is almost inherent to the nation's current social development.

Homicides in Colombia overwhelmingly affect males. The male-female ratio of homicide victims is 12 to 1, or 24,339 male victims to 1,972 female victims (INML y CF 2002). This means that 92.5 percent of all Colombian homicide victims are men. Cultural forms of masculinity reflect social position, social representations, and personal beliefs on which many men establish their social relations through various kinds of aggressive behaviors. This aggressive behavior, however, does not reflect a merely psychological distortion of their male personalities, but also learned values that are social and culturally determined, personally interpreted, and reinforced by the symbolic system in which it occurs.

Collective Crime: Young Men and Their Peers

Organized crime is responsible for a large share of violence in Colombia, especially in urban centers. The social effects of urban criminal violence extend beyond the impact on victims and their families. Violence generated by organized crime also increases feelings of uncertainty, especially among young people, and affects people's perceptions of the future (Segovia 1994). General perception points to uncertainty as an even more serious problem than violence itself. Opinion polls often rank general insecurity as the leading concern of the majority of citizens. What seems clear is that insecurity and violence are intricately tied to each other. Youth participation, particularly by young men, in these violent acts is extremely high and involves homicides, personal injuries, rapes, and aggravated robbery (National Office of the General Public Prosecutor 1993).

Whether young men target a person's economic wealth or personal integrity in criminal acts, they usually choose a form of collective action very much mediated by peer pressure and the dominant image of adult masculinity. This pattern reflects risk-taking behavior as one of the axes on which male identity is built and which is constantly undermining men's potential for responsible action. Consequently, the actions that follow a "male model of risk" as a cornerstone of male identity (Gómez and Hernán 2000) may be inscribed in the national perception of uncertainty, both social and personal, that results from crimes associated with a kind of "subjectivity of risk" (Gutiérrez 1993). Programs and policies targeting men, especially young, low-income men, need to be based on an understanding of how peer pressure and the imitation of adult male patterns result in risky and violent behavior.

Private Violence: Men in the Face of Power Exertion and Social Transitions

Domestic violence is one of the strongest expressions of private violence and therefore a subject of social analysis and policy. In 2001, 69,681 people received care for domestic violence, representing a rate of 162 for every 100,000 inhabitants (INML y CF 2002). Of the total domestic violence cases reported, 41,320, or 59 percent, were marital violence. Women were the victims in 90 percent of all reported cases, although there are indications that male victims are increasing. The female-male domestic violence ratio decreased from 14 to 1 in 1996 (14 battered women for each battered man) to 9 to 1 in 2001 (INML y CF 2002).

Domestic violence remains one of the most frequent and critical problems for Colombian women, and men remain the principal perpetrators. Although there has been considerable progress in strengthening the legal framework for prevention of and sanctions against domestic violence, such as through Law 294 of 1996, there remains a great need for integral and preventive policy making, a more detailed understanding of the risk factors faced by Colombian families, improvement of the effectiveness of protection mechanisms foreseen by the law, and a deeper analysis of the interaction of cultural and gender factors on domestic violence. The latter requires a comprehensive and contextualized gender analysis of current relationships between men and women and a better understanding of how gender identities are formed. In essence, policy making needs to go beyond punishing male aggression and assisting the victims, be they women, girls, or boys.

A related need is to develop a deeper understanding of family dynamics and configurations in Colombia, particularly with the new roles men are adopting in the public and private realms. The borders between the public and the private in the modern world are unlike any previously known. As a result of social and economic pressures, men must reflect and restate their traditional roles while repositioning themselves in relation to women, generations, families, and work. Two critical trends have been globalization, which is changing the nature of work, and increasing demands for greater gender equality in all dimensions of private and public life.

This process of reflection about private and public roles, a largely unfamiliar phenomenon for most men, often creates tension, uncertainty, and a level of discomfort. In many instances, tensions and uncertainty arise as men contrast the way they think things should be with the alternative behavioral model that they have created for themselves on a social, personal, and interpersonal level. As a side effect, a discomfort arises that is neither purely existential nor purely personal in nature, and that translates into a type of stress "between what these men need for themselves and what culture tells them they need..." (Seidler 2000, p. 176).

Men's exertion of power in domestic relations is strongly affected by these tensions and uncertainties. In fact, male participation in domestic violence "is not just a habit or the expression of a universal and personal 'disorder.' It is rather the result of a series of considerations, strategies, ways of communicating, mental assimilation, and contexts which are produced and replicated by culture, social norms, and personal experience, and which also trigger anxieties and voids in men, which they in turn express and solve through violent action" (Gómez et al. 2001, p. 4). Regarding power, it is important to remember that while from an extreme version of masculinity, exertion of power is equal to exertion of violence. There are often alternative versions that project power as constructive and respectful of those without power.

Sexual abuse, which typically occurs in private settings, is another gendered form of exerting power that plays a significant role in Colombia's current social reality. Given the profound psychological impact on the lives of victims and their families, there have been increasing efforts to analyze and design interventions to address sexual crimes. Significant insights have emerged from gender studies, although there is still a need to understand how to work with men on the prevention side.

The National Institute of Legal Medicine and Forensic Sciences reports that in 2001, there were 13,352 forensic reports for sexual crimes. This is an extremely high incidence, particularly when we consider that a large number of sexual crimes are not reported (INML y CF 2002). In all age groups, most victims (11,508 cases) were women, but the impact was particularly severe for women under age 18 (84 percent of female cases). In terms of men, 1,766 cases of sexual abuse were reported, most of which occurred among boys aged 5–14.

It is clear that the perpetrators of sexual abuse are most frequently men, known to the victim, and members of networks of relatives close to the victim. Sexual abuse, similar to homicide, is mainly exerted by men and entails a profound violation of the victim's dignity and integrity. This picture suggests complex internal dynamics within Colombian families, particularly the way in which gendered notions of power and authority are manifested. There is also a generational aspect in the way that conventional notions of masculinity impact boys and girls within family structures.

This peculiar network of cultural, psychological, and symbolic elements surrounding sexual violence is precisely what merits greater institutional attention. Although sexual abuse itself is strongly condemned by society, the condemnation does not always extend to the dominant model of male sexuality—active, penetrating, and aggressive—that is in large part related to sexual abuse. The model of masculinity expressed by sexual violence is still legitimized by social and cultural discourses promoting an aggressive masculine identity within sexual performance and relationships, as well as in society's perception of the male body. The resulting dissonance in messages and discourses may partly reflect a questioning or weakening of dominant models of masculinity, but they are yet to result in alternative models. This is precisely where gendered analysis of masculinity and the targeting and involvement of men in sexual abuse prevention can be helpful, i.e., in the cultural transformation through social education that promotes men's self-reflection and the identification and uncovering of unacceptable behavior.

Another dramatic type of private violence is suicide, which has exhibited a relatively constant rate of 4.8 suicides for every 100,000 inhabitants of Colombia since 1998, with 2,056 cases reported nationwide in 2001 (INML y CF 2002). Suicide accounts for 5.3 percent of violent deaths. Men account for 77 percent of suicides, with an average age of 36 compared with an average age of 26 for female suicides. The male–female suicide ratio is 3 to 1. This ratio has decreased from previous years, when it had remained steady at 4 to 1. Significantly, Colombian men have a particular social license to carry firearms and often resort to them for suicide (in 33.6 percent of male suicide cases), while women choose toxic substances or poisoning (53.8 percent of female suicides).

The sense of male identity is also linked to the way in which men choose to end their lives. Suicide can be understood as a desperate and extreme resolution of conflict (social, personal, familial, etc.) or as a manifestation of gender stereotypes. Popular phrases such as "better dead than defeated" or "to die on your feet is a manly death" reassert the authoritarian significance that many men assign to their own and other people's lives. An analysis of violence in Colombia therefore needs to include, as an important component, male views on power and authority and their expectations about what has been culturally prescribed as the male social role.

The trends presented above inform the work of most national and local agencies and are crucial to outlining a conceptual framework to understand the widespread and complex phenomenon of violence in Colombia. Many analysts propose approaches to finding a political and peaceful resolution to Colombia's protracted armed conflict, yet the reality is that over three-quarters of violent deaths, in which men play a dominant role, are not directly the result of the armed conflict. Civil and gender-related intolerance, in all its manifestations, is frequently the result of the need by many men to confront all social, family, and personal relationships with the use of violence.

Men in Colombia's Armed Conflict

Although Colombia's history as an independent nation can arguably be described as a succession of mostly party-based conflicts, there is agreement that April 9, 1948 inaugurated an era of brutal and pervasive confrontations between Liberals and Conservatives, commonly known as La Violencia (The Violence). That day, the assassination of the Liberal leader and likely winner of the presidential elections of 1950, Jorge Eliécer Gaitán, unleashed a wave of street riots, particularly in Bogotá, which was left half in ruins following what came to be known as El Bogotazo. Liberal-Conservative confrontations continued until 1957 when an interim military junta gave birth to the accord known as Frente Nacional

(National Front), which defined the country's administration for the ensuing 16 years and established a four-year alternation in power for the two parties.

Although the political elites in Colombia were able to negotiate a power-sharing agreement between the two main political parties, the 1950s witnessed an upsurge of violence in rural areas, including harassment, abuse, homicides, and massacres. Death squads launched a terror campaign in the countryside which included raping women and inflicting symbolic cuts and mutilations on dead bodies, a ritual intended to emphasize that the purpose of the violence was not only about killing, but "re-killing" and "counter-killing" (Uribe 1996).

The Frente Nacional accord, aimed in part to defuse La Violencia, was not successful, at least during the first two four-year presidential terms, as the desire for revenge remained unsatisfied in the countryside. Between 1963 and 1965 the leaders of the death squads (known as bandoleros, or bandits), abandoned by their political patrons, were assassinated and their members killed or imprisoned by the military.

Most observers agree that the dismantling of the death squads by 1965 marked the end of La Violencia; although it failed to bring peace, it brought an end to a historical phase of confrontations. The accord between the two main political parties, however, produced a closed political and economic system and led to rising discontent, especially in rural areas. Leftist intellectuals nourished this discontent and organized peasants into guerilla groups, leading to the creation of guerrilla movements, including the Colombian Revolutionary Armed Forces (FARC) in 1964, the National Liberation Army (ELN) in 1965, and the People's Liberation Army (EPL) in 1967. While the majority of EPL fighters laid down arms in 1991 and their strongholds were destroyed during the "dirty war" that followed, membership in the other two groups rose from a few dozen to over 40,000 in the first half of the 1990s.

The April 19 Movement (M-19) guerilla group emerged following allegations of electoral fraud during the 1970 presidential elections. The emergence of M-19 marked a new cycle of violence and hostage taking, this time with an urban character and including spectacular attacks, such as the assault on the Embassy of the Dominican Republic in 1980 and the Palace of Justice and Supreme Court in 1985. In 1990, M-19 signed a truce with the government and the movement transformed itself into a political party.

In the 1980s, drugs added a new dimension to Colombia's complex pattern of violence. By the end of the 1970s, although over 40,000 families earned a living by growing marijuana, their illicit activities were not associated with widespread violence. The emergence of coca, however, brought with it powerful and violent drug cartels. At the beginning of the 1980s, drug traffickers organized into drug cartels pressured violently for political recognition, which they considered as a logical extension of the social recognition they enjoyed, especially among low-income groups, and to protect the large rents generated by coca trafficking. The quest for political legitimacy became more urgent following the signing of an extradition treaty between Colombia and the United States and the emergence of the group

Los Extraditables, whose slogan was, "we prefer a grave in Colombia to a jail in the USA."

The cartels' growing power, political influence, and violent tactics added a more complex urban dimension to the country's violence. This included indiscriminate terrorism through bombings and the commissioning of targeted assassinations, particularly against several presidential candidates and countless journalists, judges, and policemen. Sicarios, or contract killers hired by drug traffickers, symbolized this new violence. Public attention was quickly drawn to the fact that these contract killers were teenagers or very young men from poor neighborhoods, particularly Medellín, who did not expect to live long, and who were ready to die in exchange for a short but intense life or for securing their families' economic future.

To make things worse, in the mid-1980s, new self-defense groups—this time supported by the far right as a reaction against guerilla groups—began improving their military capabilities and unleashing new waves of terror linked both to drug traffickers and the Armed Forces. Paramilitaries, as they are commonly known, persecuted and mass murdered civilians, accusing their victims of sympathizing with subversion, and even resorted, once again, to acts of brutality against the living and the dead as a ritual of enemy annihilation. Although such actions were more common in rural areas, kidnappings and selective assassinations also affected some urban areas.

Over the years, there have been several attempts to find a negotiated solution to Colombia's conflict, most notably the lengthy but failed negotiations between the Pastrana Administration and the FARC during 1998–2000. Although prospects for a comprehensive peace agreement between the FARC and ELN with the Uribe administration remain uncertain, at the time of this writing the Colombian government had negotiated an extensive disarmament and demobilization agreement with the bulk of paramilitary forces. Although an end to Colombia's conflict is key for the country's development prospects, as pointed out earlier, peace would not necessarily lead to a permanent solution to Colombia's widespread violence and its considerable economic and social costs. For this reason, and regardless of future prospects for a negotiated settlement of the conflict, it is not only useful but urgent to analyze the links between the many manifestations of violence and the prevalent constructs of masculinity in Colombia.

Links between Masculinity and Violence

A large proportion of male acts of violence and Colombia's general violence can be understood with reference to at least three relational axes: fortifying the male body, sexist rituals in the elimination of opposites, and group coercion.

Fortifying the Male Body

The first relational axis, which also serves as the foundation for the following axes, emanates from the work of Michel Foucault and Judith Butler on understanding the body not only as mere matter but also as informed substance. The result is an increasing tendency to consider gender as "embodiment", that is, the inscription in the body of historical discourses on the "correct," "appropriate," or most accepted time- and place-specific ways of defining and resolving masculinity and femininity. Another way of expressing this concept is to define gender as a linguistically informed body.

Embodiment is not neutral, since men's and women's bodies are inscribed by gender-differentiated power. In the case of masculinity, this incarnated notion of power is directly correlated with violence. Many men, for example, consider their violent actions against women legitimate because they have culturally assimilated an essentialist idea of delicacy and feminine submission in opposition to masculine aggressiveness and superiority. This may lead some men to perceive any attitude contradicting such models as insubordinate, unnatural, and in need of punishment as a way to restore "normality." The family usually represents a space that has been culturally legitimated by patriarchal archetypes that embed this kind of gender subordination. In turn, domestic violence is to a large extent the most dramatic expression of such gender hierarchy.

In Colombia, as in other parts of the world, such violent masculinity often backfires on men. As demonstrated by the research project Arco Iris[4] in its analysis of school environments, for instance, deep-rooted cultural images linking manliness to violence, competition and courage, continue to dominate school settings. It is through this and other forms of socialization that negative patterns of masculinity are consolidated. To some extent, this can be useful to explain why Colombian men, to a far greater extent than women, are the main consumers of psychoactive substances—alcohol and drugs—and the main parties involved in road accidents and all types of injuries, homicides, and suicides.

Men often go to great lengths to control their emotions, generally associating displays of emotion with female behavior. Michel Kaufman, a masculinity expert, affirms on this issue:

> "men get to the point of suppressing an entire array of emotions, needs, and possibilities, such as the pleasure of taking care of someone else, receptivity, empathy and compassion, all of which are experienced as inconsistent with male power. These emotions do not disappear, but are merely restrained or not allowed to play a significant role in our lives, which would instead be healthy, both for ourselves and for those who surround us" (Kaufman 1997, p. 70).

Some clinical psychologists and therapists have gathered considerable evidence of men's "fortification" of the body, a term they use for all body adaptation strategies that enable them to restrain needs, feelings, and emotions not consistent with predominant cultural stereotypes.

Some of these strategies include muscular tension, which makes the flow of sensations and feelings more difficult. Examples include a lump in one's throat to keep from crying; diaphragm contraction to inhibit pain or sexual feelings; facial tension to fake the absence of any expression and avoid affective contact; holding one's breath to contain the release of emotions; deviation of attention to physical feelings; and the transformation of nonmasculine emotions into emotions perceived as less threatening. In fact, studies of violent men who claim to feel anger or rage during violent reactions often show that sensations and feelings experienced prior to violence are more closely linked to fear, sadness, and fragility, but it is difficult or painful to acknowledge them. In a sense, therefore it can be argued that violence itself is a sign of fragility rather than strength.

With this understanding, violent responses can become more demanding for men in adverse conditions such as unstable employment and labor market conditions, since these are destabilizing factors for masculinity. These conditions erode one of men's main identities, that of the provider. This is a plausible explanation for the frequently high correlation between high unemployment and poverty with increased levels of marital violence, child abuse, and sexual violence.

Violent behavior also tends to increase when daily life is disrupted, as in the case of people who are displaced due to violence or natural disasters. Humanitarian and support groups often report that women fare better in these transitory or new environments, quickly organizing themselves into cooperative or mutual-support groups for specific tasks such as child care or cooking. In a sense, traditional gender roles seem to allow women greater resilience and adaptability in these settings. Men, in contrast, deprived of the opportunity to engage in any kind of productive labor, are highly prone to falling into crises of passiveness, guilt, depression, and the onset or intensification of drug or alcohol addiction. These factors often generate violent responses.

Sexist Rituals in the Elimination of Opposites

Anthropologist María Victoria Uribe (1996) conducted a pioneering study on rituals of torture and elimination of opposites in the context of the massacres perpetrated in the Department of Tolima from 1948–64, the period of La Violencia. When looking at the narratives of that period from a gender perspective, the sexist nature of most of the rituals is evident. Not just because the squads of bandoleros were evidently men-only groups, but above all due to the very nature of their actions—aroused by political bosses, they always exceeded the measures required to achieve subjugation of opposite parties. For bandoleros, it was neither enough to harass others to abandon their land nor to simply kill their enemies, with, say, firearms; they wanted to construct themselves, or at least to stage for themselves and foreigners a demonstration of toughness and insensitivity. Their crimes became representations of omnipotence and male control, and some were explicitly aimed at sexually debasing opposites.

The most common kind of torture, for instance, was to rape women several times in front of their handcuffed male relatives. Rape became a sign of territorial and body occupation that went beyond party struggle, as is clear in one woman's narrative of being raped, along with her daughter, by armed men who, in this case, had first killed the men of her family:

"Then, one of these men came and took the youngest girl to another room....Once they were gone, the girl told us that they had soiled her....They made me hand the girl to my mother and took me to another room, where two of them abused my body. Then, one of them asked me whether the dead were liberal or conservative. I answered, I don't know, and he said, go and see your children" (Uribe 1996, p. 167).

The assassination described here required that its perpetrator build toughness and a capacity to ignore the pain of and compassion for the victim, which implied a certain degree of dehumanization of the victim, and to a certain extent, of oneself. Before and during the crime, this was achieved through insults and scolding of the victim "with the aim of dehumanizing him/her and being able to sacrifice him/her and thereby also putting the necessary distance between victim and victimizer in what can be considered a symbolic treatment of contamination" (Uribe 1996, p. 167). Achieving this toughness often required an initiation rite where one of the more experienced bandoleros gave the novice a machete and said, "Here, stab any one of the corpses to drive your fear away" (Uribe 1996, p. 168).

Although victims were generally killed by a bullet, they were "counter-killed" by decapitation, and finally "re-killed" with a series of cuts that de-limbed the body, which was then symbolically reorganized, often with sexual references. Squads practiced cutting pregnant women's uteruses and extracting fetuses, leaving them on the mother's belly. This also included rituals of inversion of inferior and superior parts of the body whereby heads would replace sexual organs or the latter would be placed in the victims' mouths. Uribe (1996) finds a subjacent ritual structure in the massacres she analyzed, also characteristic of massacres that occurred during the 19th century civil wars, which suggests that these are not modern or new phenomena.

These ritualized killings have continued to the present. The tactics of the previously mentioned "dirty war" unleashed by paramilitaries in the countryside during the 1980s and later adopted by guerilla groups, drug traffickers, and even official agents, involved staging acts of brutality against dead bodies, including the relocation of limbs. For example, between October 1988 and May 1991, many of the 107 victims in the municipal district of Trujillo in the Department of Valle were subjected to gruesome torture, assassination, and dismemberment rituals carried out with chainsaws.

Group Coercion

The third relational axis that can help us understand masculinity and violence involves the dynamics of group coercion and membership. This is particularly relevant in the case of several forms of crime and social defiance committed by youths from low-income neighborhoods in large cities and grouped in gangs and criminal *parches*, or patches.[5]

In Colombia, *parche* has more than one meaning. In a general sense, it designates a gathering of individuals and is synonymous with other terms used to designate a group of friends, such as *combo* or *barra*. However, it also refers to the actual gathering place (or patch) of a group, and sometimes even to the activities carried out by such a group. A related word, the verb *parchar*, means to get together with one's clique or group. *Parchar* has come to be used derogatively to define youngsters from low-income sectors, to the point that the term is itself often associated with juvenile crime.

Most *parches* are open, versatile, horizontal groups in constant flux and with no evident leadership, and which bring together a diverse set of poor youngsters. Analysts differentiate gang and criminal *parches* from other types. Although gang members usually have the same socioeconomic background as members of *parches*—including similar unmet socioeconomic needs, lack of family structure, and lack of positive male role models—gang activities are much more restricted in scope, and they are much more closely related to crime and substance abuse. Another difference is that gangs are characterized by strong vertical and hierarchical relations, clear leadership, and a much more stable and defined group structure.

Parche initiation rites are also highly gendered. Membership is usually validated by the ability to demonstrate courage as a defining trait to peers, not only as a natural male condition but as a fastidiously chosen and constructed priority within masculinity itself. The degree of courage men are able to demonstrate and stage socially can make all the difference between "not being a man," being "not much of a man," "more manly," or "very manly." Badinter's (1993) idea of masculinity as a field of constant tests thus should be complemented by the notion of gradations or hierarchies in the condition of masculinity.

Courage in these settings means facing the challenges posed by the group with decision, firmness, and physical strength. It is not enough to claim to be courageous; to remain a member of the group, courage must be proven or staged. Those who do not demonstrate courage or who avoid staging of such a trait are collectively undermined, leading, in the worst of cases, to the member's expulsion or his becoming marginalized within the group.

Various terms are used in Colombia for a man who fallaciously boasts of being courageous: *boleta, bandera,* and *ajisoso.* In contrast, a *probón,* is an authentically brave man who takes initiative and risks and motivates others to take action. A *probón* takes on every challenge. This includes alcohol and drug abuse, use of cutting and thrusting weapons, and sometimes, use of firearms. This man is ready to engage in violent confrontations with rival groups, generally because of territorial disputes, contract killings, or other forms of crime. Sometimes, body scars which he exhibits as war trophies are proof of a *probón's* actions.

A number of programs in Colombia have attempted to reintegrate young members of these *parches*, although these efforts generally do not address the relationship between the need to demonstrate courage as proof of masculinity and the collective coercion exerted by group members. A dramatic example of this relationship is the role that organizations of drug traffickers play in recruiting poor young men to carry out military actions and acts of violence. Two aspects are particularly noteworthy. First, violent displays of courage emphasize the cohesive capacity of these organizations, which depict themselves as protective entities and simulate the symbolic paternal figure by stressing certain male traits (such as courage, intrepidness, and risk taking). Second, by emphasizing courage as a virtue, these groups channel young men's psychological and physical energy toward military actions. These reinforcing images are most tragically played out in the activities of the (usually young) character known as *sicario*, basically a hired murderer.

The need to counteract the relationship between the protective nature of these gangs and the definition of masculinity through "courageous" acts of violence could be an important consideration and entry point in efforts to address nonconflict forms of violence, or as commonly referred to in Colombia, the "other war". This is the war that, in the name of an obsessive protection of men's masculinity, imposes high social, economic, and security costs on Colombian society.

Some Efforts to Address Masculinity in Colombia

Several initiatives are working to address the link between male identities and the prevention and management of violence in Colombia. In general, pioneering actions on the issue of men have not necessarily emanated from academic or research circles, but from private service providers, particularly those working in the area of male sexual and reproductive health. Among these providers are Profamilia, which began its work during the 1970s and runs programs targeting men, including male clinics in Bogotá, Medellín, and Cali, and Oriéntame, a private organization which for several years has worked with men on sexual and reproductive health.

In the 1990s, women's reflection groups on masculinity began to appear. In 1993, Taller Abierto de Cali (Cali Open Workshop), an organization working with low-income women, organized workshops with adult, young, and indigenous men from Cauca to address issues of male identity, fatherhood and paternity, and violence. A group on masculinity founded in 1996 by Fundación Diálogo Mujer de Bogotá (Foundation for Women's Dialogue of Bogotá), as well as the First Meeting of Men celebrated in Cali the same year, were effectively the first men-only reflective and quasi-therapeutic interventions in Colombia. Also in 1996, the Network on Masculinity Studies at the National University of Colombia gathered groups of men and women to reflect on issues related to masculinity. It also disseminated information on masculinity studies and promoted debate on these issues. The Network met once a month from 1996–98.

In 1997, educators Javier Ómar Ruiz and José Manuel Hernández assembled young men and women who, under the District Inspection Office of Bogotá, organized school workshops on masculinity. In 1998, the Foundation Women and Future of Bucaramanga established a center to work with male domestic abusers, referred by local family courts in the context of the 1996 Law 294 on domestic violence. The foundation offered both individual and group therapy services, including drafting and disseminating written reflections on domestic violence and the role of men.

In July 2000, the national forum, Masculinity in Colombia: Reflections and Perspectives, aimed at various public and private agencies, scholars, and students discussed research on men and masculinity. In August 2000, the Group on Men and Masculinity sponsored an encounter at the Universidad Javeriana in Bogotá, combining exhibitions and reflections on masculinity with awareness-raising workshops. ENDA Medellín, a nongovernmental organization designed a series of program interventions with low-income men on paternity and the construction of masculinity, based on a study on paternity and the feminization of poverty.

Some state initiatives are gradually introducing a male perspective into their programs, particularly in relation to domestic violence. The Haz Paz (Make Peace) program of the Presidential Counseling Office for Social Policy has offered training in masculine roles and familiy violence, and the publication *Masculinity and Domestic Violence* targeted public servants working across state sectors (Gómez et al. 2001). In 2001–2, the city of Bogotá worked with the United Nations Population Fund (UNFPA) on a series of exchanges of private and public service providers with academics to share experiences in working on masculinity-related issues. The work also involved ten workshops to train and sensitize men on issues such as male identities, sexual and reproductive health, and exertion of violence by men (domestic, sexual, and gender violence). The workshops incorporated various work dynamics, from conceptual analysis and reflection on one's own experiences to therapeutic work with people's bodies.

The Administrative Department of Social Welfare (DABS) has served as lead agency for the program Desarmarnos con Amor (Disarming Ourselves with Love), which sponsors local activities targeting domestic and sexual violence as well as child exploitation. In 2001, the program hosted a series of conversation spaces for women, later extended to include conversation spaces for men (*conversatorios entre hombres*). The goal is to trigger cultural transformation around hegemonic gender patterns. These conversation spaces explored seven issues: male identity; men's self esteem, autonomy, and self care; body, health, and sexuality; male power (with a perspective on rights); violence in daily relationships; transformation of conflicts; and new models of masculinity. The workshops revealed that for many of the participants, this was the first opportunity in their lives to talk to other men about gender issues and to reflect on the cultural nature of dominant patterns of masculinity, particularly those associated with violence. The conversation spaces proved that it is possible to challenge the notion that violence is necessary for the construction of the male identity and that the ethics related to caring for others as much as for oneself can be used to deactivate many types of violence.[6]

In 2002, the National Police and the Universidad Javeriana, with support from the Inter-American Development Bank (IDB), organized additional training and awareness-raising workshops on domestic violence and male identities for members of the National Police. These workshops represented the first time the police force was brought together to reflect on masculinity and violence to address the sociocultural meaning of being a man in Colombia.

Research on issues of violence and masculinity can be grouped around three broad areas: (a) construction of male identities, including references to men's own narratives, opinions and reflections on their identity, analyses of male identities in relation to particular regions, cultures or socioeconomic origins, and research related to education; (b) fatherhood and masculinity; and (c) masculinity, sexuality, and sexual and reproductive health, with subthemes such as sexual practice, impact on health, and sexual and reproductive decisions and rights.

Suggestions for Future Approaches

Rather than approaching the connection between men and violence tangentially, as many of the programs addressed above have done, we believe that violence should be addressed directly, from a gender perspective. Such an approach would make the construction of male identities fully visible and highlight the elements of dominant masculinity implied in the perpetration of violence, as well as illuminate the motivations and reasons men claim for resorting to violence. Such a reflective effort requires institutional support, a full national consciousness, and a significant level of social mobilization.

A few key areas for future action emerge from the analysis presented here. The aim is not to provide a comprehensive listing of possible activities and approaches, but rather to suggest broad lines of intervention for both public policy and sociocultural initiatives. Although approaches will differ, an overriding goal is to mitigate the violence caused by social and armed conflicts by deconstructing existing symbolic and subjective patterns by which males construct their identities. Possible approaches include:

- The first step for Colombian society is to acknowledge that the prevalent and conventional way of becoming a man, although not exclusive to Colombia, plays an important role in the various manifestations of violence that continue to affect the country. Although this very violence and its social impact are leading to a gradual questioning and deconstruction of contemporary concepts of masculinity, concerted efforts to bring about cultural and social changes, especially in terms of gender norms, are necessary.
- Colombian society, policy makers, service providers, and other stakeholders need to better understand the new dynamics and family structures that have progressively replaced the conventional family. This is important not only for improving access to and delivery of public services, but also to understand how these changes are affecting Colombian men's new roles, functions, values and challenges. These changes include a blurring of what was once a strict separation between the public and private domains, women's new social and cultural roles, including greater access to the labor market, new models of masculinity, and emerging forms of collective organization.

- Managing and mitigating violence should include the treatment of aggressors, beyond mere punishment. One promising approach to the design of violence prevention policies is to seek appropriate spaces for male aggressors to express their expectations, ways of reasoning, anxieties, and fears. This is not to suggest that social sanctions and criminal prosecution should be avoided when justified, but that punishment needs to be complemented by the creation of spaces where men can rehearse and question alternative models of masculinity.
- The problem of collective coercion and its relation to the criminality of young, low-income men would benefit from being addressed from a gender perspective. Based on descriptions of the *sicario* phenomenon, it is possible to devise proposals to deactivate the logic of collective coercion that harms men as much as the rest of society. These proposals could be used to design programs based on the natural logic of group dynamics, clearly identifying and helping to challenge the role played by the dominant and hierarchical models of conventional masculinity.
- Group meetings of men, where they are asked to analyze traditional male roles and socialization patterns, are another type of initiative that can help achieve, in the medium term, significant attitude changes. "Hardened" men are at a higher risk for violence, while conscientious, self-aware, expressive men are less prone to participate in violent actions.
- The media can also play an important role, by emphasizing the connections between violent behavior and a certain way of being and perceiving oneself as a man. The prolonged and widespread dissemination of images and messages showing a refocused type of masculinity based more on affection, expressiveness, care and self-care, and respect for differences, could over time become a legitimate social reference model that is followed by men.
- A gender perspective is essential in any political negotiation process designed to end the internal armed conflict, as well as in the vision of Colombia as a post-conflict society, assuming that the country's violence is not intractable. Violence should be considered an arbitrary use of power highly legitimated by the current socialization processes experienced by many Colombian males. It would also be useful to identify the relational bonds (emotional, affective, etc.) men find in violent actions against women, boys, girls, other generations, and other men, differentiating them by political standing, ethnicity, social adherence, or sexual preferences. This could be incorporated into existing government programs which are addressing the social reintegration of ex-combatants, both adults and teenagers.

The above points imply a more profound understanding of the complex motivations men face in deciding to join armed groups of any kind. As we have argued in this chapter, men in Colombia today are motivated to participate in violence by more than political or ideological factors. We therefore posit conventional masculinity as an ideological base that broadens the affective, emotional, and relational frameworks of men enrolling in armed groups. Social analysts and policy makers must now contend with the fact that for many young and adult males, recourse to violence is not solely politically motivated or irrational. For example, analysis and program design must also focus on men's lack of security, the outcome of collective social pressure to belong to a group or movement, the constant need to prove that one is a man, and men's expression of profound rage and discomfort at increased uncertainty and changing social and family dynamics.

Designing social programs that attempt to reconcile, recover, or create a link between masculinity and an ethic of self-care represents one of the most promising areas for action by the public sector, particularly through cross-sector coordination involving education, health, and justice. The ethic of self-care implies a twofold concept: care of oneself and care of others. This concept is too often assumed to be a feminine quality and has restricted men to the realm of toughness, lack of expression, taciturnity, and risk.

Notes

1. In this respect, Colombia surpasses countries known for gender equity, such as Denmark (where women held 45.0 percent of positions), Finland (44.4 percent), New Zealand (44.0 percent), and Norway (42.1 percent); Colombia is outranked only by Sweden (55.0 percent).
2. Political empowerment refers to the equitable representation of women in decision-making structures, formal and informal, and their voice in the formulation of policies affecting their societies (World Economic Forum 2005).
3. For example, the total fatal and nonfatal injuries represents 1,422,520 of potential years of life lost—an average that remained approximately constant over the previous seven years—and 238,972 healthy years lost by intentional injuries (INML y CF 2002). In terms of intentional injuries, domestic violence accounts for 38 percent of cases and ordinary violence for the remaining 62 percent. Homicides are the category with the highest registered amount of potential years of life lost.
4. This Project was developed by the Working Area on Gender and Culture of the Central University's Research Department between 1998 and 2002. This immense effort covering 25 schools of Bogotá (and a product of 473 field diaries of observant participation) describes and explains in detail a series of teaching devices that help to understand the social construction of femininity and masculinity (García 2003).
5. Based on the study of such groups by García (1998).
6. Both assessment procedures and long-term follow-up tasks are urgently needed for this program.

Growing up Poor and Male in the Americas

Reflections from Research and Practice with Young Men in Low-Income Communities in Rio de Janeiro[1]

6

GARY BARKER

"*Voce não é homem ... voce ainda é um menino.*"
"*Eu sou homem, sim. Eu já matei alguám.*"
["You're not a man.. you're still a boy."
"I am too a man. I already killed somebody."]
Dialogue from the film *Cidade de Deus* (2002)

Although it is slightly dramatized, the excerpt above of dialogue from the recent Brazilian film, *Cidade de Deus*, about youth and drug trafficking in one of Rio de Janeiro's *favelas*, is illustrative. It hints at the connection between how manhood is defined and the violence that has come to characterize Rio de Janeiro and other major Latin American cities. In recent years, there has been growing attention worldwide on the mortality rates of young men. A variety of sources confirm that young men aged 15–24 die at rates far higher than their female counterparts, and at rates higher than men of other ages (Barker 2000b). Worldwide, the leading causes of death for young men are traffic accidents and homicides. But in much of Latin America, the leading cause is far and away homicide.

Worldwide data on violence (particularly homicide) suggest that young men in the Americas are more likely to kill other young men and to be killed than in any other region. The homicide rate in Latin America is about 20 per 100,000 per year. The highest rate in the region (and the world) is in Colombia, where from 1991–95, there were 112,000 homicides, of which 41,000 were young people, the vast majority male (World Bank 1997). WHO has estimated that in 2000 there were 155,000 deaths worldwide of young men aged 15–29 by homicide, of which close to half were in the Americas. This means that the risk of dying from homicide for a young man in the Americas is nearly 28 times higher than the average worldwide risk. Furthermore, the rate of homicide among male youths is higher than that of young women everywhere in the world, and the ratio of male-female homicide rates tends to be higher in countries with higher rates of male homicide (WHO 2002c). Similarly, in the rest of the world, while overall homicide rates are decreasing, most lethal violence is committed by men, usually younger men against other young men (Archer 1994).

Clearly, homicide is not the only form of youth violence, although it is the form most often consistently recorded across countries. Lesser forms of violence—fighting, vandalism, assaults, and dating violence—are much more common and affect many more young people than does homicide. In the United States, a nationwide study examining all types of delinquent behavior (including less violent forms, such as vandalism) found that 14.9 percent of boys compared to 5.8 percent of girls reported engaged in at least one form of delinquent behavior in the last year (U.S. Department of Justice 1997). Boys in the United States are four times more likely than girls to be involved in fights (Centers for Disease Control and Prevention 1992).

Men are victims as well as perpetrators. Many young men who use violence were themselves victims of or witnesses to violence, which, as numerous studies have confirmed, is associated with using violence. Because in most cultures boys spend more time outside the home than girls, they are more likely to be exposed to or witness physical violence.

Urban-based violence perpetrated by and against young men is related to the social exclusion, lack of employment, and curtailed educational opportunities that confront low-income male and female youth in the Americas. In addition, in many low-income urban areas in the Americas, gangs (most of which are involved in drug trafficking or other illegal activities) vie for territory and for the support, loyalties, and identities of young men. In some low-income areas—the garrison communities of Kingston, Jamaica, the *comunas* of Medellín, Colombia, Rio de Janeiro's *favelas*, inner city areas in the United States, and shantytowns in parts of Central and South America—many young people see gang leaders as homegrown heroes. Gang leaders are sought after as intimate partners by young women and emulated by many young men. They hold power, have money in their pockets and, by their willingness to use violence against police and rival gangs, possess status. To be a *bandido* in Brazil's *favelas*, a drug Don in a Kingston garrison community, or a gangbanger in an inner city area in the United States is to have a name and clout in a setting where many young people perceive themselves as excluded and disenfranchised.

From a public health perspective, we might conclude from a surface examination of the data that being a young man aged 15–24, particularly a low-income, urban-based young man in the Americas, is itself a risk factor. As one researcher in Rio de Janeiro recently described, a "male social pathology" is related to the high rate of homicide (O Globo 2002a). But to say that being a young man is a risk factor or that violence in the region is a male social pathology offers relatively little explanation of the factors at play. What is it about being a young man, and being a low-income young man in particular, that creates risk or pathology? What do we know about the young men in these settings who are not involved in drug-related and other forms of violence?

Interpersonal violence is of course only one issue affecting low-income young men in the region. This chapter examines the realities and risks that young men face across several domains. For example, there is a growing focus on young men in sexual and reproductive health and on the risks that their behavior implies for themselves and their partners. HIV/AIDS data from the Americas confirm that young men have two to three times the rates of HIV infection as young women (UNAIDS 2000a). In addition, school enrollment and educational attainment data suggest that young men in parts of the region are at a disadvantage. Low-income young men also face particular challenges in finding employment.

This chapter argues that these trends are related to macro- and microcontextual factors (the most important of which is probably family characteristics) and to social expectations of what it means to be a man—of what teachers, parents, public health workers, police, policy makers, male and female peers, and families think young men should be and do. Male risk in the Americas is associated with specific versions of male identity or masculinities. This chapter discusses how some young men are socialized into versions of manhood that encourage involvement in gang-related violence and callous behavior toward young women, while other young men interact in more respectful and nonviolent ways. This chapter uses secondary data as well as qualitative and quantitative research in which the author was involved since the mid-1990s in Rio de Janeiro and Chicago. It also includes voices of young men themselves.

The author's research reveals a complex interaction between disadvantage, generational transmission of poverty, individual and family characteristics, salient versions of masculinity, and consumer-oriented concepts of what it means to be a young person. As these connections between various kinds of risk and models of manhood are affirmed, it is necessary to recognize the diversity of young men. The author's research has often focused on those young men in low-income, violent settings who acquire other male identities, particularly those who are not involved in gangs, do not emulate those involved, and, in some cases, those who are more gender-equitable in their interactions with women than is the norm in their communities.

In reviewing this research, it is imperative to affirm from the start that the majority of low-income, urban-based young men in the region do not kill other young men, nor do they generally use other forms of serious physical violence. Indeed, most low-income young men are probably positive forces in their families and communities. In a recent interview of families in one of Rio de Janeiro's most violent *favelas*, one mother told the author, "My son never gives me any trouble, or hardly ever. He does well in school, stays out of trouble...helps out with his brothers and sisters. I have nothing to complain about." In addition, thousands of low-income young men are involved in public service projects and community initiatives throughout the region. These young men, however, seldom get the public attention that their violent counterparts do.

As a final caveat, caution is needed when examining these data not to overgeneralize from the specific context of marginalization and violence that characterize Rio de Janeiro's *favelas* (which are diverse themselves), nor from individuals whose lives and realities may not be representative of other young men in the region. The realities presented here should be seen as illustrative case studies. Examining the individual lives of some young men in depth helps one understand pathways to specific versions of manhood that may or may not lead to involvement in or victimization by violence, and other risks associated with traditional views about manhood. The analysis concentrates mainly on low-income areas in Rio de Janeiro. While these areas represent a specific reality, they are also similar in many ways to other low-income areas in Latin America, the Caribbean, and North America.

Starting with the Headlines: Violence and Gang Involment

On several occasions, the young men in low-income communities of Rio de Janeiro interviewed by the author have referred to the drug-related violence in their communities as "this war" or in some way compared the situation to a war. While this comparison may be exaggerated, the violence that plagues Rio de Janeiro's *favelas* and communities in places like Kingston, Medellín, and Chicago, among others, feels to many young people (and adults) who live there like a war. In all these settings, it is a minority of young men who participate in and are victimized by this violence, but many young people in these communities have felt or witnessed the violence, as the following narratives illustrate. These two young men are not directly involved in gangs, but have contact with gang-related violence:

> Pedro: He [the member of the rival *comando*, the Portuguese word for the drug trafficking gangs] was chasing after us on a horse...he was going to kill us. There were three of us, my brother and I and another guy [who was involved in the *comando*]. He was after my brother first, but my brother got away. Then he was after me and I ran to our house and hid inside...then my brother got there...he [the member of the rival *comando*] started to beat up my brother...beat the shit out of him. The next day we found out that the other boy [the brother's friend who was in the *comando*] was dead. This guy [from the rival *comando*] killed him (Barker 2001, p. 155).

Another young man who had friends in the *comando* told this story:

> Andre: One time...some of them [members of the *comando*] slept at my house...my mother knew them. One of them was like my brother...he was raised along with us...so then one day, he and four other friends of his who were in the *comando* slept at our house [sleeping at different residences is

sometimes a way to avoid police and rival *comandos*]. And this day I woke up...police knocked on the door and I heard them say, "We have them all, they're here." The guys in our house were armed, right...so the police said, "Open up." And the guys said, "No, if you come in we'll start shooting." So then the police broke down the door. They went upstairs and then we heard shots. I mean inside our house. Inside our house! So they [the police] sent us out of the house. I went to [a friend's] house. So then I saw them [the *comando* members]. They went out of the house through a hole in the roof...one got away, but one slipped on the roof and fell on his back on the roof. So then they started to beat him and one cop was shooting right at him [point blank]...this really bad cop. Then another police officer came and said, "He's alive. Let's take him to the hospital." But then this bad cop, he said, "Take him to the hospital? Why? I know this guy." So then they shot at him until he wasn't breathing anymore...so they took him away dead (Barker 2001, p. 155).

About 20 percent of Rio de Janeiro's population lives in low-income areas known as *favelas*. Since the 1980s, most of these *favelas* have been under the shadow of *comandos*, who traffic cocaine and marijuana and engage in armed conflict with rivals over sales and territory. To control or occupy a *favela*, *comandos* sell drugs (to residents and nonresidents), use the neighborhood to hide from police, live in the neighborhood, recruit from the neighborhood, and provide some minimal social benefits to the community, such as funding the local samba school or weekend dances (baile funk) and money lending. Residents tend to view the *comandos* with a mixture of fear, dislike, and respect. *Comando* members are often from the community itself, and while most residents oppose the violence, they frequently side with the *comandos* when violence breaks out between a rival *comando* or with police (Barker 2001).

The presence and power of the *comandos* (and the often brutal police response) is reflected directly in homicide rates among young men. As of 1999, Ministry of Health data found that 113.8 per 100,000 Brazilian young men aged 15–29 were killed by firearms, 4.1 times higher than for the population as a whole. In Rio de Janeiro, 188.8 per 100,000 young men were killed by firearms—6.8 times the homicide risk of the general population. For young men in Rio de Janeiro, the risk of being killed by a firearm is 24 times higher than the risk for young women. As of 2001, deaths by firearms represented 65 percent of mortality among young men, up from 35 percent in 1983 (Fernandes 2002). While many deaths by firearms may be related to other causes—fights, domestic arguments, and petty theft, for example— a large proportion is related to young men's involvement in the comandos.

The number of young men involved in the *comandos* is difficult to determine, but according to available estimates, only a minority participate. One study on drug trafficking in Rio de Janeiro asserted that 12,527 children aged 8–18 participate in drug trafficking, 5,773 of whom are aged 15–17. According to government household survey data, only 3,200 youth aged 15–17 are employed in other professions.

If these data are correct, drug trafficking employs more young men in low-income areas in Rio de Janeiro than does legal employment (O Globo 2002b). This same study concluded that 1.03 percent of youth from *favelas* work in drug trafficking. Similarly, a recent study sponsored by the ILO estimated that 5,000–6,000 youth in Rio de Janeiro participate in drug trafficking, or only about 0.3 percent of the city's youth population (aged 15–24) and 1.5 percent of youth living in the city's low-income areas (Souza e Silva and Urani 2002). Another study in one *favela* in Rio de Janeiro claimed, based on estimates from community residents, that about 25 percent of youth participated at least part of the time in the *comandos*, the majority of whom are young men (Meirelles and Gomez 1999).

The challenge of estimating the number of young men who participate in *comandos* is defining participation. Do we count those who work full time with the *comandos*, or do we also count those who occasionally do odd jobs for the *comandos*? Do we count those who do not sell drugs or carry weapons but allow *comando* members to hide in their houses? Whichever estimate we use, it is likely that while a minority of young men in the *favelas* actively participate in *comandos*, the violence they inflict and the version of manhood they represent are disproportionate to their absolute numbers.

Who are the young men in the *comandos*? Young men and parents interviewed in *favelas* in Rio de Janeiro say that boys as young as ten participate, and most of the people interviewed said that participation starts at about 15 (Barker 2001). Citywide, the average age of the *comando* heads has fallen; increased violence by police and rival *comandos* means that the life expectancy of leaders has decreased. In some *favelas*, *comando* heads are as young as 17.

Participating in a *comando* is a male phenomenon that generally implies projecting or adhering to a specific version of masculinity characterized by: (a) the use of armed violence to achieve one's goals and a willingness to kill if necessary; (b) callous attitudes toward women, including use of violence; and (c) an exaggerated sense of male honor and a propensity to use violence in minor altercations and insults. Of course, other young men not participating in the *comandos* may similarly adhere to some or all of these values. Indeed, some authors suggest that this version of masculinity reinforced by the *comandos* represents an extreme or exaggerated version of a prevailing or hegemonic masculinity found in low-income settings in Brazil (Zaluar 1994). However, to be a member of the *comandos* is to be in many ways a standard bearer of the most visible and fear-inspiring version of what it means to be a man. Active *comando* members are almost always men—young men. Young women in a *favela* are more likely to be indirectly involved as girlfriends of *comando* members or in the administration or accounting of drug sales than in actual trafficking and carrying of weapons.

Why do young men join the *comandos*? As discussed in this chapter, faced with a shortage of viable and stable employment, drug trafficking has become a vocational alternative for some young men, who often face family and social pressure to drop out of school to work. However, just as gang involvement in the United States and Colombia, for example, cannot be adequately explained by unemployment and poverty alone, participation in *comandos* by young men is similarly complex. One study concluded that participation was linked to a search for connection and belonging not found at home; the search for an identity, namely that of a Robin Hood-like hero fighting against a world that offers low-income youth few alternatives; and attraction to the masculinity model associated with being in a *comando*, namely having money and clothes to attract girls (Meirelles and Gomez 1999).

The ILO study confirmed that being in a *comando* provides status and access to consumer goods for those young men involved. Based on interviews with young men involved in the *comandos*, the authors conclude that outlaw activities are a concrete life and survival alternative, regardless of the risk entailed "Children and young adults seek autonomy, adrenaline, independence, and power, which are essentially expressed by their image and perceived by their peers" (Souza e Silva and Urani 2002, p. 14). In sum, young men justified their participation in the *comandos* for three main reasons: money, women, and respect.

It seems reasonable to assert that the vast majority of (heterosexual) young men in *favelas* and elsewhere want money, women, and respect. What sets the young men in *comandos* apart is the means they are willing to use (or have at hand) to acquire them. In their quest for money, women, and respect, young men in the *comandos* display extreme versions of traditional masculinity. How young men in the *comandos* treat their female partners is illustrative of this point. The ILO study reported that 22.5 percent of young men interviewed who were involved in *comandos* were married or in a stable union. This is higher than rates of marriage for other young men in the same age range, suggesting that the income from drug trafficking allows young men to have access to female partners and form families earlier than their non-*comando* peers. As one young man said, "A hard worker can go months without a girlfriend, but a *bandido* always has two or three women" (Barker 2001, p. 123). By various accounts, being a *bandido* means having several female partners and being able to demand absolute loyalty from them. A young woman connected to a *comando* member, even after she has broken off from him, cannot be seen with another man in the community. And if she were to sexually betray him while he was imprisoned, she would likely face death. As a young man (not involved in the *comandos*) in one *favela* stated, "We just beat our women when they deserve it. The *bandidos* beat their women like dolls" (Barker 2000a, p. 270).

What about income derived from drug trafficking? Young people involved with the *comandos* say they earn R\$240–320 per month as informants and up to R\$1,200 as "sales managers" (O Globo 2002b).[2] This compares with a monthly per capita income of R\$134 in low-income neighborhoods and a city average of about R\$700 (Souza e Silva and Urani 2002). However, possibly more important than the amount of income is the status that a stable income confers. Various studies of male socialization and identity worldwide have confirmed the importance of work and the resulting income as being central to how societies and individuals define what it means to be a man. Gilmore's (1990) review of ethnographic research on male socialization concludes that almost universally, cultures promote an achieve-ment-oriented masculinity that emphasizes men's primary roles as providers (workers) and protectors.

Indeed, if work defines male identity, having stable employment (legal or ille-gal) that offers respect and income is central to achieving status before the male peer group, before family, and in the community. For young men interviewed by the author, having stable employment is to achieve both adulthood and adult man-hood and is generally necessary for starting a family. In a low-income setting, work also provides access to consumer goods that are craved by young men themselves and attractive to potential female partners, as the following quotes suggest:

> Author: Why do women like guys in the *comando*?
> João (age 19): Because they have the best clothes. [A girl says]: "Huh, I'm gonna go out with a guy without money? He doesn't give me anything." But a gangster [*bandido*] can give a motorcycle or whatever she wants because a gangster never goes without money....But if a girl goes out with a hard worker, you know how it is, he'll have a hard time finding a job and getting money. So girls prefer to go out with the gangster because it's rare to find a guy (around here) who's a hard worker (Barker 2001, p. 123).

In another interview:

> Author: ...what does it mean [for a man] to work?
> Murilo: You have to work. Because you want to have your [own] things and at least when you're 20 or 25, you want your things organized...together [have a family and support yourself]. And if you don't work, you're gonna have to rob to make a living. You're not going to be [as a man], walking around with nothing to do or wear. I prefer to work [than to steal] (Barker 2001, p. 109).

To not have work and the associated income and status, as these young men sug-gest, is to be a nobody, to lack status in the eyes of one's family and potential and actual female partners. Various ethnographic studies in low-income areas in the United States and elsewhere have confirmed the negative impact on men and their self-image, health, and well-being when they lack meaningful work that confers sta-tus (Anderson 1990; Wilson 1996.) For low-income young men who often lack other means of affirming their identity, being without work and income is not merely a question of material poverty or unemployment but it is an affront to their very sense of self and how they define who they are in their social setting. Young women in these same settings may find meaningful, albeit limited, social roles and senses of self as mothers or partners of men, but young men rarely find a socially recognized identity in carrying out domestic chores or caring for children.

Being in the *comando* also brings respect on other fronts. For young men who have few other sources of social recognition, being tough or being an outlaw may be all there is. Research on gang involvement and delinquency in the United States and Western Europe identifies similar patterns. Ethnographic and qualitative research on violence and adolescent boys has found a survival and instrumental function of violence for young men in low-income communities. For many low-income males, many of whom have little else which gives them meaning and clear roles in society, violence can be a way of maintaining status in the male peer group and of preventing violence against oneself (Majors and Billson 1992; Anderson 1990; Archer 1994; Schwartz 1987).

Writing about delinquency and adolescent males in the British and American contexts, Emler and Reicher (1995) suggest that delinquency for many adolescent males is a deliberate "reputational project," an effort to demonstrate a delinquent identity to others to fit into the antisocial peer group—particularly for those young men who see mainstream goals and identities as beyond their reach (or who feel they have been rejected by mainstream social institutions, such as schools or conventional workplaces). Given that most delinquent behavior happens in groups and that most delinquent acts are committed by a relatively small number of adolescent boys, there is strong validity in the view that violent and delinquent behavior by adolescent boys is an identity and not merely a series of isolated acts.

To give an example from Rio de Janeiro, in a recent group activity organized in one *favela* in which the author works, a *comando*-involved young man with an automatic weapon in hand insisted on using the restroom in the space being used for the group activity. He made an obvious and visible point of showing his weapon to the group and watching their reaction. The young man seemed pleased by the fear he could instill, and clearly defined for the other young men who he was—a *bandido*. Now compare this scene of a young man brandishing an automatic weapon before his peers to the exclusion and discrimination that young men from *favelas* often face when they venture outside their communities. The following narrative is from a young man from a *favela* (who did not participate in a *comando*) describing an incident in which he was parking cars and a white, middle-class woman asked him to wash her car. When the woman returned, she claimed that he did not wash the car:

> João: When she came back, it was already washed but she started just saying like shit, you didn't wash it, and cussing at me. And I just stayed quiet because I knew if I started to argue, someone would call the police and pretty soon they'll be saying I'm trying to rob her. And I'm quiet, and she says: "You didn't wash shit." And I said: "Yes ma'am, I did." "You washed nothing," she says. And then I said: "Ma'am, some day you'll be robbed or something like that and people say we [blacks, residents of *favelas*] just do that but here you are cursing me." But she didn't want to hear any of that. She just got in her car and left. Just because I was black. She's racist, just likes to take advantage of others. There are times when it makes you want to hate, but I just let it go. I'm used to just letting it go. Like sometimes when I'm walking along Lagoa [the lake in the middle-class neighborhood in Rio de Janeiro], some whites will like walk away from you when they come in my direction. Some will walk around a different way to

avoid me. I don't say anything. But sometimes I'll talk to them. I'll say: "Don't worry, I'm not a thief." But they walk by looking at me like all strange. Blacks get a lot of discrimination (Barker 2001, p. 124).

These two examples lead to an important point. If status, money, women, and a lack of other means to attain these things are what motivate young men to join *comandos*, how does one explain the majority of young men in the same settings who do not join? In addition to the factors previously discussed, the author's qualitative research on young men not involved in *comandos* suggests that family stress, family disorganization, and lack of family coping skills are also crucial to explain involvement in or staying out of *comandos*. Young men who join, or who previously participated, seem to have "nothing else to lose," as one young man told the author. Compared to non-*comando* young men, those in *comandos* seem to have less optimism or faith in the future (i.e., they are more fatalistic) and have a shorter time horizon. As several young men told me, their desire for status in the short run is greater than the fear associated with being involved in the *comandos*. Of young men interviewed who participated in the *comandos* and were able to get out, fear was often a major motivator for leaving, whether fear of being killed by a rival *comando*, by the police, or by members of their own *comando*. In many cases, this fear was also associated with a family member, a child, or a partner who the young man perceived would suffer if he were killed or imprisoned (Barker 2001).

Young men not involved in gangs who were interviewed by the author in Chicago and Rio de Janeiro showed a variety of similar characteristics that seemed to explain how they stayed out of gangs and *comandos*, including: (a) having a valued, stable relationship with a parent, a grandparent, or a female partner (or multiple relationships) who would be disappointed if the young man became involved with gangs; (b) having access to alternative identities or some other sense of self that was positively valued by the young man and by those in his social setting, particularly the male peer group (for example, being a good student, athlete, or musician or having a good job); (c) being able to reflect on the risks and costs associated with the violent version of masculinity promoted by gang members; and (d) finding an alternative male peer group that provided positive reinforcement for nongang male identities (Barker 1998b, 2000b, 2001).

Other researchers have identified similar factors. One study comparing young men in Rio de Janeiro who were juvenile offenders with their nonoffending siblings identified a number of protective factors that worked in favor of the nondelinquent young men (Assis 1999). The nonoffending siblings: (a) showed more optimism toward their life settings; (b) were more verbally expressive; (c) were either the first-born or youngest siblings in the family; (d) had calmer temperaments; and (e) reported stronger affective connections with parents and/or teachers.

For young men in Chicago and Rio de Janeiro who had been involved in a *comando* or gangs and gotten out, a number of factors seem to have made it possible for them to leave. These included fear, becoming a father and assuming a relationship with the child and child's mother, moving out of the neighborhood or community, or becoming a member of an evangelical church (Barker 1998b, 2001). Other research in the United States uncovers similar patterns. When young men in low-income and violent settings find conventional means to attain identity and status—finishing school; acquiring legal, stable, and reasonably well-paid employment; having family members they can connect to; having nondelinquent peers; forming their own family—most young men stay out of gangs and other delinquent behaviors.[3]

The research suggests that the factors that explain whether young men get involved in gangs is a complex interaction between specific family, peer group, and individual characteristics. Overlapping and interacting with these factors are the salient versions of masculinities in these communities, in particular a "hard worker" version of masculinity associated with conventional employment competing with a hypermasculine, violent version of masculinity promoted by young men in *comandos*. These two versions compete for the loyalties and identities of young men, but they also have much in common. Both are identities (overwhelmingly heterosexual and generally homophobic) that emphasize men's roles as providers (and the need to have stable income to be recognized as a real man), access to consumer goods, and access to women as stable or occasional partners. Becoming a member of the *comandos*, and using violence (or risking being a victim of violence) is partly a conscious choice to adhere to an exaggerated version of manhood.

It should be emphasized that aspects of this exaggerated manhood are found in the wider local culture beyond the *favelas*—a culture that promotes a man's right to respond to insults to his honor and his right to expect loyalty from female partners, among other things. It is probably no coincidence that as the *comandos* have expanded their influence in Rio de Janeiro's *favelas*, in middle-class bars in the city, groups of middle-class young men (some called "Pit Boys" after pit bulls) have been in the news for starting fights with bouncers or with other young men. These fights, from press reports, have generally been related to altercations over girls, being denied entrance into clubs or bars, or disputes between rival peer groups. Indeed, the *comandos* are not the creators of violent versions of masculinity in Brazil, just as gang members in the United States and elsewhere are not. They recreate and sometimes exaggerate these identities from a wider social context that promotes violent versions of manhood.

Low-Income Young Men and Educational Attainment

How do young men in these settings fare in the public education system? Does the education system suit their needs? Is the way boys are socialized in Brazil and elsewhere conducive to their success in the formal education system? Recent data on school enrollment and school performance in Brazil clearly confirms that young men are faring worse than young women. But what can be said about the causes of these gender differences? What is happening with young men in the school system? This section explores these issues in some detail.

As a result of government priority, primary school enrollment is close to 100 percent in Brazil, but completion of primary education and enrollment in secondary education continue to lag. A recent UNICEF report using national census data found that only 33 percent of young people aged 15–17 are in middle school (O Globo 2002c). Examining national educational enrollment data for 15–24 year-olds, 57 percent have not completed primary schooling; in the state of Rio de Janeiro, 47.5 percent have not completed primary education. In addition, 21.7 percent of youth who are enrolled in school are behind their age-grade level and 25.8 percent of young people in this age range in Rio de Janeiro have left school. In low-income areas of the city, these rates show even more disparity: 69.8 percent of youth have not completed primary school, compared to 52.2 percent in the state as a whole (Fernandes 2002).

Looking specifically at gender, there is even more disparity. As of 1996, men in Brazil had an average of 5.7 years of formal education, compared to 6 years for women (World Bank 1996). Gender disparities start showing up around age 10 for boys when they begin to leave school at higher rates than girls, or when a greater proportion of boys both study and work (outside the home). At ages 15–17, 43.8 percent of boys in Brazil as a whole are in only school and 27.8 percent study and work. For girls in the same age range, 57.5 percent are only studying and 17.3 percent work (outside the home) and study. In the same age range, 19.2 percent of boys only work and do not study, compared to only 8.5 percent of girls (IBGE 1998). Data also show that women have lower rates of illiteracy than men in Brazil. In 2002, 7 percent of men aged 15–24 were illiterate compared to 4 percent of young women (World Bank 2005a). In a recent survey of young people in one low-income neighborhood in Rio de Janeiro, among 225 youth aged 13–19, 20.6 percent of girls compared to 42 percent of boys had missed at least one entire year of school (CEPSI/USU and Promundo 2000). These data suggest that boys are faring worse than girls in the education system in Brazil, with an even greater disparity among low-income youths.

Despite indications of an emerging gender gap in education in Brazil, there has been relatively little policy discussion and scant research on the causes. The traditional argument has been that boys are more likely to drop out of school early because they are more likely to work outside the home.[4] Indeed, as previously discussed, there are clear social expectations that boys should work to support themselves and their families, particularly in low-income settings. But qualitative research in Brazil and elsewhere in Latin America suggests that another possible factor is the way that boys are socialized, specifically the tighter control and closer monitoring of girls' activities compared to boys. Time-use studies confirm that girls are more likely to work in the home or be in the home care of younger siblings or carrying out domestic chores, while boys are more likely to work outside or be outside the home hanging out on the streets, playing or working.

Researchers in parts of Australia, the Caribbean, North America, and Western Europe are beginning to ask what specific factors impede boys' academic achievement, particularly that of low-income boys (Barker 2000b). This research has focused on several issues, including the possibility that socialization in the home for girls encourages positive study habits and staying on task, and that the school environment is often more conducive to the ways that most girls are socialized in their interaction and ways of learning. For example, research from Jamaica, where girls are outperforming boys at the secondary and tertiary levels, suggests that boys are generally socialized to run free while girls are confined to the home. As a result, girls may learn to concentrate on tasks, sit still for longer periods, and interact with greater ease with female authority figures. Research on low-income boys in North America and the Caribbean suggests that teachers (the majority of whom are women, at least in primary and middle levels) sometimes hold stereotypical images of boys, which may become self-fulfilling—they think that boys will be disruptive and drop out of school or be expelled, and that boys in turn behave accordingly (Figueroa 1997b; Taylor 1991).

The author's own research with low-income young men in Rio de Janeiro lends additional support to these arguments. Informal conversations with teachers and observations of classrooms suggest that some female teachers may have a difficult time controlling or dealing with the sometimes disruptive and aggressive energy of boys (Barker 2001). Boys spend more time outside the home socializing with predominantly male peer groups, whose style of interaction and aggressive energy is probably not conducive to the more passive educational style that requires sitting still for hours at a time. One female teacher pointed ominously to several boys in the classroom and stated she knew they had family members in a *comando*. While she genuinely seemed to want to help the boys stay in school, her comments also suggested that some boys are identified as potential troublemakers because of their ties to a *comando*.

Another possible factor in boys leaving school may be the nature of the male peer group. The author's qualitative study found that many young men started dropping out of school around age 11 or 12, when they began hanging out with an antischool male peer group (Barker 2001). These male peer groups often convinced young men that playing soccer and just hanging out were more interesting than attending school. Only when families were extremely vigilant were they able to counter the male peer group and strive to keep their sons in school. The following quote from a young man in a *favela* illustrates the importance of the family in countering this tendency:

Anderson: I think school is something that I don't want to stop now. Because when I was little, I didn't have...[the chance to study], well I guess I did have it, but I wasted it. You know, when you're younger, you don't want to worry about anything, just goofing off. My mother would call me to go to school and I would say that I wasn't going. [He was hanging out with his male friends in the street.] And I'd take off running because there was no man at the house...a man who could run after me and catch me and make me go to school. My mother couldn't catch me. Today, now that I'm older, shit, I'm gonna study. Without an education...it's already hard (Barker 2001, p. 134).

As a contrast to the style of passive learning that often characterizes public schooling in Brazil and elsewhere, it is useful to look again at what it means to be in a *comando*. The ILO study states that it implies action, alacrity, tuning in, and maintaining a state of alertness (Souza e Silva and Urani 2002). These are all traits that may be keenly suited to the way boys are socialized outside the home. Of course, activities such as conventional work, being part of a musical group, or participation in a soccer team may also be interesting and engaging to boys for the same reasons—they imply action and require tuning in and maintaining alertness. The point is that the public education system in Brazil, particularly in low-income areas, probably provides few spaces or opportunities for boys (and girls, for that matter) to feel engaged in these same ways.

Other relevant questions are, first, whether schooling is worth the time and effort for low-income boys, and second, whether low-income young men perceive that schooling provides a return on the investment. An analysis of average income by educational attainment suggests that for low-income youth (male and female), educational attainment does not provide the same returns in terms of income gains as it does for middle-income youth. The ILO study compared average earnings by years of schooling for greater metropolitan Rio de Janeiro as a whole and for low-income areas. For greater Rio de Janeiro, the average income with just four years of schooling is nearly equal to the average earnings for those with 11 years of education from low-income areas in the city. In addition, among low-income residents who reach university level, average income is less than half the average earnings for a person with university-level education for the city as a whole (Souza e Silva and Urani 2002). This data suggests that marginalization for low-income youth is more that just a lack of access to education. Class, race, and gender barriers, along with limited social capital, have a measurable impact on their employment status and earnings. In low-income, urban settings, it becomes even more difficult to motivate a young man to stay in school, which is compounded by the likelihood that being in school provides relatively little status or identity compared to working or being in the *comando*. These issues have not been widely studied.

What are the implications of these trends? In Australia, Canada, the Caribbean, the United Kingdom, and the United States, there has been some initial discussion and program development on the special challenges that some boys face in school (Barker 2000b). Australia is probably the most advanced; it has started discussions with public education staff and policymakers on how to offer special services and structure education in ways that may be more suitable to learning for boys, particularly low-income boys.

The challenge with such initiatives is to avoid reinforcing gender stereotypes, by suggesting, for example, that all boys learn one way and all girls a different way. Many boys fare well in school, and seem to adjust well, just as there are girls who fare poorly in school. In examining these gender differences, it should be kept in mind that individual differences and class differences may be equally or more important than aggregate gender differences. Nonetheless, there is a need for special attention to boys' needs in public education in Brazil. The response should be to consider the ways that gender socialization can create specific challenges for girls and boys. Girls, for example, often drop out due to unplanned pregnancies, while boys drop out for some of the previously cited reasons. The point is that both boys and girls in low-income settings too often drop out or are pushed out of school for gender-related reasons.

Low-Income Young Men and Employment

Previous sections highlighted a number of challenges related to employment and the meaning and importance of work to young men. This section examines some of the recent trends in greater detail and further discusses challenges that low-income young men in Brazil face in terms of finding employment.

A review of employment trends in Brazil and many countries in the region suggests that unemployment is a chronic and growing problem, particularly for young, less-educated workers (Arias 2001). Unemployment rates in low-income communities in Rio de Janeiro are around 12.4 percent, compared to a national average of 7.3 percent and a citywide rate of 5.2 percent (Souza e Silva and Urani 2002). In recent years, there has also been an increase in employment in the informal sector in all age groups, including 18–24-year-olds in Brazil, although this has not always been synonymous with lower wages. For some workers, informal sector employment has actually meant increased wages (Arias 2001).

In addition, due in part to increasing (but still low) educational enrollment and to efforts to reduce and eradicate child labor, participation of 15–17-year-olds in the labor market has been declining. At the same time, there has been an increase in unemployment among youth aged 18–24, whose unemployment rates are about twice national rates (Souza e Silva and Urani 2002). Data from 1991–2000 show a decrease in the number of working youth (aged 15–17) from about 30 percent to just under 15 percent for boys and from less than 20 percent to less than ten percent for girls in the Rio de Janeiro metropolitan area as a whole. Nonetheless, in low-income areas of Rio de Janeiro, the proportion of youth who work continues to be high, nearly double the workforce participation rates for the city as a whole. In some low-income areas, nearly 50 percent of young people work, with even higher rates for boys (Souza e Silva and Urani 2002).

As previously mentioned, young men are far more likely than young women to be working outside the home. For youth aged 15–19 in Brazil, 42 percent of young women were working outside the home compared to 61 percent of young men in 1999. For the 20–24-year-old group, 64 percent of young women were working in 1999 compared to 89 percent of young men. Among the adult population aged 25–44, an increasing percentage of women are working outside the home while the percentage of men working has remained stable (Arias 2001).

How do young men themselves perceive these trends? Even when young men are employed, the question is whether the work that is available and attainable meets their needs for stable income and for status. Access to work is fundamental to low-income young men beyond the income it provides. Various young men

reported that having stable, dignified employment was the difference between joining the *comando* or not. The following quote is from a young man who participated
for a time in a *comando*, and who said he joined because he needed the money to
support his mother and grandmother:

> Anderson: [Work isn't] everything, but almost everything. You know [if you
> work], you'll have some money in your pocket. I mean if you don't have
> work, you see men get involved in all kinds of trouble. You want to kill some-
> one with a knife in your hand. I've seen a lot of hard workers get a weapon
> and start to rob buses just to make ends meet. You need the money. When a
> guy is working, he's not gonna get rich, but he'll get by. When you have
> work, you're better off, better for yourself, and nobody wishes you a hard
> time [bad luck] (Barker 2001, p. 146).

Interviews reveal that many kinds of informal sector work, particularly itinerant selling (on buses, in the street, or in a marketplace), are often seen as demean-
ing. It is seen as a last resort and generally pays less, is less stable, and does not bring
status. Young men and their families generally coveted public sector jobs with
stability (and with benefits), not unlike much of the middle class. For low-income
men interviewed, formal sector employment also provides another immediate benefit—with stable employment, most employers offer an identification card for their
workers. For young men in *favelas*, who are often harassed by police for presumed
participation in the *comandos*, this identification card is extremely useful. Although
with job stability, a man can form and support a family and attain status in the community, formal sector jobs are increasingly scarce. While the informal sector may
provide higher income for some workers, informal employment is inherently
unstable and may not help young men gain status in their communities.

Indeed, many of the young men and their families interviewed by the author
perceived that it was increasingly difficult to become a "hard worker," a man with
sufficient income and job stability to form and support a family. In one focus-group
discussion in which adult and young women from the community participated, an
adult women said:

> The way things are going, I think it's hard to find a good man [which she
> used to mean a man who did not hit women and who had a job]. I got lucky,
> thank God [and found a man who is a hard worker] but my [woman] friends
> haven't had this luck.
> ...these days looking for work is hard [for a man]...he'll look but he won't
> find anything, and when he finds something it will pay just a little. So then
> he'll start a family when he's still young. They'll have children right after that
> [and he has to support them]... I mean, I think it's difficult for men. The
> doors don't open... Look at this group. There are 30 young men [who have
> the opportunity to participate in this course], but how many men do you

think there are in our community [who need an opportunity like this]? (Barker 2001, p. 165).

Young men themselves complained about how difficult it was to achieve the hard worker identity and status, particularly having low educational attainment and being low-income, black young men:

Author: How is it as a young man trying to find work?
João: It's harder for a man than a woman to find work, because…there are more opportunities for women, like an opening for being a cook. Not for a man, but for a woman, or like someone to work a counter. They say they want a woman. A man will try, but there will be this mistrust: "Shit, he must be a thief." Or like the boss will be racist and he doesn't want to let you (a black guy) work. And they'll accept women more, it's easier for women. If they have an ID they can get a job really fast (Barker 2001, p. 128).

Another barrier for many young men in *favelas* is the lack of social capital, specifically having contacts and direct experience with the formal labor market. Given high rates of female-headed households and chronic unemployment and underemployment, many of the young men interviewed lack contacts with fathers, stepfathers, or other adult men in the family who present models of a working man. Given that most of the young men interviewed had only four or five years of schooling (for young men whose average age was 16 and should have had up to nine years of formal education), many lack notions of punctuality, perseverance, and other social skills required for most formal sector jobs. This lack of contact with working men and the lack of familiarity with the formal sector workplace probably heightened the fear that some of the young men expressed when talking about looking for work. In this setting, having little social capital to facilitate finding formal sector employment was both a subjective and objective barrier to finding stable employment. The social codes of the formal workplace and even those necessary for many kinds of informal work are simply unknown to many young men in Rio's *favelas*, and probably to thousands of other young men in low-income, urban settings like this. Such concerns must be taken into account in job training and employment creation initiatives in the region.

Relating to Women: Implications for Sexual and Reproductive Health and Women's Well-Being

How low-income, urban-based young men relate to women and deal with their own reproductive and sexual health needs are also important issues to consider. Since the mid-1990s, there has been a growing international consensus on the need to more adequately include boys and young men in reproductive and sexual health initiatives and gender-based violence prevention, most notably at the 1994 International Conference on Population and Development. Various ministries of health, local health authorities, and NGOs throughout Latin America have affirmed the need to include boys and young men in reproductive and sexual health initiatives and in gender-based violence prevention.

This growing attention to young men and sexual and reproductive health is crucial for young men and young women. From research with young women and young men in Brazil and elsewhere, we know it is frequently men who decide and control how and when the sexual activity of young women happens. By holding greater power in sexual relationships, by having more sexual partners, and by starting their sexual activity earlier than young women, young men are also at the center of the HIV epidemic in the Americas and in many cases control the reproductive choices of young women. Furthermore, from a developmental perspective, men's styles of interaction in intimate relationships are "rehearsed" during adolescence. Viewing women as sex objects, using violence against women, and seeing sexual and reproductive health as "women's issues" generally begin in adolescence (and probably before) and may continue into adulthood, providing yet another rationale for focusing attention on young men (Barker 200b).

What does research tell us about young men, sexual and reproductive health, and gender-based violence? There are several reviews of the literature on young men and reproductive and sexual health (see Green 1997; Barker 2000b, 2002). This section provides a short overview, using the author's research from Brazil for illustration.

In most of Latin America, young men generally have penetrative sex earlier and with more partners before forming a stable union than do young women, although in recent years there has been a general approximation between the median age of first vaginal intercourse between boys and girls (Singh et al. 2000). After forming stable unions, young men are also more likely than young women to have occasional sexual partners outside their stable relationships. Furthermore, studies throughout the region suggest that the meaning of sexual activity is often different for boys than for girls. Young men often view sexual initiation as a way to prove that they are real men, that is, to affirm their identity and to have status in the male peer group (Marsiglio 1988). In qualitative research carried out with lower-income and lower middle-income young men in Rio de Janeiro, having had (heterosexual) sex and acquiring employment were seen as the two milestones for becoming a man (Barker and Loewenstein 1997).

Various studies also find that boys often share their conquests with pride with the male peer group, while doubts or lack of sexual experience and any homosexual experiences are hidden or denied. In interactions with young men, we have seen how not being sexually active, and sometimes having just one female partner or having experienced same-sex sexual attraction, can be sources of ridicule in the male peer group. These conclusions are key for understanding the sexual behavior of young men because they imply that changing such behavior generally entails promoting changes in peer group norms, and not simply at the level of the individual.

Although changing young men's sexual behavior is complex, there are some positive signs that change is occurring. For example, condom use among young men in Brazil, and in much of Latin America, has increased in the last 10 years but is still inconsistent and varies according to the nature of the partner or relationship (for example, occasional, regular, or sex worker). National data on condom use in Brazil found that in 1986 fewer than 5 percent of young men reported using a condom during first sexual intercourse, compared to nearly 50 percent in 1999 (UNAIDS 1999a).

At least part of this increase in condom use is probably related to changing peer group and community norms on increased awareness of HIV/AIDS. Nonetheless, there are still many barriers to promoting young men's increased condom use and attention to sexual health matters. These include the sporadic nature of their sexual activity, lack of information on correct condom use, reported discomfort, social norms that inhibit communication between partners, and rigid norms about whose responsibility it is to propose condom or other contraceptive use. In many settings, because reproductive health is seen to be a female concern, women must suggest condom use or other contraceptive methods. At the same time, the prevailing norms frequently hold that it is the man's responsibility to acquire condoms, since for a young woman to carry condoms would suggest that she planned to have sex, which is often seen as promiscuous.

One of the results of inconsistent condom use by young men is high rates of sexually transmitted infections (STIs) and HIV/AIDS. In a study carried out with 749 men aged 15–60 in three neighborhoods in Rio de Janeiro (two low-income and one middle-income), 15 percent of all men reported having had an STI at least once, but only 42 percent said they informed their partner (Promundo and NOOS 2002). Other studies have confirmed that although young men have high rates of STIs, they sometimes do not seek treatment or rely on self-treatment (Barker 2000b).[5] Related to relatively high rates of STIs among adolescent boys is the increased risk of HIV infection. An estimated one in four persons infected by HIV/AIDS in the world is a young man under age 25 (Green 1997). As previously mentioned, in Latin America and the Caribbean, including Brazil, young men have consistently higher HIV prevalence rates than young women, generally two to three times higher (UNAIDS 2000).

In much of Latin America, boys are frequently socialized to accept polarized notions of what is masculine and feminine. As we have confirmed in our work in low-income settings in Rio de Janeiro, young men who diverge from these norms, including those who have same-sex orientation or behavior are likely to be ridiculed or criticized. At the same time, research from around the world finds that 1–16 percent of young men report having had some same-sex sexual contact (PANOS Institute 1998; Lundgren 1999; Barker 2000b). Our study of adult and young men found that 6.6 percent of 749 men aged 15–60 said they had a sexual relationship with another man at least once. One result of these tendencies is that young men who have sex with men are stigmatized. In the survey, 32 men affirmed that they would never have a gay person as a friend (Promundo and NOOS 2002). The rigid socialization of boys into gender norms, which includes using homophobia to criticize boys who act in nontraditional ways, hinders the promotion of more gender-equitable behavior and hinders HIV prevention and sexual health promotion efforts.

Related to sexual and reproductive health is the issue of fatherhood. Adolescent fathers and young men's roles as fathers have been largely absent from research and program development related to adolescent reproductive and sexual health, and youth programming in general. Research on young men's attitudes toward fatherhood, their experience and needs as fathers, and their involvement or desire for involvement as fathers is lacking. Yet we know that fatherhood is part of many young men's experiences. For example, in the previously cited baseline research with young men, 28 percent of 225 young men aged 15–24 interviewed were already fathers, and 38 percent of those had more than one child.

What do we know about the realities of young fathers? Several studies from Latin America suggest that young fathers, like young mothers, may face social pressures to drop out of school to support their children and are less likely to complete secondary school than their nonparenting peers (Barker 2000b). Research suggests that many young men may initially deny responsibility and paternity when faced with a possible pregnancy, often because of the financial burden associated with fatherhood. Research in Mexico concluded that an adolescent father's employment and financial situation were key factors in determining how he responded to pregnancy and fatherhood (Atkin and Alatorre-Rico 1991).

Young fathers often face stereotypes on the part of their parents, the parents of their children's mother, the mother herself, and service providers. Young fathers who do not marry the mothers of the children, for example, are frequently seen as being irresponsible. In some cases, young fathers may want to be involved with their child but the child's mother will not allow it. Young fathers who are unemployed may feel constrained in their parenting role because they do not believe they have the right to interact with their child if they are not financially providing for the child. Such nuances have not been widely studied and are often neglected in discussions about young fathers (Lyra 1998). Indeed, only recently have a handful of programs in several parts of the world started to examine the multiple roles of fathers and to promote greater involvement by fathers in child care and maternal health.

A final issue related to the ways that young men interact with women, is that of gender-based violence. Research suggests that up to 30 percent of women in Brazil have been victims of physical violence from male partners, and an estimated 300,000 women report being victims of violence by a male partner each year, with similar tendencies elsewhere in Latin America. Research of men aged 15–60 in Rio de Janeiro found that 26 percent said they had used physical violence at least once against an intimate female partner; the highest rates were among young men aged 20–24 (Promundo and NOOS 2002).

What factors are associated with men's use of violence against women? Our research and other studies confirm that having been a victim of or witnessing violence in one's home increases the likelihood that a man will use violence in his own intimate relationships. In our study, 40 percent of men had witnessed physical violence by a man against a woman in their home of origin and 45.5 percent reported having been victims of physical violence in their homes. In both cases, men who reported being victims of or witnessing violence in their homes were more likely to report using violence against a partner. Other factors include men's greater power in relationships, women's fear and inability to seek legal recourse and men's traditional views about gender, among others. Adult and younger men who had more traditional views about gender and men's roles were more likely to report having used violence against women (Promundo and NOOS 2002).

In looking at all four issues—sexual and reproductive health, condom use, young men's roles as fathers, and young men's use of violence against women—the question of traditional views about what it means to be a man emerges consistently. In the settings we work in, four prevailing sets of views are common among young and adult men: (a) reproductive health is a woman's responsibility; (b) men are allowed and expected to have occasional sexual partners while women must be faithful; (c) men's involvement in domestic tasks, including child care, is limited; and (d) many men tolerate and use violence against women. Although these are the prevailing views, there are also many young men who question them. For example, in our interviews and interactions with young men in various communities in Rio de Janeiro, we heard the voices of young men who oppose violence against women. Many of these young men came to question violence against women because they had a space or a person to whom they talked to about the violence. We have also encountered young men who are actively engaged as fathers and others who seek greater equality in their relationships with young women.

Three key factors emerged in interviews with these more gender-equitable young men: (a) having family members or other influential individuals who modeled or presented alternative, more equitable views of gender roles; (b) having experienced some pain as a result of traditional versions of masculinity (a father who abandoned the family or used violence against the mother) and being able to reflect about the "cost" involved; and (c) finding a peer group or social space where alternative views about men were presented (Barker 2000a). These findings and these more gender-equitable young men are fundamental to finding ways to promote greater gender equity in settings where traditional gender norms prevail. Using these results, we have worked at the community level to: (a) promote or support alternative male peer groups; (b) promote discussions in group educational activities about the costs of traditional versions of masculinities; and (c) engage community leaders and families to promote alternative views of manhood.

Together with a network of NGOs in the region (Promundo, Ecos, and PAPAI in Brazil and Salud y Género in Mexico) we have incorporated some of these elements into a set of manuals with group educational activities that focus on promoting reflections about the costs of traditional views of manhood. These materials have been field-tested in five countries in the region and are gaining widespread acceptance in ministries of health and among NGOs. We have also developed a perceived norm scale—the Gender Equitable Attitudes in Men Scale (GEM Scale)—that assesses young men's attitudes related to gender roles and masculinities and is also used to measure changes in attitudes based on participation in group activities and other community interventions. As in the case for young men and gang involvement, this intervention seeks to learn from the realities of young men in low-income communities who question some of the negative versions of what it means to be a man.

Rethinking Young Men in the Region: Reflections from Program Development

There is a small but growing number of nongovernmental and governmental efforts in Latin America to work with young men from a gender perspective—that is, examining how the ways boys and young men are socialized affects their health and well-being.

In 1998–99, Instituto Promundo collaborated with WHO on an international survey of programs working with adolescent boys in health promotion (WHO 2000c). This survey of 77 programs from around the world (17 in Latin America) found a variety of creative approaches for reaching boys and young men, ranging from health centers with special hours for boys to mentoring programs that connect young men with positive male role models. Many programs focus on sexual health, recognizing young men's unmet needs in this area, but others work on general health promotion, vocational training, counseling, educational support, and violence and substance-abuse prevention.

Among the 17 Latin America programs, the most pressing needs of young men were reported to be: (a) vocational training; (b) reproductive health services and information; and (c) counseling or group spaces where young men can discuss and deal with issues related to identity, gender, self-esteem, and the pressure to adhere to prescribed gender roles. Some programs, particularly in the United States and the Caribbean, are focusing considerable staff time and resources on working exclusively with young men because they see men as an at-risk population that merits specific attention. However, the majority of organizations offered special activities, including special clinic hours or boys-only discussion groups, for young men within their overall work with adults and/or adolescents. In addition, the majority of these programs working with young men in health promotion were NGOs, probably a reflection of the fact that NGOs in the region first called attention to adolescent boys. However, it is encouraging to note that in some countries, it has been possible to incorporate a focus on young men within public health centers and hospitals or within university teaching hospitals, as in the cases of Argentina and Brazil. Emerging practices in terms of working with young men included engaging young men via the military, media campaigns to promote changes in peer group and community norms, and efforts to reach even young boys. One promising project in Chile, which is being carried out in collaboration with the Pan-American Health Organization, delivers messages about health promotion and gender equity to young boys via their soccer coaches.

Although there are a number of ideas and approaches to reach young men on these issues, there has been almost no serious impact evaluation of these efforts and relatively few efforts to scale them up. For example, in the WHO review of 77 programs, only one (from the United States) had been subjected to a rigorous impact evaluation. Another finding was that many programs were like "jewel boxes," well crafted programs reaching a small number of young men. The major challenge, then, is scaling up.

Conclusions and Recommendations

Summarizing some of the points covered in this chapter, the analysis confirms a number of areas where more research and more policy and program development are required, including:

THE NEED TO INCLUDE GENDER AND DISCUSSIONS ABOUT MAS-CULINITIES IN THE CLASSROOM. While data from several countries in the region confirms boys' underperformance in school, there is little research on the issue. There is a need for greater understanding of what is happening to boys in schools, as well as discussions at the levels of ministries of education, and at the local level, on possible gender-based challenges that many young men seem to face.

THE NEED TO INCLUDE GENDER IN THE WORKPLACE AND IN WORK-FORCE TRAINING. Vocational training is, of course, widely offered to youth throughout the region, although by most accounts there are still large unmet needs for job training. Such training generally focuses on technical skills, which although vital, fails to consider the lack of contact with the world of work that many low-income young men (and women) face. There is also a need to pay more attention to the impact of unemployment and underemployment on men's identities and the stress that being without work often generates.

FOCUS ON CHANGING PEER GROUP AND COMMUNITY NORMS. In recent years, there has been significant questioning of simplistic and mechanistic models of behavior change that focus on individuals in the HIV/AIDS and public health fields. Research consistently confirms the role of peer group and community norms. Peer and community norms are highly influential for young men who often feel the need to affirm their status and identity before their male peer group. Thus, rather than focusing exclusively on behavior change and attitude change among individual young men, interventions should focus more on these community and group norms. This means that gender work should include all those involved in the socialization of young men—teachers, families, peer groups, community leaders, schools, the military, and the media, among others.

MAKING GENDER VISIBLE FOR YOUNG MEN. The discourse on gender has for the most part focused on young or adult women. The result is that gender has become visible for women in many important ways, but it is also necessary to understand and affirm that gender matters for boys and young men—and understand how young men are socialized and the costs or stresses from their socialization. This is not to convert young men into victims or to downplay the many ways that women face serious and pervasive disadvantages in the current gender order. Rather, making gender visible for young men means understanding that young men have gender and that the gendered identities they adhere to can mean the difference between poor health or good health, between having meaningful or superficial relationships, and between life, death, or imprisonment, as many authors have stressed (see for example, Kaufman 1993).

Finally, it is important to keep in mind that gang involvement, violence, and callous attitudes toward women are not male destinies. The plurality of male identities, even in low-income settings, holds the key to understanding and promoting change. There is no typical low-income, urban-based young man in the Americas. There are multiple pathways to manhood for young men—pathways where individual, family, community, and cultural factors intersect. The author's research has repeatedly emphasized young men who stay out of gangs and who act in gender-equitable ways. These young men illustrate possibilities for promoting change and clarify the fact that the elements of change can often be found within low-income communities themselves when they are supported by creative NGOs, community efforts, families, individuals, and a favorable policy environment. For some young men, to be a man is to be violent. For others in the same setting, being a man means working to support oneself and family, caring for one's children, respecting the rights of women, and caring for one's own health. Our challenge is to support more young men to follow similar pathways.

Notes

1. This chapter is excerpted from the book *Dying to Be Men: Youth, Masculinity and Social Exclusion* (Barker 2005).
2. At the time, US$1 was equal to about 3.5 Brazilian reais.
3. I have deliberately given little attention to issues such as temperament or biological factors that may lead young men to be more violent on average than young women, or make some young men more prone to the use of interpersonal violence than others. This is for two reasons. First, terms such as "disposition" and "temperament" are often inadequately defined in the literature and in research. Second, the majority of research confirms that if there is a biological tendency toward aggression and violence for boys and men, the role of biological factors is extremely limited in explaining the range of behavior of young men.
4. Girls work at rates nearly as high as boys, perhaps even higher, when their unpaid domestic work is included.
5. This section is focused mainly on sexual and reproductive health needs. Nonetheless, research from various settings confirms similar trends with other health needs. In much of the world, boys are generally raised to be self-reliant, not to worry about their health

and not to seek help when they face stress. Young men often see themselves as being invulnerable to illness or risk, and may just "tough it out" when they are sick, or seek health services only as a last resort. In other cases, men may believe that clinics or hospitals are "female" places (Barker 2000a).

Fearing Africa's Young Men

Male Youth, Conflict, Urbanization, and the Case of Rwanda

7

MARC SOMMERS

M̲ale youth are Africa's vanguard. They are leading the charge in cities, which are rapidly transforming the historically rural-based African population into a mostly urban one (Hope 1998). Male youth are featured in military outfits across the continent. They are being devastated by the AIDS epidemic, and their place on the margins of most reconstruction and development efforts in Sub-Saharan Africa threatens to undermine efforts to improve African lives.

Perhaps more than any other Sub-Saharan African nation, Rwanda is at a cross-roads. For years, Rwanda was the least urbanized country in the world. Now it has the world's highest urbanization rate. Victimized by arguably the most efficient genocide in modern history, Rwanda's population is riding a wave of government reforms. At the same time, most male youth, some of whom were foot soldiers of the 1994 genocide, remain pinioned on the margins, receiving precious little attention or support. This is a potentially disastrous situation, given male youths' significant demographic numbers, their legacy of being drawn and forced into acts of extreme violence, and limited opportunities for them to contribute to Rwanda's development.

This chapter proposes to set the case of Rwanda's male youth within the larger context of Sub-Saharan Africa's urbanization and burgeoning youth population. It will begin by investigating the pervasive images of male urban youth as a menace to Sub-Saharan Africa's development and its primary source of instability. It will then turn to the Rwandan case, examining the desperate conditions Rwanda's young men (and women) faced before and during the civil war (1990–94) and the 1994 genocide. It will then draw on field interviews with Rwandan youth to consider the situation male youth face in the postwar, postgenocide era. The chapter will conclude by situating the Rwandan case within the debate on whether concentrated numbers of Sub-Saharan African male youth are dangerous, as well as future prospects for Rwanda's male youth population.

Fearing Young African Men

Young Sub-Saharan African men are fearsome, particularly those in big cities. This, at least, is how they continue to be depicted. It is certainly the case that young urban men scare or, at the very least, deeply unsettle, some foreign visitors to urban Sub-Saharan Africa. In his book *African Madness*, Alex Shoumatoff characterizes Sub-Saharan African cities as strange, even macabre. Here, he connects urban Sub-Saharan Africa to social dysfunction:

> It is only when large cities begin to appear on the landscape, as they did in the [1970s], when eleven cities in Central Africa grew to have populations of more than a million, that a societal madness begins to occur; that detribalized young men, lost souls wandering in the vast space between the traditional and the modern worlds, can be heard howling in the streets of downtown Nairobi in the middle of the night; that stark naked aliénés can be seen rummaging in the ditches of Bangui (1988, p. xiv).

Shoumatoff also quotes a Ugandan woman explaining that "most of the people who run mad in the villages move to the towns, I think because there are more things for them to do" (1988, p. xv).

The idea that young urban men in Sub-Saharan African cities have both become disconnected from their cultures and cause social madness are themes that Robert D. Kaplan has expanded on to powerful, and influential, effect.[1] Kaplan's work seems intended to terrify. He describes the young men who throng West African cities not as fellow humans but "out of school, unemployed, loose molecules in an unstable social fluid that threatened to ignite" (1996, p. 16). Strangely, he adds, "Their robust health and good looks made their predicament sadder."

In Kaplan's view, the world that these young men inhabit is repellent. He describes, for example, "rotting market stalls of blackened bile-green" (1996, p. 15), a rural horizon as a "writhing, bumpy green carpet" (p. 26), and cities as a cultural wasteland where "forest cultures" decay and are replaced by "high-density concentrations of human beings who have been divested of certain stabilizing cultural models, with no strong governmental institutions or communities to compensate for the loss" (p. 29). Young men in a bar in a poor urban neighborhood are automatically considered the robbers of the wealthy. He describes the immediate area as having a "decaying, vegetal odor." The young men and the stench collectively inspire Kaplan to announce, "Nature appeared far too prolific in this heat, and much of what she created spoiled quickly" (p. 19). Given the tapestry of horror that Kaplan describes, it is perhaps not surprising that he also predicts, albeit with little or no direct evidence, that "the perpetrators of future violence will likely be urban born, with no rural experience from which to draw" (p. 12). Taken together, there appears to be nothing redeemable whatsoever about young Sub-Saharan African men and the urban environs they inhabit.

Kaplan's frightening Sub-Saharan African urban male youth baton of the 1990s has been handed over to more recent supporters of the same dark vision—the proponents of the youth bulge, which Urdal defines as "extraordinarily large youth cohorts relative to the adult population" (2004, p. 1). The underlying youth bulge idea is that presence of large numbers of male youth inevitably sets the stage for violence. The short answer to the question of why are youth bulges so often volatile, Cincotta, Engelman, and Anastasion assert that there are "too many young men with not enough to do" (2003, p. 44). The connection to Kaplan's earlier predictions are direct, and are made explicit in a 2002 speech by George Tenet, then Director of the Central Intelligence Agency (CIA), who noted that the "sizable 'youth bulge'—what Robert Kaplan calls 'unemployed young guys walking around,' [is] a strong indicator of social volatility" (Tenet 2002, p. 5).[2]

Since the alarmist, deterministic youth bulge thesis is examined at length by Urdal, it will not be explored in this chapter, except for a handful of observations about the debate it has inspired. It is useful to note, for example, that while the youth bulge thesis purports to be scientific and predictive, it is frequently hammered home by members of the U.S. security community, many of whom are connected to federal intelligence institutions. The connection made between young people and terrorism is illustrated in the following CIA statement in an unclassified letter to the U.S. Senate's Select Committee on Intelligence dated April 8, 2002:

> While we are striking major blows against al-Qa'ida—the preeminent global terrorist threat—the underlying causes that drive terrorists will persist. Several troublesome global trends—especially the growing demographic youth bulge in developing nations whose economic systems and political ideologies are under enormous stress—will fuel the rise of more disaffected groups willing to use violence to address their perceived grievances (CIA 2002, p. 5).

John L. Helgerson, formerly Chairman of the U.S. National Intelligence Council and currently Inspector General of the CIA, is among those who have highlighted the threat of young men in urban Sub-Saharan Africa as a cause for particular alarm. After noting that Sub-Saharan Africa is the only region in the world where youth bulges are not expected to decrease in the next two decades, Helgerson states:

> The inability of states to adequately integrate youth populations is likely to perpetuate the cycle of political instability, ethnic wars, revolutions, and anti-government activities that already affects many countries. And a large proportion of youth will be living in cities, where opportunities will be limited (2002, p. 3).

While Urdal has found that a high proportion of youth in a society can be seen as both a "blessing and a curse" (2004, p. 17), Hendrixson takes youth bulge proponents to task more directly. Hendrixson first connects the youth bulge thesis to a discipline known as strategic demography, which "uses population characteristics such as age, ethnicity, geographic location and numbers to help locate terrorist or criminal threats" (2004, p. 1). She even locates the origin of the youth bulge thesis: Gary Fuller, a demographer who developed the idea while serving as a visiting scholar at the CIA in 1985 (Hendrixson 2004, p. 2). The youth bulge thesis also supported a related theory introduced by Princeton professor John DiIulio in the mid-1990s: the "superpredator" theory, which "equated a rise in the proportion of young men in a given population with a rise in the numbers of criminal young men" (Hendrixson 2004, p. 3).[3] The superpredator theory specifically referred to youth of color in urban areas in the United States.[4]

Hendrixson (2003) argues that the youth bulge theory is likewise "personified as a discontented, angry young man, almost always a person of colour," who resides in huge numbers in Africa, the Middle East, and parts of Asia and Latin America and forms an "unpredictable, out-of-control force" (p. 8). Conflicts arising from high concentrations of young men constitute serious security threats because they "are capable of spilling over into neighboring countries" and even other regions such as the United States, making them "an immediate threat that must be stopped" (Hendrixson 2003, p. 8). Hendrixson further notes that the theory "reinforces a view of Southern cities as pathological," underestimates "their functionality," and exaggerates "their violence" (2003, p. 12).

The security-driven response promoted by youth bulge proponents, Hendrixson argues, highlights both the pressure of high concentrations of youth facing limited educational and employment opportunities (2003) and the fact that "angry young men" are "driven to violence by their very biology" (2004, p. 10). Thus, the youth bulge theory implies that young men with constricted options will automatically and necessarily respond with violent rebellion.

Hendrixson also asserts that the resulting policies fundamentally misunderstand the source of the problem. The issue is not that there are too many angry male youth. Instead, it is how resources are used. She cites the example of Egypt, where "development problems are often framed in terms of population pressures" instead of issues such as escalating disparities between the rich and poor, foreign aid undermining local food production, weakening public welfare institutions and, most significantly, expanding military budgets (2003, p. 2). Hendrixson adds that there is a need to acknowledge that Sub-Saharan African cities "make sense" (2004, p. 16).

Curiously, in many Sub-Saharan African cities, the dreadful future that youth bulge proponents highlight—of too many male youth packed into cities—has long ago become a location for high concentrations of male youth. Indeed, men (most of them young) have demographically dominated some Sub-Saharan African cities almost from their inception: colonial Nairobi, for example, prohibited workers from bringing their families with them, resulting in "an overwhelmingly male urban population" (Kurtz 1998, p. 78). Since the predicted danger of large numbers of young men concentrated in urban areas has long ago come to pass across Sub-Saharan Africa, one can reasonably ask why Sub-Saharan African cities are not much more dangerous. How is it possible that cities containing high numbers of young men are reasonably peaceful?

The youth bulge thesis stains all youth in certain places—most frequently those in the Middle East and Sub-Saharan Africa—with the mark of danger. At its core, the thesis is not based on an argument but rather a closed statement containing an unsupportable premise: if young men are inherently violent, then high concentrations of them inevitably lead to massive violence and even warfare. While African cities are hardly oases of tranquility and content, they are not centers for major conflict. Nor is it apparent that all urban male youth are manifestly dangerous. To this day, from Somalia to Sierra Leone and Sudan to Mozambique, Sub-Saharan Africa's wars have been largely rural-based conflicts at their roots. Rebellions have emanated from the hinterlands (where male youth are generally not densely settled), not the capitals (where they are). One is thus inclined to interpret phrases such as, "Urbanization concentrates precisely that demographic group most inclined to violence: unattached young males who have left their families behind and have come to the city seeking economic opportunities," as overblown (Office of Conflict Management and Mitigation 2005, p. 7).

Reading about the youth bulge and depictions of urban Sub-Saharan Africa by Shoumatoff, Kaplan, and others is to recoil from urban Sub-Saharan African realities and to turn one's eyes toward rural Sub-Saharan Africa, perhaps, as Shoumatoff notes, to "groove on the scenery" (1988, p. xvii). Indeed, given the dreadful picture of an urban Sub-Saharan Africa clotted with hordes of threatening young men, the response is usually not to address urban Sub-Saharan African problems with direct assistance. A common response to the perceived urban youth threat is to essentially invest elsewhere. This denial of the obvious has many adherents. After all, the presence of so many people in cities seems counterintuitive, at least in economic terms. Hope has observed, "African countries are substantially more urbanized than is justified by their degree of economic development" (1998, p. 356).

The popular postwar practice of reintegration illustrates the widespread tendency for Sub-Saharan African governments and international agencies to persist in directing much of their development investment toward rural areas, even as migrants pour into urban areas. Reintegration has been largely spurred by the need to help former combatants return to live in their former rural homes. The ex-combatants who have received assistance in formal programs are mainly male youth. Typically, large numbers of female youth who have been active with military groups are not targeted (see Mazurana et al. [2002], McKay and Mazurana [2004], and Verhey [2001]. Some programs engage in community reintegration, which is based on the view that assistance is required to facilitate the successful reintegration of all community members, not just ex-combatants.

It may thus be assumed that international agency support for the reintegration of postwar communities is both necessary and effective. While this could be the case, recent documentation and field research raise questions about this assumption, particularly as they relate to assistance for, and the location of, youth.

First, postwar community reintegration frequently concentrates programming in rural rather than urban communities. This approach may be partly based on the assumption that urban youth, including ex-combatants, will return to rural communities once investments arrive there. An international donor official interviewed in Liberia illustrated this view by asserting that, "The way forward is for youth is agriculture, whether they like it or not." Many youth, however, do not like it—few urban youth in Sub-Saharan Africa appear to ever return to live in their former rural communities (Ogbu and Ikiara 1995; Sommers 2003). Urban youth may not want to farm or live in rural communities partly because they fear retribution and partly because war experiences changed their aspirations. A woman interviewed in rural Democratic Republic of Congo (DRC) shed light on such changes when asked why her ex-combatant son migrated to town. "Maisha ya kizungu" (the white man's life), she stated, an allusion to her son's interest in the urban lifestyle demonstrated by foreign aid workers residing there.

Second, much community reintegration work aims to reconstruct communities. During an interview, a foreign official in DRC described his agency's community work in the following way: "We go for rehabilitation rather than new construction because we want to support something the community has already done something about." Yet this approach does not address the possibility that what community leaders did before the war helped cause it. Recent research in Burundi reveals that international agencies have unintentionally helped to rebuild structures of inequality that were a central cause of civil war. Their concentration of support in the "favored" zones (such as reconstructing destroyed permanent structures) while largely overlooking "neglected" zones (where few such structures or opportunities for advancement existed) appears to have greatly exacerbated geographic, ethnic, and class disparities and is a potentially destabilizing factor that could help fuel a return to violent conflict (Sommers 2005).

In postwar Liberia, Richards et al. (2005) similarly warn that "communities will sink their differences temporarily in order to qualify for a grant," suggesting that reintegration efforts may "empower certain groups over others" and provide, at best, temporary positive results (p. ix). They add that many young people "are no longer able, or willing, to integrate within a traditional social system based on family land and social deference" (Richards et al., p. ix). As a result, "marginalized youth (including ex-combatants) see only a choice between rural dependency and exploitation of their labor, and the 'freedom' of life in urban areas" (Richards et al., p. ix). The authors imply that the urban option is by far the most popular.

Rwandan Youth in Context

Is there a better example of fearsome male youth than the notorious *Interahamwe* (variously interpreted as "those who work together," "those who stand together," and "those who attack together") militiamen of Rwanda? It is a well-known fact, and is consistently related in literature on the genocide, that unemployed, undereducated male youth made up most of the foot soldiers of Rwanda's 1994 genocide.

The genocide itself was quite possibly the most efficient in modern history, with an average, on peak killing days, of one murder every two seconds (Peterson 2000, p. 252). It is thought that somewhere between 500,000 (Mamdani 2001) and 1.1 million (Reyntjens 2004) of Rwanda's approximately 7.6 million people perished during the genocide. Kuperman (2001) and Des Forges (1999) both conclude that slightly more than three-quarters of all ethnic Tutsi citizens in Rwanda were killed during the operation. Reyntjens asserts that, in addition, "hundreds of thousands of [ethnic] Hutu died at the hands of other Hutu or the RPF" (that is, the Rwandan Patriotic Front, the military force led by [ethnic] Tutsi refugees who invaded Rwanda in 1990 and assumed power in Rwanda after the genocide) (Reyntjens 2004, p. 178). What has been much less studied is just how many thousands perished during the civil war, which began in 1990, and the tentative truce that followed in 1992, which immediately preceded the genocide. Des Forges offers an estimate of RPF killings during and soon after the genocide ranging from 25,000 to 60,000 people (1999, p. 16).[5] Perhaps 200,000 more Rwandans lost their lives while in exile following the genocide (Economist Intelligence Unit 2005a, p. 17), most of them in DRC. Taken together, this is a staggering loss of life—as much as 18 percent of Rwanda's population from 1994–96, and perhaps more. Yet Rwanda remains, to this day, the country with "the highest overall and rural population density in Africa" (Economist Intelligence Unit 2005a).

A lesser-known fact about Rwanda is the degree to which the country's youth have been overlooked. The literature on Rwanda, for example, is conspicuously thin on information about youth in the postwar and postgenocide period. International agency and government investment on youth remains similarly low. Few programs or opportunities exist for Rwanda's youth. The Rwandan government has a national policy regarding youth but it has limited investment levels. On its face, this appears to be both a counterintuitive and startling state of affairs. Young men, after all, demonstrated their capacity to be drawn (and coerced) into exterminating their fellow citizens.

What follows is a review of the plight of Rwanda's male youth before and during the 1994 genocide. It is designed to lay the groundwork for the subsequent section, which will explore the situation facing young Rwandan men since 1994, and the world they now live in.

Before the Genocide (and Civil War)

In prewar and pregenocide times, Rwanda was characterized by grinding poverty; intense population pressure on land; pronounced lack of education; social and geographic immobility; a dominant, controlling, authoritarian government with an extensive record of human rights abuses; an unusually prominent Catholic Church; a small and intimidated civil society; an influential yet frequently pliant international development community (quite often generating decidedly underwhelming results; see Uvin [1998] for extended discussion of this issue); and truly profound social inequality and exclusion.

Uvin draws a frightening picture of how these and other factors combined to create a life of crushing entrapment and frustration for the vast majority of Rwandans. Prior to the genocide, Rwanda was the poorest country in the world, with 86 percent of total population below the poverty line; half of its people were characterized as "extremely poor" (Uvin 1998, p. 117). Clay, Kampayana, and Kayitsinga (1997) add that 26 percent of its rural population lived on less than half a hectare of land, without schooling or nonfarm income (p. 108). Ethnic, class, and geographic favoritism were rampant. From 1982–84, for example, 90 percent of all public aid (mostly financed by international donors) was directed at only four provinces: Kigali, Ruhengeri, Gisensyi, and Cyangugu (Uvin 1998). Expanding landlessness, dramatic reductions in life opportunities for most poor Rwandans, and corruption and clientelism among the elite, all helped create a rural life that Uvin characterized as a "prison without escape in which poverty, infantilization, social inferiority, and powerlessness combined to create a sense of personal failure" (Uvin 1998, p. 117).

This confinement was by no means illusory. The government also had a historic fear of urbanization. Forced immobility, indeed, was a deliberate and consistent government policy that dated back to the colonial era and merely continued following independence. In 1953–54, the population of Rwanda's capital, Kigali, was, at most, 3,000 people (Voyame et al. 1996, p. 50). The government's mandate that almost all Rwandans remain in rural areas hit young men especially hard because they had far less land than their fathers and were incapable of supporting families or even marrying. By the early 1980s, according to one source, hundreds of thousands of young men could neither attain education nor inherit land and were in a permanent search for low-paid, temporary jobs, mostly in vain. They were blocked in their educational advancement, were limited in their employment and migration options, and lacked the resources to make a decent living in agriculture (Uvin 1998). The road from enforced misery to participation in extreme violence, in other words, was already being built.

In principle, the government developed an option for such youth within an education system designed to allow very few students into secondary school. Called the Centres d'enseignement rural et artisanal integrés (CERAI) vocational education system, it was mainly intended to produce "modern farmers or local artisans in their place of origin" (Hoben 1989, p. 108). The results were consistently disappointing. Hoben noted three central flaws: (a) community members had to pay for much of the cost of equipping CERAIs in their communities; (b) communities had no experience in making manpower assessments or forecasts, which frequently made their choice of CERAI courses inappropriate; and (c) government policies restricted the movement of CERAI graduates. This last factor "did not help to disperse growing pools of youth with similar training out of areas that could support only one or two" (1989, p. 113). Hoben added that while the problems of poor training and immobility were serious for boys, "it was worse for girls, who were leaving the CERAIs trained to cook dishes with ingredients unavailable in the countryside, to sew, or to embroider" (1989, p. 119). Hoben also argued that "forcing the formal school system to carry the main burden of vocational preparation is a mistake" (1989, p. 114).

Primary schools and the CERAIs were mainly supposed to provide a rural work force. For those who left primary school and did not attend either secondary schools or the CERAIs, there were limited options. These included the Centres de formation des jeunes (CJF), organized by the Ministry of Youth and Cooperatives, which largely provided limited courses in practical skills and cooperative organization to out-of-school youth, and Jeunesse ouvrière catholique (JOC), Catholic centers aiming to provide "Christian morality and the work ethic with a practical approach to improving the lot of aspiring young workers" (Hoben 1989, p. 88). Unfortunately, little data existed that allowed an evaluation of the situation of the majority of Rwandan youth who did not attend either CERAIs or secondary schools.

Most youth in prewar and pregenocide Rwanda thus subsisted in rural areas with truly limited prospects for advancement. A 1989, survey found that while most young men and women in Rwanda sought to become farmers, 85 percent of youth, and the majority of their parents, "believe that they will not inherit enough land for the subsistence needs of their families (Clay, Kampayana, and Kayitsinga 1997, p. 109). The sense of "life as a prison," in short, was palpable.

Youth and the Genocide

From the outside, the tens of thousands of young men who were forced or recruited into the notorious *Interahamwe* embodied much of what proponents of the superpredator and youth bulge theories had warned. Rwandan male youths seemed out of their minds, were unspeakably vicious, killed thousands upon thousands of innocent civilians, and killed in awful ways.

Yet another reality lay beneath journalistic reports of societal madness and rampaging young men during the 1994 genocide. The organizers of the genocide had carefully developed an extraordinarily effective plan which, among other things, engaged the entire government in the pursuit of genocidal objectives. As Des Forges observed, "By appropriating the well-established hierarchies of the military, administrative and political systems, leaders of the genocide were able to exterminate Tutsi with astonishing speed and thoroughness" (1999, p. 8). Uvin (1998) further noted how massacres and other human rights abuses perpetrated by the government against Tutsi civilians during the civil war years met with, at most, muffled responses by the international community. This international timidity continued across the weeks and months of the genocidal operation and has been extensively documented. Limited international protest or resistance against genocidal operations (as well as direct support for those administrating the genocide)[6] helped the organizers of genocide advance their objectives.[7] Uvin characterized the failure of the international community to react to the situation in Rwanda as "the absence of external constraints" (1998, p. 221).

Among the elements of destruction at the easy disposal of the genocide organizers was the enforced entrapment and pervasive hopelessness of Rwandan youth.

Their situation had been inflamed by the invasion of the RPF and the civil war that followed, which combined to make a bad situation exceedingly worse (Des Forges 1999, p. 1). By 1994, there was widespread drought and displacement, which exacerbated food and land shortages. Extremists within and outside government, who eventually formed the Hutu Power movement, beat the drum of fear of and revenge against ethnic Tutsi with political maneuvers and relentless, venomous propaganda against the Tutsi (Des Forges 1999, p. 4). Uvin observed that the racist, anti-Tutsi prejudice, already a longstanding strategy of legitimization of the Hutu-dominated government, was also "a means for ordinary people, subject to structural violence and humiliation, to make sense of their predicament, to explain their ever-growing misery through projection and scapegoating" (1998, p. 217). Mamdani has asserted that "the combined fear of a return to servitude and of reprisals thereafter...energized the foot soldiers of the genocide" (2001, p. 233).

All of this made poor, unemployed male youth easy pickings for those organizing the genocide. Malvern argues that the conditions on the eve of the genocide made it "almost impossible for the youth of the country, most of them unemployed, not to get involved" (2004, p. 24). Coercion mixed with promises of material gain. In 1992, the youth wing of President Habyarimana's ruling party began to transform them into the massive *Interahamwe* militia. Recruitment was countrywide and targeted unemployed young men (African Rights 1995, p. 56) and armed them heavily. Des Forges, for example, observed, "Businessmen close to Habyarimana imported large numbers of machetes, enough to arm every third adult Hutu male" (1999, p. 5). The *Interahamwe* and other young men were eventually authorized to terrorize and murder Tutsis not only with complete impunity, but with the urging of superiors.

What followed during the genocide was a near-complete engagement of youth at the forefront of involvement and victimization, a story that will not be told here but has been covered at length by others.[8] It includes how young people became killers and the killed, rapists and the raped, and looters and the looted. Young people were forced to join in the killing or were threatened with execution as Tutsi collaborators. Some were among those who risked their lives to save the lives of Rwandan Tutsis (Des Forges 1999, p. 11). Some young people became refugees or were internally displaced. The traumatic experience blanketed thousands of young people and left "hundreds of thousands of orphaned children and nearly 100,000 people in jail facing charges of genocide" (Economist Intelligence Unit 2005a, p. 17).

Male Youth Since the Civil War and Genocide

This section sketches the current situation of Rwanda's male youth, set within the context of government reforms, and introduces perspectives from Rwandan male youth about their plight and prospects.

Surveying Some Statistics

Before Rwanda's 1994 genocide, nearly 95 percent of Rwanda's population lived from farming (Taylor 1999). This is changing rapidly. Rwanda has not only joined the continent's surge toward cities, but it has quite suddenly assumed the lead, not only in Sub-Saharan Africa but worldwide. As of 2001, Rwanda was the least urbanized country in the world, with a mere 6 percent of its population in cities (Nationmaster 2005).[9] It still retains the position of having "the highest overall and rural population density in Africa" (Economist Intelligence Unit 2005a). Most of Rwanda's citizens continue to live with at least one foot in their farm plots, although these plots are increasingly under pressure. High population densities in rural areas, together with soil depletion and other agricultural challenges, led a former Rwandan préfet to characterize land scarcity as "our time bomb" (Sommers 2006, p. 90).

At the same time, Rwanda's capital, Kigali, "has been growing at a phenomenal rate," dwarfing the growth rate in other urban areas of Rwanda (Economist Intelligence Unit 2005a). In 2000, Rwanda's urban growth rate was estimated at an extraordinary 18.4 percent, more than twice the rate of Liberia, which ranked second (7.8 percent). By 2005, the rate had fallen to 11.6 percent, which was still the world's highest and nearly two times the rate of the second-ranking country, Burundi (6.5 percent; Global Health Council 2005).

How can Rwanda still be overwhelmingly rural while simultaneously urbanizing at such a high rate? The answer lies in the fact that, as noted, a succession of Rwandan administrations has kept Rwanda's urban areas unusually small. Kigali is much larger than it has ever been, but this does not mean that most Rwandans will soon live in cities. In fact, the United Nations Population Division has estimated that the percentage of Rwandans living in urban areas in 2030 will be 14.2 percent. This is unprecedented by Rwandan standards, but it is fourth-lowest when compared to all other nations. The three lowest countries in this ranking have less than 150,000 inhabitants (2002).[10]

A brief statistical review helps flesh out Rwanda's current situation. Rwanda had by far the world's highest rate of armed forces growth between 1985 and 2000 (1,246 percent; Nationmaster 2005c). Rwanda's population is estimated to be 8.6 million and is projected to rise to 10.6 million by 2015 (United Nations Population Division 2002). Forty-five percent of the population is under age 15. Rwanda is also one of the world's poorest nations, ranking 159th on the UNDP's latest Human Development Index (Sierra Leone, at 177th, is last). Life expectancy at birth is an alarmingly low 38.9 years. Rwanda is 129th out of 144 countries in building the capacities of women even though, impressively, Rwanda has the world's highest proportion of women holding seats in national parliament (45 percent; Polgreen 2005). There are two doctors for every 100,000 Rwandans. The contraceptive prevalence rate is only 13 percent, in a country where 5.1 percent of Rwandans aged 15–49 are infected with HIV. Forty-one percent of the population is considered undernourished. There are, of course, promising developments in Rwanda, such as in education: the adult literacy rate is 69.2 percent (as of 2002) and the youth literacy rate (age 15–24) is 84.9 percent (Nationmaster 2005c; UNDP 2004). At the same time, a quarter of all primary-age children are not in school (Obura 2003), and the percentage of its pupils reaching grade five is third-lowest in the world at 39.1 percent (Nationmaster 2005b).

Primary schools endure exceedingly difficult circumstances. Since the end of the civil war and genocide, Obura notes that "the retention rate has decreased, the repetition rate remains high, teachers' salaries are extremely low and schools lack essential books, materials, supplies and equipment" (2003, p. 147). In addition, "Boys drop out [of primary school] due to 'lack of interest' while girls drop out due to work for their families" (Obura 2003, p. 146). An encouraging sign is the expanding level of students enrolling in secondary school. As of 2003, there were an estimated 157,210 secondary students, "up from about 3,000 in 1994 after the war [and genocide], and...approximately 55,000 in 1993" (Obura 2003, p. 126). In 2000/01, 37 percent of primary school graduates reportedly entered secondary school, a remarkably high rate for Rwanda, compared to 9.2 percent in 1990 (Obura 2003).

For the purposes of our discussion, however, perhaps it is most significant that 94 percent of all adolescents are out of school (Obura 2003) and that "less than 5% of secondary [students] are from the poorest 20% of households" (Economist Intelligence Unit 2005a, p. 18). Most youth, in other words, remain out of school, and the poorest youth have little chance to advance in the education system.

A Changed World?

When the RPF began to assume control of the Rwandan government near the end of the genocide, it faced a *tabula rasa* of colossal proportions. Large swaths of the country were practically empty, since most of the inhabitants had been killed, internally displaced or had fled over borders in search of refugee asylum. A field visit to the northwest Rwanda a few weeks after the end of the genocide illustrated this in remarkable fashion: the hillsides, once dense with peasantry, were practically empty, and the town of Ruhengeri had precious few inhabitants. Rwanda was also a shambles: Reyntjens notes that the material damage included "infrastructure destroyed, banks and businesses plundered, the civil service, judicial system, health care and education services in ruins, and crops and livestock lost" (2004, p. 178).

Visits to the Ministry of Education building soon after the genocide illustrated the degree of destruction that the country faced. The interior structure had been severely damaged and its contents had been looted to such a degree that it suggested an effort at once clinical and energetic. The few doors that remained were shot up or cracked nearly in two. Nearly everything, from furniture to window panes, was gone or ruined. There appeared to be nothing worth salvaging. To an extraordinary extent, the new government was starting from scratch.

Amid the wreckage, the new RPF government simultaneously faced the enormous task and opportunity of starting fresh. Descriptions of what has transpired in
postgenocide Rwanda, particularly the government's still-towering role over political and social life, have run the gamut from complimentary to scathing. It is but
one way to illustrate the startling contrasts that the last 11 years have inspired.
Rwanda has been a scene for sweeping reforms, only some of which will be mentioned here.

Decentralization of the government—not a minor reform in a country as historically hierarchical and authoritarian as Rwanda—has been widely viewed as a
new opportunity for Rwanda (Unsworth and Uvin 2002). The promising
Ubudehe program hopes to eventually provide Rwandans at the lowest political
segments (cellules) with approximately $1,000 annually for small development
projects (National Poverty Reduction Programme and Ministry of Local
Government and Social Affairs). Misser reports that the Rwandan government has
the long-term aim to transform the "rural-based economy into a services centre
for the region" (2004, p. 2). A World Bank report delivers an upbeat assessment of
many aspects of the Rwandan scene:

> Considerable progress [in Rwanda] has been achieved over the last ten years in
> a range of areas. Peace and stability have been maintained. Traditional Rwandan
> values, such as community participation, group solidarity, support to the poor,
> and Gacaca—the concept of conflict resolution through communal efforts—
> have been instrumental in advancing reconciliation and accountability follow-
> ing the Genocide (López, Wodon, and Bannon 2004, p. 1).

Other observers have taken a starkly different view. Human Rights Watch has
condemned, among other things, the government's move at the end of 1996 to create new villages, known as *imidugudu*, as they constituted a "drastic change in the
way of life of approximately 94 percent of the population that resulted in violations
of the rights of tens of thousands of Rwandan citizens" (2001, p. 1). International
actors were also harshly criticized: "Praise for the generosity and promptness with
which donors responded to the housing program must be tempered by criticism of
their readiness to ignore the human rights abuses occasioned by the rural organization program [that is, *imidugudu*] that operated under its cover" (Human Rights
Watch, p. 74). Pottier further castigates the emergence of new commentators on
Rwanda who have almost no expertise, employ a "hasty, haphazard and uninformed
approach" (2002, p. 232), and effectively support the "official discourse which legit-
imates the use of violence and makes some, leaders and led, *génocidaires*" (p. 207). But
most of the criticism is aimed at the Rwandan government. The Economist
Intelligence Unit, for example, has observed that "the democratic process remains
heavily constrained and real power rests exclusively in the hands of the president,
Paul Kagame, and his party, the Rwandan Patriotic Front (RPF)" (2005b, p. 7). It
has also expressed concerns about government corruption and asserts that the government's behavior has inspired a reduced level of standing and support from

Western governments due to "concerns about political liberty at home and the controversial involvement of the country's security forces in the Democratic Republic of Congo (DRC)" (2005b, p. 7).

Of all recent assessments of Rwanda's current plight, Reyntjens (2004) provides probably the most comprehensive critique of the government's current role in Rwandan society. It is a shattering and damning assessment, as well as a somewhat peculiar one. Rather than communicating balance, the author boldly announces that his argument will intentionally be skewed toward the negative because the donor community continues to highlight government achievements, and because, in the author's view, the Rwandan government receives "favourable prejudice" that has had the same "blinding effect that caused major warning signs to be ignored" prior to the genocide (Reyntjens 2004, p. 179).

While the breadth of Reyntjens' critique of the Rwandan government and its international supporters are not shared here, some of the author's primary assertions will be briefly mentioned. The article moves across issues of flawed local and national elections, a broad array of examples describing the government's refusal to tolerate dissent, favoring the Tutsi, human rights violations, and the government's role in regional instability (2004, p. 185). International agencies—donors, UN agencies, and NGOs—are accused of a complicity of silence that has minimized criticism of the current regime due to what Reyntjens terms the genocide credit: "...the 1994 genocide has become an ideological weapon allowing the RPF to acquire and maintain victim status and, as a perceived form of compensation, to enjoy complete immunity" (Reyntjens 2004, p. 199). In his chilling conclusion, Reyntjens asserts, "There is a striking continuity from the pre-genocide to the post-genocide regime in Rwanda" (2004, p. 208). The list of similarities is long, and includes the complacent attitude of the international community. Reyntjens also describes "most Rwandans" as again suffering from exclusion, frustration, anger, and desperation, just as they had before the genocide.

Youth Developments

Is Rwanda once more descending toward massive and extreme violence, as Reyntjens suggests? While this question will be revisited in the concluding section, it is useful to note that given Rwanda's youth bulge, the prodigious expansion of its capital, and the established vulnerability of unemployed Rwandan male youth to being exploited and directed to carry out acts of extreme violence, one might presume that considerable attention would be accorded Rwandans' plight.

More than a decade after the genocide and civil war ended, this has simply not been the case for male or female youth. Most Rwandan youth are poorly educated, out of school, unemployed, and bereft of promising opportunities. A survey showed that "every second adolescent [in Rwanda] had no money at all at his personal disposal" and less than a third had regular paid income (UNDP and International Council on National Youth Policy 2003, p. 1). One international agency official working in Rwanda commented that about 1.5 percent of Rwanda's national budget is earmarked for nonformal education and out-of-school children and youth. Another international agency official related a conversation with a Rwandan government official who explained that the Ministry of Gender does not work on youth issues (the Youth Ministry's involvement is also limited). The international official also related that while the government is expanding investment in vocational education, the lessons learned from the earlier CERAI legacy are not being heeded, such as not basing its programming on labor market information. Consequently, most graduates (reportedly as much as 60 percent) do not find jobs after graduating. As Suzanne Kaplan has recently noted, "today the [Rwandan] youth struggle to rebuild their lives with little help in a society that has been completely devastated" (2005, p. 30).

There are precious few international and nongovernmental programs targeting Rwandan youth, and programs that do exist appear to be limited and unable to reach significant numbers of youth. They tend to be skewed either toward well-adjusted, educated youth or to youth facing particular circumstances, such as orphans and street children. Nonetheless, a few programs hold considerable promise. One such program aims to provide training, mentoring, and job placement for participants in Kigali.[11]

The government's approach to the youth challenge is mainly informed by its National Youth Policy. The official policy document opens with a useful statistical overview of the dire situation confronting most Rwandan youth. It then identifies a number of key youth actors in the country, including new youth representatives ranging from the grassroots to the national political level and the insertion of vice mayors charged with youth affairs into district affairs. The policy vests national leadership for youth matters in the Ministry of Youth, Sports and Culture (MIJESPOC). Several other ministries and commissions, the document outlines, are also involved with youth concerns, including education, HIV/AIDS, and the National Unity and Reconciliation Commission. Intriguingly, the focal point, think tank, coordinator, and implementing agent of the National Youth Policy is the Maison des Jeunes de Kimisgara, a youth center based in Kigali, and not the Ministry of Youth, Sports and Culture. This is hardly the approach one anticipates from a government that dominates so much of the nation's social and political life, and it suggests the low priority that youth issues continue to receive. In addition, it may well point to the low priority accorded to MIJESPOC and its objectives.

The National Youth Policy nonetheless makes a number of important assertions, including:

- In addition to income generating activities, there is a need for what the document terms "youth empowerment" and "youth advocacy" activities in order to make youth self-conscious and resistant to political indoctrination. This statement reveals a government view of most youth as malleable and vulnerable to manipulation.

- Two interventions are to receive priority through programs that are large in scale and decentralized, job creation and income generation,
- The success of the new policy will be judged by the involvement of youth on grass roots level. This bottom–up approach is to be carried out via the involvement of youth representatives in relevant decision making processes (UNDP and International Council on National Youth Policy 2003).

Perhaps most significantly, the next steps are merely stated in a suggestive fashion, namely that if jobless youth would be included in poverty reduction projects, a high amount of vocational training would be needed. Trainers would have to be motivated to undertake on-the-job training in this field in addition to teaching entrepreneurial skills. No concrete steps for achieving these ends are provided.

All of this said, the government's recognition that youth concerns need to be dealt with stands as a potentially significant step forward because the policy puts youth issues on the political and development map. Another promising sign is that international aid agencies appears to be increasingly interested in supporting Rwandan youth, although it is too early to gauge whether such emerging initiatives will be able to address the concerns of so many Rwandan youth.

Youth Views: Considering Two Questions

The following comments from and concerning Rwandan male youth have been culled from a series of field research visits to Rwanda since 1994.

WHICH MALE YOUTH ARE MIGRATING TO KIGALI? In 1994, while carrying out field research on Rwandan youth needs for UNESCO and the Academy for Educational Development (AED), less than two months after the genocide, the author interviewed five youth who informed him that they had entered Rwanda two days previously from Bukavu, Zaire (now the Democratic Republic of Congo). All of them had been born in Democratic Republic of Congo to refugees of the ethnic massacres in Rwanda in 1959–64 that drove tens of thousands of Rwandan Tutsis out of the country. All the interviewees proudly announced that they were very glad to be "home" in Rwanda for the first time in their lives. Some explained that their parents had sent them ahead to get their family's return to Rwanda started. Two days into their adventure, they had not yet found work in the capital. Already, they were frustrated, and one mentioned that he was ready to join the army (this description is drawn from Sommers [1995]).

Several years later, from 2000–2002, the author carried out seven field research visits in rural Rwanda to evaluate the impact of the Conflict Management Group's Central Africa Project.[12] One of the findings arising from interviews with male youth in a rural village in northeast Rwanda concerned migration to Kigali. Few youth from their village had even attempted to migrate, the youth reported. To most youth, it seemed impossible. They explained an array of problems. Urban migration had little precedence. They had no education and no work set up there. They had no relatives in the capital. "Youth can't go to Kigali," one explained, "because they don't know anything and they can't go just to wait around" for employment. Traveling to Kigali, moreover, appeared to be intimidating: two youth invitees to a workshop in Kigali did not leave the village until the mayor of the district approved their trip. Rwandans still carry cards listing their place of residence and identity (ethnicity, a pregenocide and prewar requirement, is no longer listed).

It is not yet clear which Rwandan youth are managing to migrate to Kigali and other cities and towns. Some information is available about a narrow portion of migrants, however. A survey of some of the thousands of street children in urban Rwanda, many of them orphaned by the genocide, found that they were mainly male youth: "approximately half of street children are 15 years or older, and of these the majority are male" (Veale and Doná 2003, p. 264). Beyond this population, little has been documented. Informal interviews with some Rwandan government and international agency officials suggest that a significant proportion of youth in Kigali are ethnic Tutsi refugee returnees, who traveled to the capital after returning to Rwanda following the genocide; the route that the youth from Bukavu followed, as mentioned above. Surely those with the networks, capital and education to start a life in the capital are present. Such information, however, remains merely suggestive and ultimately unreliable. What remains unsubstantiated is which Rwandan youth are managing to migrate to Kigali, why they migrate, and what they are doing in the city. Many basic details about Rwanda's urbanization thus remain largely unknown.

WHAT DOES RURAL YOUTH LIFE LOOK LIKE? A sequence of interviews with male youth in a Rwandan village from 2000–2002 revealed lives of elemental frustration. Land holdings are tiny. One leader explained that most families live on a mere half hectare of land. Government officials want youth to form cooperatives and farm together, but a government leader related that it was difficult to get youth to collaborate. One meeting with youth, for example, descended quickly into an argument. Unmarried male youth accused their married counterparts of not contributing their share of labor to their cooperative farm work. One married young man said he could not, due to family obligations. Unmarried youth challenged his stance. During a subsequent visit, I was told that the cooperative effort they were discussing had since collapsed.

The scarcity of land for a growing population was a widespread concern. A government leader present at a provincial meeting about land later related that the general feeling among the leaders present was that "there's no way out." Another leader said, "Poverty and land shortages make the youth feel hopeless. They have no vision of the future." Solutions were hard to come by, even for educated youth, and conflicts between neighbors and relatives were widespread. Some conflicts turn into unresolved feuds that can last for years.

As the amount of land available for inheritance withers, the chances for young men to build houses on their own land and then marry, as is expected of them, grow increasingly scarce. This was a persistent worry among male youth interviewed. Many regularly hunted for low wage, temporary employment. Some had clearly turned toward drink: the many bars in the village center teemed with young men. The lives of many young men seemed to largely alternate between wandering in search of an opportunity and waiting. "Struggling for life and being patient," one related, "is very, very difficult."[13]

Conclusions

The concluding section addresses four central concerns: the fears and realities of youth, Rwanda's urban outlet, the integration of youth in urban areas, and the invisibility of young women.

Fears and Realities: A Silent Emergency

A recent study suggests that early adolescent males, with high levels of testosterone in their blood, are easily influenced by their peers. If they are surrounded by peers engaged in delinquency, they are likely to copy that behavior. However, if they are around those engaged in positive activities, they are likely to become leaders. The authors of the study found that "testosterone was related to leadership rather than to antisocial behavior in boys who definitely did not have deviant peers" (Rowe et al. 2004, p. 550).

This example illustrates the serious distortions introduced by youth bulge theorists and others, who have essentially fingered male youth as elementally dangerous. "Too many" young Sub-Saharan African men in one place just may be a possible recipe for danger—but even then, only potentially. Youth may have excellent reasons to be frustrated, and government and international donor policies, in all likelihood, may merely be making a dire situation much worse.

Years of fieldwork in Sub-Saharan African cities suggests that if marginalized urban male youth interact with government officials, it is likely that those officials work in law enforcement. In most cases, programs and investment for them remain scarce, most particularly for members of the marginalized majority. Indeed, the answer to the youth challenge is not to further marginalize or paint male youth as fearsome security threats. That can only inspire increased alienation and a sense of being cornered. It is, in fact, quite the opposite: unemployed, undereducated young men require positive engagement, appropriate empowerment, and participatory financial and program support. Doing so promises to allow the array of assets that youth offer—namely their energy, enthusiasm, creativity, resourcefulness, and adaptability—to flourish. Most fortunately, the literature on the need to positively work with and support youth is gaining some momentum (e.g., Ebata et al. 2005; Kemper 2005; Lowicki and Pillsbury 2000; Newman 2005; Office of Conflict Management and Mitigation 2005; Sommers 2001; Thorup and Kinkade 2005; UN-Habitat 2004; UNICEF 2002a, 2002b; World Bank 2005b).

The case of Rwanda's male youth illustrates the inherent weakness of the youth bulge theory and the arguments of others who charge that high concentrations of Sub-Saharan African (and other) male youth is inherently dangerous. As Uvin (1998) has described, before the 1994 genocide, male youth were largely trapped in lives of crushing poverty, frustration, immobility, and humiliation on densely populated and increasingly scarce amounts of farmland. Most could neither migrate nor find a reasonable means for constructing a hopeful future. Yet despite their high demographic concentration in rural areas, there is no evidence that they were in any way unusually violent or threatening prior to the government's determination (and those of their allies) to exploit and direct male youth frustrations toward violence and genocide. Mention of unemployed young men, such a staple of literature about the 1994 genocide, scarcely exists in the prewar and pregenocide literature—as well as most literature produced since 1994. There was nothing intrinsically and predictively violent about male youth in Rwanda. On the contrary, a much better assertion would be to wonder at their remarkable peacefulness in the face of truly wretched conditions and a strong sense of hopelessness. The young Rwandan men of 1994, in short, were most certainly desperate and vulnerable. But their violence only emerged when their desperation and vulnerability were exploited. Indeed, if out of school, unemployed Rwandan male youth are so truly dangerous, one might expect more attention and investment paid to their needs. That is only beginning to be the case, and interest in youth concerns remains limited. An international agency official familiar with the issue recently commented that "the Rwandan Government is becoming quite concerned about youth."

Maintaining a cynical perspective of youth (even while youth are being supported) is underscored, of course, by youth bulge proponents. Yet, their frightening, predictive message, together with others bearing similar messages (such as Shoumatoff, Kaplan, and Huntington) reveals more about the proponents of such arguments than their male youth subjects. It may be more useful to ask why certain people are so threatened by some young men rather than why those young men seem so threatening. It is also useful to bear in mind the central irony surrounding Sub-Saharan Africa's urban youth: "...they are a demographic majority that sees itself as an outcast minority" (Sommers 2003, p. 1). The situation confronting most Rwandan youth, and most all of their counterparts in most of Sub-Saharan Africa—female and male—remains alarming. Their plight constitutes a largely silent emergency. Tragically, their general peacefulness makes them all the more invisible.

Rwanda's Urban Outlet

To borrow a famous phrase from the late Julius K. Nyerere, are Rwandan male youth "voting with their feet" by urbanizing? Given the spectacular failures of international assistance and government policies prior to Rwanda's civil war and genocide, when rural "development" was the only option (e.g., Uvin 1998), and increasing indications of serious difficulties in the postgenocide era (e.g., Economist Intelligence Unit 2005a, 2005b; Human Rights Watch 2001, 2003;

Klippenberg 2004; Reyntjens 2004), the answer certainly appears to be yes. The current Rwandan government is now facing something that has proven challenging for its counterparts across Sub-Saharan Africa to keep up with—massive urban migration.

The situation facing Rwandan youth today is likely not as punishing as before the 1994 genocide in large part because an urban outlet, to some degree, exists. But that does not mean that life for Rwanda's youth has transformed from mainly hopeless to primarily hopeful. The plight for the overwhelming majority remains extremely serious, and their access to available and appropriate opportunities lies, for most, somewhere between negligible and nonexistent. Rwanda's contracting social and political environment and grossly inadequate advocacy for and investment in youth rights and development threatens to worsen an already dire situation for most of Rwanda's youth population. Moreover, the picture of life in one Rwandan village provided in the section just above is eerily similar to descriptions of pregenocide life noted earlier in this chapter.

The situation for nearly all of Rwanda's youth population, then, remains bleak. As mentioned previously, Rwanda's National Youth Policy provides a potential platform (or, perhaps, part of a platform) for positive movement in support of youth. What is not yet sufficiently clear is whether and how recent Rwandan government and nongovernment actions directed at youth will impact youth lives, which youth are ready and able to take advantage of the urban outlet, what will become of those who continue to feel frustrated and trapped regardless of their location, and how the tightening social and political environment is impacting youth lives. Research and action on these and related issues is urgently required.

Urbanizing Youth: Reflecting on Postwar "Integration"

If positive engagement and appropriate support for members of the marginalized male and female youth majority in Sub-Saharan Africa (and elsewhere) is to be enacted, as is strongly recommended, then it will be necessary to remember that location matters. A component of successfully working with youth is to do it where they reside. Again, the example of postwar, community-based reintegration work is instructive. The term reintegration, in fact, inaccurately describes what is actually required because it assumes that people seek to reintegrate. They may not. Youth in cities, for example, may wish to integrate into new communities, not reintegrate into old ones—a decision that should be recognized, respected, and supported.

Similarly, people in rural or urban communities may have very good reasons to avoid reintegrating themselves into social and economic arrangements that existed before war. War likely altered the roles and aspirations of just about everyone—older men and women, youth and children, and most definitely ex-combatants. Powerful but unpopular leaders able to silence opposing views and funnel investments through them often present an additional challenge. Into this environment arrive government and nongovernment actors interested in, among other things, supporting people whose capacities almost certainly changed because of war and for whom empowerment and reintegration may lead in opposite directions. The backward glance inferred by reintegration may be precisely what many people, youth in particular, do not want.

Integration is thus a much more appropriate term for post-war community work than reintegration, and flexible programming needs to support youth and others creating new lives in their new communities (such as in cities). A rule of thumb for working with youth is to avoid the term "should." In this case, it means that governments, donors and programmers need to work with youth not where they think youth should be, but where youth already are.

Removing the Veil of Silence

Finally, the fact that this chapter addresses the fear and invisibility of Sub-Saharan Africa's male youth should in no way obfuscate the even greater invisibility and needs of their silent colleagues—female youth. Research in 20 war-affected countries since the early 1990s has illuminated how no population group is more at-risk and overlooked with more regularity than adolescent girls and young women. The contrast between their plight and those of their male counterparts is instructive. In too many contexts, the relatively few youth programs and organizations that exist are dominated by male youth. Meanwhile, existing women's programs and organizations are often dominated by more senior women. Stating this is in no way intended to undermine or question the needs of other war-affected populations. On the contrary, it is intended to shed light on the unnoticed lives of most female youth in war-affected contexts (if not in general). The results for them are frequently harsh and hidden. Nordstrom speaks of the "veil of silence" surrounding the treatment of girls in war (1999, p. 75). This veil, in fact, cloaks most young women as well, before, during, and following wars. It must be lifted so that all of Sub-Saharan Africa's marginalized youth majority can be engaged and supported with appropriate, proactive, empowering, and truly inclusive measures.

Notes

1. Reportedly, when Kaplan's famous 1994 article, "The Coming Anarchy," was published, it was subsequently "faxed to every American embassy in Africa, and has undoubtedly influenced U.S. policy" (Richards 1996, p. xv).
2. Tenet made these remarks in his acceptance speech at the Nixon Center, where he received the 2002 Distinguished Service Award for his "lifetime of public service in intelligence and national security" (Tenet 2002, p. 2).
3. DiIulio later became the first Director of the White House Office of Faith-Based and Community Initiatives in the George W. Bush administration.
4. The superpredator theory is not the only one to emerge from the United States concerning American urban youth. Uvin, for example, notes mention of "the so-called riffraff theory and the wild youngsters theory" to explain urban violence in the 1960s

and 1970s in the United States. Uvin considers these theories to be "without any proof apart from [their] political convenience" (1998, p. 219).

5. Robert Gersony, author of a United Nations report that was never released, estimated that between 25,000 and 45,000 people were killed between April and August 1994. Seth Sendshonga, an early RPF member, put the estimate at 60,000 between April 1994 and August 1995.

6. See, for example, Prunier (1995), which contains a remarkable, first-hand account of French complicity.

7. More recent examples of this literature include Dallaire (2004), Melvern (2004), and Power (2002).

8. Two of the most detailed are African Rights (1995) and Des Forges (1999).

9. It was just ahead of Bhutan (7 percent) and Burundi (9 percent).

10. These are Pitcairn, Tokelau, and the Wallis and Futuna Islands.

11. The program involves a consortium of international actors, including USAID, Nokia, the International Youth Foundation (IYF), and the Lions Clubs International Foundation. [http://www.iyfnet.org/document.cfm/30/626].

12. The program is examined in Sommers and McClintock (2003). The Conflict Management Group was founded by Harvard Law School Professor Roger Fisher as a 501(c)(3) nonprofit organization specializing in negotiation and leadership skills training and consulting services. In 2004, it merged with Mercy Corps to become Mercy Corps Conflict Management Group.

13. A more extensive description of field research findings is located in Sommers (2006).

Young Men and the Construction of Masculinity in Sub-Saharan Africa
Implications for HIV/AIDS, Conflict, and Violence[1]

GARY BARKER AND CHRISTINE RICARDO

G ender is increasingly used as a framework for analysis and for youth program development in the Africa region In most cases, gender refers specifically and often exclusively to the disadvantages faced by women and girls; given the extent of gender inequalities in the region, this focus has been necessary. However, a gender perspective and gender mainstreaming have too often ignored the gender of men and boys.

Two of the most pressing social issues in Sub-Saharan Africa—conflict and HIV/AIDS—are directly related to how masculinities are socially constructed. Most gender analyses of conflict focus on sexual violence against women or on the relatively small number of female combatants. These analyses generally conclude that those who use weapons are usually young men and that those who suffer the consequences of conflict are women and girls.[2] Similarly, most reports on HIV/AIDS focus on how women are made vulnerable by the sexual behavior of men. Indeed, too many women have been made vulnerable by the behavior of men in conflict and sexual relationships. However, development literature and many policy statements on gender generally present Sub-Saharan African men in simplistic and overtly negative terms, or ignore men's gender. As White states, "...men appear very little, often as hazy background figures. 'Good girl/bad boy' stereotypes present women as resourceful and caring mothers, with men as relatively autonomous individualists, putting their own desires for drink or cigarettes before the family's needs (1997, p. 16).

This chapter argues for applying a more sophisticated gender analysis that requires us to understand how men and women, and boys and girls, are made vulnerable by rigid notions of manhood and gender hierarchies. It seeks to answer two key questions. First, what does a gender perspective mean when applied to young men in Sub-Saharan Africa? And second, in terms of conflict and HIV/AIDS, what are the program, policy, and research implications of studying the gender-specific realities and vulnerabilities of young men?

We take that the perspective that specific versions of manhood are socially constructed, fluid over time and across settings, and plural. There is no typical young man in Sub-Saharan Africa and no single version of manhood. The concept of masculinities—referring to the plurality of ways of being men—has been used for more than 10 years in the field of gender studies (Connell 2003). There are, in turn, numerous and changing Sub-Saharan African masculinities. There are indigenous versions of manhood, defined by tribal and ethnic group practices, and historically newer versions shaped by Islam, Christianity, and Western influences.[3]

The Socialization of Boys and Men in Sub-Saharan Africa

A near-universal feature of manhood is that it must be achieved—it requires behaving and acting in specific ways before one's social group (Connell 2003; Gilmore 1990; Pollack 1998). Achieving manhood is judged by other men and women; young men frequently report a sense of being observed and watched to see if they measure up to culturally salient versions of manhood (Barker 2005). Research in Nigeria concludes:

> Through both formal and informal means, such as jokes, social ridicule and insinuations, a man is informed of what society expects from him. A non-conformist is made aware of his difference. The society exerts strong pressure upon anyone that deviates from the socially accepted gender roles, letting a male know when he is failing "to be a man" (Social Science and Reproductive Health Research Network 2001, p. 97).

These categories of manhood, however, are fluid and rarely mutually exclusive. Young men perceive multiple and sometimes conflicting notions of what it means to be a man. Young men's lives and identities also have multiple dimensions. Although Sub-Saharan African men are largely seen in monolithic and negative terms, they are rarely examined in terms of their domestic lives—for example, as fathers and partners—or in terms of how their motivation to work interacts with their other social roles (Lindsay and Miescher 2003). The migration of southern African men in search of work is often couched in negative terms and linked to the increase in female-headed households. Traditional gender analysis typically condemns men's behavior, emphasizing accounts of men's alcohol use and violence against women and children. While men's neglect of family responsibilities must be highlighted, it is also important to understand the complexity of men's cultural antecedents and roles in households.

Accounts of conflict often portray young men as barbarians and vicious killers—"imagine a whole sub-continent of Lord of the Flies," one journalist remarked (Grout 2002). Reports from the Democratic Republic of Congo (DRC), Liberia, and Sierra Leone, however gruesome and shocking, do not speak for all young men in Sub-Saharan Africa, or even for all men in these countries. Such reports frequently fail to probe for underlying factors that lead young men to use or participate in this violence.

What Makes a Man in Sub-Saharan Africa

The main social requirement for achieving manhood in Sub-Saharan Africa—for being a man—is attaining some level of financial independence, employment, or income, and subsequently starting a family. In much of Sub-Saharan Africa, bride price is commonplace, and thus marriage and family formation are directly tied to having income or property. A young man in Lira in northern Uganda put it simply: "To call oneself a man it is simplest after (one is) married with children. No children and you are still a boy." Focus group discussions with out-of-school, mostly underemployed young men in Kaduna, Nigeria (the site of recent clashes between Christian and Muslim youth) confirmed this association between work, marriage, and manhood. Many young men described themselves as being trapped in youth. Because they were not employed, they were not socially recognized as adults and thus could not marry. Some of the young men said that being employed also brought social recognition beyond their family, as unemployed young men were frequently harassed by military forces sent to areas where riots had erupted. Thus, having stable work, which might be identified by having a uniform or an identity card, was also coveted for the protection it offered. Police and soldiers respect young men with stable employment, but they expect that unemployed young men will be troublemakers and treat them as such.

In rural Sub-Saharan Africa, where men work primarily in subsistence agriculture, manhood, marriage, and work are highly associated with access to land. Young and adult men in internally displaced person (IDP) camps in northern Uganda affirmed that if they had no land "to dig," they could not be considered men. Among ethnic groups in Sub-Saharan Africa that rely on cattle herding for subsistence, manhood begins when a father bestows land and livestock to a son, which in turn can serve as bride price and enable him to achieve manhood and form a family. Thus, achieving manhood depends on an older man—one who holds more power—an issue that recurs throughout this analysis.

An employed man is also expected to support his extended family. The resulting pressure bears some relation to his willingness to engage in illegal or unethical activities. Similarly, Townsend's 1997 thoughtful account of men's migration in Botswana finds that men may support two or more households, depending on their age and role in the extended family. Men may support a residential family consisting of a wife, children, and some of the wife's family members, as well as another household consisting of their own parents. Because young, unmarried men have to contribute to their parents' households, they rarely establish their own households before the age of 40. In this setting, the social norm for young men is to care for the livestock of their fathers, grandfathers, brothers, and uncles. In many cases, young men are subject to their father's authority until he dies (Bennett 1998). Young men in such social structures express understandable frustration with the multiple demands on them.

Men's social recognition and their sense of manhood suffer when they lack work. For example, in Yoruba regions of Nigeria, there are documented accounts of women belittling husbands when they are not able to provide financially for the family and of men reported feeling emasculated when they cannot contribute to family income. In such settings, relationships between couples may become tenuous or stressed; some young married women keep their possessions in their father's house as a precaution in case of having an "economically unviable" husband (Cornwall 2003). Accounts from out-of-work men in Tanzania and South Africa suggest that some compensate this feeling of emasculation by taking on outside sexual partners or by drinking.

Accordingly, men go to great lengths to meet the cultural expectation of work. Migration for work is commonplace in parts of southern Africa. In South Africa, as of 2000, there were an estimated 350,000 black male workers working in mines, 95 percent of whom were from rural areas in South Africa and from neighboring Botswana, Lesotho, and Mozambique. The majority of these men live away from home in same-sex residences (Campbell 2001).

There is a growing body of research on the versions of manhood that have emerged among mine workers in South Africa. Ethnographies have described a culture of sexual encounters with occasional sexual partners, the daily fear of death and injuries, and the stress associated with seeing friends and coworkers injured or killed. Some mine workers describe the risk of HIV as minimal compared to their occupational risks. Many mine workers show a remarkable sense of obligation to their families, which motivates them to continue working in hazardous conditions. While there has been significant attention to the HIV risk behaviors of mine workers, and a tendency to blame men for taking HIV back to their wives, most authors now see mine workers as living up to a specific version of manhood. They seek to achieve socially prescribed versions of manhood—being sexually active and providing for their families—even when they rationally understand the risks of their occupation and sexual activity (Campbell 2001; Moodie 2001).

Studies confirm that not just any employment is sufficient to achieve manhood, and that men's definition of what is gender-appropriate work is fluid. A study in Mozambique found that lack of formal employment was driving low-income urban men into street commerce, traditionally a women's area of work. Men reported that due to unstable employment, they were frequently unable to pay bride price and more likely to enter into less formal unions with women. In effect, they were reshaping definitions of manhood and family formation in the face of economic change (Agadjanian 2002).

These limited examples confirm the importance of achieving a socially recognized manhood. This issue is important to highlight precisely because the link between work and manhood is seldom factored into economic policies, especially the need to understand employment and job creation beyond income-producing purposes. Young men who do not achieve a sense of socially respected manhood are more likely to engage in violence. They are precisely the young men drawn into ethnic clashes in Nigeria, conflicts in Liberia and Sierra Leone, and gangs in South African townships.

Rites of Passage

Many cultural groups in Sub-Saharan Africa carry out initiation practices, or rites of passage, as part of the socialization of boys and men. These rites (there are frequently analogous processes for young women) include seclusion from families (and from women and girls) and informal learning sessions, during which older men impart information or skills considered necessary to be an adult male. These sessions may include how to hunt, how to treat women, how to build a house, warrior or fighting skills, and historical information about the cultural group and its rituals.

Numerous studies have confirmed the cultural power of these rites as "agents of political and social incorporation, notably of young men who are most likely to be the warlike element in any society" (Ellis 1997, p. 6). They may become particularly important for creating cultural and collective identities when more formalized public institutions, such as schools and religious and political structures, are weak. These rites provide a combination of social control, support, and guidance to young people making the sometimes confusing and tense transition from childhood to adulthood, and they generate a sense of cultural or tribal identity and social cohesion.

Many of these rituals include references to abandoning boyhood in favor of manhood, especially through a clear demarcation between children (boys) and men and between men and women. Some of the rites include a cathartic moment of being out-of-control, drunk, or under the control of evil spirits before achieving a defined and mature adult identity. The age-specific peer groups, sometimes called secret societies, along with the initiation rituals, set parameters for conflict resolution, male-female relationships, family and community life, and adult roles. While some aspects of this socialization reinforce patriarchal gender norms, they have deep cultural resonance and often serve as a form of positive social control. Indeed, whether in research or in the autobiographies of people such as Jomo Kenyatta and Nelson Mandela, these rituals are often seen as central to men's personal development. Rituals represent a way to gain access to elders, where men interact with the chief and other leaders to resolve conflicts and act as training grounds for assuming political power.

While many of these rites reinforce traditional, patriarchal gender hierarchies, they sometimes act as a form of social restraint. They teach boys how to be warriors, a skill that has sometimes been coopted for armed insurgencies, but in the case of violence against women, they serve as a form of restraint on men.

The "Big Man" and Intergenerational Tensions

In most of Sub-Saharan Africa, tribal society traditionally has been and often still is based on the authority and supreme manhood of chiefs and on rigid community and tribal hierarchies that leave young men in waiting to become men. According to Lindsay and Miescher, "The African 'big man' provides perhaps the most enduring image of Sub-Saharan African masculinity. Across the continent and for a long sweep of history, ambitious people (usually men) have worked to enlarge their households and use their 'wealth in people' for political and material advancement" (2003, p. 3). This arrangement has been key to social organization in the region. In parts of Namibia, for example, "...male power was equated with men who had their own livestock, houses, wives, and juvenile dependents—men who were 'senior' and who performed the social role of 'fathers.' Such power was reproduced through their ability to determine the criteria and candidates for becoming 'real men' by getting married and setting up their own households" (Lindsay and Miescher 2003, p. 10).

In the countryside, the big men commanded respect, dispensed rights to land, and were at the top of the social hierarchy. (Big men were follwed in the hierarchy, in decreasing order of power, by other adult men, uninitiated young men, boys, women, and girls.) In some settings, older men still control most resources, including those earned by young, unmarried men. As Townsend concludes, "From the point of a view of a man in rural Botswana, moving through the life course is a process of negotiating a way through a series of overlapping and competing claims for the products of his labour" (1997, p. 419).

Colonization undermined some of the powers of the traditional big men and created new big men backed by colonial authority. From the time of colonization, Sub-Saharan African men and manhood have often been constructed in relation to European manhood. The term "boy," for example, means maleness, but also social immaturity and inferiority before adult men, particularly white men. The word was used as an insult by European men toward Sub-Saharan African men and also by Sub-Saharan African elders to keep the younger generation of men "in their place" (Lindsay and Miescher 2003, p. 5). The literature on Sub-Saharan African manhood reveals numerous examples of colonizers who questioned or criticized the masculinities of the people in the countries they colonized.

The concentration of power in the hands of big men and male elders leads to power struggles between older and young men, and is related to some insurgencies in Sub-Saharan Africa. The institutionalized stratification of age groups frequently puts younger men at the service of elders, and the control of property and women by older men creates a structural conflict between younger and older generations of men. A major tension is over access to women. In much of Sub-Saharan Africa, adolescent women often marry older men, sometimes much older, in part because older men have the resources to pay bride wealth or bride price. In many countries, the proportion of married adolescent girls is 20–60 percent, compared to less than 6 percent for young men (Bankole et al. 2004). While such data have often been used to highlight the vulnerabilities of young women in relation to their older spouses, these data also suggest that older men's greater access to younger women comes at the expense of younger men.[4]

This intergenerational tension manifests itself in numerous ways. In South Africa, for example, there have been conflicts between rural elder men and wage-earning younger men who migrate to cities. Most of these migrants send income to their families, thus maintaining a status as men even if not physically present. Migration has become a way for young men to usurp the power of elders and, in some settings, has become part of a new rite of passage. By moving to the city, young men escape rural power hierarchies and earn money, which allows some independence and access to women.

Gang violence and street cultures represent another form of manhood. The common discourse among rural elders is that urban young men are not respectful of traditional customs and hierarchies (Carton 2001). Intergenerational struggles in the KwaZulu Natal region of South Africa in the late 1980s and early 1990s led to the deaths of 15,000 men (Morrell 1998). At the root of this struggle was an attempt by older men to hold onto their traditional rights and the efforts of a younger generation to break free from patriarchal control.

Indeed, power struggles between older men (who are sometimes seen as representing corruption and cronyism) and younger men are often related to conflicts across the continent. Young men interviewed in Kaduna, Nigeria showed anger toward Al-Hajis (Islamic men who had made the pilgrimage to Mecca, and thus had some wealth) and their social equivalents. Another "young" man (young because men up to age 40 are considered youth in parts of Nigeria) expressed rage at older men and the challenges he faced in acquiring employment. He was 39 when he finally acquired a civil servant job, for which he said he had to pay a bribe, which had cost him years of itinerant work to pay.

Masculinities, Urbanization, and Social Change

Manhood in Sub-Saharan Africa must also be studied within the context of social change, urbanization, and political upheaval, including civil unrest and, in some countries, lack of functioning social institutions. Conflict in the region is related to how versions of manhood are socially constructed, while manhood and masculinities are also affected by conflict and social change. For example, nationalist and independence movements generated a highly respected version of "struggle masculinity" around the men who led these movements. While this tendency was strong in South Africa and Zimbabwe, it also existed in independence struggles in Angola, Mozambique, and Tanzania. In South Africa, struggle masculinity was a version of manhood shaped by constant confrontation with the police, the apartheid-era military, and the white minority. Male leaders of the antiapartheid struggle were coveted by women and emulated by younger men. Yet while black men were subordinate to whites, they maintained gender privilege over women and were generally more visible and held more power than women in the antiapartheid movement. Morrell writes, "Where black men resisted class and race oppression, they were also, simultaneously, defending their masculinity. This often involved efforts to re-establish or perpetuate power over women" (2002, p. 311).

Urbanization, the expansion of formal education, and the increased enrollment of girls are also leading to changes in definitions of manhood and, more generally, gender roles. The net effects of migration on manhood are complex, but various accounts suggest both positive and negative aspects. On one hand, young men who move to cities lose connection to and perhaps feel little affiliation with their rural roots; they may also be distant from positive forms of social control once exercised by clans and elders. At the same time, cities may expose young men to more gender-equitable versions of manhood, or force them to question male stereotypes. As Sommers notes, "In Africa and elsewhere, cities force people to mix and become familiar with members of groups whose paths might never cross in rural areas" (2003, p. 7). Indeed, while migration to cities can create tinderboxes for conflicts between social groups, cities are also spaces where rival groups come to see each other as "human," struggling for the same things—to gain an education, find work, and maintain families.

Formal schooling clearly impacts the social construction of masculinities, and is a space for creating or reinforcing specific versions of manhood. Young men interviewed in Kaduna, Nigeria affirmed that people with greater education were the least likely to participate in ethnic conflicts. Indeed, most secondary and post-secondary public education facilities have both Christian and Muslim students. While some in-school youth were involved in the rioting, we observed teachers mediating tensions between Christian and Muslim youth and promoting a critical reflection about the riots, factors that likely serve to diminish tensions among those young men. Our observations suggest that male teachers in this secondary school modeled a version of a modern, rational, and educated man who was able to deconstruct ethnic tensions through critical reflection.[5]

Research in southern and eastern Africa suggests that schools may present gender-equitable messages while simultaneously reinforcing rigid, sexist norms. Studies of in-school youth in Ghana, Malawi, and Zimbabwe found that men's and boys' use of violence against women was accepted and even encouraged, while girls were largely socialized to be tolerant and to passively accept such violence (Leach 2003). Another study in Zimbabwe found that schools reinforced traditional roles while promoting a discourse of equal rights of girls to education (Gordon 1998). Teachers and headmasters were usually men, who, along with male students, reinforced a discourse that women were sexual instigators and temptresses. Girls, on the other hand, described themselves as victims of sexual violence and harassment. The study found a contradictory discourse by boys and girls: although girls had equal rights to education, beliefs about sex-specific professions (i.e., women should become nurses or work in caring professions, while men should work in technical professions) lingered.

Similarly, research in rural schools in Botswana found that boys and girls espoused gender equality and women's need to work, but they saw equal rights for women as something foreign (Ansell 2002). Another study on gender roles in Botswana found a similar dual discourse: girls and boys acknowledged the sexual harassment that girls face, while time they were open to new gender roles as part of development and modernization processes (Commeyras and Montsi 2000).

Other accounts find rigid gender socialization of boys in schools, along with reinforcement of intergenerational hierarchies, suggesting that boys chafe under rigidly defined versions of manhood and age-specific hierarchies and make girls vulnerable by seeking to live out socially proscribed misogynistic tendencies. Kariuki's (2004) analysis of student unrest in Kenyan schools in 2000–2001 finds clear and rigid gender orders contributing to violence against girls, teachers, and headmasters. These included a highly publicized incident of adolescent males raping female students who did not agree to participate in riots they initiated, which the boys alleged caused them to lose face. The male head teacher commented that the young men did not want to hurt the girls but "only wanted to rape them" (Kariuki 2004).

Other incidents included murders of headmasters by male students, apparently over longstanding grievances and power struggles. In a 2001 incident, 68 students were burned to death when classrooms were set on fire by male students angry over exam results and increased pressure to pay school fees. In a thoughtful analysis of these events, Kariuki states:

> The self-image of the adolescent male student as an oppressed and powerless individual is a devastating blow in the light of the pervasive socialization that the adolescent male student receives from his parents, teachers and other forces of socialization. Having been groomed to react aggressively and violently through socialization, the adolescent male student is caught in a Catch 22 situation where he has to respond aggressively or passively risk being seen as 'un-masculine.' Only then do the boys begin to organize their line of attack on the calculated basis of their powerlessness. Student violence in the schools should thus be viewed as the embodiment of a power struggle where one of the stakes is the societal meaning attached to masculinity (2004, p. 7).

Kenya Ministry of Education data from 2000–2001 found that 13 percent of secondary schools suffered from unrest and riots, including damage to school property, injuries, and deaths. Nonetheless, as Kariuki states, "The gendered politics of boy's actions were...kept out of the general accounts of these acts of student violence" (2004, p. 1).

These examples highlight the problematic nature of gender socialization and gender hierarchies in school settings. Too many young men are socialized into versions of manhood that encourage sexual aggression toward girls. A 2000 study in

South Africa of 30,000 young people found that one in four men said they had forced a girl to have sex at least once. As Leach states, "Having a girlfriend, competing over girls and boasting about conquests were clearly essential features of dominant male peer culture" (2003, p. 390). Male teachers often set the tone for how boys treat girls, although boys and girls perceived that many male teachers proposition female students. Some young men condemned male teachers not for sexual harassment and misuse of authority but for taking the available girls.

While the traditional discourse on educational attainment in Sub-Saharan Africa has shown that boys had preferential treatment and greater access than girls, which on the whole has been the case, the story is not so simple. For example, a recent study of boys in 12 junior secondary schools in Botswana and Ghana finds many low-income boys acting in ways that resemble low-income boys other parts of the world, including aggressive behavior, lack of attention, challenging authority, and subsequently underperforming academically. Girls in such settings were encouraged to focus on finding a mate, and being too smart was seen as decreasing the likelihood of a good marriage. These accounts suggest that the traditional gender discourse about education in Sub-Saharan Africa, while correct on aggregate, fails to account for gender-specific vulnerabilities faced by girls and boys.

Indeed, literature and interviews with key informants suggest that while on aggregate boys have higher enrollment rates and stay in school longer, there are at least some low-income boys who are not performing well and whose access to schools is, like girls, precarious. In parts of Botswana, young men drop out of school early because of social expectations related to work (Townsend 1997). Young men interviewed in Nigeria had to drop out when a father died, while young men in northern Uganda were forced to drop out when the family moved to an IDP camp.

As a final note on gender norms in Sub-Saharan Africa's education systems, it is worth mentioning positive examples. The public education system in Sub-Saharan Africa, for all its challenges and shortcomings, is also a valuable space for instilling a discourse on nation building, modernization, and civic participation. In several focus group discussions and site visits to schools in Nigeria and Uganda, young men showed an impressive sense of optimism and duty and what might be called a civic-minded version of manhood.

Sexuality and the Social Construction of Manhood in Sub-Saharan Africa

Sexual experience for young men is frequently associated with initiation into manhood. This fosters a perception of sex as performance and a means by which to demonstrate masculine prowess. Young men in many cultures experience peer pressure to be sexually active and to have multiple partners in order to be seen as men. These sexual experiences are viewed among peers as displays of sexual competence or achievement rather than acts of intimacy (Marsiglio 1988; WHO 2003). Moreover, the status that a sexually active young man attains among his peers can be more important than the intimacy that comes from the sexual relationship itself (Lundgren 1999), and this pattern of sexual bravado as a means to peer acceptance often continues into manhood (Barker 2000b). This association between sexual activity, manhood, and identity has important implications for HIV/AIDS prevention. It implies, among other things, that changing sexual behavior among young men must consider how this behavior is linked to the sense of self and the desire to achieve a socially recognized version of manhood.

Although young men's sexual experiences are, in general, more self-willed than those of women, it is important to acknowledge the extent to which social pressures govern young men's behaviors and choices. In many settings, a young man's reputation among his peers may suffer if he does not have sex with a girl (Gorgen et al. 1998; MacPhail and Campbell 2001). A significant minority of young Zulu men report that they would prefer abstinence before marriage but that they feel obliged to have sex for fear of social rejection (Varga 2001) from male peers and from young women, who young men believe have a role in reinforcing traditional views about manhood and sexuality.

The notion that men have a right to multiple partners is reinforced in numerous ways across Sub-Saharan Africa. The tradition of polygamy is closely linked to the norm by which masculinity is expressed as sexual conquest and prowess, particularly as represented by fertility (Silberschmidt 2001). These links have important implications for sexual behaviors and choices, particularly in terms of number of partners and use of condoms. While polygamy nearly always places men in a role of power over their wives, in its traditional form it restricts extramarital affairs. In some settings, however, the tradition is now more informally interpreted as a man's right to have as many sexual partners as he wishes. And while polygamy has been dismantled by various socioeconomic factors and limited by law in some countries, normative discourse about a man needing more than one partner continues.

Although peer and traditional norms frame sexual activity as a defining issue in achieving and maintaining socially recognized manhood, premarital sexual relations are still generally viewed as taboo in many (if not most) settings in Sub-Saharan Africa. Thus, young men face conflicting pressures in terms of sexual behavior. Many young men interviewed in this and other studies preface discussions about sex by commenting that although the social, and in many instances religious, norms argue for not having sex before marriage, most young people were in fact having sex.[6]

Young men's sexuality can be significantly shaped by socioeconomic, political, and cultural forces. While there is limited research on how economic forces influence young men's sexual behaviors, some of the literature suggests that men may seek additional sexual partners when economic disempowerment threatens their sense of manhood (Silberschmidt 2001). For example, a study in an Eastern Cape township in South Africa suggested that the lack of economic and recreational opportunities for youth led to the use of sexual relations as a means to gain respect and social status (Wood and Jewkes 2001). Low-income young men frequently express frustration over the fact that young women are largely attracted to men with income. Older men, who tend to have more money, also seem to be "watching and showing off their money" to compete with younger men (Mataure et al. 2002). Since social structures determine that mostly older men control land or generally have access to jobs and income, it is mostly older men that are able to marry and have occasional sexual partners. This can contribute to intergenerational tension, in which young men see older men as having more access to women, jobs, and resources, and having subsequently greater power.

Under prevailing norms in Sub-Saharan Africa and worldwide, young men are expected to be knowledgeable, aggressive, and experienced regarding sexuality and reproductive health (Barker 2000b). By adhering to these prescribed gender roles, young men by default often have a disproportionate share of power and voice in intimate relationships with women. Frequently, however, young men have little accurate information on these matters and fear admitting their ignorance, which may lead them to engage in unsafe behaviors that put them and their partners at risk (Rivers and Aggleton 1999). In these cases, tension may develop between the emotional vulnerabilities of young men and the behavior they are expected to adopt in order to be accepted as masculine (Holland et al. 1994). On the surface, many young men may display bravado, but this may in fact be an attempt to compensate for insecurities or doubts about their sexuality.

Finally, despite strong social and peer pressures to engage in sexual activity, young men do not seek sexual relationships solely to prove their masculinity; they also seek companionship, intimacy, and pleasure. However, most of the research has focused on quantitative indicators of young men's sexual behavior, including age of initiation; number of partners; frequency of encounters; and links between social norms, pressures, and sexual activity (Varga 2001). Less is known about the nature of young men's sexual relationships, including types of partners, sexual practices, desire, and sexual pleasure.

Socialization and Young Men's Views of Women

It is worth examining some examples of young men's views about women, as they have direct implications for HIV/AIDS and gender-based violence. For example, young men often categorize women, distinguishing between girls suitable for long-term relationships, including marriage, and girls with whom they have short-term, sexual relationships. In Nigeria, young women who had sex before marriage, either to earn income or favors or because they wanted to, are classified as "harlots." In other cases, young men described women as inferior and morally weak, or as property to be given to the husband's family. While some young men criticize young women for using sex to acquire income, it is important to note that some men make an effort to understand the difficulties that young women face and are keenly aware of the negative treatment and harassment they face. While their attitude may not be entirely empathetic, some men believe that this sexual harassment is unjust.

A few young men go beyond simply observing the unjust treatment and sexual harassment of young women and openly state that such treatment is wrong. For example, when the peers of a young Muslim man in Nigeria were criticizing women, describing them as untrustworthy, one young man said, "Girls should be given the same opportunities, just as boys have." Other young men, although usually a minority, voice a similar sense of indignation over the unfair treatment of young women. These examples suggest the need to engage young men in efforts to reconsider their views about young women, a necessary step for promoting gender equality and safe sex.

Young Men and Perceptions of Gender-Based Violence

Violence and coercion, including verbal threats and forced sex, are common features of young people's sexual relationships and adults' intimate relationships in Sub-Saharan Africa (MacPhail and Campbell 2001; Wood and Jewkes 2001). For example, in a study in a South Africa township, young men aged 13–25 admitted having tricked young women into sex, lying about the use of condoms, and using physical violence against women with too many partners (MacPhail and Campbell 2001). In another study, more than half of the girls reported having experienced physical assault by a boyfriend (Jewkes 1998).

Some young men may view violence against women as a socially sanctioned extension of male authority in the private realm (Wood and Jewkes 2001). In focus group discussions, some young men spoke of violence as a means to make a woman "understand"—essentially, violence was used as a means of discipline. The most commonly reported motive for using violence against a woman is proven or suspected infidelity. Another motive was a woman refusing to have sex. Young men in Uganda explained that such a refusal might mean that the woman has another lover and should thus be considered a sign of infidelity.

Many young men interviewed saw sex as contractual. If the woman accepted favors or said she would go out with him, sex was expected, in a way that paralleled traditional, rural Sub-Saharan African views about bride price. As a young man in Uganda related, it would be acceptable to use violence against a woman, in this case "a slap," at "times when you take her out, have negotiated [sex] and then she refuses."

The literature and our field research point to a range of perceptions among young men of what qualifies as violence against women. Many of the young men interviewed in Nigeria and Uganda considered a slap as mostly acceptable; greater violence was considered dangerous because it could seriously harm the woman and might bring a reprimand from the elders or official authorities.

Most young men interviewed recognized that it is not appropriate to use violence against a female partner, yet reported that it occurs often. Others reported an association between anger and substance abuse, particularly alcohol. At the same time, many young men seemed to believe that women provoked violence through infidelity or nagging. Silberschmidt (2001), writing about men in east Africa, argues that "successful masculinity" among one's peers requires having many and attractive sexual partners and having the ability to control them. Young men, particularly low-income men, are constantly at risk of losing face because older men and men with money are more likely to attract partners. Silberschmidt argues that to compensate for this lack of power, some men use other strategies to achieve and secure their authority over women, including aggressiveness and violence.

In some settings, the use of violence to discipline women is reinforced by local traditions, such as bride price. In research conducted by Law and Advocacy for Women in Uganda, for example, the majority of the focus groups identified bride price as a direct cause of domestic violence (Human Rights Watch 2003b). Presumably, domestic violence is mainly due to the social norms of male "ownership" of women and the female duty which it perpetuates. In another Uganda study, one in four men and women (from a 3,106-person sample) believe that a woman cannot refuse sex, even if she knows her partner has HIV/AIDS (Blanc et al. 1996).

The literature also reports the internalization of violence against women as a norm among young men and women. Some studies show that boys and girls might interpret the use of violence due to infidelity as reflecting the level of emotional investment, that is, when a man uses violence against a woman, it shows that he cares for her. In focus groups in Uganda, several young men mentioned how women will think a man does not love her if he does not hit her. Wood and Jewkes (1997) report that young women interviewed in townships in South Africa spoke of physical assaults as a male strategy for "getting you to love him," and many young women did not recognize forced sex with their partners as rape.

Other forms of violence against women have been the subject of recent research in Africa, including sexual coercion and sexual harassment. In a recent South African survey of nearly 12,000 youth, 98 percent of young men reported that they really wanted their first sexual experience, versus 71 percent of young women (Pettifor et al. 2004). In another South African study, female participants indicated that the majority of men engage in relationships to satisfy their own sexual needs and that women perceive themselves as powerless to define relationships on other terms (MacPhail and Campbell 2001).

It is clear that not all young men use violence against women. Just as there are social norms that encourage such violence, there are social norms and socialization forces—traditional clan structures, extended families, and rites of passage—that may serve to reduce violence against women. Nonetheless, norms supporting the acceptability of men's violence against women are internalized and reproduced by young men and women and can have grave implications where couples are not able to communicate effectively (Wood and Jewkes 1998).[7]

Although girls are more likely than boys to be victims of sexual abuse or sexual coercion, many boys are also victims. Apart from research on young men's experiences of sexual abuse and rape in specific contexts, including living on the streets (Swart-Kruger and Richter 1997) and in prison (Gear 2001), there is still very little research on the extent and nature of young men's victimization by sexual violence in Sub-Saharan Africa.

Young Men, Violence, and Conflict in Sub-Saharan Africa

As of 2002, approximately half of Sub-Saharan Africa's countries and about one in three persons were directly or indirectly affected by conflict. The number of affected persons increases substantially when other forms of violence and criminal activity are considered. Although each conflict has its own specificities, it is clear that manhood and masculinities are at play in all these conflicts. Many leaders of liberation struggles have played on generational issues, emphasizing young men's grievances toward adults and sometimes reinforcing the intergenerational divide (Stavrou, Stewart, and Stavrou 2000). Some of the armed insurgencies may have clear ideological motives, but many are directly related to an attempt by young men to acquire power, question the power of groups of older men, and live up to a specific version of manhood.

In discussing how cultural versions of manhood in Sub-Saharan Africa are related to violence, we must also discuss voices of dissent and restraint. For example, while rites of passage and secret societies are frequently criticized for promoting warrior skills, much of the traditional socialization can also promote restraint from violence. Similarly, there is tremendous diversity in the region in terms of whether violence by young men is socially sanctioned or subject to social control. For example, accounts of young men's socialization in South Africa suggest a clear difference between ritualized fighting and fighting that is either out of control or carried out to cause harm. Traditional rites of passage often emphasize the former and condemn the latter.

Young Men and the Dynamics of Armed Conflicts

Young combatants have been ubiquitous in the region's conflicts. There may be as many as 300,000 child soldiers worldwide, the majority of which are in Sub-Saharan Africa and male (Verhey 2001). When reports on child soldiers mention gender, they frequently focus on the smaller percentage of girl combatants or on sexual violence against girls. These issues need urgent attention, but the process by which young men and boys become combatants also needs to be better understood.

At the most basic level, boys involved in brutal armed insurgencies become big men by being in control of a setting and being able to exert violence on those around them. In addition to survival, they achieve and wield power. Young men who become combatants are often bombarded with violent images of manhood, whether in the form of violent films, gangsta rap, or the idolization of big men such as Charles Taylor. Some observers of conflicts suggest that the violence feels like a performance by young men who are acting out a violent version of manhood and seeking to instill fear in a terrified audience. They are acting out a socially recognized role of manhood taken to its extreme. As Ellis states, "In many of these wars...observers have detected an element of youth out of control, adolescents and even children who, in societies with strong gerontocratic traditions, seize power by force" (2003, p. 110).

Rites of passage and indoctrination play a role in young men's participation in conflict. Nearly all armed movements and wars involve some kind of initiation ritual, which can involve use of violence against family members and threats of murder for noncompliance. Many insurgencies have tapped into the traditional socialization of young men as warriors, using elements of these rites in their own, brutal indoctrination (Stavrou, Stewart, and Stavrou 2000). In some cases, leaders have made deliberate links to initiation rituals and rites of passage. In Liberia, Charles Taylor's warlords used traditional elements such as talismans and tattoos to make made young men believe that they were immune to enemy fire. Cross-dressing that is part of traditional male rites of passage was subverted, so that rebels sometimes dressed as women when carrying out war atrocities. Indoctrination may also include forms of brutality and violence. Former abductees and combatants interviewed in Uganda talked of forced cannibalism and being forced to rape young women—part of a deliberately traumatizing and shame-creating indoctrination. Some authors argue that armed movements have in effect become newer versions of rites of passage, continuing to draw on traditional elements, such as seclusion from the tribe, dominance of men and boys, and cathartic or out-of-control moments (Ellis 1997).

As Richards points out in the case of West Africa (chapter 9 of this book), joining an insurgency may be a rational choice for some young men. Other accounts find that some young men may be coerced while others participate voluntarily in the same conflict. For example, Schafer's (2001) study of young men involved with the Mozambiquan National Resistance (RENAMO) questions the view that all young combatants were coerced and psychologically brutalized to become crazed killers. She concludes that some were coopted or recruited rather than coerced in dehumanizing ways; while most young men said their recruitment was involuntary, they did not describe being brutalized. Some young men saw participating in the insurgency as a viable economic activity in the face of rural poverty. In other cases, young men find camaraderie with male peers in insurgency groups, or they find male role models, surrogate fathers, and substitute families.

Armed movements with a clear ideology tend to exert some restraint on the use of violence. The worst violence seems to happen when there is a political vacuum and violence becomes an end in itself, providing young men with power, sexual partners, and income. Many of the newer armed movements—the Lord's Resistance Army (LRA) in Uganda, the Revolutionary United Front (RUF) in Sierra Leone, and those in Liberia mostly lacked a clear ideology and often revolved around a cult of an individual or a handful of leaders trying to acquire power at all costs. These groups were not able to win over or alienated people in the countryside, relying instead on forced recruitment of those most vulnerable, namely young, unemployed, low educated men (Abdullah 1998). In some cases, the same insurgency may have different meanings for different young men. For higher-educated young men, the rebellion may have political undertones, but for less-educated young men, it is mostly about following a big man who distributes weapons and war booty, and offers status by participating in violence and terrorizing.

Insurgency groups in Liberia, Sierra Leone, and northern Uganda often chose the youngest sons and boys, who are more likely than older boys to feel a sense of powerlessness and who are also the most susceptible, malleable, and traumatized by conflict experiences. In Liberia and Sierra Leone, drugs were often included in conflict indoctrination as a means to causing boys to lose control and carry out acts of brutality. It is no coincidence that in the socialization of boys and men around the world, drugs and alcohol often form part of rites of passage and of first sexual encounters. Young men often describe drugs and alcohol as giving them the courage to do the things required of them to be seen as men.

In thinking about the factors that contribute to young men's participation in armed conflicts, particularly those that lack political ideologies and have used brutal forms of violence, it is important to affirm that this violence is produced. It is not a natural state of the behavior of boys and young men, nor is it biologically programmed.[8] This violent behavior is reinforced by social structures at the community level and sometimes at the family level. It is learned violence—learned by modeling, reinforcement, shame, overt threats, and coercion. Some insurgency groups have learned through experience and their own brutalization to efficiently manipulate the social environment to create this violence. Young men coerced to join rebel groups sometimes become the next generation of leaders and in turn coerce other boys to join. It is thus difficult to distinguish what begins as coerced behavior and what is subsequently voluntary. If young men and boys could so easily be induced to kill and use violence, or were willing to use violence of their own volition, and if violence were an inherent part of young men's temperament, this kind of indoctrination would not be necessary.

There has been significant discussion of the means that armed groups use to recruit and coerce young men; nearly absent is any reflection about those indigenous sources of strength which allow or keep young men out of conflict. Accounts from Mozambique found that many adult and young men tried to stay out of the conflict and that some went to great lengths to try to protect their families from such violence (Schafer 2001). In the town of Bo in Sierra Leone, youth-serving organizations were able to keep young men from the RUF by recruiting them into civil defense units through local football clubs (Peters, Richards, and Vlassenroot 2003). Whether because of personal convictions, the ability of their families to help them escape, fear, community mobilization, or some combination of these things, some youths manage to stay out of armed groups. These accounts may be particularly useful in understanding and building on social capital and protective factors that may prevent young men's future involvement in violence.

Young Men Affected by Conflict and Violence

Young men are affected by and react to conflict in gender-specific ways. One of the most telling patterns is young men's propensity to migrate. In virtually all conflict and postconflict settings, young men are more likely to migrate than women and old men (Cockburn 1999). Young men are also more likely to migrate to cities as a reaction to conflict, which increases the number of young men on the streets and leaves them vulnerable to recruitment into new forms of violence. While migrating to cities appears on one level to be a protective factor for young men, it also means that young men are separated from their communities and families (Stavrou, Stewart, and Stavrou 2000). Sommers (2001b) found that young Burundian refugee men in Tanzania often become outcasts or are seen as second-class citizens.

Ex-combatants face many challenges in returning to civilian life, but for most young men the most troubling concerns are a return to second-class status and of again being powerless and marginalized due to prevailing intergenerational power differentials. Having wielded power, some young men are reluctant to return to settings in which they are subordinate to older adults (Peters et al. 2003). Similar concerns were voiced by young South African men who were on the "front lines" with the African National Congress (ANC) and now perceive themselves as relegated to second-class status (CSVR 1998).

There is a considerable research on the reintegration of underage combatants and the specific traumas they face. Young men interviewed in northern Uganda reported trauma from coping with the consequences of being forced to rape girls, being put on the front line as a buffer when the military approached, being forced to kill a family member, and being forced to practice cannibalism. Some former abductees live in constant fear of reabduction—one young man we interviewed had been abducted, had escaped, and had been abducted again. Others fear the military, as boys have sometimes been killed by the military who suspect them of being members of LRA, even when they are not.

Other challenges include lingering fears and prejudices by communities and families, who believe that as former combatants they may use violence again at any time. Given the stop-start process of many conflicts, this is a reasonable fear. Some former combatants in northern Uganda reported that their families treated them as outcasts, and were scared of them when they returned. "When I returned [from being abducted by the LRA] my in-laws took away my wife and child. They were afraid I might kill her. Now I stay with my mother," said one ex-combatant. Others lost the chance to pay bride price and marry.

Frustration is high for young men in refugee camps who are ex-combatants or abductees or who have been displaced by violence. Young men interviewed in northern Uganda camps reported a sense of idleness, little hope for the future, and that they may turn to alcohol and other substances. Many young men reported that they cannot marry and in the process achieve a socially recognized manhood. One young man said, "In the past, we would have the opportunity to dig [farm a small plot of land] and produce things and get married. Now we are displaced and it is very different." Forced settlement in camps weakens men's ties to their land, leading to fears that others will take their land and that they will have nowhere to return. Similar conditions prevail in camps of Burundian refugees in Tanzania, where young men were described as seeking to "recuperate the masculinity that they perceive to have lost in the camp" (Turner 1999, p. 1). They frequently complain that women do not respect them and some sense that camp administrators have become the new big men.

One manifestation of a sense of "demasculation" in refugee camps is sexual violence. Somali young men refugees interviewed in camps in Kenya said that because they could not get married, they would use sexual violence against women. This is a serious issue in cultural groups in which premarital sexual activity is highly sanctioned and marriage is delayed because young men cannot achieve the conditions for marriage in refugee camps (Sommers 2001a).

Programs to assist ex-combatants and youth affected by violence face tremendous challenges. Many such programs exclude youths—male and female—who were affected by violence but not directly involved as combatants. Evaluations in Liberia have highlighted the lack of jobs and educational opportunities outside targeted programs, and the mismatch between market demands and income and employment possibilities. Program reviews have found examples of young men being trained as auto mechanics, only to return to villages where there are only two or three cars (Peters, Richards, and Vlassenroot 2003). Some programs have created dependency, while others are too short-term, raising expectations and then leaving young men frustrated when programs end. Most programs to assist youth to return to school provide scholarships last for a year or less. In many instances, the young men consider themselves too old to return to school, although there have been useful experiences of accelerated educational programs for young men who have missed several years of schooling.

Few of these programs seem to have incorporated a discussion of how gender comes into play—that is, how efforts to engage young men must also consider their desire to achieve a socially recognized version of manhood, and intergenerational tensions between groups of men. To be sure, the gender-specific needs of young women and men have not been incorporated into most reintegration programs, but there has been more discussion about the gender-specific needs of girls and young women.

Young Men, Ethnic Unrest, and Criminal Activity

Although other forms of violence are prevalent in Sub-Saharan Africa and are clearly linked to masculinities, there is little research or data on criminal activity and delinquency in most of the region other than South Africa (Shaw and Tschiwula 2002).[9] As Peters, Richards, and Vlassenroot (2003) point out, the annual homicide rate in South Africa is nearly double the estimated death rate from conflict in Sierra Leone. Various studies confirm gang activity, predominantly involving young men, in urban areas in Sub-Saharan Africa, including in Mozambique, Nigeria, and South Africa. In the Western Cape region of South Africa, 90,000 young people are reported to be members of gangs (Barker 2000b).

South Africa is said to have one of the highest homicide rates in the world (as of 2004), and one of the highest rates of sexual violence in the world. An estimated 52,733 women are raped per year, and 11,000 persons die of gun-inflicted wounds

(South Africa Police Service 2004). Homicide is currently the leading cause of death for young men aged 15–21. Worldwide, 80 percent of homicide victims are male, compared to 88 percent in South Africa. In 2002, more than 45,000 young people under age 26 were in South African prisons, representing 36 percent of sentenced prisoners in South Africa. Among those on trial, 27,000 were young people and the vast majority were young men, accounting for 53 percent of people awaiting trial (Palmary and Moat 2002).

Young men were protagonists in South Africa's antiapartheid struggle. They had status and were associated with a hero version of masculinity linked to Nelson Mandela, Stephen Biko, and other ANC and antiapartheid leaders. Similarly, Mangosuthu Gatsha Buthelezi declared Inthaka to be a movement based on masculine values, enjoining Sub-Saharan African men to participate in the struggle against apartheid in the name of the Zulu culture that had historically resisted white rule in South Africa. The socialization of young men in these movements made specific references to weapons and their use to achieve freedom. In the ANC, the AK-47 was a visible symbol associated with young men involved in the liberation movement (Cock 2001). Zulu nationalist images project a man carrying a spear and other traditional weapons and in some traditional Zulu areas, rites of passage for young men include learning how to be a stick fighter. In low-income urban areas (townships) and in rural areas, however, wielding a gun is a sign of status, male affluence, and power. For much of the past two to three decades in many parts of South Africa, white and black young men were often socialized into a militaristic version of manhood through the formation of a brotherhood of combatants, whether for or against apartheid.

South Africa's townships currently experience much of this violence. With the end of apartheid and the realization that long-standing economic inequalities do not have short-term remedies, some authors suggest that more young men are turning to crime and violence, sometimes in the context of gang activities. Many of these accounts discuss the "...heroes of yesteryear who have become the villains and felons of today" (Xaba 2001, p. 107). Some researchers see this as a form of compensatory manhood marked by sexual violence–men seeking to regain a sense of manhood through criminal activity and violence against women. Numerous accounts affirm that township life in South Africa is based in part on the "toughness" of men, which can be positively channeled into sports or negatively channeled into criminal activity (Morrell 2001).

Interviews and analyses of young men involved in criminal activities in South Africa find that an array of factors are associated with their participation in violence, including family conflict and violence, the inability of families to provide social control and positive guidance, socialization into violent versions of manhood, and attaining quick financial rewards. As a Centre for the Study of Violence and Reconciliation (CSVR) study states:

> ...the money made from crime does not only address their need arising from poverty in the home. It supports a particular lifestyle that is hedonistic,

glamorous and revered. It is a lifestyle that allows the amagents (delinquent young men) to literally and figuratively transcend the confines of the world—the here and now... It turns these youngsters into objects of attraction, rather than repulsion in their own communities (1998, p. 10).

As in accounts of delinquency from Western Europe and the Americas, research suggests that delinquent acts in South Africa's townships usually start small, gradually intensify, and are nearly always carried out by gangs.[10] Gangs are described as providing a sense of belonging when other social institutions—family, community, and school—fail. Prison in South Africa has lost much of its stigma as many of the antiapartheid heroes spent time in prison in what was seen as a new rite of passage for young men (CSVR 1998). Other accounts of gang activity suggest that they reinforce traditional gender norms or values in which women are seen as property. As such, sexual violence (in the form of gang rape) may be a form of gang initiation (Vetten 2000).

Young men may be also involved in forms of organized violence that are neither traditional gangs nor armed insurgencies. These include vigilante groups, such as those in Nigeria, or groups of young men hired by white farmers and black businessmen in South Africa in the 1990s to hunt criminals and carry out summary executions. Violence against oil companies in Nigeria's delta region has also been mostly perpetrated by young men. This violence emerged largely from perception that local communities do not benefit from oil extraction and that revenues have been squandered by corrupt regimes. Political organization has led to large-scale protests and civil disobedience. Many of the protesters perceived the failure of nonviolent action, which along with repression by the police was key to the young men turning to violent action. Ukeje (2001) writes, "Each military regime deployed armed soldiers, as well as the notorious mobile police paramilitary branch, popularly called 'Kill-and-go,' to quell community disturbances" (p. 354).

Subsequent violence against oil companies is also at least partly linked to ethnic conflicts in Nigeria, which have been about perceptions of which ethnic group are favored by oil companies and the local government. Young men involved include educated and highly politicized youth and less-educated youth; less-educated young men tend to lead the militant wing of a movements, while their more educated counterparts lead the political wing.

Young men's involvement in conflict is associated with easy access to arms, historical ethnic rivalries, brutal police response, and lack of employment. Politically motivated violence can sometimes disintegrate into general mayhem. Often, once groups of young men are armed and encouraged to use weapons, what might have started as politically-focused violence can turn into general hooliganism and harassment. As such, militant groups that once mostly or only attacked oil company staff and their installations now create havoc in some major cities. Movements that once had a political basis sometimes devolve into violence as a means to acquire and maintain power for their own sake.

Another example of out-of-control violence is the case of vigilante groups in Nigeria, one of the most famous of which is the Bakassi Boys, which initially started as a self-defense group to protect market sellers from robbery but is now subsidized by the government as a public security project. The Bakassi Boys wield significant extrajudicial power in parts of Nigeria and carry out summary executions at the whim of local politicians. Although these boys have reduced crime in some cities, they also kill human rights activists or those who dare to speak out against them (Human Rights Watch/CLEEN 2002).

Young Men, Social Unrest, and the Youth Bulge Argument

Much of the literature on conflict points to youth frustration about corrupt and repressive regimes, which erupts as armed insurgencies or simply as social unrest. While most of this literature does not focus on gender-specific aspects of youth unrest, it points out that youth are the most visible actors. Although there are marked differences between the student-led violence in apartheid-era South Africa and the violence carried out by boys and young men in Liberia, Sierra Leone, and similar settings, the socialization of boys often plays into such unrest and violence. Authors have suggested that in addition to intergenerational tensions, the development or formation of a specific youth culture is also at play. Parents, teachers, and religious leaders in South African townships are commonly believed to have lost their relevance and legitimacy for youth. Several researchers portray young men as out of work, with a tremendous amount free time on their hands, loosely connected to any social institution, and likely to create their own language and culture. Although most of these accounts are presented in a negative light, some reports point out that unemployed young men in such settings are a major voice for cultural expression because they are able to survive through music and mingling of different tribal groups and their creative informal economic activity (Sommers 2003).

To what extent is Sub-Saharan African young men's violence a function of simply having many young men in society? A recent World Bank report states, "Large-scale unemployment, combined with rapid demographic growth, creates a large pool of idle young men with few prospects and little to lose" (Michailof, Kostner, and Devictor 2002, p. 3). Sub-Saharan Africa has a very young population; nearly half of its people are aged 5–24. In Sub-Saharan African countries hardest hit by HIV/AIDS, the population pyramid, which once had a wide base and a narrow tip, now has a wide base and a very thin middle, as adults are dying of AIDS. Unemployment is also a major issue for economies with rapid population growth. In South Africa, youth unemployment rose from 45 percent in 1995 to 56 percent in 2000 (ILO 2005).

Many researchers have examined the connection between large youth cohorts and violence. Much of this work presents out-of-work young men as a menace, suggesting that they will be sucked into violence at any moment. Mesquida and Wiener (1999) make a strong and convincing case that one of the most reliable factors to explain conflict (coalitional aggression) is the ratio of young men (under age 30) to older men (over age 30). In analyzing data from more than 45 countries and 12 tribal societies, Mesquida and Wiener find (controlling for income distribution and per capita GNP) that societies with a high ratio of 15-29-year-old men to over-30 men have higher conflict rate. In a similar vein, Cincotta, Engelman, and Anastasion (2003) state:

> Why are youth bulges so often volatile? The short answer is: too many young men with not enough to do. When a population as a whole is growing, ever larger numbers of young males come of age each year, ready for work, in search of respect from their male peers and elders. Typically, they are eager to achieve an identity, assert their independence and impress young females. While unemployment rates tend to be high in developing countries, unemployment among young adult males is usually from three to five times as high as adult's rates, with lengthy periods between the end of schooling and first placement in a job (2003, p. 44).

Urdal (2004), after reviewing 1950–2000 demographic data, concludes that countries with large youth cohorts do indeed have higher rates of conflict than countries with smaller cohorts but he contends that there is not a clear threshold as to how many young men make countries more prone to conflict. Urdal adds that youth bulges are more likely to cause armed conflict when combined with economic stress:

> The generational approach has some serious shortcomings with regard to the explanatory power of the relationship between youth bulges and violence. The development of generational units may explain the formation of youth movements that can function as identity groups. Identity groups are necessary for collective violent action to take place. But it is not necessary that identity groups are generation-based for youth bulges to increase the likelihood of armed conflict. Furthermore, the generational approach does not offer explanations for the motives of youth rebellion nor does it provide sufficient explanation for the opportunities of conflict (2004, p. 3).

While the youth bulge argument is compelling, it is important to reaffirm that in any of these settings, only a minority of young men participate in conflicts. For example, the vast majority of young men, even those unemployed and out of school, were not involved in conflicts in Liberia and Sierra Leone. It is also impossible and unrealistic to separate age distribution from income distribution and political repression. These issues clearly interact to produce violence, along with socially relevant versions of manhood. There are, to be sure, many young men without access to work who are thus vulnerable to being recruited into insurgency groups and other forms of unrest. But from a more sophisticated ecological perspective of human development, this demographic argument does not account for the vast majority of young men, who even in the poorest countries with the highest youth ratios do not become involved in conflict.

The inability of governments to provide opportunities for young people must also be considered. Indeed, a large youth cohort need not be a problem if societies find ways to engage young people in meaningful, democratic national projects. As Ellis states, "The recent history of West Africa...includes the experience of young people who were offered the vision of state-led development, and of prosperity, only to become frustrated in the economic and political conditions obtained since the 1970s" (1999, p. 12). The same could be said for much of Sub-Saharan Africa. Perhaps the problem is not too many young men, but rather the collective inability to respond to their needs. Applying a demographic prophecy to young men in Sub-Saharan Africa is ultimately a racist and sexist oversimplification that dehumanizes low-income Sub-Saharan African young men.

Young Men and HIV/AIDS in Sub-Saharan Africa

There are nearly 10 million young men and women aged 15–24 living with HIV/AIDS in Sub-Saharan Africa, of whom more than 75 percent are women, a statistic that reflects the worldwide feminization of the epidemic (UNAIDS 2003, 2004). The unequal balance of social power between young men and women in Sub-Saharan Africa, combined with the patterns of risk behaviors among young men, suggests that young men play a key role in shaping the course of the epidemic. Specifically, we must consider how their risk behaviors are learned and reinforced, and ultimately, how they can be engaged as protective forces.

Although there has been increasing research on gender-related aspects of HIV, the majority of this research has focused on the specific needs and risks of young and adult women. Only recently has there been growing attention on the need to also engage men, particularly young men, in HIV prevention efforts (Nzioka 2001; Varga 2001). Despite this increasing attention, there is still little in-depth research on the underlying norms that drive young men's attitudes and behaviors in various contexts (Wood and Jewkes 1998).

This section reviews how the socialization and behavior of young men contributes to the spread of HIV/AIDS in Sub-Saharan Africa. It is not an exhaustive review, but rather an effort to highlight patterns and provide a conceptual framework for the more salient trends and issues. It seeks to identify some of the various contextual realities that underlie young men's HIV-related knowledge, attitudes, and behaviors and points out how gender relations and behaviors are shaped by economic, social, and cultural realities.

The tremendous diversity among young men in Sub-Saharan Africa leads to a spectrum of experiences when we discuss vulnerability to HIV/AIDS. Young men in Sub-Saharan Africa, including young boys living on the streets in Johannesburg, university students in Lagos, military conscripts in Malawi, or the ex-abductees of the LRA in Lira, form distinct, yet interacting ethnic, cultural, religious, and socioeconomic identities. In order to appropriately address the needs of each group in the context of HIV prevention, it is necessary to understand how young men are made vulnerable by or protected by various elements in their socialization, education, and economic prospects and their access to health services.

In recent years, there has been a growing focus on how young men are socialized, particularly in terms of sexuality. Studies show that while many young men are beginning to report a reduction in partners and an increase in condom use, there is mixed reactions to HIV, including limited verbal communication with partners and low perception of risk to the disease (Varga 2001). There are also many gaps in research and program efforts, particularly in regard to certain groups: young men who have sex with other men, young men who assume the role of caregivers, and young men living with HIV.

Sexuality and HIV/AIDS

There is evidence that adolescents worldwide are becoming sexually active at an earlier age (Moore and Rosenthal 1993; UNAIDS 1999a). Of major concern is the high number of reported STI and HIV infections among adolescents, suggesting significant unprotected sexual activity (Barker 2000b). Even when adolescents (and adults) possess adequate information about HIV, they still engage in risky behavior. Research has shown that while factual knowledge of HIV transmission is important, it is not a sufficient predictor of safe sexual behavior (Moore and Rosenthal 1993). Working to fill the gap between knowledge and behavior requires an understanding of the underlying determinants that lead adolescents to engage in unsafe behaviors.

Numerous researchers have affirmed that gender norms are among the strongest underlying social factors that influence sexual behavior (Gupta and Mahy 2003). Ideals of masculinity, such as those which espouse male sexual needs as uncontrollable, multiple partners as evidence of sexual prowess, and dominance over women, can place young men and women at high risk of HIV infection. Studies have shown that in all cultures worldwide, men tend to have more sexual partners than women; thus, on average, men have more exposure to risk and can be expected to infect more partners in a lifetime (UNAIDS 2000b). Women, in contrast, are expected to be passive and innocent on sexual matters and are thus placed at heightened risk of infection (Rivers and Aggleton 1998).

The intersection of these different gender roles has perpetuated HIV infection risks for young men and women, while significantly shaping expansion of the epidemic (Rivers and Aggleton 1998). Data from the U.S. National Survey on Adolescent Males found that beliefs about manhood was the strongest predictor of risk-taking behaviors; young men who adhered to traditional views of manhood were more likely to report substance use, violence and delinquency, and unsafe sexual practices (Courtney 1998). Research in Brazil that applied an attitude scale (the Gender Equitable Men Scale) found a strong association between adherence to traditional gender norms and self-reported issues such as use of violence against women and STI symptoms (Pulerwitz, Barker, and Segundo 2004). In this context, it has become increasingly important for sexuality research to prioritize young men. The topic has been substantially ignored, particularly on qualitative levels, and only recently is there a growing literature on male sexuality throughout the region (MacPhail and Campbell 2001; Varga 2001).

In Sub-Saharan Africa, young men have an average window of five years between their sexual debut and marriage. Within this window, men usually have a higher number of partners than young women, which combined with inconsistent condom use, means that men and their partners are vulnerable. A young Sub-Saharan African woman entering into marriage or a sexual relationship with a male partner (who is likely to be several years older) is thus highly vulnerable. This highlights yet again the need to engage young men before and as they initiate sexual activity, in order to reduce their own vulnerabilities and those of young women.

Cross-Generational Sex and HIV/AIDS

On average, young women in some parts of Sub-Saharan Africa form partnerships with men 5-10 years older, whereas young men have relationships with women of similar age or slightly younger (Gregson et al. 2002). This pattern means that women are likely to be infected by HIV at a younger age than men, and that young men's risk of HIV increases as they get older and have more partners (Mataure et al. 2002). Men over age 25 had HIV rates ten times higher than 15–19-year-old boys (PANOS 1998). In some settings, older men deliberately seek young women and girls as sexual partners because they believe that young women are less likely to be infected. This perpetuates the HIV transmission chain from older men to younger women, who in turn may infect younger men.

In many parts of Sub-Saharan Africa, particularly in the most impoverished countries, there has been a reported increase (or at least increased attention to) in the number of older men, or "sugar daddies," who offer money and gifts in exchange for sex with younger women (Luke and Kurz 2002). There are cases in which young women are actively or passively encouraged by parents and guardians to pursue these offers (Gage 1998; Silberschmidt and Rasch 2001). This situation has had a dramatic impact on young women's vulnerability to HIV, as evidenced by an increasing number of young women being infected by older partners (Luke and Kurz 2002). At the same time, the young male sexual partners and companions of these young women are also vulnerable, as they may seek sexual relations with even younger female peers or with female peers who exchange sex for favors with older men. Focus group discussions with young men in Nigeria and Uganda suggest that some young men criticize or resent young women for exchanging sex for favors or money, while others seem to understand the conditions that lead young women to enter into such relations. In addition to the direct risk of HIV infection, the phenomenon of sugar daddies reinforces young men's perceptions of power dynamics along gender, age, and wealth lines, fueling resentment toward older men.

There are also reports of young men paying and being paid for sex. One national survey in Kenya revealed that up to 17 percent of unmarried boys aged 15–19 had paid for sex with money or gifts (CBS, Ministry of Health, and ORC Macro 1998). There are also reports of young men involved in transactional sex with older and married women, know as "sugar mummies" (Mataure et al. 2000). These relationships are often propelled by economic need and status among peers. In settings where bride price is practiced, a young man might become involved with an older woman in order to help raise the necessary wealth to get married. Or, in countries such as Uganda, where a young man might face charges of defilement if he has a sexual relationship with a young woman under the age of 18, he may prefer older women because they are legally safer partners.

Young Men, HIV/AIDS Knowledge, and Attitudes

Awareness about HIV/AIDS and STIs has increased in most parts of Sub-Saharan Africa in the past 10 years, and research shows that at least 90 percent of young men and women aged 15–19 have heard of HIV/AIDS (Bankole et al. 2004). Despite higher awareness, young people continue to practice unsafe sex and hold misconceptions about preventive behaviors, including condom use and the disease itself (Harrison, Xaba, and Kunene 2001; Varga 2001). Research on youth behavior and knowledge is lacking in a number of areas, including the difference between HIV and AIDS, the link between STIs and HIV risk, and the window between infection and possible detection (Varga 2001). Knowledge is an insufficient predictor of safe sex. In focus group discussions in Kenya, young men reported experiencing conflicting pressures between their knowledge (about HIV/AIDS and safe sex) and their behavior, or between what they know they should do and what they actually do (Nzioka 2001).

Most young men in Sub-Saharan Africa are aware of HIV and know how to use condoms (Bankole et al. 2004), but there are barriers to condom use, including self-risk perception, access to condoms, and negotiation with a partner. Several studies suggest that many young men associate HIV with high-risk or out-of-the-ordinary sexual encounters, such as rape, sex with commercial sex workers, and excessive alcohol use, making young men believe that all other sexual encounters are safe (PSI 2003; MacPhail and Campbell 2001). Although an estimated 50–80 percent of young Sub-Saharan African men know that appearance does not necessarily reveal infection status (Bankole et al. 2004; WHO/UNAIDS 2002), some rely on outward appearance as a means of identifying infected individuals (PSI 2003).

In other studies, young men associate HIV with promiscuous women, and some young men believe that girls and women are more promiscuous than men (PSI 2003). Indeed, many young men seem to shift the risk or blame of HIV to women, just as some young men do for sexual violence. Other studies suggest that some young men view STIs as a sign of virility (Nzioka 2001; WHO/UNAIDS 2002). For example, a study in rural Malawi found that young men boast about the likelihood of being HIV-positive, since it is a badge of manhood among their peers

(Kaler 2003). These examples suggest the complex ways in which knowledge is filtered through attitudes and social norms, particularly those related to gender.

Young Men, HIV/AIDS Prevention, and Condom Use

There have been lengthy debates on the relative merits of the ABC approach (abstinence, partner reduction, and condom use). In national sample data from various countries in Sub-Saharan Africa, young men have a low awareness of all three ABC methods (Bankole et al. 2004). Studies show that many young men do not view abstinence as a reasonable prevention option, unlike girls who are more likely to see it as desirable and report that they would prefer to delay their first sexual experience (Harrison, Xaba, and Kunene 2001; PSI 2003). Young men are also less likely than young women to identify monogamy as a way to avoid HIV/AIDS. The prevention method most cited by young men is condom use. In several settings, condom use was the only preventive behavior spontaneously mentioned (Bankole et al. 2004).

Consistent and correct condom use is critical in terms of HIV prevention. Young men's condom use, however, is still much lower than desired, lower than reported knowledge about condoms and HIV/AIDS would suggest, and varies according to the nature of the partner or relationship (e.g., occasional partner, regular partner, or sex worker) (Bankole et al. 2004; Harrison, Xaba, and Kunene. 2001; Nzioka 2001). While 20–80 percent of young men in Sub-Saharan Africa have ever used a condom, fewer than 40 percent of young men aged 15–19 used a condom the last time they had sex (Bankole et al. 2004). This disconnect between knowledge and behavior suggests a continued resistance to condom use, partly due to how young men view gender roles and sexual activity but also due to how they perceive infection risk and the effectiveness of and access to condoms (Nzioka 2003; Harrison, Xaba, and Kunene 2001; PSI 2003).

VIEWS ON CONDOMS. In some settings, masculinity is associated with unprotected ("flesh to flesh" or "live sex") sex with numerous partners, which is often reinforced among peers (MacPhail and Campbell 2001). Young men's peers may belittle them for using condoms and, as we saw in our focus group discussions, condoms are often perceived to be ineffective or defective (MacPhail and Campbell 2001; Nzioka 2001). Condoms as contraceptives can also militate against young men's notions of pregnancy as proof of masculinity and pride (Abdool, Preston-Whyte, and Abdool 1992; MacPhail and Campbell 2001; Preston-Whyte and Zondi 1991).

NEGOTIATION OF CONDOM USE WITH PARTNERS. Many young men believe that condoms are unnecessary in steady relationships, should only be used with casual partners, and are unnecessary with a virgin (Harrison, Xaba, and Kunene 2001; Mataure et al. 2000; MacPhail and Campbell 2001). Young men interviewed for this study reported that condoms are most often used for casual encounters, and as a young man in Uganda related, "[once] you begin to trust your partner you stop using a condom." This is because suggesting using a condom with a steady partner may disclose or insinuate a man's hidden sexual history, while a woman who carries a condom is perceived as promiscuous (Nzioka 2001; Varga 2001). In a study in South Africa, girls reported it was easier to refuse sex than to negotiate condom use (Harrison, Xaba, and Kunene 2001).

Substance Abuse and HIV/AIDS

The connection between substance use and HIV has long been confirmed. Worldwide, men account for approximately four-fifths of intravenous drug users and they are more likely to share needles and not to use condoms (UNAIDS 2000b). Men and boys also use other substances at higher rates than women and girls. In Kenya, boys are more than twice as likely as girls to have tried alcohol and marijuana (Erulkar 1998). For many adolescent and adult men, substance abuse helps prove manhood or helps them fit in with the male peer group. In a survey in South Africa, young men were twice as likely as young women to report having had sex under the influence of alcohol (Pettifor et al. 2004). Substance abuse is also higher among vulnerable groups, including young refugee men, combatants, ex-combatants, and men living in migrant worker camps or on the streets (Swart-Kruger and Richter 1997). While usage rates are still relatively low, there are indications of increasing intravenous drug use among low-income young men in Lagos and other major Sub-Saharan African urban centers (WHO/UNAIDS 2001).

HIV Testing and Living with HIV/AIDS

In various countries in Sub-Saharan Africa, only 1–9 percent of young males aged 15–19 have been tested for HIV, although most say they would like to be (Bankole et al. 2004). In a study of 11,904 youth in South Africa, young men were less likely to have sought HIV testing and 15 percent of young men compared to 25 percent of young women had been tested (Pettifor et al. 2004). Other studies have found that young men are often traditionally excluded from information about maternal and child health, which is often a point of entry or source of information about HIV for young women (WHO 2003). HIV testing thus follows traditional gender norms related to health seeking. In addition to having limited access to health services, many young men have the perception that clinics are female spaces and that real men do not get sick. A group of HIV-positive fathers in a focus group in South Africa said that men wanted to avoid testing and disclosure, and that women are braver when it comes to testing.

There is limited research on the reactions and behaviors of young men who are HIV-positive. Some reports suggest that there are few sources of support, particularly for unmarried young men. Interviews for this study and other research suggest that both adult and young men are less likely than women to care for their health and are reluctant to reveal their HIV status. This social isolation leads to stress and can directly impact the health of men (Foreman 1999). Some discourses by young men suggest that being HIV positive flies in the face of traditional ideals of being virile, healthy, productive, and working. As one young HIV-positive father interviewed in South Africa said, "If you are not working and you are HIV positive, like many of us, that is the worst state that a man can be in."

Conflict and HIV/AIDS

There is a significant literature on the links between HIV/AIDS and conflict. In Sub-Saharan Africa and throughout the world, young men represent the majority of military personnel and are one of the professional groups most affected by the epidemic (UNAIDS 2004). According to UNAIDS, STI rates among armed forces are often two to five times higher than civilian populations. HIV prevalence among soldiers is 10–20 percent in many countries, and as high as 50–60 percent in others (Elbe 2002). A recent British Broadcasting Corporation report based on a study of 500 Nigerian naval officers found that AIDS may be responsible for more than half of all deaths in the armed forces (BBC 2004). While there is an urgent need for awareness and testing among the military, there is also a need to address the influences of socialization and militarization on the behaviors of young men in the military. Young soldiers are indoctrinated with values of fearlessness, violence, and norms that reinforce gender inequities (Malaza-Debose 2001). Sexual prowess is often integral to the self-image of being strong and aggressive. Soldiers are generally young, sexually active, consume large amounts of alcohol, have money to pay for sex, and are separated from family. During periods in which they are away from home and from their regular sexual partners, sexual activity—consensual and coerced—may increase.

Rape by armed groups is often a deliberate war tactic. In Rwanda, for example, 200,000–500,000 women were raped. Some women genocide survivors were told by the men who raped them that they would eventually die of AIDS. HIV rates are indeed high among rape survivors; one study in Rwanda of 1,200 genocide survivors found that two-thirds were HIV positive (Elbe 2002).

Applying a Gender Perspective in Working with Young Men

Although it is generally small in scale, a growing array of program, research, and policy initiatives seek to engage men in promoting gender equality. These include clinic-based efforts to engage men in primary health care and specialized reproductive and sexual health clinics. There is also increased attention to the role of men as fathers. UNICEF and other UN agencies have begun to discuss ways to engage men more fully in promoting the health and development of their children. A handful of NGOs in parts of Sub-Saharan Africa have started educational sessions, group discussions, or support groups for adult and adolescent fathers. Others have carried out media campaigns to promote positive images of men's involvement in the lives of their children. HIV/AIDS programs in parts of Sub-Saharan Africa and elsewhere are engaging men to prevent mother-to-child transmission. A few organizations have started support groups for HIV-positive fathers to promote their own health and to encourage them to support their partners and children. UNAIDS focused its 2000–2001 World AIDS Campaign on men and boys, giving it the slogan "Men Make a Difference" (UNAIDS 2000b).

Programs that work with young men traditionally target discrete risk groups. They largely focus on unidirectional communication of information or service delivery and rarely address the underlying impact of gender socialization and men's behavior norms. In addition, most of the research and programs on male involvement focus on adult men, while work with young men has been mainly limited to small-scale projects that often work in isolation.

This dual gender perspective on young men has rarely been applied in the field of violence prevention and postconflict reintegration, although some initiatives have focused on young men. There is a growing body of research on the gender-specific realities of young men in conflict and postconflict settings, and on the ways that the socialization of boys and young men makes young women vulnerable. Overall, however, a gender perspective has not been applied to young men in post-conflict settings.

A number of lessons and common operating principles emerge from the program experiences reviewed for this study:[11]

EXPLICIT DISCUSSIONS OF MANHOOD/MASCULINITIES. Nearly all the group activities include some discussion of men, masculinities, and gender norms. In the case of the Men as Partners (MAP) initiative and Stepping Stones, discussions are systematized in curricula, which are made available to partner organizations. These discussions about gender and masculinities are not simply "feel-good" discussion groups or group therapy. Rather, they are concrete and deliberate efforts to engage young men in critical analyses of gender roles, which when well structured can lead to changes in attitudes and behavior (Barker 2005).

CREATING ENABLING ENVIRONMENTS. Most programs seek to change social environments. By applying an ecological approach (even if it is not explicitly mentioned), they seek to engage peer and social groups or entire communities to promote changes in social norms related to gender, violence, and HIV/AIDS.

ALLIANCE BUILDING. Many of these examples, particularly MAP, seek to build broad-based alliances at the local and sometimes national level to change discourses about men and manhood. By engaging the armed forces, the police, trade unions, and others, a small program can increase its reach and influence.

INCLUDING THE MULTIPLE NEEDS OF YOUNG MEN. Many programs, even when they focus primarily on HIV/AIDS or gender-based violence, recognize that young men, particularly low-income young men, need employment. Programs often face major challenges in providing stipends and salaries to young men work-ing as peer promoters. The reality is that most low-income young men in Sub-Saharan Africa devote much of their time to working, seeking work, or developing social networks to assist in the search for work.

Conclusions and Recommendations

Gender-specific needs and vulnerabilities of Sub-Saharan African young men and women have not received adequate attention in policies, programs, and research. Too many gender analyses merely focus on the percentage of males or females in a given category or those facing a specific need. When they are discussed, Sub-Saharan African young men are often stigmatized and seen as criminals, trouble-makers, or predators. The long-standing use of pejorative terms points to the historical existence of a group of marginalized young men, often urban-based and mostly out-of-school, who are seen as potentially dangerous. Indeed, young men are on the front line of conflicts in the region, but this is nearly always a minority of young men. Sweeping generalizations that young men or the youth bulge are the cause of conflict create self-fulfilling prophecies, strip young men of their indi-viduality and subjectivity, and fail to explore the plurality of their experiences. Similarly, most reports on HIV/AIDS focus on how women are made vulnerable by the sexual behavior of men. This chapter has argued that many of the negative or harmful behaviors of young men are frequently part of public affirmations of male identity that are defined within narrow social constructs of what it means to be a man in Sub-Saharan Africa.

In Sub-Saharan Africa and elsewhere, changes in gender norms are taking place independent from policy efforts, especially in terms of increased educational attain-ment greater access to labor markets by girls and women, which in some cases is eroding men's economic advantages relative to women. Young men acknowledge the importance of women's education and incomes and perceive them as good for families. Although some males are changing how they view women, others hang on to traditional views.

Changing gender norms, however, is a slow process which is made slower by the fact that decision makers often have deep-seated gender biases and are frequently resistant to others questioning those biases. Questioning the sexual behavior of men in Sub-Saharan Africa, for example, has sometimes faced resistance from national leaders who perceive that Sub-Saharan African men are being bashed or maligned. Some programs and research are in fact prescriptive and represent outside-in approaches in which foreigners are attempting to change Sub-Saharan African men and cast them in a negative light. The challenge is to tap into voices of change and pathways to change that exist in Sub-Saharan Africa. Ultimately, the voices of young and adult men and women will promote change.

In terms of policy directions, a first priority for governments and development agencies is to broaden gender policies to recognize the gender-specific needs and realities of men and to support strategies for their meaningful involvement in the promotion of gender equality. Examples of such policies, such as the new constitution in South Africa, include several clauses on gender equality related to men. The Truth and Reconciliation Commission in South Africa invoked the issue of manhood, suggesting that "for many, acceptance and forgiveness have been incorporated into new self-understanding of what it is to be a man" (Morrell 2002, p. 30). Similarly, youth policies need to include gender from both a female and a male perspective. Many youth policies do indeed recognize gender as a variable but the application is only to young women. To be sure, a focus on the inclusion of females in youth programs and organizations—which are mostly male-dominated-is necessary, but the absence of a gender perspective in working with men weakens their effectiveness.

With regard to programming, a number of recommendations emerge, including working with young men through mainstream youth organizations; using community-driven development to reach young people and their families; and using social marketing to promote change in gender norms. Sector-specific entry points include: (a) utilizing the education system for socializing young people and addressing gender and social constructs of masculinity; (b) ensuring that national AIDS programs include explicit components on young men and gender, including efforts to engage men on gender equality and safer sex behaviors; (c) ensuring that job creation policies and programs, when they exist, take into account the gender-specific realities of young men; (d) reexamining juvenile justice systems and policies with a view to understanding the gender-specific realities of young men; (e) addressing young men and gender within the framework of postconflict disarmament, demobilization, and reintegration programs; and (f) investing in research to better understand how the changing nature of masculinity affects adolescent boys, the developmental differences between younger and older adolescents, and the potential of different protective factors to promote safer sexual behaviors and nonviolence in Sub-Saharan Africa.

Notes

1. This chapter is based on a larger study carried out for the World Bank, which was based on: (a) a review of literature on men, masculinities, conflict, and HIV/AIDS in Africa and consultations with colleague organizations to identify promising program examples that apply a gender perspective to work with young men in the region; (b) 50 key informant interviews with staff at organizations working with young men in Botswana, Nigeria, South Africa, and Uganda; (c) 23 focus group discussions and interviews with young men in Nigeria, South Africa, and Uganda; and (d) four in-depth individual interviews of young men who showed compelling gender-equitable attitudes (Barker and Ricardo 2005.)

2. See, for example, the Conceptual Framework section in International Alert's Toolkit, Inclusive Security, Sustainable Peace: A Toolkit for Advocay and Cation, accessible at: http://www.international-alert.org/pdfs/TK1_coneptualframework.pdf.

3. In analyzing the literature, carrying out site visits and analyzing the discourses of young men interviewed for this work, we loosely applied an ecological approach to understanding young men and masculinities. An ecological model of human development, attributed

initially to Bronfenbrenner (1986), has been widely used in youth development studies to represent the multiple levels at which youth interact with and respond to their environment. These levels include the intrapersonal, family, local community, and wider context of social, political, and cultural norms. Applied to gender socialization, this model suggests that young men are not passive receptors of social norms related to gender, but rather active participants in internalizing, reframing and reproducing gender norms that are passed on to them from their social settings, their families and their peers. In this model, the given behaviors of a young man—such as involvement as a combatant or use of sexual violence against a woman—are not attributed to one specific factor. Instead, they are examined in their full and interactive complexity.

4. Most researchers suggest that for women, there is no analogous intergenerational tension since in many parts of Africa, women marry and begin childbearing at early ages. Where polygamy is practiced, there may be tensions between first and subsequent wives, but these tensions are not necessarily generational.

5. At various times during the focus group discussions in this secondary school, a male teacher would intervene when students argued emphatically for one religious group over another. Through questioning (essentially, using the Socratic method), this teacher diffused or minimized ethnic tensions.

6. In much of Europe, Latin America, and North America, homophobia is often part of the socialization of boys, enjoined to act in certain ways or risk being stigmatized by being called gay. In this way, homophobia is used as a way to reinforce prevailing norms on gender-appropriate behavior. This appears to be somewhat less an issue in Africa, in that being a "real man" is not being not-gay, but more about being not-woman, not-girl, and not-child. In some groups, a culturally recognized concept of same-sex attraction does not exist, is denied, or is repressed to the extent that the problem is not so much homophobia as it is denial and lack of familiarity with same-sex attraction. With a few notable exceptions (South Africa is the most obvious one), there are no strong gay minorities in Africa that have created identity politics in ways common in other parts of the world. There may in fact be significant same-sex attraction and sexual encounters in Africa that are invisible or hidden precisely for this reason.

7. These findings related to gender-based violence also have implications for HIV/AIDS; numerous studies affirm that sexual violence increases HIV risk. Research in South Africa found that violence (sexual or physical) and feeling unable to discuss sexual matters with a male partner were related to higher sexual risk (Wood and Jewkes 1998; Dunkle 2004).

8. Recent research on violence and delinquency in the United States and Western Europe has sought to identify early childhood predictors of violent behavior, including biologically-based tendencies, such as temperament, aggressiveness, and hyperactivity. Overall, these predictors of violent behavior for young men are relatively weak in their explanatory power. Many authors have concluded that while there is some evidence for the early propensity of aggression in boys, the majority of violent behavior is explained by social factors during adolescence and childhood. Boys are not born violent—they learn to be violent, mainly by seeing other boys and men use violence; by witnessing violence; by being victims of violence in the home, at school, and in their neighborhoods; and by

seeing violence as an effective means to acquire income, power, respect and to attract women (Sampson and Laub 1993; Barker 2005).

9. There is growing research, program development, and policy attention on violence and delinquency in South Africa, and considerable analysis of how this violence is linked to culturally salient versions of manhood.

10. One study in South Africa suggests that, among other factors, the greater involvement of young women in pro-social groups in South Africa (the church is the prominent group) serves as protective factor for keeping girls out of gangs (Vetten 2000).

11. The programs were: Climbing into Manhood (Kenya), Conscientizing Male Adolescents (Nigeria), The Fatherhood Project (South Africa), Men Sector (Botswana), Men as Partners (South Africa), Soul City (South Africa), Stepping Stone (regional), Targeted AIDS Intervention (South Africa), and Positive Men's Union (TASO-Uganda). Additional details on these and other programs can be found in Barker and Ricardo (2005).

Young Men and Gender in War and Postwar Reconstruction

Some Comparative Findings from Liberia and Sierra Leone

9

PAUL RICHARDS

ender and youth categorizations are products of organizational challenges faced by all human groups—for example, youth undergo training and women bear children—and a range of localized institutional considerations—for example, culture-specific ideas about ancestors and ancestor worship as the proper guide to relations between (living) generations. This dual inheritance leads to gender and youth being seen as troublesome and contested categories. Most Sub-Saharan African countries have signed into law the UN Convention on the Rights of the Child and the Convention on the Elimination of All Forms of Discrimination against Women. It is now (in principle) illegal for those under age 18 to carry arms, or for a woman to be denied her own property. But these universal standards often clash with local expectations. In parts of rural West Africa, for example, it is still assumed by most men that a woman's property belongs to her husband, and that male children should participate in village civil defense activities (and bear arms when adults deem it necessary).

The clash of universal and local norms is only part of the story. Tensions are also the result of social change and demographics. The report of the (Blair) Commission for Africa provides an illustration. In a section entitled "Through African Eyes," two contesting positions on gender and youth emerge. A remark that Sub-Saharan African "culture was strong on kinship ties" introduces a defense of "big man" culture, patronage, and the continuing (beneficial) persistence of "the relationship between elders and non-elders" (Commission for Africa 2005, p. 30). This is immediately followed by the blunt and contradictory judgment that "many African cultures nurture a sense of denial and passivity, or encourage the abuse of women, or pay respect to the elderly with such deference that they exclude the young" (Commission for Africa 2005, p. 31).

These differences of view reflect social and demographic change in contemporary Sub-Saharan Africa. Greater female participation in goods and labor markets fosters demands for greater equality, for example in political representation or in responsibility for domestic tasks. Rapid population growth has undermined respect for elders by vastly increasing the number of youths relative to elders. Patrons can no longer keep up with demand for help (for example, for educational expenses). Land and property have been increasingly subdivided, threatening livelihoods, especially in the absence of agro-technical change. Extreme poverty and loss of options for sustaining livelihood undermines confidence in established modalities for maintaining social cohesion.[1]

This chapter aims to show how a focus on gender and youth in times of war and postwar reconstruction takes us to the heart of social change and the causes of violent conflict in contemporary Sub-Saharan Africa. The analysis makes recommendations about ways to involve marginalized groups of young men and women in creating postconflict societies that are more fair and peaceful. Youth and gender are treated as products of societal change that involve both local and global aspects. To understand recent Sub-Saharan African conflicts, postwar reconstruction, and the twin notion of youth empowerment and the creation of a responsible citizenry, we must first place gender and youth in specific historical and social contexts (Government of Sierra Leone n.d.).

Two Types of War

Wars do not simply "break out." They require organization, leadership, command-and-control tactics, strategic planning, and mobilization of fighters and resources. In short, wars are social projects, but purposes vary (Richards 2004). Some wars (WAR I) pursue technical and rational goals (control of the state, territory, or economic resources), while others (WAR II) are dominated by dramaturgical manifestations that express anger, fear, and frustration. WAR II is often a response to acute tensions induced by rapid and uncontrolled social and institutional change, where rational objectives may be hard to discern.

Although their relative importance varies, elements of both types of war are found in most conflicts. Some argue there is a higher element of WAR II in recent Sub-Saharan African conflicts than currently recognized given a dominant analytical tendency to interpret these conflicts as driven by "greed not grievance" (Berdal and Malone 2001; Collier 2000).

Both types of war impact young and old women and men, although the people fighting in all wars are predominantly youthful and male. Heavy equipment tended to limit the participation of children and younger teenagers in mechanized 20th century conflict, but the lightweight equipment used in jungle wars of contemporary Sub-Saharan Africa has made child soldiers more common. When women were excluded from the battlefield in 20th century mechanized warfare, they were recruited in large numbers into factories and noncombat military roles, positively affecting struggles for female political and economic emancipation.

WAR II is often a specific manifestation of unresolved societal tension around youth and gender.[2] Young women were induced to fight in the recent wars in

Liberia and Sierra Leone because they were frustrated at their loss of economic opportunity or angered by government corruption. But civilian women and children also pay a heavy price. Expressive war often vents its rage on those seen to be the nurturers and caregivers in a hated social system, and seeks to "convert" populations to its cause by the dramaturgical use of violence and atrocities (Richards 2003).

Three general points can be made regarding types of war:

- Although all wars are combinations of types I and II (technical and expressive warfare), Sub-Saharan African bush wars of the early 21st century tend toward type II.
- Both types of war reflect and transform gender and youth categorizations, although in different ways. WAR I often empowers women, albeit unintentionally, while WAR II gives expression to the frustrations of those marginalized by societal norms related to gender and youth and often severely damages those who continue to live within the limits of established categorizations.
- The impact of type II wars on existing gender and youth categorizations opens up social chasms which postwar reconstruction must seek to close.

Interconnected Wars on the West African Forest Frontier

This chapter draws on social assessments prepared to support community-driven reconstruction processes after damaging civil wars in Liberia and Sierra Leone (Richards, Bah, and Vincent 2004; Richards et al. 2005). These two wars will be used as examples to discuss gender and youth issues in armed conflict and social reconstruction. The two wars in question belong to a regional nexus of conflicts, including rebellions in Casamance (Senegal), Guinea Bissau, Guinea and an insurrection in Côte d'Ivoire, that have revived the organizational and expressive modalities associated with wars of the late 19th century.

Milieu is a key factor connecting recent West African conflicts. All these conflicts have taken place in or adjacent to the Upper Guinean forest block, which stretches from Senegal to Ghana, and forest resources have played an important role in sustaining conflict (Richards 1996). Colonial governments were sometimes happy to use forests to mark international boundaries, but in some cases what divided states linked peoples. This is especially true of Liberia, where 15 of 16 recognized ethnolinguistic groups have close transborder family, marital, and cultural links with adjacent groups in Côte d'Ivoire, Guinea, and Sierra Leone. The forest is crisscrossed with tracks along which local people move easily on foot; security forces, however, have difficulty patrolling the forest.

Population dynamics and their historical context are important in the context of West Africa. From 1930 to 2005, the population of West Africa increased from 40 million to an estimated 290 million; by 2020, the population is expected to reach 430 million (Bangoura, Minard, and Perret 2005). The slave trade, which began in the 16th century, depleted the region's population by removing perhaps 10 million West Africans and killing many more through internal warfare and ensuing famines and disease. Rapid population growth in the second half of the 20th century has strained local institutions, including chieftaincy, land tenure, marriage, and education. If we define "youth" broadly as those of school age or preparing for and seeking first employment (aged 5–25), this group accounts for more than 45 percent of all West Africans.

Further stresses are due to population movements away from dry rural districts in the Sahel toward forest cash crop areas and coastal cities. Urban areas now account for 45 percent of the region's population, which is projected to rise to 63 percent by 2020. The Upper Guinean forest region (southern Ghana and Côte d'Ivoire, in particular) and associated coastal capitals (notably Abidjan and Accra) have been major magnets for this moving population, many of whom are young people.

During the colonial period and for some decades after, the resource-rich Upper Guinean forest attracted young people from overpopulated districts into a range of activities, including tree crop planting, diamond and gold mining, timber exploitation, and hunting. Knowledge of the eastern and western ends of this forest frontier contributes to an understanding of West Africa's conflicts and how, despite regional links, these conflicts vary in character and impact (Richards 1995, 1996; Ellis 1999; Chauveau 2005).

A planter economy began to emerge at the western end of the forest in the first decades of the 20th century. The British put down an uprising of forest chiefs in 1898 and then built a railway to the Liberian border, opening up possibilities for palm oil, coffee, and cocoa exports from the eastern forests. The Liberian presidency extended its rule into the interior at the beginning of the 20th century through a combination of armed conquest and co-optation of traditional rulers under a system of indirect rule borrowed from the British in Sierra Leone (Ford 1989). The constitution allowed indigenes usage rights to cleared forests but claimed all other forested land on behalf of the state. Citizens (i.e., settlers) were permitted to acquire government land with approval of the executive mansion. This allowed extension of rubber planting throughout the interior, often as joint ventures with foreign companies. Tensions between planters and indigenes fed ethnic politics that eventually undermined the Americo-Liberian political elite and ushered in a period of military rule from 1980. Liberia plunged into an ethnically-based civil war beginning in 1989, when a Libyan-backed dissident (Charles Taylor) tried to seize the presidency with the help of ethnic factions from the northeast of the country (Ellis 1999).

In Sierra Leone, the plantation economy of the forests bordering Liberia was superseded by alluvial diamond mining from around 1950. Mining sustained a circular migration in which young people worked in diamond pits, but continued to draw upon subsistence livelihoods in villages ruled by customary law chiefs (Zack-Williams 1995). The system ran into trouble in the 1970s and 1980s amid signs that deposits were declining. Facing state corruption and reduced educational and employment opportunities, young miners sensed they were trapped in rural poverty, oscillating between violent and exploitative mine bosses and predatory village chiefs, unsure of their identity either as peasants or proletarians. A crisis of identity and loyalty rendered them vulnerable to mobilization by the Revolutionary United Front (RUF), a Libyan-supported group of insurgents. Sierra Leone's war was distinctly less ethnic than Liberia's (Richards 1996). In rallying multiethnic groups of young miners, the RUF attempted to use a rudimentary ideology focused on class conflict and revolution. But RUF recruits were no more proletarians than they were peasants, and the conflict took on a life of its own.

At the eastern end of the forest, the planter economy spread westward from Ghana and southeastern Côte d'Ivoire toward the dense forests of western Côte d'Ivoire and the Ivorian/Liberian border (Chauveau 2005, 2006), based on the institution of the *tutorat* (state approved tenancy agreements between planters and petty chiefs, who were deemed to have spiritual authority over the land). A large labor force was recruited from Sahelian districts to the north, and some laborers later became planters under the *tutorat*. Other planters came from the southeast of the country. Many young indigenes of the western forests moved to Abidjan. A sharp downturn in the world price of coffee and cacao in the late 1980s, however, and subsequent economic downturn made urban life difficult for these unskilled migrants. Some prepared to go home.

Migrants returning to western forest communities found migrant planters strongly entrenched, while new land for cash crop expansion was now difficult to find. Youths accused elders of squandering their birth right. A youth political movement emerged that stressed neotraditional values and opposed migrant–planter interests.

The fate of Côte d'Ivoire, Liberia, and Sierra Leone became intertwined from the outset of the Liberian conflict in 1989, as authorities in Côte d'Ivoire turned a blind eye to the activities of Charles Taylor and fellow insurgents who had earlier helped Blaise Compaoré topple Thomas Sankara in Burkina Faso. To repay earlier support from its Libyan-trained cadres, Taylor then assisted the RUF in launching an insurgency in eastern Sierra Leone. War spread in Sierra Leone when the army split into warring factions and international mercenaries intervened, attempting to enforce a peace. Taylor was elected president of war-weary Liberia in 1997, but he continued to play a role in the increasingly bitter war in Sierra Leone, which finally ended when UN and British forces consolidated a fragile peace in 2000. Assisted by Côte d'Ivoire, and Sierra Leone, armed opposition groups then launched a third phase of conflict in Liberia, eventually forcing Taylor's exit in August 2003. The UN switched its peacekeeping efforts to Liberia. Fighting then broke out in Côte d'Ivoire—the original launching pad for the two Mano River conflicts—when an army rebellion divided the country along north-south lines in 2002.

Different local factors have predominated in each of these three forest conflicts. In Liberia, violence can be linked to the ethnic factionalism stirred by Monrovia's divide-and-rule tactics in opening up the country to a planter class. The Sierra

Leone war reflects a diamond-based system of localized circulatory migration which prevented young people from forming clear peasant or proletarian identities. War in western and west-central Côte d'Ivoire increasingly draws upon intergenerational tensions over land (embedded in a wider conflict between ruling elites and northern migrants). But in addition to these specific aspects, common elements underlie all three wars. Tensions concerning youth and gender are important among these common elements, and peacemaking and postwar reconstruction requires a thorough grasp of youth and gender issues.

Institutional Shaping of Youth and Gender on a West African Forest Frontier

Male and Female Sodalities

The use of initiation rites to turn children into adults is common throughout the Upper Guinean forest. Poro (a men's association) and Sande (a women's association) are found in an arc across the northwestern part of the forest and adjacent districts, the so-called Poro belt (d'Azevedo 1962). Other associations are found in eastern Liberia and western Côte d'Ivoire, and alongside Poro in some parts of its range (Ethnologische Zeitschrift Zuerich 1980). A basic function of these "secret societies" was to "swallow" children through secret initiation rituals and "bring them back to life" as fully-gendered adults.

The sodalities carry out other social regulatory functions in addition to the initiation of children, including conveying knowledge of topics such as agriculture and reproductive health (sodalities are sometimes referred to as "bush schools"), maintaining a moral order, and curing sicknesses caused by breaches of societal rules. These functions vary according to whether the sodality is in the underpopulated heart of the forest or in the more densely populated fringes.

In the heart of the forest (in eastern Liberia and western Côte d'Ivoire), settlements are small, commerce is limited, and social stratification is minimal (Massing 1980). Here, initiation serves essentially to differentiate society into gendered age cohorts linked to the division of labor (young men undertake gang labor for farming and forest clearance, women of childbearing age cooperate in giving birth and child care, and male and female elders regulate disputes). Leadership is diffuse in these remote forest communities (Massing 1980). Elders attract respect but enjoy little executive power. Young males and females largely regulate their own affairs, manifesting "mechanical" solidarity (i.e., the perceived basis for social order is similarity, and differences based on individual success are viewed with suspicion). Where young Ivorian migrants return to the village to find chiefs have granted land rights to migrant planters, they feel the social order has been threatened (Chauveau 2005, 2006).

On the more densely populated fringes of the forest, which have a longer history of external penetration, sodalities have become stratified, especially under the leadership of trade-oriented or warrior chiefs. The cohort differentiation and instructional roles survive, but powerful chiefs of the 19th century remodeled the sodalities to serve political purposes, especially by ensuring that decision-making authority depended on initiation into higher ranks accessible only through wealth (Little 1965; Jones 1983).

The sodalities remain very important in the Upper Guinean forest. Initiation rituals create strong collective bonds among young people, which are useful as social capital for the poor and are important for community development and civil defense (Richards et al. 2004). The expectation that male teenage initiates should undertake civil defense has been revived in recent wars. Poro-based civil defense against the RUF was organized by junior army officers. The national civil defense force deployed against the RUF in Sierra Leone starting in 1996 also made extensive use of secret initiation to bond, discipline, and empower its recruits (Fithen and Richards 2004).

Many Liberians and Sierra Leoneans consider that "disrespect" by government and outside agencies of the sodalities is a source of current moral and social malaise, or even a cause of war. From time to time, political leaders—even warlords—seek initiation to enhance their political prestige (Ellis 1999). Another viewpoint is that the sodalities, dominated chiefly by elites, exploit young people from poor backgrounds (Murphy 1980; Bledsoe 1984). Sodalities' lack of public accountability also makes them problematic in an era of democracy.[3] Initiation generally takes place at the behest of parents, and perhaps without the full consent of the youngest initiates. Lodges serve a quasijudicial function in many parts of rural eastern Sierra Leone or northwestern Liberia, where Poro and Sande membership approaches 100 percent of rural populations.

Slaves and the Freeborn

Unlike the egalitarian village republics of the interior forests, the societies that emerged from the 19th century trade wars were based on a fundamental social distinction between the freeborn and domestic slaves. Slaves were property, not persons; they lacked rights and were dependent on the personal beneficence of their owners. Most became slaves through capture in war, but some entered into slavery due to debt (Grace 1977; Holsoe 1977). In war, young people were acquired as booty and female slaves were redistributed by warrior chiefs to fighters or clients. In the late 19th century, slavery was the bedrock of the society and economy of the northwestern Upper Guinean forest. When the British took the interior of Sierra Leone in 1896, it was estimated that more than half of the population was enslaved—the legacy of which remains strong to this day.

The freeborn were much less numerous. They were categorized as "children of the chief" and they had rights protected under customary laws. The laws were enforced by chiefs' courts and the sodalities. The rights of freeborn women, which were never as strong as the rights of freeborn men, were nevertheless not negligible. Among the Mende of eastern Sierra Leone, women even aspire to paramount chieftaincy. A leading family may prefer to offer a talented or strong-willed female candidate for chieftaincy if it feels its interests will be better served by such a woman than by a man. But property rights were (and remain) highly gender-asymmetric, even among children of the chief. A woman in the strongly patrilineal societies of the Upper Guinean forest risks losing houses, land, and even children to her husband's family at divorce or after his death.

Following abolition in Sierra Leone, although slaves could no longer be bought and sold, British-supervised customary courts enforced the rights of owners against runaways. Whereas slaves dropped to less than 20 percent of residents of rural districts close to Freetown, they remained as high as 50 percent in chiefdoms along the Liberian border in the late 1920s (Grace 1977). Forced labor, which was sometimes thinly disguised as chiefly rights to command community service from young men, was essential to the road-building and farming activities of the rural planter class, which was largely comprised of local land-owning families (Fenton 1948). The situation was comparable in Liberia, except that thanks to a settler constitution, Monrovia planters joined chiefs in making use of various forms of coerced labor to establish a plantation economy.[4]

The historian of slavery in Sierra Leone, John Grace, points out that exploitation of the youth labor from the former slave classes continued after abolition through "other customs linked to slavery...polygamy, forced labor and pawning [of young people, for debt]" (1977, p. 429). Even today, young people from the former slave classes remain vulnerable to labor exploitation through such means. It can be argued that the extensive development of patron-client relations in postslavery Liberia and Sierra Leone is less an expression of African social inclusiveness and family responsibility (as the Commission for Africa wishes to suggest) than the survival of a system in which dependents are granted protection not through their rights as persons but through attachment to an owner.

Marriage

Marriage can be defined as a socially-recognized partnership through which generational succession is achieved. Durkheim regarded it as the foundation of social life, since it showed how cooperative division of domestic tasks can go hand in hand with affection and respect to create social cohesion and durable partnerships (1964 [1893]). Successful marriage can take many forms, but it should be seen primarily as a social process which has great bearing on the shaping of childhood, gender identities, and the social commitments of young adults. To prevent, disable, or ignore marriage is a recipe for undermining social cohesion.

Marriage systems in the Upper Guinean forest (where chiefs typically practiced polygamy) were conditioned by 19th century warfare and a slave-based division of labor. In the 19th century, Vai chiefs on the Liberian border sometimes had 20–40 wives, and a few had more than 100. A document from 1812 notes that when asked why they had so many wives, the chiefs responded that they needed many women to work for them (Jones 1983, p. 189). This control by a few elite men of the labor of a majority of young women through marriage has been well described as "wealth in people" (Bledsoe 1980).

Chiefs accumulated women for more than work. They also controlled and redistributed women's sexual and reproductive services to form political alliances, sustain clients, and reproduce a slave class. In the 19th century, chiefs were given wives as a token of respect or to strengthen a friendship. Slaves could only marry if they were given a wife by their master. Jones writes, "Adultery cases outnumbered all others in judicial proceedings: in 1850, for instance, all but two of the 32 prisoners held in chains at Gendema were there for adultery with Prince Mana's wives" (1983, p. 189). A poor but free young man sometimes paid off a large fine by laboring on the farm of the chief whose wife he seduced.

Marriage is closely linked to wealth in people. Writing about the Kpelle people in northwest Liberia, Gibbs notes the different marriage prospects of "rich people," "children of the soil," and "clients" (1985, p. 215). A man's wealth was measured not only in terms of money and goods but also in his control over women and children. From the male perspective, the three classes Gibbs identifies can be labeled as "wife givers," "wife keepers," and "wife borrowers." The three classes were, in effect, the freeborn, slaves, and pawns. The freeborn used their capacity to contract polygamous marriages to underwrite their labor needs. The *toh nuu* (upstanding or prominent person) might allow some of his wives "to become consorts of poor men of the lower class who become his tii keh *nuwai* [workmen or clients]...another source of labor to work on the patron's farms" (Gibbs 1985, p. 215). Slavery was thus reconstituted as clientship through marriage.

Two marriage systems are widely used in the Upper Guinean forest (Currens 1972). One is the avunculate, a type of preferential cross-cousin marriage involving no bride wealth (Leopold 1991), which is often used to build political alliances among freeborn lineages (Murphy and Bledsoe 1987). The other system involves a bride wealth or bride service payment between the wife receiver and wife giver (Etienne 1997). In its formal aspects, the bride wealth system stabilizes marriage (undoing transactions is difficult and expensive) and creates durable bonds between wife-giving and wife-receiving lineages (the wife givers frequently seek to marry up to a wealthy man not only to gain resources but also to enter into stable client relationships). The bride wealth system can have adverse consequences, however. A young man from a poor family may be too poor to marry and instead offers free labor as bride service to his wife's lineage, to the detriment of his own dependents. A young woman may find herself locked into an abusive marriage, unable to leave because her family is too poor to repay bride wealth (Richards, Bah, and Vincent 2004).

Bride wealth makes village marriage generationally asymmetric—older men marry much younger women because only older men have the resources to pay. The average ages of marriage in rural central and eastern Sierra Leone is typically 40–50 for men and 15–16 for women (Richards, Bah, and Vincent 2004). Many village women are not only married to men with several partners but become widows at an early age. Multiple marriages to elderly men also encourage clandestine liaisons between young married women and village youth. Husbands sometimes exploit this possibility, forcing the woman to confess the name of a lover (often through beatings which result in false confessions), who is then charged in a customary court to extract substantial damages (often paid as farm labor). The courts and jails deal with many young men accused of "woman damage" (adultery) who face fines they cannot pay. An option is to run away. Outlaws and vagrants accumulate in the diamond districts or forest reserves as a result.

Polygamy and the enforcement of bride wealth and woman damage in local courts perpetuates asymmetric intergenerational marriage and blocks a route to social cohesion based on marriage as a freely contracted union between consenting young adults. It keeps poor men as youths, with limited family (and thus social) responsibilities well into their middle age. Those who join militia forces are sometimes explicit that inability to marry was an important motivation. Some young men become fighters to accumulate bride wealth, while others use sexual violence to express rage and frustration at a system that denies them the chance to form recognized families.

In a large-scale quantitative study of ex-combatants in Sierra Leone, Humphreys and Weinstein (2004) found that few combatants mentioned diamonds as a motivation to join the RUF but as many as 25 percent stated they had received a marriage partner for joining. The RUF abducted women into its combat wives unit to serve this purpose. Disarmament, demobilization, and reintegration planners in Liberia and Sierra Leone encountered larger-than-expected numbers of combatants with children and partners. The formation of often stable marital partnerships within the RUF may have been a factor in the group's desire to seek peace in 2000.

Metayage

Fenoaltea's (1984) "extended" transaction-cost model of slavery shows that coerced unwaged labor is effective in low-skill activities but tends to be replaced when skill requirements rise. For example, slavery is historically common on cotton and rice plantations but rare in olive and wine production. The legal abolition of slavery in Sierra Leone and Liberia was unaccompanied by major change in agrarian skill requirements. These are the kinds of conditions in which slave-based production tends to be substituted by *metayage* (sharecropping). Too poor to pay wages, land owners offer land and perhaps seeds to sharecroppers who grow their own food and pay back by splitting the harvest with the land owner.

Sharecropping is well-developed in the cocoa belt on the eastern flank of the Upper Guinean forest (Robertson 1987) and is an aspect of the *tutorat* in Côte d'Ivoire. But sharecropping is not strongly developed in rural production systems at the western end of the Upper Guinean Forest. *Metayage* is more important as an aspect of mining, especially in Sierra Leone.[5] Starting in about 1930, minerals replaced cash crops as Sierra Leone's leading export. Neither hematite, the first export, nor alluvial diamonds, the second export, starting the 1950s, generated much wage labor. During its first two decades of existence, the mining company DELCO (Sierra Leone Development Company) depended mainly on "target migration," or short-term labor contracts for workers who returned to farming when they were laid off. SLST (Sierra Leone Selection Trust, the diamond mining company) carried out intensive industrial mining in a limited area of Kono, but from the mid-1950s allocated much of its concession to artisanal miners.

In the 1950s, the government and SLST offered low-yield areas of its huge eastern concession to local miners. The official reason for this was to limit illegal mining, but Zack-Williams (1995) suggests the real reason was to address local militancy. Chiefs received payoffs from the mining company, while villagers received nothing. Chiefs and government could offer local concessions to key figures who might otherwise become a focal point for the dissidence triggered by the contrast between diamond wealth and rural backwardness.

The artisanal mining system that emerged was a type of *metayage* that required very little equipment. Gang masters recruited seasonal labor in farming villages and acted as protectors and patrons to young men. License holders and tributers split the proceeds. The system was riddled with opportunities for cheating, and violence was an endemic mode of control. Government taxes and unofficial exactions bled wealth from the system. These exactions were handed down the line to the tributers who lived on extremely meager returns until finally slipping back into agrarian subsistence when the mining pits failed.

Zack-Williams (1995) points out several essential features. For an expatriate company mining only the richest part of the concession but that is keen to buy the product of unskilled African mining activity, a compliant (even venal) government partner and (above all) a subsistence agricultural system viable enough to feed young tributers and provide them a fallback when their mining ventures failed. Without farming as backup source of income and nourishment, many tributers would have starved to death, but the circulatory migration of young rural labor between farms and mines meant there was little scope for the emergence of skill-intensive farming systems.

The system was held together by the patriarchal values and patrimonial social institutions associated with post-slavery societies. It remained viable as long as some diamond wealth continued to flow, but increasing numbers of young people, limited land for fallow farming, and exhaustion of the best gravels posed severe challenges. Political interference undermined chiefly rule from the 1970s. As high-quality Kono gravels began to be exhausted, and tributers explored new niches, especially in and around the Gola Forest on the Liberian border. Although these forested areas were isolated from Freetown, they were influenced by economic and political powers in Liberia.

New political doctrines crossed the border, including Libyan leader Muammar al-Gaddafi's *The Green Book*. Patrimonial values were questioned in mining camps and farms. As the poverty of uneducated laborers trapped in a vicious cycle of declining mining and farming opportunities intensified, a rough radicalism took root. The disillusionment with customary institutions, confined at first to the renegades from rural society who first supported the RUF, became more general among poor rural youth as the war progressed. In the aftermath of the war in Sierra

Leone, even the civil defense volunteers who fought against the RUF seemed at times intensely disillusioned with their chiefs (Archibald and Richards 2002; Richards 2005). Fighting in the bush near the diamond fields intensified the privations and low rewards associated with alluvial diamond mining. Ex-combatants know they lack the skills to find new jobs in urban areas, but are unenthused by the thought of return to tributer life. Modern farming has attracted some, including several groups of ex-RUF cadres keen on agricultural cooperation, but they are skeptical about unreconstructed rural institutions built around customary law, clientage, and traditional marriage payments.

Young diamond miners are hypermobile and politically volatile in a world of circulatory migration linked to diamond production which renders them neither peasants nor proletarians. This is one reason why the WAR I elements of the RUF program developed so quickly. The movement directed a vicious vengeance against rural people, processes, and institutions it viewed as prolonging social exclusion. Hand cutting atrocities disabled the mechanical solidarities—for example, group labor for subsistence production—through which the system of diamond-based *metayage* was maintained. Sierra Leone's war can thus be seen as a kind of slave revolt against a system that blocked rural youth from finding a stable basis for community life. Peace requires an increase in the skill content of the work undertaken by impoverished young Liberians and Sierra Leoneans. The modernization of both mining and agriculture is essential.

Who Fought and Why?

Theories to explain the Upper Guinean forest conflicts have invoked rootless urban youth—lumpen elements and criminal gangs (Abdullah 1997; Kandeh 2001). Mkandawire (2002) sees a pattern applicable to several African conflicts— urban malcontents take to the countryside hoping to rouse the peasantry, and when the peasants fail to respond, the insurgents turn on those they intended to recruit. Evidence on demobilized Sierra Leonean fighters, however, fails to confirm the lumpen thesis. Urban youth fought in the army, but the great majority of RUF and Civil Defense Forces (CDF) combatants were from rural backgrounds. RUF cadres murdered helpless villagers, but this was rural-on-rural violence; the violence was really directed across generations and classes. RUF fighters in particular were young and poor. The largest intake came from rural schools. The second-largest group were farmers before the war (Humphreys and Weinstein 2004; Richards 2004).

This pattern of fighting matches the one already suggested—of violence directed against chiefly classes by exploited farm or diamond laborers. Few ex-combatants reported that they had joined the RUF for diamonds, but a quarter of them reported that by joining the movement they had gained a marriage partner (Humphreys and Weinstein 2004). Village marriage systems reproduce the clientelistic order of a society rooted in domestic slavery. The frustrations of rural young men appear to have been shared, at least in part, by impoverished rural young women. Up to a quarter of all RUF fighters were women.

Can the slave revolt thesis be confirmed from the mouths of the fighters themselves? The following statements come from interviews completed as part of Liberian and Sierra Leonean social assessments (Richards, Bah, and Vincent 2004; Richards et al. 2005), supplemented by material on the RUF supplied by Krijn Peters and extracts from focus group sessions with villagers in 1999–2000 undertaken for the Governance Reform Secretariat (for further information on sources see Archibald and Richards 2002 and Richards 2004). Labor exploitation by chiefs and the malfunctioning of village justice, governance, and marriage systems figure large in the ex-combatants' interpretations of the war.

Chiefs victimize youths by imposing heavy and unjust fines; criminal summonses make youths run from the village (youth focus group, Kamajei Chiefdom, 2002).

Heavy fines levied by chiefs on youths have led to many leaving the village, and the chiefs are concerned that these youths will return and seek revenge on them (elders focus group, Kamajei Chiefdom, 2002).

Chiefs withhold benefits meant for the community, resulting in defiance by youths...chiefs protect their own children from doing communal work (youth focus group, Kamajei Chiefdom, 2002).

Nobody was willing to help the young men...when ministers or the paramount chief visit any village they ask us to contribute rice and money, instead of bringing development...That inspired us to fight...to have justice in the country (male RUF ex-combatant, eastern Sierra Leone, 2001).

Most...young men and women were suffering...our chiefs and some elders were doing wrong to our young...some preferred to go and join the RUF, either to take revenge or to protect themselves (male CDF ex-combatant, eastern Sierra Leone, 2001).

Even if you have a minor problem [the chiefs] exaggerate it...taking it to a district chief, then you the young man cannot handle the case...and you have to run away...I was accused, so I ran away and hid...then I heard about the Kamajor Society [CDF] and decided to join (male CDF ex-combatant, eastern Sierra Leone, 2001).

[The chiefs] levy high fines on the youth, if you are sent to do a job and you refuse...up to now the chiefs are pressuring us (male SLA ex-combatant, eastern Sierra Leone, 2001).

[We] joined the RUF willingly—seven girls and thirteen boys [in my village]...the main reason was lack of job...and lack of encouragement for youth (female RUF ex-combatant, eastern Sierra Leone, 2001).

We have problems with our elders...They force young men to marry...If you refuse they cause more problems...than even being in the bush as a rebel. They charge you to court for smiling at a girl... But the bride price is not reasonable. You will be required to do all sorts of physical jobs for the bride's family, like brushing and making a farm for the family...sharing the proceeds of your own labor, harvest or business...You will be forced to give them 70 percent [of your drum of palm oil], or you will lose your wife and be taken to court...Most of us...avoid the scene. [In Tongo Field] you can...marry a woman of your choice. [Village] marriage is the same as slavery (male RUF ex-combatant, eastern Sierra Leone, July 2003).

[Talking of whether it is better to be married to a younger, poor man or older, wealthier man a young woman says] Of course it is preferable to have a young husband, but it would be hard for [such a] husband to get his own farm. Because of bride service he will work for my father and brothers for many years to come...in fact, for the rest of his life [laughing].Yes, he will remain poor, but my daughters will marry, and my husband can rest on the bride service the daughters attract (female youth, Kamajei Chiefdom, 2003).

We cannot run away from any chief any more because this is a democracy...if you, as a bad chief, send us anywhere to brush some land...we will refuse (CDF male ex-combatant, eastern Sierra Leone, 2001).

Heavy fines...[are] imposed by [little] respected chiefs...with no love for the youths (CDF focus group, Wonde Chiefdom consultation, July 2000).

The youth of Dasse have been suppressed by the ruling elite for too long...[Court Chairmen] use intimidation tactics to extort revenue...resulting in justice being denied (youth focus group, Dasse Chiefdom consultation, December 1999).

A CDF group reported that during the war there was a good relationship between the fighters and the chiefs, but that with the war effectively over the chiefs no longer have respect for nor recognize the sacrifice of the CDF (ex-CDF fighters, Dasse Chiefdom, December 1999).

The war started long ago, in the house. The men took too many wives and had too many children. They then abandoned them because they could not support them. The children grew angry; they wanted revenge on their fathers. War was the opportunity they needed (male elder, Lofa County, Liberia, August 2004).

I joined the rebel forces to fight inequality in the country, and because of this issue I also encouraged my three children to join (female ex-combatant, Margibi County, Liberia, August 2004).

This war was caused by poverty and injustice. Our (youth) poverty is caused by having no education, no training, no money and no jobs. [The chiefs] fine us too much for any small thing. Because we are poor, we cannot pay. So somebody 'buys' our case, and then we have to work for that person, and for the chief. This means we cannot work for ourselves, so we get poorer, so some have to steal to survive and, when...caught...get fined again. We don't call this justice...it [is] jungle justice...the only outcome will be back to war (participant in a youth focus group, Margibi County, Liberia, August 2004).

New Gender and Youth-Oriented Bases for Social Cohesion

If Durkheim's model of social harmony is a successful marriage partnership in which sharing tasks nourishes affection, then behavior of rural youth in the Upper Guinean forest conforms more to one of Durkheim's three major social patholo-gies—social schism as a product of a forced division of labor (Durkheim 1964 [1893]; Lockwood 1992; Rawls 2003). A minority group among these youth obtain the majority of educational opportunities and jobs regardless of aptitude, while the rest of the group is unable to see its social value reflected in the work it undertakes. Cooperation and solidarity are undermined, causing social unrest. The result (according to Durkheim's model) is civil war. And the antidote to social unrest and conflict lies in addressing the underlying division of labor.

As the above analysis has attempted to show, this division of labor is deeply enmeshed in the history of postslavery social institutions on the West African forest frontier. Labor exploitation, embedded in systems for access to land, skill forma-tion, marriage, and justice, leads to the formation of a large vagrant underclass in which young men and women lack stakes in or commitment to the wider society. Expressive violence takes on the character of a crusade against society itself. Reversing this trend requires close attention to the underlying institutional prob-lems, and considerable strategic acumen.

The Central Importance of Jobs and Skills

Talking to ex-combatants in Liberia and Sierra Leone reveals a real desire by a majority of these people to be incorporated into the social mainstream. For main-streaming to happen, however, a focus on skill formation and waged work is necessary (Fithen and Richards 2005; Richards et al. 2003; Utas 2004). Postwar reconstruction brings money into rural areas, opening up potential job opportu-nities for the underclass, whose basic problem is lack of skills. Most have lost what little education they had, but some formed skills in combat. These are mainly skills of cooperation, which in some instances are being put to use in ex-combatant agricultural projects. More ex-combatants may follow down this route if there is better agrotechnical training and innovation suited to local conditions, coupled with the availability of land leases and credit.

Dead-end jobs for ex-combatants need to be avoided over any long period. Brushing roads for $2 per day (as in Liberia) can only be a temporary expedient. The work is no more attractive—or a suitable basis to develop stable social relations, nor for young men to establish a family and complete the transition to adulthood—than laboring on tree crop plantations before the war. When the benefits of the road or plantation flow mainly to outside elites, young, displaced indigenes feel resentful.

Skill formation is key for the reintegration of young, rural ex-combatants, but skill formation should not focus exclusively on this cohort. Because the group of potential future recruits is much larger and needs to be treated in the same way as those who fought, too much attention to actual combatants simply creates incentives for young marginalized noncombatants to follow their example. A major difficulty to overcome is the relevance of the skill formation offered. Agencies offer the training they are able to supply, not necessarily what is appropriate to the local society and economy or what ex-combatant or marginalized youth can absorb. Business skills can be critical. Skills for rural road maintenance may be quickly taught but skills to run a small repair business and successfully compete for contracts are of a higher order.

Addressing Metayage

Metayage presents special challenges, as it embeds a division of labor that feeds extreme social discontent, especially where it is the organizational basis for alluvial mining. Here, precapitalist labor relations exist alongside the international jet-set lifestyles of successful mining entrepreneurs. The diggers contrast the affluence and the educational success and overseas jobs of the children of the diamond nomenklatura with their own oppression and lack of progress. This clash of postmodern global with postslavery local values feeds some of the resentments which have fed conflict in the region. And yet diamond mining *metayage* has actually been boosted by war and postwar circumstances. It was the operational modality used by both army and RUF to tap the resources that funded their campaigns. The postwar democratic government in Sierra Leone has reverted to the modality as a way of tying large numbers of otherwise unemployed ex-combatants into the national economy.

It is ironic that the violence associated with diamond mining is interpreted by some as "greed not grievance" because for the diggers the work is as backbreakingly unattractive and as poorly paid as the subsistence agriculture to which they often revert (OTI 2000). As Humphreys and Weinstein (2004) show, the opportunity to mine diamonds is not an incentive to fight. Mining appeals only as a lottery, but as Douglas and Ney (1998) argue, lotteries represent a preferred option only when all confidence in social hierarchies and human justice is lacking. Thus, mining is not a source of greed nor a viable livelihood option, but a gamble on a lucky strike. It is perhaps no coincidence that RUF cadres, when they were bombed out of their secure forest bases, resorted to a randomized violence against villagers, which RUF termed its "lottery of life and death."

Diamond diggers dream of escaping mining by acquiring other skills. One young man in the depths of the Gola Forest just prior to the outbreak of war cross-examined me closely on biotechnology (Richards 1996). Many diamond diggers in Sierra Leone work diamond pits in the dry season and grow rice for subsistence in the rainy season. However, the standard innovation for rice in Sierra Leone, increasing labor-intensive swamp production, extends cultivation into the dry season, which is not good for miners. The young man interested in biotechnology asked me whether I thought that crop biotechnology would boost rainy-season, dry-land rice cultivation without the need to hold secure land tenure or interfere with the labor demands of alluvial mining. Potentially, yes, yet it remains to be seen if the new rice varieties, which are engineered to bring some of the hardiness of native African rice into higher-yielding Asian varieties, are the answer. The general point, however, is that it is difficult to raise skill levels under *metayage*. There may be operational obstacles (such as seasonality), but perhaps more importantly, the various parties to the *metayage* contract must agree before skill-enhancing investments can be made. Devising the necessary win–win scenarios requires ingenuity.

The divergent interests of diggers and diamond interests at the western end of the forest may be too great to bridge without an overhaul of the entire system. In Sierra Leone, major political will is required to support a technological revolution in mining, including major investments, establishment of a mining college, and a considerable tightening of the systems of mining permits and safety controls. It is still too easy for a politically well-connected supporter to send, at low outlay, a gang of laborers to dig and sieve inefficiently for diamonds in the bush and then post a reliable family member (often as a student) in Europe to sell the product, thus storing up social resentment as well as picking low-tech holes in the national resource base.

At the eastern end of the Upper Guinean forest, *metayage* is mainly agricultural and may offer some scope for developing new local skills and technology-based approaches. While technological approaches may alleviate some stresses in the *tutorat* in Côte d'Ivoire, they would not directly address a major cause of the war in the western part of Côte d'Ivoire (i.e., returning migrant urban youth who consider the elders to have broken an intergenerational bargain by granting land to the planters). The challenge in this case is to carve a place for indigenous youth in the agrarian landscape. As in Liberia, the parental generation actually invested its hope in sending young people to the city. In Liberia, having a youth posted to Monrovia is seen as an asset because in this highly centralized country, resources are perceived to be accessible only through brokerage by those with connections in the capital. Youths returning from war or youths returning to rural areas from Monrovia are regarded as having failed not only personally but also for having undermined family welfare. General economic weakness (exacerbated by war) lies behind this breakdown of a tacit intergenerational contract. Economic revival and decentralization (to reduce the need for the high-risk gamble of sending poorly-educated youths to the city in the hope they will one day help the wider family) will therefore be important keys to peace.

Education Reforms

Education was a key issue in Sierra Leone's conflict. This reflected the country's heritage as a 19th century beacon of modern education for much of anglophone colonial West Africa, but also the perception—especially by those trapped in unskilled diamond-mining *metayage*—that their own labor contributed to the social mobility of land-owning elites. If the underclass stayed in the village, their plantation labor (and often, their fines) helped pay for the education of the chief's children, who escaped community labor by being at school in town. Underclass children attended the village school, which was often dilapidated and staffed by untrained teachers. Alternatively, these children could seek work in the diamond fields. Thus underclass sweat contributed to the education of the children of politically-connected diamond elites.

Diamond pits were full of diggers whose education had been terminated by poverty or misfortune. In 1987, President Joseph Momoh's claim that education was a privilege, not a right, stirred up widespead anger. Diamond diggers fell into the arms of the RUF, a movement run by secondary school graduates and trainee teachers and led by a former army noncommissioned officer. According to Humphreys and Weinstein (2004), as many as 47 percent of the RUF intake was mobilized or abducted directly from impoverished and collapsing rural primary schools (about 6 percent of soldiers were secondary school graduates). Those who fought the RUF knew early on that education was as much an issue for the rebels as corrupt government. "We knew this," one CDF interviewee said, "because of the pamphlets and letters they dropped in the villages they attacked" (Peters and Richards 1998). Several RUF camps operated a rudimentary system of free education, staffed by trained teachers it had recruited or abducted, for its cadres.

The marginalization of rural education must be addressed when mainstreaming youth and gender issues into postconflict reconstruction. Families with sufficient resources send their children to town, but this undermines the educational chances of children who remain, since it reduces the pressure to build and staff schools in then-smaller communities. Even if there is a school in such communities, there is no incentive structure to attract qualified teachers. The curriculum (dominated by capital-city-educated elites) is not fully oriented to the needs and interests of forest children, and pass rates (for entry to junior secondary education) are abysmally low, typically no more than 5–7 percent.

Lack of good rural primary schooling is especially damaging to girls. The hazards girls face when they are sent to the city for education are much higher than the hazards boys face, including pregnancy (which in any case terminates her education under prevailing mores) and informal marriage in which the parents have no hand. Thus, many parents prefer to keep their daughters at home, seeking early marriage to a village big man whose bride wealth payments and protection provide some degree of security to the girl's family. The typical age of first marriage for most girls in rural upcountry Sierra Leone is about 15 years; the average fell during the war due to closure of rural schools (Richards, Bah, and Vincent 2004).

And yet girls probably benefit more (intrinsically) from rural primary education than boys. A literate and numerate mother has better access to health messages affecting her own children, commands basic skills to run a small part-time craft or trading business, helps her own children develop good educational habits, and is better able to participate in village-level representative institutions (especially parent-teacher associations). Although it would be hard to understate the importance of the Millennium Development Goals on primary education and gender equality for war-affected countries in West Africa, achieving these goals will require a considerable change in orientation (Humphreys and Richards 2005). A vicious circle of tradition and insecurity will continue to deny girls decent basic education unless steps are taken to spread schools and well-qualified teachers into remote rural localities and reform the curriculum to fit local realities and needs.

Reform of Women's Property Rights and Marriage

Women's property rights and marriage rights in the West African forest devolve from institutional arrangements prevailing in a society once based on slavery. Certain rules are perpetuated by customary courts to the advantage of chiefly, landed elites. Men and women from a rural underclass are subordinated by these rules. Customarily, a woman may lose property rights (including rights to her marital home and her children) on the death of her husband unless she submits to the levirate (marry another man proffered by her husband's patrilineage). If she seeks divorce, she typically loses her property rights.

In Liberia, after Charles Taylor stepped down, the women's caucus placed a bill before the Senate to extend constitutional property rights, hitherto ruled by lineage custom, to upcountry women (Republic of Liberia 2003). The bill allows women to own property from a marriage, grants them rights to their children, and legislates against compulsory levirate. The law is especially interesting on the implication of marriage for gender relations. Bride wealth transactions are permitted only as gifts and cannot be recovered through court action. "Woman damage" cases are circumscribed by rendering it illegal for a polygamist to encourage his wives to take lovers in order to seek damages, or to force a woman to confess the name of a lover.[6]

Sierra Leone has adopted international human rights conventions (on women and children) as national law so that any judgment from a customary court in favor of the husband's lineage can be struck down on appeal. The problem is how to appeal.[7] One possibility is for human rights' lawyers to pursue test cases (equivalent to a class action in the United States) to publicize the issue and establish the principle. Fighting and winning one such case would establish precedent.

Reform of customary law is planned in postwar Sierra Leone, and the country would do well to consider some of the formulations adopted in Liberia to reduce the incidence of polygamy and intergenerational marriage (perhaps even to ban polygamy outright). In addition to legal reforms, administration of justice will play a key role. Officials in local courts need to be better trained in marriage law, and there needs to be better documentation and supervision of cases tried in local courts, not least to facilitate appeals.

Land Leasing and Resettlement

A second item for the justice reform agenda with considerable potential to bring marginalized young men and women into the social mainstream is the issue of land rights. Availability of land for farming is a contentious issue in some areas (for example, northwestern Liberia) as a result of extensive land alienations by planters. A degree of restitution may be necessary in some cases, as part of a long-term peace process.

In Liberia, land grabbing was associated with political cronyism under the True Whig Party, and the controversies generated continue to feed local ethnic dissidence. In other instances, land reform (as commonly understood) is not the main issue. What is perhaps more important are flexible land leasing arrangements to allow young people without jobs to make farms, perhaps on a cooperative basis. In Liberia, the state already has the power to make such land grants.[8] In Sierra Leone, a group of ex-combatants (the ex-RUF Bansal Project) successfully petitioned the Paramount Chief of Magburaka for land lease for cooperative boliland farming, and claims over 600 members.[9]

Where there is likely most need for policy intervention is in helping groups of young people negotiate fair and unambiguous land leasing contracts that are understood by the parties and protected by a well-administered local court system capable of enforcing contractual agreements (FAO 2004). If it is correct that the rural youth of the Upper Guinean forest frontier have been marginalized by a forced division of labor, then a degree of labor mobility is needed to help with reintegration. For many ex-combatants in Liberia and Sierra Leone, mobility within the rural sector will be especially important. While these people have no skills for urban living, they prefer not to return to communities that in some cases they helped to destroy. Leasing of agricultural land in areas where they are unknown to the local population, and where they can thus make a fresh start, may be the key to mitigating violence and forming wider social solidarities among groups feeling marginalized.

Women's land rights require special attention (Davison 1988). It is common for African women to be heavily engaged in farming but to be given only secondary land rights (i.e., through a husband or a male family member). In cases of divorce or widowhood, a woman risks losing all rights to specific plots of land. It could be said, therefore, that women in Africa have rights to land but not to specific pieces of land. African women need inheritance reform, a property regime for marriage, and credit programs to fund land purchases.

For some young women who participated in armed violence, there are further problems. These women are rejected by their communities for having offended against local taboos on women fighting and killing. In some cases, female ex-combatants have been stripped of their weapons by more powerful commanders at demobilization in order to accommodate noncombatant partners in the demobilization process. Meanwhile, the wider society has tended to ignore or deny the existence of female fighters. After being scattered across the region, those who were excluded from demobilization have a tendency to drift into highly disadvantageous marriages with village polygamists (under conditions approaching domestic slavery) or to become urban sex workers (Richards et al. 2003). These young women have special rehabilitation needs.

Taking Youth and Gender Policy Seriously

Given the huge demographic increase in young men and women in West Africa over the past half century, it is not surprising that countries in the region now have ministries of gender and youth. Typically these are add-on or offshoot agencies, i.e., they mix a range of concerns such as gender, youth, sports, and culture, or perhaps emerged as a devolved subsection of the ministry of education. This seems to be the wrong institutional approach. Youth and gender are overarching policy concerns, and the relevant minister should be coordinating a range of key activities, including education, employment, social welfare, health, and security. Basic requirements are a national youth policy and a serious budget to allow, among other things, experimentation in youth activities designed to foster social cohesion. Sierra Leone, for example, has a National Youth Policy document, but the Ministry has a miniscule budget (Government of Sierra Leone). Donors bypass it in favor of discussing reconstruction with traditionally important ministries such as education or agriculture. Youth and gender-based civil society organizations are at times equally neglected by donors seeking to strengthen civil society. Organized as sports clubs or mutual aid groups, for example, they remain invisible to donors concerned with "big" issues (such as democracy). This should be reversed—mainstreaming youth and gender issues in national reconstruction is hardly likely to happen unless they are mainstreamed at the level of the state and civil society.

Youth and Women in Postwar West Africa: An Agenda for Action

A number of changes would ensure greater involvement of youth and women in the development of postwar West Africa. These include:

- Recognize that low skill/low wage work acts as a trap to the self advancement and transition to adulthood of a majority of young men, undermining social cohesion and fostering violence.
- Work to reverse the low skill/low wage trap by improving the technical content of alluvial mining, forest-edge agriculture, and forest exploitation. Provide appropriate training opportunities open to all.
- Engage employers, trade unions, and governance institutions (for example, the national anticorruption commission) to ensure openness, transparency, and accountability of employment procedures, ensuring that jobs are allocated on merit, not according to patronage.
- Improve basic education and ensure that all marginalized groups have access to education; in particular, take steps to guarantee better rural education for village girls, for example, build schools in remote areas and offer incentives for

qualified teachers. Work with village parents to promote girls' education and discourage early marriage.

- Reform women's property rights. Legislate to ensure that women own joint shares in assets created by marriage; establish widow's rights in regard to children, land, and housing; and abolish customs such as compulsory levirate and forcible recovery of bride wealth.
- Encourage national debate on ways to resolve possible contradictions between international human rights law and customary practice affecting women and youth (in families, schools, and sodalities). Reform customary law to bring it in line with national and international law; offer better training to customary court officials; and ensure that court officials are selected from a wide societal cross section, including women and migrants.
- Reform customary marriage laws. For example, abolish woman damage and forced confession of lovers, prevent husbands encouraging extramarital liaisons for the purposes of indebting young men, and legislate against polygamy.
- Ensure better documentary procedures in customary courts and better monitoring by government court inspectors of cases involving women and youth, in particular punishment regimes (for example, arbitrary detention and fines). Prevent the "buying" of cases by payment of fines in return for unpaid labor.
- Encourage legal activism (for example, by pro bono human rights lawyers) in appeals likely to be of special significance to the interests of women and youth (these include cases concerning enforcement of land leasing contracts or protection of women's property).
- Pay special attention to land tenure, especially to land leasing arrangements that can accommodate mobile young people (for example, government land grants to cooperative groups of young farm settlers, especially ex-combatants and unemployed youth). Develop and publicize country-specific good practices for agricultural land leasing arrangements that incorporate FAO good practice guidelines.
- Grant women land rights in their own name and recognize and protect women's secondary rights to land or land-linked property, for example harvesting rights in forests.
- Pay specific attention to the resettlement needs of female ex-combatants, including tracking and releasing those who have fallen into transboundary rural domestic servitude that is thinly disguised as village marriage.
- Ensure that local courts are competent in administering land and labor contracts, including leases granted under guaranteed short-hold tenure. Closely monitor adherence to contract law as applied to land and labor cases.
- Strengthen ministries of gender and youth and ensure they have resources and capacity commensurate with their policy role. Ensure that national gender and youth policies are elaborated, implemented, and monitored. Encourage gender and youth-based organizations to mobilize, federate, and enter policy debates and democratic politics.

- Ensure that community-based social funds address issues relating to involvement of youth and women in postwar reconstruction and community-driven development.

Notes

1. Whether patrimonialism is an intrinsic aspect of African culture or a product of the modification of social values associated with slavery is controversial. Indeed, whether "culture" can be introduced as an independent, explanatory variable in social development is challenged by some (see Douglas 2004).
2. There was a strong element of WAR II in the "women's war" of eastern Nigeria in the 1920s, which was sparked by unpopular colonially-imposed chiefs and taxes that threatened women's trade (Van Allen 1997 [1971]).
3. Richards (2000) argues that chiefly dominance of women and youth via existing sodalities accounts for the widespread belief in Liberia and Sierra Leone in imaginary "counter sodalities" of chiefly "cannibals." See Ellis (1999) for a different view which stresses the reality of these criminal associations.
4. On the importance of domestic slavery among the Gola of northwestern Liberia until emancipation in 1930, see d'Azevedo (1969–71). Sierra Leone (in 1928) and Liberia (in 1930) were among the last countries in the West African coastal belt to emancipate domestic slaves. Getz (2004), using the examples of Senegal and Gold Coast (the former Ghana), argues that emancipation of domestic slaves was slow in West Africa because French and British administrations needed the collaboration of merchant and chiefly elites with vested interests in prolonging domestic servitude.
5. The following account draws extensively on Zack-Williams (1995).
6. It is not clear how quickly (if at all) this law will take effect. Awareness in rural Liberia does not yet seem high, but given the centrality of the issues the law addresses in fostering socially responsible marriage (and thereby strengthening social solidarity), it seems that other parts of the Upper Guinean forest frontier might take note (especially Sierra Leone).
7. Customary cases appealed to higher courts are assessed by the Local Appeals Division, in which a judge of the Supreme Court of Sierra Leone is advised by two experts in custom (Local Courts Act 1963, and subsequent amendments).
8. An unemployed school leavers' association in Buchanan, upon recognizing that government jobs disappeared, proposes to petition the state for such a grant.
9. This is not to argue that traditional land tenure institutions are as flexible as some commentators claim (Bassett 1993). The idea that there is a traditional system is perhaps a misconception. Judgments in land cases often represent current or past political bargaining strengths. The 19th century picture for the Upper Guinean forest frontier may have been close to what Ranger claims for 19th century Zimbabwe: "There were no rules of succession in Shona chiefships in the nineteenth century and...successful contenders depended upon force and fraud and the backing of a powerful faction in a constant competition with other contenders and factions for power and spoils. Land

was part of the spoils of the victor in these competitions, along with cattle and women and other captives of war; the members of the losing faction lost their lands and fled to the shelter of a rival chiefdom" (1993, p. 356, quoting David Beach).

Collapsing Livelihoods and the Crisis of Masculinity in Rural Kenya

10

MARY AMUYUNZU–NYAMONGO AND PAUL FRANCIS

hanges in gender roles and relations in Kenya have been occurring since the onset of colonialism, yet they have been particularly marked since the mid–1980s especially with regard to normative masculinity. There are several reasons for this, including intensifying poverty and inequality, increasing unemployment, the erosion of livelihood systems, and women's changing role in providing for the household. These changes affect relative gender power relations in the household. Empowerment has been defined as a process by which the powerless gain greater control over their life circumstances, including control over resources (physical, human, intellectual, and financial) and ideology (beliefs, values, and attitudes; Batliwala 1994). It implies not only greater extrinsic control but also a growing intrinsic capability—great self-confidence and an inner transformation of conscience that enables an individual to overcome external barriers to accessing resources or changing traditional ideology (Sen and Batliwala 2000, p. 18). Empowerment is also a social action process that promotes the participation of people, organizations, and communities in gaining control over their lives (Jejeebhoy 2000, p. 205). Empowerment is therefore a dynamic term, encompassing both process and the result of that process (Batliwala 1994). It is also a collective, as well as an individual, process. As discussed in this chapter, rural Kenyan men have experienced the reverse of empowerment in the last two decades. Disempowerment is understood in this context as a process that has resulted in men's loss of power over the circumstances of their lives, mainly due to changes in livelihoods. This has affected their self-esteem and decreased their ability to overcome barriers to self actualization.

Despite the aspirations and progress of the 1960s and 1970s, Kenya's economy stagnated starting in the early 1980s, largely due to adverse world prices for its cash crops, corruption, mismanagement, and failure of the government to identify and support indigenous institutions and capacity (UNDP 2005b). Disappointing economic growth, which was well below Kenya's population growth, was compounded by increased vulnerability of the population, rising unemployment, and reduced access to basic services. Pastoral communities came under increasing pressure, while migration opportunities were limited by growing unemployment. The level of income poverty reached 57 percent in 2004; UNDP's Human Development Index for Kenya declined from 0.533 in 1990 to 0.520 in 2004 (UNDP 2005b). The increased hardship, however, has not been shared equally among Kenyans. According to UNDP, Kenya is the world's fourth most unequal society, with the top 10 percent controlling 48 percent of national income. And according to participants in the study, "the rich are getting richer while the poor are getting poorer" (UNDP 2005b).

This chapter utilizes data collected between February and May 2005 as part of a national study on social vulnerability in Kenya. During the study, the research team was struck by the different ways in which men and women have responded to economic crises and the impact these changes are having on relations within the household. The capacity of men to support the household appears to have been eroded by the undermining of livelihood systems. As women have taken on increasing responsibilities for household provisioning, men appear to have opted out. Although the household is the unit of analysis, gender is the variable used to examine the impacts of these changes, especially on gender-based and intergenerational violence and general community criminal activities. The overall aim of the chapter is to provide a broader understanding of factors that contribute to the marginalization of men and ultimately to their disempowerment. The analysis indicates that men have been and continue to be sidelined in development, especially the poor in rural areas. This marginalization has led to their disempowerment. Men's efforts to reassert themselves include, in some cases, turning to violence to reassert their masculinity. It is the contention of the authors that strategies aimed at empowering women may be creating new forms of vulnerabilities for them and that these should be redressed if meaningful social and economic development is to be realized, especially in rural areas. The concept of masculinity should be reconstructed to fit new socioeconomic realities, taking into account women's empowerment, migratory labor, HIV/AIDS, and unemployment. A different perception of manhood is necessary to empower men to live differently and to become more responsive to household and community needs within a changing socioeconomic context.

The Changing Context of Masculinity in Kenya

> Precisely because of patriarchal structures working to the detriment of women, hardly any attempts have been made to investigate and analyze the impact of socioeconomic change on men's lives, and how men are dealing with their new situation (Silberschmidt 2001, p. 658).

The realization in traditional gender discourse that men's issues have been neglected has led in recent years to a growing body of literature on masculinity in Sub-Saharan Africa. Men have traditionally been depicted as being at the center of development, while women are at the margin. Although this may be true in many contexts, it represents a stereotype that has led to a skewed development focus and exclusive attention to women because of their presumed vulnerability. Traditionally, elderly men commanded respect, dispensed rights to land, and were at the top of the social hierarchy, and were followed in decreasing order of power by other adult men, uninitiated young men, boys, women, and girls. In pastoral communities, for instance, old men had control over land use and cattle, and thus over young men as well, a fact that has also been reported in other Sub-Saharan African countries. For example, as Townsend observes, "From the point of view of a man in rural Botswana, moving through the life course is a process of negotiating a way through a series of overlapping and competing claims for the products of his labor" (1997, p. 419).

The concentration of power in the hands of the generation of older men continues to affect people in Kenya and in other parts of Sub-Saharan Africa, leading to ongoing power struggles between older and young men.[1] In parts of Namibia, for example, male power was vested in men who had their own livestock, i.e., those who were senior and performed the social roles of fathers (Lindsay and Miescher 2003). Women, in this case, were a source (but not the only source) of power for men. Male power in most Kenyan communities has been steeped in patriarchy that traditionally has been reinforced through rites of passage, bride wealth payments, and patrilocal residence. However, changes in the communities are challenging traditional norms. For instance, although bride wealth payments and patriarchal residence rules are still prevalent, their enforcement is being challenged by pervasive socioeconomic changes that are affecting all aspects of people's lives. These changes, however, are occurring within long-established patriarchal systems that are built on many years of socialization and enculturation and that retain the notion that men exert dominant power over households and communities. Women have also been socialized to believe in this power and their own subordination, contradictions that are discussed below taking into account their increasing role in household survival. Dolan (2003b) observes that precolonial, colonial, and postcolonial messages led to a normative model of masculinity that set stereotypes of what women and men are like, what they should do, how they should relate, and what their respective positions and roles in society should be. A number of researchers point out that men's ability to achieve some of the key elements in the normative model of masculinity into which they have been socialized has been severely reduced (Silberschmidt 2001; Dolan 2003b; Luyt 2005). For most men, however, it is difficult to acknowledge the increasing role of women in their households and in society, although they recognize that women are taking on more responsibilities. This chapter looks at these changes in rural communities in Kenya in an effort to better understand the wide-ranging effects of collapsing livelihoods on gender roles, i.e., moving the debate from economics to more intrinsic levels of household survival and relations.

Analytical Framework and Methodology

The study adopts a three-pronged conceptual framework. It looks at drivers, impacts, and responses to the changes in masculinity occurring in Kenya.

Drivers

The most important of the changing conditions faced by rural households in the last two decades, drivers, have often undermined rural livelihood systems. The working hypothesis is that the role of men has been rendered ineffective by an interlocking set of processes, including pressures on livelihoods and assets (for example, declining agricultural and pastoral economies and the decline or collapse of markets and marketing institutions), higher exposure to risk, and women's increasing contribution to the economy.

Impact

Impact of changes is traced to the household level in terms of increasing challenges and stresses that have had an influence on gender and intergenerational relations. The drivers and impacts enumerated in this chapter have continued to add to the domestic and economic burden of women. With the erosion of their customary roles and economic disempowerment, men often withdraw from an active role in household provisioning and planning. The resulting strains are reflected in growing levels of conflict in households, including violence against women. At the same time, tension between parents and their children has increased because youth have few productive or legitimate outlets. Conflicts increasingly arise as parents perceive their children as taking little responsibility for contributing to the household, while youth (particularly young men) see the older generation as incapable of devolving control of household resources to the next generation or unable to provide viable role models. The fact that access to employment opportunities is determined by reasons other than merit creates further strain on the households, especially when the fathers do not have the necessary connections to access jobs or places in institutions of higher learning.

Response

The third element of the conceptual model is response, which defines the way in which households and communities have actively responded, positively and negatively, to drivers and impacts. The responses addressed in this chapter include alcohol brewing and consumption and depression; fear and anger are also discussed as responses by women toward men's disempowerment.

It is evident that social value is fundamental to both men's and women's identity, self-esteem, and to gender and intergenerational relations (Silberschmidt 2001). Several authors (including Cornwall and Lindisfarne 1994; Connell 1995; Bourdieu 1998; Silberschmidt 2001) have shown linkages between masculinity,

Table 10.1 **Study Sites in the Six Districts**

District	Division	Cluster
Isiolo	Garba Tulla	Manyatta Demo
	Kinna	Rapsu
	Central	Bulla Pesa
Nakuru	Rongai	Bongoloa
	Keringet	Chemaner
	Kuresoi	Tiloa
Bungoma	Kanduyi	Namasanda
	Chwele	Kilimani
	Sirisia	Kimabole
Kisii	Suneka	Bogiakumu
	Masaba	Ramacha
	Marani	Gesonso
Kiambu	Limuru	Ngecha
	Githunguri	Karia
	Kikuyu	Kiamburi
Kwale	Matuga	Mazu Malume
	Kubo	Tiribe
	Kinango	Ndavaya

Source: Authors.

sexuality, and manifestations of sexual power and violence. There is also recognition that masculinity, like femininity, is always subject to internal contradictions and historical disruptions.

The study was conducted in six districts representing six provinces of Kenya: Isiolo (Eastern), Nakuru (Rift Valley), Bungoma (Western), Kisii (Nyanza), Kiambu (Central), and Kwale (Coast). Three clusters were selected, in consultation with district leaders and research teams, to represent the study districts, as shown in table 10.1.

The main criteria for selecting the clusters was diversity of livelihood sources (crops versus livestock, ecological zones, and distance from the district headquarters). A combination of quantitative and qualitative tools was used to collect data. A range of participatory tools was used to gather qualitative data, including in-depth interviews with key informants, focus group discussions (FGDs), social and institutional mapping, gender analysis, pair-wise matrix ranking, and participant observations. In total, 51 FGDs involving groups of women, men, and male and female youth were conducted. All the groups were segregated along gender lines to allow for free discussions, and all the FGDs were tape-recorded and later transcribed and translated into English. Case studies were also collected paying special attention to the drivers, impacts and responses to the various socioeconomic changes experienced by the communities. The qualitative tools were complemented by quantitative data collected through an interviewer-based questionnaire administered to 710 people in the six districts. Slightly over half of the respondents were male, close to two-thirds had attained up to primary education, and over 70 percent were not in gainful employment. In addition, data generated by Kenya's Central Bureau of Statistics (CBS) were analyzed to capture reports on domestic violence.[2]

Data were collected over a period of slightly more than two months (February 27 to May 3, 2005). Prior to data collection, the research teams visited the various district offices and the communities for mobilization. The teams spent six working days in each district. The morning of the first day was spent in discussions with the district commissioners and other senior staff to gather an overview of development issues in the district. After this meeting, the study teams traveled to their first cluster where they spent the day collecting qualitative data. In each of the clusters, community members converged at a central place (school, dispensary, tea factory, or church), where they engaged in focus group discussions, in-depth interviews, and the participatory activities. On the second day, the research teams went from house to house conducting one-on-one interviews. Being in one cluster for two consecutive days allowed the research teams to follow up on issues that may have been left pending during the qualitative data collection process and to collect or complete case studies.

Development Changes Shaping Household Relations

All six districts involved in the study have experienced varying degrees of socioeconomic change since the mid-1980s (or for longer) due to the nature and form of the main livelihood sources. Kisii district is one of the most fertile areas in Kenya and the most densely populated rural district. The main source of livelihood is agricultural products: tea, coffee, and pyrethrum (a type of flower). The main livelihood activity for Bungoma district is also crop farming. There, sugar, maize, and, in limited amounts, coffee are grown. Some parts of Nakuru district are fertile, while others (including Bongoloa, one of the clusters in the study) are semiarid. The main form of livelihood is agriculture (pyrethrum, tea, horticulture, and livestock). Kiambu is known for its large tea and coffee farms, and for its dairy farms. Kwale is less agriculturally productive than the other four districts but it is linked to the tourism economy on the coast. Farmers in Kwale produce coconuts, cashew nuts, and an assortment of fruits (including mangoes, oranges, and lemons) for local and export markets. The inhabitants of Isiolo are pastoralists whose fortunes have changed over time due to insecurity and drought, conditions that have limited crop farming in parts of the district.

Changes in Sources of Livelihood

A high proportion of Kenyans (65 percent) live in rural areas, where agriculture remains the most important source of livelihood (CBS and GOK 2001). Agriculture, however, has undergone major changes since the mid-1980s that have led to a general decline in the quantity and quality of goods produced locally. For example, it is estimated that the downturn in the coffee industry has affected 5 million rural households in Kenya. The study participants observed that the coffee industry is not performing well because of arguments among farmers, poor performance of the cooperative movement, and political interference. While private farmers are able to sell their coffee directly, the marketing for small-scale producers has been problematic to the extent that some demoralized farmers have uprooted coffee trees or have planted other crops, including maize, legumes, and vegetables, between the coffee trees in Kisii, Kiambu, and Bungoma districts.

Although the sugar industry provides direct employment to 35,000 workers, is a major income source for 100,000 small-scale farmers, and supports over 2 million people in western Kenya, it has also suffered a decline (UNDP 2005b). The industry is associated with rampant corruption, official complacency fueled by inappropriate policies, poor internal management, and heavy taxation, all of which have negatively impacted poor farmers. Sugarcane, the most important cash crop in Bungoma district, is mainly grown under contract with large companies. Farmers sign a five-year, three-harvest contract with the company, under which the company provides farmers with inputs and implements but harvests the cane itself. Farmers are responsible for planting, weeding, and managing the crop. At harvest time, deductions are made for the services provided by the companies. Farmers involved in our study complained that these deductions are not explained to them in advance and some felt they were being conned.

The pyrethrum subsector has suffered almost complete collapse. Although Kenya was once the world's largest producer of pyrethrum, with 65 percent of global production (followed by Australia), its production has declined from an annual production of 17,710 tons of dry flowers in 1992/93 to about 7,000 tons in 1997/98, despite favorable international prices (CBS and GOK 2001). The Board owes farmers in excess of K Sh 1.2 billion (equivalent to $16 million), which has left many farmers impoverished.

Radical and permanent changes in the livelihoods of pastoralists in Isiolo district date from the tragedy of the *Shifta* war.[3] Although this conflict took place in the mid-1960s, male study participants perceived it to be the single most important driver affecting their ability to fulfill their obligations. It is estimated that the war claimed about 40 percent of the population (based on in-depth interviews with the retired chief and on FGDs with male participants). The Boran pastoralists lost almost all their livestock during the conflict to consumption, destruction by the security forces, and diseases contracted during confinement. Without livestock at the end of the war, most pastoralists were forced to learn new coping mechanisms: farming, charcoal and wood selling, and casual labor. Subsequent banditry and cattle rustling activities further impoverished communities. The collapse of the Kenya Meat Commission, a state marketing enterprise that cushioned farmers during the dry season, was seen by the community as a final blow to their fledgling pastoral economy.

A downturn in the marketing of agricultural products also had an adverse effect on rural livelihoods. In Kenya, market institutions were organized as farmer cooperatives, which also served as a link between the farmers and national institutions. Government boards controlled the processing and marketing of farm produce. Some of these marketing institutions were created as legally constituted corporations and operated as monopolies with dual marketing and regulatory roles. Examples include the Coffee Board of Kenya, the Pyrethrum Board of Kenya, and the Kenya Meat Commission. Most of these institutions, largely controlled and managed by men, were one-stop shops for farmers that provided services ranging from transportation of the produce to banking. These institutions offered important advantages to farmers, including price stability and access to international markets. (International markets would have been extremely difficult or impossible for small-scale farmers and cooperatives to reach without these institutions.) These large public entities, however, were generally managed by incompetent and corrupt political appointees and failed to adapt to the changes brought about by globalization and new business practices. As these large parastatals failed, the cooperative movement declined, affecting mainly the small-scale farmers, some of whom have sunk deeper into poverty.

Farmers have also been affected by increases in agricultural input prices that have outstripped output prices, exerting further pressure on poor rural households. For instance, a farmer in Ngecha (Kiambu district) reported that in the 1980s, farmers earned K Sh 18.70 for a kilogram[4] of milk but the same cooperative society currently pays K Sh 15.00. Ironically, the cost of dairy feed in the 1980s was K Sh. 300–400 but the same feed currently costs K Sh 900–1,000. How does a farmer provide for his family without a viable income?

HIV/AIDS also exerts enormous pressure on rural livelihoods. Kenya's HIV prevalence of 6.7 percent makes it one of the most affected countries in the world (CBS et al. 2004). Although women have higher infection rates than men across all age groups, HIV/AIDS destabilizes many areas of society—including employment, health systems, agriculture, mining, transport, and marketing. There are also important macroeconomic effects, including the effects of HIV/AIDS on government revenues and expenditures, and the government's ability to make progress toward achieving the Millennium Development Goals (UNAIDS 2004).

Changes in the Form and Content of the Marriage Contract

The form and content of the marriage contract have been changing since the mid-1980s. The constitutional recognition of three types of unions—cultural, legal, and religious—has reduced the power base of men. The rising cases of "come-we-stay" (informal) unions are posing further challenges, especially to patriarchy. Indeed, as more young people find it difficult to pay bride wealth, which is a common thread in the six districts studied, the more prevalent are come-we-stay unions. Furthermore, with increasing exposure and interaction among the youth, inter-marriages are becoming common, which is weakening some cultural mores. Marriages that are not sanctioned through bride wealth sometimes deny men traditional rights over women. Under these circumstances, the women are better placed to exercise autonomy than those for whom bride wealth has been paid (Kibwana and Mute 2000). Furthermore, although the changing context of marriage challenges traditional norms, it is also creating new vulnerabilities for young women and men, particularly for the poor.

In Isiolo, Bungoma, and Kwale districts, where polygamy is widely practiced, young men decried that young women were married off to elderly men able to pay bride wealth while they are left pondering their own fate. Several cases were cited in Isiolo district of young girls aged 16–18 being married off to men aged over 80. Even though the girls were against the marriages, they had no option because the elderly men had already paid bride wealth (Barker and Ricardo 2005). The younger women, however, have some measure of power in their households because they are better able to move around in search of livelihood, which makes the men dependent on them. A young women in Isiolo district looked at her elderly husband and remarked, "He married me because he wanted someone to work for him. He stays at home while I go to the forest to get wood for sale or to burn charcoal. If I do not do that we would all starve to death."

Although traditionally polygamy was a status symbol, our study indicates that polygamous men are some of the most isolated people in their households. The potential for conflict between children and their fathers is also higher in polygamous households.

Development Focus on Women

One of the significant changes that has occurred over time is the role and place of women in their households and communities at large. As they become increasingly responsible for their household's income, women acquire a new awareness, autonomy, and feeling of self-worth (Silberschmidt 2001). Indeed, women are beginning to demand their own space, which is an indication of a significant reduction of men's power. Through the efforts of development agencies that focus on gender empowerment, emancipation of women, girl-child protection, and affirmative action, women are acquiring status that can no longer be ignored even by the men in their households. It is notable that when women have access to their own income, they become more assertive because they are more aware of their pivotal role in the household. Women have been found to be better able to form and work in groups compared to men, which gives them access to labor, information and credit that they invest in their households and on their own development. Through such groups women have been able to gain access to information on a number of areas, including family planning, investment and credit opportunities, and improved health practices, which is not always available to men (Boulay and Valente 1999). Women's groups are especially effective in conveying information on gender empowerment and women's rights, which can further strengthen women's sense of empowerment (Mwenzwa 2004).

Women who are engaged in social groups reported that even with meager incomes, they were able to pay for their children's schooling and to meet their household needs, while men's contribution to these areas remained minimal and sometimes absent. Women depicted themselves as hard working while men were portrayed as lazy and unwilling to do certain kinds of jobs, including child care and working on other people's farms. What emerged from the discussions in all the districts was the fact that although women may be structurally subordinate to men, they have found ways to survive in a changing environment and have gained some control over their lives. As men have withdrawn from their traditional responsibilities amid socioeconomic changes, women have acquired new roles as they seek to survive. It is important to note, however, that although some men were considered responsible by women, they tended to be religious men, and those with formal employment who seemed to care and provide for their households, i.e., they were able to practice normative masculinity.

Male Disempowerment and Women's Vulnerability

The inability of many men to fulfill expected roles in their households and communities has led to significant changes in all six districts in the study. These changes, in what has traditionally been a male domain, have resulted in shifts in gender and intergenerational interactions. "Women were in the past submissive and respectful to their spouses compared to now" was a view expressed by men in all study sites. The respondents reminisced about the past when children respected their parents and parents fulfilled their obligations. Alongside the socioeconomic changes that have occurred in Kenya, women's participation in formal and informal labor markets has increased, thus contributing significantly to household incomes (UNDP 2005b).

Discussions with women and men suggest that once a household's means of primary livelihood changes, men's role as household provider is reduced as women look for alternative survival means. Because of the forces underlying changing livelihoods, under which male economic activities are often eroded and new female opportunities develop, women are better placed to adapt to livelihood changes. Table 10.2 presents responses by study participants in Manyatta Demo (Isiolo district) regarding the economic activities undertaken by men and women as presented by a group of women during a gender analysis exercise.

It is clear from table 10.2 that the women were engaged in a range of activities from which they earned some form of income. Most of these activities were small scale (for example, collection of wild fruits) but essential for the survival of their households. Women also participate in activities that have traditionally been considered men's domain, such as burning charcoal, collection of herbal medicine, and shopkeeping, implying that women are more flexible and have greater scope to generate alternative incomes compared to their male counterparts. The same trend was observed in Nakuru, especially in pyrethrum-growing areas. Men were more affected by the failure of the pyrethrum industry compared to the women, one of whom stated that "the children have to eat and attend school." Women, in other words, believe that they have to work to generate the income to meet their households' basic needs.

Table 10.2 Economic Activities in Manyatta Demo (adult females)

Activities	Men	Women	Both
Charcoal burning and selling			√
Miraa selling			√[1]
Firewood selling		√	
Mat and basket weaving		√	
Livestock marketing			√[1]
Wild fruit and berry collecting		√	
Vegetable selling		√	
Shopkeeping			√
Ornaments and cultural artifacts, producing and selling			√[1]
Herbal medicine collecting and selling			√[1]
Honey selling	√		
Building materials selling			√
Egg selling		√	
Milk selling[2]		√	
Bread making[3]		√	

Source: Authors.
1. Activities are mainly undertaken by women.
2. Women buy milk from Somalis and sell it in the community.
3. A women's group in Manyatta Demo bakes bread.

The diversification in agriculture and income-generating activities seems to have favored women. For example, in Nakuru, as farmers have shifted from traditional cash crops, which are the responsibility of men, they have turned to potato and vegetable farming, which are entrusted to women. Pastoralists who have been forced to make changes in their way of life have adopted farming, gathering of wild fruit, or small-scale trade, activities that are mainly undertaken by women. In some districts, such as Bungoma and Nakuru, respondents indicated that it is easier for women to get casual jobs compared to men, perhaps because they are perceived as more trustworthy or are able to do a variety of chores concurrently, including cooking, caring for children, and other household activities.

What was evident in all the districts was the ability of women, unlike their male counterparts, to organize themselves into groups. Group membership allows individuals to save money, which is later used as capital to initiate income-generating activities for women, even if those activities are only small-scale. As the options available to men narrow, women seem to have a resilience that allows them to cope with the changing circumstances and lack of labor market opportunities. Women's role in the community has also been enhanced by development agencies that require their increased participation in development initiatives and through increased literacy and funds allocated for women's empowerment (Atieno 2001). Moreover, it is no longer natural or acceptable for women's groups to be headed by men. Although clearly not all women belong to groups and not all groups are effective or productive, there has been a marked increase in the number of women's groups in Kenya since the mid-1980s (Toulis 1990). These groups often play an important role in supporting and helping communities to cope with changing work opportunities.

In all the districts except Isiolo, people expressed sentiments to the effect that children favored their mothers (while alienating their fathers). For the women, the logic was simple: "The children see us struggling to feed, clothe and educate them, while their fathers are either doing nothing much or spend most of the day idling or taking alcohol." Children were therefore increasingly turning to their mothers for material and emotional support. Women also emerged as more concerned with the education of their children compared to men, who seemed more skeptical of the merits of education given increased competition and high unemployment. In Nakuru, Kwale, and Isiolo districts, it emerged that once a girl completes primary schooling (grade 8), she is deemed by adults ready for marriage. Any further investment in her education was considered largely a waste of resources. Women perceive the education of their sons as a key to future well-being or as an investment for old age, although they also perceive that men were doing little for their households. In this paradox of normative masculinity, although their partners may be failing in their duties, women hoped that their sons would be different in adulthood and that they would make a greater contribution to household livelihoods than their fathers. Education of children beyond the secondary level varied between districts. Parents in Kisii and Kiambu were more likely than parents in other districts to educate both boys and girls, which may be explained by higher socioeconomic development in these districts.

Although women are increasingly involved in generating household income, men still control most household spending decisions. This presents an obvious contradiction in roles and responsibilities (Mwenzwa 2004). Dolan (2003b) notes that even as traditional male roles—father, protector, and provider—become harder to fulfill, they do not become less desirable; on the contrary, they become more desirable as they provide anchors and points of leverage in the midst of economic, social, and political uncertainty. This implies that as men become less able to provide for their households, they are more likely to cling to their decision-making role and to seek to stamp their authority on the household.

The contradiction in male and female control over resources is illustrated by an incident in Bungoma district. While in a discussion with a women's group, the owner of the shop in which the meeting was taking place described the process to acquire a loan from the Kenya Women's Finance Trust in order to build a small shop. The loan required a woman to obtain her husband's signature because he was holder of the title deed to the land. At that very moment, her husband was talking to a male researcher, telling him how he had put up a shop for his wife, taking credit for his wife's initiative. In another discussion, members of a women's group told the research team that while they were responsible for everything in their households. their husbands took credit for the achievements. Women bought clothes, paid school fees, and supplemented food supplies, while their husbands whiled their time away socializing or drinking. In one group in Bungoma district, an elderly woman said that she supported her sons' families because her sons were jobless. The research team sought clarification regarding the women's views from a group of married men. In response, one of the participants noted, "She is my wife. I paid bride wealth. She uses my land and lives in my house free of charge. Therefore, if she buys sugar, I have bought it and if she buys a cow it is mine."

The same sentiment was reported in Kiambu, where a male participant informed the research team that sometimes men return home empty handed in the evening after failing to get casual employment to find women preparing good food (for example, *chapati*, rice and beef stew). Although the men knew that another man must have paid for the food, they eat it because they have no options. Similar incidents—of women being obliged to have liaisons with butchers or other traders to ensure that there was food on the table—were narrated in Kisii and Kwale districts. Women seemed to be driven to such desperate and risky strategies to generate income by the need to avoid violence from their spouses. Some women even bought cigarettes and alcohol for their husbands for the sake of peace in their households. Men's economic dependence on their spouses, however, seems to exacerbate their violent behavior toward women.

Domestic Violence

Domestic violence is a major problem in all the districts. Men cited culture as a reason permitting them to "discipline" their wives, and women to have accepted this as a way of life. A key male informant in Rapsu (Isiolo district) noted, "Nowadays women have a lot of liberties. In the past they were not allowed to talk in the presence of their spouses, they had to wait until later when they were just the two of them for the men to explain issues to them."

Domestic violence was explored in detail during the 2003 Kenya Demographic and Health Survey (CBS et al. 2003). The data were reanalyzed for this study and the results on women's experience of violence are presented in table 10.3. It is clear from the data presented that domestic violence transcends all social and demographic characteristics, including education and employment. In Nakuru, both emotional (E) and physical (P) violence were more frequent among women who had completed secondary schooling and above, while physical violence was higher among those in gainful employment. Women who were wealthier encountered higher levels of physical violence. In Bungoma, women with limited education encountered more emotional violence than those with higher education, while women with higher education suffered more physical violence than women with limited education. In Kisii, both emotional and physical violence were high for all categories of women, although women in gainful employment encountered more physical than emotional abuse. In Kiambu, there were fewer reports of violence among well-educated women, and physical violence was more frequent than emotional. In Kwale, violence was high for women who were employed. The findings

Table 10.3 Marital Violence[1]

Characteristic	Nakuru E	Nakuru P	Bungoma E	Bungoma P	Kisii E	Kisii P	Kiambu E	Kiambu P	Kwale E	Kwale P
Marital status										
Currently married	25.7	28.5	50.9	69.0	37.1	55.2	11.9	28.3	19.5	23.0
Once	24.5	27.5	51.8	68.3	34.2	53.1	11.7	28.0	20.5	17.7
More than once	51.7	51.7	39.1	78.9	61.7	73.5	15.2	35.1	17.5	33.3
Divorced/separated	55.5	55.9	23.7	82.2	65.4	65.1	46.5	66.6	37.8	17.4
Educational attainment										
No education	28.7	10.2	29.9	10.0	42.0	69.2	0.0	0.0	33.2	25.9
Primary	25.9	25.3	52.4	74.7	38.5	52.9	19.3	44.0	14.4	21.5
Incomplete	23.7	22.6	52.9	79.6	48.4	64	31.5	48.2	16.5	24.3
Complete	28.2	28.3	51.4	64.2	23.5	35.9	9.8	40.7	6.6	11.4
Secondary +	33.7	46.0	42.4	51.4	47.2	66.9	16.7	28.5	0.0	0.0
Incomplete	29.4	36.0	59.2	68.6	53.9	79.7	21.1	41.0	0.0	0.0
Complete	25.9	42.2	19.3	25.9	41.6	56.9	13.6	29.2	0.0	0.0
Completed +	36.3	52.2	18.7	27.3	29.4	33.0	14.9	23.1	0.0	0.0
Higher	56.7	71.9	16.9	31.4	18.8	12.1	17.0	13.1	0.0	0.0
Employment status										
Employed for cash	27.7	39.9	52.4	56.9	38.3	56.3	19.5	37.7	32.8	29.1
Employed, not for cash	26.9	25.6	48.9	80.6	34.4	56.9	16.0	37.2	4.6	15.2
Not employed	30.8	23.2	41.4	73.9	50.3	55.8	14.9	26.4	14.1	17.4
Wealth index										
Poorest	0.0	0.0	51.3	80.1	60.8	77.1	0.0	0.0	26.1	32.5
Middle	7.2	17.9	43.0	71.9	43.1	61.8	35.5	46.7	23.2	30.3
Richer	41.9	28.0	57.6	66.1	14.7	28.8	18.6	38.0	18.3	15.6
Richest	29.6	46.8	43.4	33.4	30.6	54.7	13.8	30.5	0.0	0.0
Total	28.8	31.3	48.9	70.0	40.2	56.3	17.7	34.7	21.4	22.4

Source: CBS, Ministry of Health, and ORC Macro (2004).

1. Table measures percentage of married, divorced, or separated women who have ever suffered emotional (E) or physical or sexual violence (P) at the hands of their current/last husband according to selected background characteristics. Data for Isiolo District were not analyzed because the sample was too small.

illustrate the potential tension between the contribution of a working woman to her household's income and the challenge this may pose to the man. Violence may arise due to a woman's relative independence and feelings of worthiness, which may be at odds with the man's ego and sense of social value. The sense of irrelevance faced by men whose wives are educated or in gainful employment, coupled with poverty, undermines men's self-esteem and may lead to disruptive behavior intended to "put the woman in her rightful place" (Dolan 2003b).

The study participants in Bungoma and Kisii districts referred to violence against women as cultural and a form of discipline. A male respondent in Bungoma noted that "a woman must be beaten by the man to instill respect and a sense of discipline." Women expressed the view that once bride wealth had been paid and the couple had children, there was nothing they could do other than persevere. Thus, domestic violence is largely a power play with the men exerting their authority. It is presumed that as women gain more economic independence, men's domestic violence increases to "put them in their rightful place." The extreme position accepted by some women was expressed by a participant when she noted that "my husband is my god on earth, even if he beats me there is nothing I can do." This woman was at that time responsible for all household needs (while her husband was a renowned local drunk), but she still seemed to hold him in high esteem. Men can still rely on gender ideology to shore up their waning position in the household, although they may not be fulfilling their marital and parental responsibilities. This observation reinforces the notion that men must conquer and dominate even when they are not meeting societal expectations commensurate with the community definition of masculinity. The case of Esther Cheptoo in box 10.1 illustrates the difficult situations some women find themselves in. The harder they try to provide for the household, the more difficult it becomes for them to cope with the men in their households, reflecting a resistance toward the woman's achievements, more so if they are earning more money than men.

Box 10.1 Family Conflict

Esther Cheptoo is 24 years old. She is a second wife and a mother of seven children. Her parents arranged her marriage to a man who operates a kiosk at a shopping center. She belongs to a merry-go-round group that meets every Thursday. Although she works hard to till the small piece of land and cultivate potatoes and maize, her husband takes all the proceeds. She is often beaten when she complains but she perseveres for the sake of her children. In fact, her husband sold the only milk cow she had and used the money to purchase locally-brewed alcohol. When she complained, she was beaten thoroughly. She has regular conflicts with her cowife, with whom she shares a compound. She complained that her husband always sides with the first wife.

The changing roles of women and men was identified by FGD participants as an issue of concern to both sexes, but more so to men who felt they were not "as powerful as they used to be in the past." In some parts of Nakuru, the collapse of the pyrethrum industry left many men without viable income-generation options. Although the women and children took care of the pyrethrum farms when the sector was still vibrant, men managed the income by virtue of owning the land. The situation has since changed. The shift in agricultural production to potatoes, peas, and vegetables has reduced men's control over resources, since these are considered women's crops. Furthermore, these crops do not generate as much income as pyrethrum and are not absorbed into an institutionalized marketing structure. When asked what the impact of the collapse of the industry has been on men, women cited increased alcohol consumption. One woman said, "The men are idle most of the time and end up spending their time and the meager household resources on alcohol." A female FGD participant in Nakuru stated that when her husband comes home after drinking alcohol, the children run away for fear of violence. Essentially, women have been left to fend for themselves and their children, and many women are in constant fear of violence at the hands of husbands.

Alcohol Consumption

Alcohol brewing and consumption are responses that have been adopted by communities in the face of collapsing livelihoods. Male youth and adult men are the main consumers of alcohol, as opposed to the past, when elderly men were the main consumers. When asked to consider the trend in alcohol consumption, respondents in all sites

---

Box 10.2 Case on Male Dominance

Caroline is a mother of eight. Her youngest child is four years old. Her husband, a construction worker, is a heavy drinker of locally-brewed alcohol. Some of her sons ran away from home due to quarrels with their father. Her daughters got married just after being circumcised. Caroline cannot start any business, despite living very near the shopping center, because her husband will not allow her to. When he comes home in the evening drunk, he quarrels very loudly so that even the neighbors hear. He always complains of being hungry and wants to be served immediately when he gets into the house. He insults everyone he meets along the way and sometimes batters his wife and children. Caroline takes care of her father-in-law who is blind and cannot fend for himself. Although Caroline feels the need to engage in income-generating activities to cater for the needs of her large household, she is unable to do so because of her husband. She is terrified of him, while her children are not in a position to provide any substantive support because they are no longer at home or they are insufficiently educated to obtain any meaningful form of employment.

noted that it was on the increase among men. This could be due to three main factors: (a) men have become increasingly idle and therefore pass the time drinking; (b) women have turned to alcohol brewing in order to make a living, thus inadvertently increasing the amount and reducing the price of alcohol in the community; or (c) due to poverty, men can only afford local brews, which has enhanced the popularity of these drinks. Whatever the case, both men and women linked alcohol abuse to underdevelopment, crime, intergenerational tensions, and gender-based violence. Box 10.2 illustrates the role of alcohol in household disintegration and distress. The man may be consuming alcohol in attempt to cover up his inadequacies, and his aggression may be a means to cope with his failure as a husband and father or his inability to care for his own father. In Nakuru and Kiambu, women narrated stories of men who went out drinking in the evening and came home late, demanding food and sex. These women have therefore begun to prepare their children's meals early in the evening, before their husbands return and disrupt the household.

Depression

The study also explored depression as a consequence of social and economic change. This issue was investigated by assessing participants' personal, household, and community experience with depression. Table 10.4 presents responses to four questions asked of participants in the study: Are there people in your community who are depressed? Have you ever been depressed? Has any member of your household experienced depression? Do you know anyone (personally) with depression?

The results show a high proportion of reported depression in all the communities involved in the study but fewer reports of personal depression. The numbers of males and females who reported ever having suffered depression was similar. On average, cases of personal depression were highest in Kiambu, followed by Isiolo and Bungoma districts. It is, however, important to note that the differences in

Table 10.4 **Reports of Depression by District (percent in community)**

District	Presence of depressed people in community	Ever been depressed	Household member ever been depressed	Know someone who is depressed
Isiolo	65.3	41.3	33.1	52.9
Nakuru	61.9	28.0	28.0	48.3
Bungoma	56.1	34.1	31.7	46.3
Kisii	68.1	33.6	28.6	54.6
Kiambu	90.0	58.3	61.7	74.2
Kwale	56.9	27.5	26.6	35.8
Total	66.3	37.1	35.0	52.0

Source: Authors.

Table 10.5 **Causes of Depression by District
(percentage of responses)**

District	Poverty/lack of finance	Social pressures	Domestic violence	Unemployment	Sickness	Hunger
Isiolo	17.6	3.9	3.3	2.2	5.5	2.9
Nakuru	16.9	4.8	7.3	6.8	4.5	2.5
Bungoma	20.6	3.8	8.1	5.7	4.1	0.8
Kisii	14.8	2.5	13.7	1.4	3.6	1.7
Kiambu	24.4	2.2	6.1	15.6	10.3	2.8
Kwale	21.4	2.4	5.8	4.3	4.6	2.4
Total	19.9	3.2	7.9	7.2	5.4	2.2

Source: Authors.

proportions could be due to the terminologies used. Except for Bungoma and Kwale, where the researchers were able to get direct translations for depression (*chingunyi* and *mukunguru*, respectively), a collection of terms was used to describe the condition in the other districts. In Kiambu, people were asked whether "they experienced too many thoughts that could lead to illness," while in Kisii they were asked "whether they experienced deep thoughts capable of causing illness."[5] When asked to state causes of depression, participants identified finances and poverty among the leading factors (see table 10.5).

It is clear that poverty or lack of finance (expressed by the study participants as *ukosefu wa pe*, or scarcity of money) is the leading cause of depression in all the districts. This was followed by domestic violence, mainly cited in Kisii district (13.7 percent) and unemployment, reported most in Kiambu district (15.6 percent). It is important to note that hunger was not a problem in Bungoma compared to Isiolo and Nakuru districts (Bongoloa). The latter two districts experience frequent droughts and famine, which lead to perennial food insecurity. It is notable that although unemployment was reported to be high in all districts, it was not seen as an important factor in depression. This could be due to the fact that a person can earn an income without necessarily being formally employed. In FGDs, people expressed the view that with access to microfinance, they could generate income from the informal sector and thus do not necessarily require formal employment.

Although there were some reports of suicide in the communities, these were few and far between. Some cases were mentioned in Bungoma and Kwale, mainly related to scarcity of resources. All the communities involved in this study treat suicide as an abomination. The body of a person who has committed suicide is often cleansed to remove the curse from the household; the event is something that people are unwilling to discuss. This could explain the few instances of suicide reported to the research team. Perhaps to illustrate the disempowerment of male youth, a young man committed suicide because his father had disinherited him before he died—implying that the young man could not get a share of the family land.

The clan elders felt that they could not go against the wishes of the dead man and removed the boy from the list of inheritors. Without land and an education, the young man felt there was no need to continue living—disinheritance implied that he would have no base to exercise his masculinity. Having land provides a man the foundation to marry, thereby establishing his identity as an adult male and allowing him to gain control over his household.

Youth as Victims of Male Disempowerment

There is no doubt that tension between parents and their children is high in Kenya. A systematic review of media reports spanning five years (1999–2004) showed a steady increase in reported parent-children conflict. This could be due to increased media coverage or the fact that as poverty intensifies the potential for conflict increases. Thus, as more young people stay at home jobless with parents who are unable to provide for them, there is an increased likelihood of them quarreling or disagreeing over access to and use of resources. Respondents in Isiolo district indicated that the education system alienates the male youth from the traditional way of life (herding), but does not provide them with viable alternatives. Idle youth are prone to taking up drug abuse, including chewing *miraa* (khat), which causes tension at home because they can ill afford the drug. It was noted in Kisii, Bungoma, and Nakuru districts that fathers who abused alcohol had a higher chance of causing or being involved in tension and conflict at home compared to those who went to church and those in gainful employment. It was also reported that tensions between children and their parents were more likely in polygamous households, especially when one of the units felt discriminated against.

Study participants were asked to mention the causes of intergenerational violence in their communities by responding to the question, "What causes intergenerational violence in this community?" Table 10.6 summarizes the results. The results indicate that land is the leading cause of tension in Kiambu, Nakuru, and Bungoma districts, while alcohol is the driving force in Kwale and Isiolo districts. It is notable that the leading cause of tension in Kisii district is lack of school fees. As land becomes too fragmented, education emerges as an alternative investment for the community and the main source of livelihoods. Therefore, lack of access to education signifies lack of a meaningful source of livelihood, which heightens the potential for conflicts in the households.

The respondents to the questionnaire were also asked to state whether they personally knew of conflicts between parents and their children and whether they knew of intergenerational killings. All the districts showed a high incidence of parent-child conflict, with over 50 percent of respondents having knowledge of such conflicts. The highest incidence, greater than 70 percent, was in Kisii and Kiambu districts. Conflict in Kisii was mainly associated with lack of access to education, while for Kiambu it was related to financial resources. There were more killings reported in Kisii, followed by Bungoma, than in Isiolo and Nakuru, which had the least. Kisii has featured in media reports as one of the areas with high levels

Table 10.6 Causes of Intergenerational Violence
            (percentage of reports)

Cause	Kiambu (N=78)	Kwale (N=10)	Isiolo (N=5)	Kisii (N=58)	Nakuru (N=39)	Bungoma (N=40)
Lack of food	7.5	17.4	32.2	30.3	25.4	11.4
Inadequate access to livestock	0.8	3.7	12.4	7.6	15.3	6.5
Lack of access to land	65.0	9.2	4.1	48.7	33.1	32.5
Alcohol consumption	52.5	22.0	34.7	52.1	25.4	27.6
Lack of school fees	23.3	16.5	26.4	55.5	11.9	13.0
Money/finances	20.8	17.4	26.4	42.9	13.6	8.1
Arranged marriages	1.7	2.8	27.3	10.1	3.4	0.8
Parents' fighting	10.8	4.6	9.9	14.3	7.6	2.2

Source: Authors.

of domestic violence leading to loss of lives, a fact that has also been observed by Silberschmidt (2001). Other causes of conflict mentioned by youth included forced early marriages (Nakuru and Isiolo) and teenage parenthood (Kisii and Kiambu).

Perceptions held by parents regarding the youth reflect intergenerational differences. The view of a parent in Nakuru, that "children are lazy, don't work but expect to be fed ..." was common in all the districts despite respondents' acknowledgment that young people have few economic options. In Rapsu (Isiolo district), youth observed that their lives would change if a microfinance institution supported them. Although they were willing to farm commercially, they lacked farm implements and inputs. They also faced immense problems in marketing their crops due to the poor road infrastructure. Characterizing such groups as lazy would be ignoring the major challenges they face in generating income. Essentially, the collapse in livelihoods has contributed to negative perceptions between generations, which have further lowered the position of men in their communities.

Alcohol consumption and drug use by the youth were also cited as contributing to tensions, conflicts, and physical violence at home. Women in Kiambu district noted that when a young man comes home drunk, he demands food and becomes violent, thus making women victims of their sons who vent their anger and frustrations on them. It is important to note that this is the generation of future husbands and fathers who, feeling disempowered in their youth, are more likely to seek to reassert a dominant masculine role by exerting power over those around them as adults. In most cases, those around them will be women, children or subordinate males (younger males or servants).

There is evidence that violence can be a last resort for men unable to achieve normative masculinity. In a study conducted in South Africa, young and poorly educated men who strongly supported traditional masculinity were more inclined to aggression than older, well-educated men who endorsed traditional masculinity

(Luyt 2005). In our study, occurrence of violence at the community level was explored by asking participants their views regarding trends in rural criminal activities. Respondents indicated that criminal activities have increased in the last five years, accompanied by unprecedented brutality. Reports of criminals killing innocent people, destroying property, and raping women have been prevalent in the media and were cited by study participants in Bungoma and Kisii. Community members alluded to the fact that these crimes could be due to frustration, that is, an expression of anger experienced by men, mainly male youth. In Ngecha (Kiambu), a key informant noted, "We are producing clever thieves. Young people are educated up to university level but they are jobless. Such people will use their knowledge to steal or they become so frustrated to the extent of venting their anger on innocent community members."

Although insecurity in the past was mainly an urban problem, rural areas are increasingly experiencing severe forms of crime and violence. Kisii, Kiambu, and Bungoma have been highly affected by criminal activities. Poverty was cited as the main driver of crime in rural areas. Also noted was the disparity in wealth at the community level. As some people become richer others are getting poorer, feelings of unfairness and frustration increase. To redress the imbalance in wealth, some men have adopted force, which they sometimes use on innocent people.

Discussion

The data generated from this study clearly illustrates an economic decline that has greatly affected the livelihood of men and women in rural areas of Kenya. The findings also indicate that men and women have responded differently to these changes. While men have increasingly withdrawn from their traditional responsibilities because of their inability to fulfill their roles as providers, women have been forced to take on new roles under harsh conditions, if for no other reason than to ensure their and their children's survival (Silberschmidt 2001). The socioeconomic changes that have occurred since the mid-1980s have largely impacted aspects of the male domain, including cash crop farming, livestock, and formal and informal employment. In addition, the failure of cooperative societies has affected poor farmers, pushing them to the margins of survival. This is illustrated by the collapse of the pyrethrum industry and the near collapse of the coffee and sugar industries. Farmers who had invested heavily in the crops are owed large sums of money or have seen a marked decline in their incomes. Consequently, many households have withdrawn their children from school and many men have increasingly turned to alcohol consumption, leaving women to cater to household needs.

The disenfranchisement of men stems from their socialization and from expectations of themselves and the community regarding what a man should be. Although the main axis of patriarchal power is still that of male dominance, material conditions have seriously undermined the basis for men to assert themselves in the six districts. Men's authority has come under threat and, most importantly, so has their identity and sense of self esteem (Dolan 2003b; Silberschmidt 2001).

The study results indicate that although the conceptualization of masculinity has changed, men (whether as husbands or partners) still cling to the breadwinner role and their position as the household head. Men's grip on these roles has much to do with patriarchy, i.e., the unequal power relationship between them and women and control of women's behavior (Endeley and Happi 2002). However, this grip is increasingly challenged as women's roles in their households expand and as they begin to command respect from their children and society.

Men report that they are isolated in their homes and that women are "alienating their children." Most men, therefore, were lonely. This could be occurring due to a variety of factors: (a) children see and appreciate their mothers struggle to fend for the household; (b) children have been socialized to expect certain roles of their fathers and when these are not fulfilled they feel less responsive to their presence; (c) due to their own frustrations, men pull away from their households and spend more time with their friends weakening their ability to relate to their children; (d) women may take every opportunity to tell their children and remind their husbands that they are the ones doing everything for their households; and (e) women are exercising their dominance over their children. Men observed that if a woman does anything for the household, she ensures that people know that she is the one who has done it. This again could be due to socialization. As women realize they are going beyond what they are expected to do for their households, they attempt to exert some influence and to gain respect from the household members. Whatever the case, increasing dependence of households on women is leading to domestic conflicts. Indeed, women's economic independence has been shown to threaten the male ego, worthiness, and honor, leading to a marked level of tension and conflict (Dolan 2003b; Silberschmidt 2001; Connell 1995). Women who were educated and engaged in income generation were more susceptible to physical abuse—an indication that their positions threatened the men who tried to physically reassert their dominant place in the household.

Men's inability to cater to their households' needs increases the potential for conflict with their children. The fact that men are unable to create employment opportunities for their children (because access to jobs is mainly based on contacts—on a who-you-know basis) or to provide alternative means of survival creates tension in households. It is also clear that youth may not have role models in their households, especially in homes where the men drink alcohol excessively or abuse their wives, or where women are the main income earners. Men's feelings of frustration at their marginalization may lead them to aggressively dominate their children, who are the most accessible and vulnerable targets (Masanja and Urassa 1993; Silberschmidt 2001). The aggressive behavior is then transferred to young men, who in turn demand services from their mothers and other female kin. Some male youth physically confront their fathers, while others project their anger to outsiders. The high prevalence of crime in rural areas was seen as related to poverty and feelings of hopelessness among the youth. Some youth have taken up alcohol consumption, among other substances, which leads them into criminal activities to finance their needs.

Fear and anger, especially among women, were commonly expressed in all the study sites as reactions to household poverty. Fear of violence affects the ability and willingness of women to engage in income-generating activities, thereby limiting their potential to support their households and cope with collapsing livelihoods. However, women who were able to generate income for their households expressed feelings of anger against the men who were unable to fulfill their culturally-prescribed roles as household providers. Women were equally unhappy with male youth, who mirrored the behavior of their fathers and demanded support. Such anger further reinforced the men's sense of failure. Because they were unable to do what was expected of them, men felt pushed away from their homes. The fact that women were relatively closer to their children intensified men's feelings of marginalization and lack of self worth, which was then translated into domestic violence and intergenerational tension and violence. Furthermore, these were the same emotions that pushed some men into substance abuse and depression. Some women may have been driven into depression by the increased burden they shouldered and their disappointment in men, young and old, who seemed to have relinquished their household responsibilities.

Impacts of social change clearly go beyond physical consequences to psychological and to the overall quality of life of the affected individuals. Lack of employment contributes to frustrations and desperation; especially among men who have no alternative means of livelihood or whose livelihood opportunities have collapsed. Although lack of employment may spur some individuals to innovate, most young men involved in this study alluded to the fact that they were idle and unhappy with their situations. They felt alienated in their own country, and they were angry with people who were amassing wealth while they remained poor or became even more impoverished. They also alluded to corruption as hindering their ability to access employment. One young man in Isiolo expressed a widely-felt sentiment: "Jobs are given to people with connections." Corruption continues to limit Kenya's potential to serve its youth (UNDP 2005b).

Depression and alcoholism often have psychological explanations. When a man's situation in life contradicts moral and social expectations and obligations, his identity and perception of self in relation to others are invalidated. It has been noted that if the self-image does not correspond to the actual social reality, an identity crisis occurs (Jacobson-Widding 1983). The 2003 Kenya Demographic and Health Survey (CBS et al. 2004) shows that women with higher status were more likely to report physical violence in all the districts. Thus, violence is used to enforce gender hierarchies, particularly when men feel powerless because their social position makes them appear as failures; men thus develop low self esteem (Burazeri et al. 2005; Dolan 2003b).

Conclusions

Men's position in the six districts has been impacted similarly by divergent socio-economic changes that have largely resulted in loss or decline in livelihoods.

In Isiolo, the main driver of change has been the depletion of livestock, while in the other six districts it has been declining agricultural production and the collapse of major agricultural industries and marketing institutions. In Kiambu, the situation has been exacerbated by the near collapse of the cooperative movement. Men have been greatly impacted. In the agricultural districts, they own the land and receive most of the payments from farm production, and in most cases women received what the men decided was appropriate. Some women received nothing in return for their labor. The income generated from these enterprises allowed men to fulfill their obligations: provision of shelter, education for their children, and other household provisioning. However, with the changing fortunes, men have found themselves in a paradoxical situation. On the one hand, they continue to be regarded as household heads and decision makers while on the other hand, more and more of them cannot meet the normative standard set for them. They find themselves caught between cultural expectations that they can hardly meet and the powerlessness they feel due to their inability to meet their families' economic needs (Silberschmidt 2001).

These changes have significant impacts on the relationships between people and among households and communities. The intensification of poverty has been linked to the increase in moral collapse. Anecdotal evidence by study participants indicates that the consumption of alcohol intensifies following the decline in the main source of income. In the study districts, this has been the collapse or poor performance of traditional agricultural activities. Men are facing difficulties in adapting to changes in livelihoods, trapped in a stereotypical definition of male identity and unable to redefine their roles in the local economy or within the household. The frustration is channeled into antisocial behavior, such as substance abuse and crime, intrahousehold violence, and mental health problems.

Economic collapse and changes in livelihood are leading to the disempowerment of men at a time when, out of necessity, women are developing new coping strategies and greater empowerment. The focus of the government and development agencies on women and girls and the empowerment and emancipation of women and affirmative action have largely sidelined men, who increasingly find themselves dependent on the women who seem better able to develop alternative income-generation activities. The fact that women easily organize themselves into groups that provide opportunities for saving and group support enhances their ability to consolidate their limited resources. However, it is important to note that not all men find it difficult to adapt or cope with livelihood changes. Some men have ventured into small businesses, formed or joined solidarity groups, and are generating income or have concentrated on farming in spite of the low returns. However, the fact remains that many poor men find it difficult to survive, which is compounded by the lack of access to quality public services. For instance, men's inability to access healthcare for their families intensifies their feelings of worthlessness. "What kind of a father cannot treat his sick child?" was a statement made by a man in Nakuru that captured the sense of loss by some men.

This study has several policy implications. First, there is a great need for economic empowerment of both men and women in an effort to facilitate common grounds for development. Focusing on women has increased their burden and contributed to violence against them, which has intensified their sense of fear and anger. Further, it is critical to focus on poor people in rural areas. The collapse of the cooperative movement, coupled with the poor performance of the agricultural sector, has affected household survival and relations. A revival of agricultural industries and cooperative societies is critical for rural development. In addition, there is a need for discussions with communities on how gender roles have been affected by socioeconomic change. Through such dialogue, it may be possible to facilitate value-based community development that brings together households rather than targeting specific individuals or groups. It is clear that targeting women may increase their vulnerability to violence at home. Mechanisms to address gender violence should be put in place taking into consideration social, cultural, and economic contexts. A more household-oriented approach would require reassessing the gender rights approach with a view to making it contextually relevant and ensuring that new kinds of vulnerabilities are not created. Reempowerment of men may be required if real growth and greater social cohesion is to be achieved in rural areas, especially where there have been agricultural-based shocks that have resulted in male marginalization.

Youth continue to be the main victims of unemployment, which significantly contributes to intergenerational tensions and conflicts at the household level. Although opportunities exist for income generation, people who are "connected" grab these opportunities, further marginalizing the poor. This is partly responsible for the high levels of insecurity and increasing violence in rural areas, further hampering development prospects. Clearly, there is a need to revitalize rural economies to generate new income-generation activities and employment and to enforce the rule of law to improve security, but there is also a need to better understand the causes of violence. In many instances, violence is related to changing gender dynamics and the inability of men to rehearse and adopt new versions of masculinity. Without addressing these underlying causes through targeted programs and efforts within the education system and other community activities, there is a danger that as women become more empowered, violence in the household and society at large will continue to increase. Although this study has attempted to document these processes, there is an urgent need to analyze the types of programs that can be effective in supporting a redefinition of male identities and their role in Kenyan households.

Notes

1. Most researchers suggest that there is no analogous intergenerational tension between women, since in many parts of Sub-Saharan Africa, women marry and begin childbearing at early ages. In the parts of Africa where polygamy is practiced, there may be tensions between first and subsequent wives, but these tensions are not necessarily generational.

2. The analysis of quantitative data was done using the statistical package SPSS, while the qualitative data was analyzed manually.
3. *Shifta* is an Amharic word for bandits. This is a period referred to as *daaba* by the local people meaning "when life stopped."
4. The government uses kilograms when referring to milk producer prices.
5. Amuyunzu et al. (1996) have discussed the difficulties of translating English terms, including depression, health and illness, into local languages.

Gender and Its Discontents

Moving to Men-Streaming Development

11

MARIA C. CORREIA AND IAN BANNON

A central premise of the gender and development discourse since the 1970s has been the ways in which men exercise power over and dominate women, resulting in inequities, discrimination, and the subordination of women. Virtually all the main actors in international development subscribe to this basic premise.

This is only half the story. Gender is also about the way social structures and authority give men power over other men, thus resulting in their marginalization, discrimination, and subordination. To ignore this other side of gender is to ignore a critical variable in some of the most pressing issues the development world is tackling today—including the spread of the HIV/AIDS pandemic, pervasive patterns of war and conflict, urban crime and delinquency, insecurity, and even terrorism. Addressing male gender issues is also central to securing the illusive goal of women's equality.

Serious attention to the issue of men and gender in development is long past due. While a body of knowledge on the topic of masculinity has been growing and the gender and development model—with its focus on gender relations—has been in use since the mid-1980s, men have only recently appeared in the gender and development discourse. Even so, this rarely translates into any noticeable change in policy and practice. Gender and development today thus remains very much a female bastion. Men, when mentioned at all, appear as hazy background figures and are only included to the extent that they contribute to the needs and interests of women, not as a development issue in and of themselves.

This book reinforces and adds credence to a few key messages that have emerged over the years from the literature on men and masculinities. First, a dominant form of masculinity across societies and cultures—hegemonic masculinity—is commonly the basis by which men are judged and assess themselves. Second, for many men, particularly low-income and poor men, there is a huge gap between this dominant model and the reality of what they can achieve. Due to a range of factors, including chronic poverty, inequality, and exclusion, declining economic conditions, and conflict, men are unable to fulfill these external and internalized expectations of what it is "to be a man." Third, faced with the pressures of proving their manhood but unable to do so, too many men are led to destructive, and sometimes violent, illicit, or criminal behavior, against themselves and women. Because these behaviors impose high costs on developing countries, they can no longer be ignored.

In this chapter, we elaborate on these key messages, discuss prevailing gender development policy and the reasons it excludes men, present programmatic examples of efforts to address male gender issues, and offer recommendations and basic principles for moving forward on the "men-streaming" development agenda. Men-streaming in this context refers to the explicit inclusion of male issues as gender issues and the relational aspect of gender, which has hitherto been almost absent.

Key Messages

ACROSS SOCIETIES AND CULTURES, A DOMINANT FORM OF MASCULINITY—HEGEMONIC MASCULINITY—IS THE BASIS ON WHICH MEN ARE CRITICALLY JUDGED AND ASSESSED. While there are many ways of being a man, some ways are more socially valued than others and men feel social pressure to conform to the dominant ideals of manhood. Men who are unable to achieve these ideals are often socially sanctioned, belittled, or ridiculed. The term "hegemonic masculinity" refers to these dominant representations of manhood (Carrigan, Connell, and Lee 1985). As Dolan notes:

> "The model is hegemonic in that it largely precludes alternatives and is buttressed by major forms of social and political power. It is normative in that men are taught they should aspire to and judge themselves by it, and state and society in turn judge and assess them against it. The hegemonic model rests on polarized stereotypes and models of what women and men are like, what they should do, how they should relate to one another, and what their respective positions and roles in society should be. At its simplest it can be described as based on sexist, heterosexist, ethnocentrist and adultist premises, and as entailing economic responsibilities and a particular relationship with the state" (2003b, p. 60).

The first prerequisite for being a man is the ability to work and achieve financial independence. Ethnographic research and numerous studies and reviews of male socialization and male identity have confirmed that almost universally, work and income are central to how societies and individuals—women and men alike—define what it means to be a man. Studies also confirm the negative impact on men's self-image, health, and well-being when they lack meaningful, status-providing work. For a man, it translates into being "a nobody," lacking status (in the eyes of his family) and potential and actual female partners (Barker, this volume). For low-income young men who often lack other means of affirming their identity, being without work and income is not merely a question of material poverty, unemployment, or underemployment, but an affront to their sense of self and identity and how they define themselves in their social setting (Barker 2005).

A second prerequisite for being a man in most cultures, particularly socially traditional ones, is becoming a husband and father and exercising control over one's family. Being able to provide the material needs of wife and children, as well as physical protection for the family, is part of societal expectations placed on men (Dolan 2003b). Thus, in many cultures, having income is not enough; a man will continue to be perceived as a boy until he is married and has fathered a child (Dolan 2003b). As described by Barker and Ricardo (2005), not being able to meet these expectations carries severe consequences. In certain parts of Nigeria, unmarried men are forbidden to hold certain titles to land and in the event of death, cannot be buried like a married man. Unmarried men are also viewed with suspicion and often precluded from occupying certain social positions. Moreover, they are often looked upon as irresponsible and can be accused of being homosexual. In the parts of Sub-Saharan Africa where bride price is commonplace, marriage and family formation are directly tied to having income and/or property or access to land (Barker and Ricardo 2005). When the men are unable to meet this condition, they find themselves trapped as youth—unable to acquire employment and, as such, get married and transition to adulthood and manhood (Richards, Sommers, this volume).

Another nearly universal feature of manhood is that it must be achieved—it requires behaving and acting in specific ways before one's social group (Connell 2003; Gilmore 1990; Pollack [1998, as cited in Barker and Ricardo 2005]). Achieving manhood is in effect judged by other men and women; young men in diverse social settings frequently report a sense of being observed and watched to see if they measure up to culturally salient versions of manhood (Barker and Ricardo 2005). In many countries, society exerts strong pressure on men who deviate from socially accepted gender norms of behavior, which lets a male know when he is failing to be a man. In contrast, for a woman, at least in general terms, it is enough for her to fulfill her biological or caring functions. Stated another way, a woman performs her part by merely *being*; for the man, it requires *doing* something, accomplishing something, or performing something (Chevannes 2001b).

For young men worldwide, achieving manhood means becoming sexually active. As described in Barker and Ricardo (this volume):

"Sexual experience for young men is frequently associated with initiation into manhood. This fosters a perception of sex as performance and a means by which to demonstrate masculine prowess. Young men in many cultures experience peer pressure to be sexually active and have multiple partners in order to be seen as men. These sexual experiences are viewed among peers as displays of sexual competence or achievement rather than acts of intimacy (Marsiglio 1998; WHO 2003). Moreover, the status that a sexually active young man attains among his peers can be more important than the intimacy that comes from the sexual relationship itself (Lundgren 1999), and this pattern of sexual bravado as a means to peer acceptance often continues into manhood (Barker 2000b)."

Power is an element of hegemonic masculinity, and in most cultures, men are expected to exert power, control, and authority over women. Men exercise power over women in the domestic sphere (male-female relationships, family life, children's socialization, etc.) and in public settings (Kimmel 2002b). The latter refers to the institutional arrangements in a society that favors masculine traits and behaviors in the economy and polity and reproduces the gender order.

Consciously or subconsciously, women are complicit in the reproduction of hegemonic masculinity. As mothers, grandmothers, aunts, sisters, girlfriends, sexual partners, or teachers, women come in contact with boys and men and directly and indirectly pass on messages on gender norms and expectations (Barker and Ricardo 2005). Young women influence men's sexual behavior, for example, through negotiations about sex and condom use. Mothers influence the behavior of boys and men by relating messages on appropriate masculine activities and discouraging attitudes or behaviors they perceive to be associated with femininity, girls, and women.

FOR MANY MEN, PARTICULARLY LOW-INCOME OR POOR MEN, THERE IS A HUGE GAP BETWEEN THIS DOMINANT MODEL AND THE REALITY OF WHAT THEY CAN ACHIEVE. For many men, because they live in low-income, economically marginalized, or conflict-affected areas, or because they are disabled, it is extremely difficult and sometimes impossible to fulfill the roles contained in the hegemonic masculinity model.

The situation is perhaps most acute in Sub-Saharan Africa, where economic performance and average income per capita have declined significantly since the 1960s. In some countries, per capita income has dropped by more than 50 percent (World Bank 2000b). Rapid demographic growth has contributed to the problem, resulting in large-scale unemployment or underemployment across Sub-Saharan Africa. Many rural areas are particularly affected. Despite rapid urbanization, most Sub-Saharan Africans continue to live in rural areas and subsist through agriculture, which has undergone profound structural changes in the last decades. Amuyunzu-Nyamongo and Francis' research (this volume) on rural Kenya shows how the decline of the sugar and coffee industries, the collapse of pyrethrum production, and subsequent decline of marketing boards and cooperatives have led to a decrease in men's livelihoods, authority in the household, and self esteem—and ultimately to their disempowerment. Silberschmidt (2005) documents similar trends in East Africa, where labor surpluses have resulted in loss of income and earning power in both rural and urban areas, with corollary effects on men's employment and economic activity, household stature and authority, identity, and self esteem. In both cases, men have resorted to violence and aggression against women and children, because it is one of the few remaining ways they can demonstrate power over others and feel like a man.

The situation is also bleak in low-income areas of the Americas and the Caribbean, a region that has some of the worst indicators of inequality in the world. Frustration and anger over the unequal distribution of opportunities are breeding grounds for violence (Barker 2005). The plight of young men in meeting expectations of manhood in Brazil, which is the world's tenth largest economy but is characterized by extreme social division and income inequality, is chronicled in Barker's chapter.

Conditions are most extreme in conflict or war-affected areas of the world, where economies have collapsed, whole populations have been displaced, and insecurity reigns. In Sub-Saharan Africa, almost half of the continent is conflict affected or emerging from war, and 13.5 million people are internally displaced (Norwegian Refugee Council). The collapse of masculinity in conflict regions of Uganda is documented by Dolan (2003b). He notes that in northern Uganda, which has suffered pervasive conflict for the better part of the past 30 years, 50 percent of the population is internally displaced and has limited access to subsistence farming, income-generating opportunities, education, employment, or legal and physical protection from the state. Prior to war, families held their wealth in the form of cattle and other livestock. These forms of livelihood now have been largely wiped out. For men who want to marry, the absence of cattle and cash to provide bride payments presents a major obstacle. For those men able to marry, the insecure environment compromises their ability to protect their families, further undermining their sense of manhood.

Cultural patterns favoring adults over young people make matters worse. Young men in Sub-Saharan Africa are often dependent on older, more powerful men for transitioning into socially recognized manhood (Barker and Ricardo, Richards, this volume). These older men—fathers, chiefs, or elders—determine when young men may own land, whether they have access to family goods or wealth, and when and whom they may marry. This institutionalized stratification of age groups puts younger men at the service of elders, and the control of property and women by older men creates a structural conflict between younger and older generations of men, including tensions between older and younger men over access to women.

FACED WITH THE PRESSURES TO PROVE NORMATIVE MANHOOD— BUT UNABLE TO DO SO—MEN ARE LED TO DESTRUCTIVE, AND SOMETIMES VIOLENT, ILLICIT, OR CRIMINAL BEHAVIOR. For many men, particularly those in low-income or conflict settings, there is a disconnect between expectations and ability to live up to the normative model of masculinity into which they have been socialized. Opting out is not an option—even in the face of difficult social and economic circumstances, men cannot afford not to try to live up to the expectations of being a man (Dolan 2003b). This may lead men to seek other ways of asserting their masculinity, including resorting to illicit and criminal behavior to earn income and status or taking out their frustration and anger through the use of violence, alcohol and substance abuse, and suicide. Taking out their frustrations through the oppression of less powerful individuals, such as women and youth, is also a common reaction. At its extreme, men's thwarted masculinity, frustration, and anger can leave them vulnerable to engagement in conflict and war.

Indeed, research has found that beliefs about manhood are the strongest predictor of risk-taking behavior. Young men who adhere to traditional views of manhood are more likely to report substance abuse, violence, delinquency, and unsafe sexual practices (Barker and Ricardo, this volume). As such, the definition of masculinity is associated with male violence (Kimmel 2002b). Violence is lower in societies that allow men to acknowledge fear. Levels of violence are likely to be high, however, in societies where masculinity is defined by bravado and the repression and denial of male fear.[1]

Gangs and Illicit and Criminal Activity

In urban settings in the Americas, where poverty intersects with racism to create high levels of social exclusion and marginalization, some young men turn to urban gangs, which act as a substitute for what social and economic institutions cannot provide them, including a respectable level of income, a sense of belonging, and respect (Barker this volume). As Barker's research shows, these gangs—most of which are involved in drug trafficking or other illegal activities—compete for and actively recruit young men. Because gang leaders have power and money, they are often seen as local heroes by the community and young women and men. Being a gang member thus means having status, money, and power in settings of exclusion and disenfranchisement. Similar accounts have been recorded in the Caribbean and townships of South Africa, where gangs have been described as providing young men with a sense of belonging that few other social institutions—family, community, or school—can provide.

Conflict and War

In its most extreme form, men's vulnerability, powerlessness, and sense of impotence can contribute to violent behavior and even conflict and war. Gómez and García (this volume) report that in Colombia, which has experienced protracted violent conflict, the destabilization experienced by men in the face of social change, the ancestral masculine exertion of power, and peer pressure exerted by men have been factors in men's violent behavior. In Rwanda, unemployed, undereducated male youth formed the majority of the foot soldiers in the 1994 genocide in which some 500,000 to 1.1 million Rwandans perished. Before the genocide, youth were largely trapped in lives of crushing poverty, immobility, frustration, and humiliation (Sommers, this volume). The Rwandan government's mandate that people remain in rural areas hit young men especially hard because they had far less land than their fathers and were incapable of supporting families or even marrying, all of which are prerequisites for achieving manhood. These men, in turn, made easy pickings for the organizers of the genocide. Conflict in West Africa was similarly traced back to the extreme marginalization of male youth, who were exploited for their labor by traditional chiefs and customary law, thereby trapping them in a perpetual state of "youth"—unable to marry, transition into adulthood, and achieve manliness (Richards, this volume). Indeed, young men in Liberia, Sierra Leone, and other countries in conflict were attracted to war through the promise of being able to marry, which they otherwise could not do (Richards, this volume). In Uganda, youth were believed to have joined the army to get "free women"—i.e., women for whom they did not have to make bride payments (ACORD [2000] as cited in Dolan [2003b, p. 71–72]).

The relationship between the perpetuation of war and men's frustrations and humiliation brought about through their inability to meet societal expectations of manhood is documented by Dolan (2003b) from his research in northern Uganda. According to the accounts of a man there, "The local population lose their human dignity; they feel unprotected by the national army and or rebel forces and that their lives are not valued. They become aggressive in self-preservation." The man further noted, "People who get victimized take sides in the war with the spirit of revenging the atrocities against them or their families." Men also linked aspirations with decisions to join armed groups in discussing discrimination against youth: "They defy culture by joining war in order to achieve what they have been denied" and "since they are denied economic opportunity by elders the youth take short cuts through taking up arms" (Dolan 2003b). Dolan further asserts that militarization has undermined civilian men's sense of their own masculinity by creating a large economic disparity that favors soldiers over civilians. Soldiers have considerably more disposable income than their civilian counterparts and are therefore able to attract local women as temporary wives. Militarization has also created a local power hierarchy among men: some men have no power (mostly youth); others exert power in the household over wives and children; and others (notably military) sit at the top of the power structure, exercising power over other men as well as women (Dolan 2003b, p. 77).

HIV/AIDS

For young men (and young women), economic disempowerment has had important implications for their sexual behavior. Studies have shown that in the absence of economic and recreational opportunities, young men seek sexual relationships as a means to gain respect and social status (Barker and Ricardo, this volume). Indeed, studies demonstrate that men view STIs as a sign of virility (Barker and Ricardo 2005). Men in Malawi boasted about the likelihood of being HIV positive, since having HIV would be a badge of manhood before their peers (Kaler 2003 as cited in Barker and Ricardo 2005). In some settings, the notion of masculinity is associated with the ideal of unprotected sex, often with numerous partners. Research has further shown that young men may be belittled by peers for using condoms. Research in Tanzania by Silberschmidt (2005) shows that men compensate for feelings of inadequacy and despair by engaging in extramarital sexual activity, including with casual partners. Silberschmidt writes, "As one man put it, 'if you cannot be a successful breadwinner, you can be a successful seducer.' The fact that more than 30 percent of the sexually active population is HIV positive was of no concern to him" (2005, p. 198). Gender role norms are among the strongest social determinants of sexual behaviors (Barker and Ricardo, this volume).

Terrorism

While not explicitly dealt with in this volume, the events of September 11, 2001, have led some to speculate on the relationship between gender and terrorism. In writings on gender, class, and terrorism, Kimmel (2002a) compares Mohammed Atta, Adolf Hitler, and Timothy McVeigh. He posits that what unites the three men was gender and masculinity, that is, their sense of masculine entitlement and thwarted ambitions. They accepted cultural definitions of masculinity and needed someone to blame when they felt that they failed to measure up. Kimmel writes that Hitler was a failed artist, having been unsuccessful at almost all positions he had held with the exception of dictator. McVeigh, who had dropped out of college, excelled in the military during the Gulf War, for which he received a commendation for his exemplary performance. However, success led to disillusionment when he fell out of Green Beret training after two days, preventing him from getting his ideal job. For his part, Atta was the odd man out in his family, constantly denigrated by his father for not having become a doctor (as his two sisters had become) when he was the "man in the family." Defeated, humiliated, emasculated, a disappointment to his father and a failed rival to his sisters, Atta retreated into militant Islamic theology, which eventually led him to command one of the doomed planes on September 11.

In examining the intertwining of masculinity and warfare over time, Braudy (2003) describes terrorism as a "gender war," drawing a parallel between acts of fundamentalism today—where war is waged through acts of terrorism by men seeking honor—and the old world of heroic warriors and mythical figures. He argues that the enemy of the Islamic terrorists is intrusive Western civilization, in which gender is a "continuum" rather than a polarity of absolute male-female differences—the fear being that masculinity is being undermined. Indeed, the image of the resurgent masculine warrior has been used as a galvanizing symbol of the Islamic terrorists. Thus, unlike conventional wars that vie for territory, material goods, and resources, Islamic terrorism is a symbolic war aimed at restoring the gender order and a primitive "warrior masculinity" in which men are *real* men and a man is constantly being tested to prove his manhood.[2]

The above suggests that the consequences of thinking more seriously about gender as it pertains to men and prevailing notions of manhood are far reaching. As noted by Kimmel (2002a):

> "The terrors of emasculation experienced by lower-middle-class men all over the world will no doubt continue, as they struggle to make a place for themselves in shrinking economies and inevitably shifting cultures. They may continue to feel a seething resentment against women, whom they perceive as stealing their rightful place at the head of the table, and against the

governments that displace them. Globalization feels to them like a game of musical chairs, in which, when the music stops, all the seats are handed to others by nursemaid governments."

Constraints to Men-Streaming Gender

"Gender identify is clearly as much an issue for men as it is for women. This is just beginning to be recognized in development practice, with men's groups organized to discuss fatherhood or tackle issues of alcoholism or violence in the home. These are, however, marginal initiatives. Mainstream development takes men's gender identities for granted, and even the move from 'Women in Development' (WID) to 'Gender and Development' did little to shake the overwhelming preoccupation with women" (White 1997, p. 15).

The above excerpt is from a book published by Oxfam in 1997 entitled *Men and Masculinity*. Almost a decade later, the situation has not changed much. Why is this the case? If gender is relational and male gender issues are clearly consequential for development, why do men and masculinity continue to be virtually absent in gender and development policy and practice? Why does gender continue to be synonymous with women? What is locking the gender system in place?

An argument put forward by gender advocates is that until the disadvantages faced by women are redressed, the needs of men and boys should be secondary. Indeed, in many parts of the developing world, women's position has not improved much for centuries, and many developing countries continue to face an unfinished gender agenda. Gender advocates also argue that men have been the main beneficiaries of development and that it would therefore be unjust for women to have to share with men the few development resources available for gender. However, as experience has demonstrated—and as the chapters in this book confirm—gender is relational, and as such, interventions directed at women are often ineffective or unsustainable if men do not cooperate or are not involved. In rural areas in Kenya, for example, development activities have continued to focus on empowering women. Meanwhile, men are losing their economic livelihoods and becoming disempowered, leading many of them to take out their frustrations on women through domestic violence and alcohol abuse (Amuyunzu-Nyamongo and Francis, this volume). On the question of resources, the argument put forward by gender advocates assumes a zero sum game, which may indeed not be the case. As pointed out by Jacobsen (this volume) and others, it is in fact likely that a more comprehensive, male-inclusive gender paradigm will attract additional resources for gender work by, *inter alia,* reallocating resources from other programs that do not have a gender focus but that benefit men.

There are likely other more profound and unspoken reasons for the omission of men in gender and development work. As Cornwall (2003) and others have asserted, the conventional gender and development paradigm has thrived on the oppositional, two-dimensional "women as victim, men as a problem" stereotype.

To now admit that men also face gender issues and to bring men into the gender world would be to "undermine the most sacred of all cows: the oppositional categories 'women' and 'men' that are so potent a framing device for development intervention in the name of 'gender'" (Cornwall 2003, p. 6). There is also much fear among those who have fought the gender war over the years that bringing in men would be the equivalent of letting in the enemy. This is exacerbated by concerns that men would "take over" control and monopolize gender resources, which is threatening to those who have run the gender show (Cornwall 2003).

From an institutional perspective, many development organizations prefer to take the less troublesome route of designing and supporting small, symbolic projects for women, sidestepping the uncomfortable and complex issues associated with changing gender relations between women and men. Moreover, since demand for addressing women's issues so outweighs the demand for addressing men's issues—men, after all, are the privileged ones and thus are not supposed to complain about their conditions—development organizations can legitimately direct their efforts at women without having to worry about the male gender agenda. In an era of scarce resources, where the focus is on meeting client demands, this is not an unsurprising response. In the current parlance, international development agencies have no incentives to deal with men-streaming.

Lastly, resistance to address men's gender issues also comes from men (and women, generally) at a personal level. Program and policy decisions are often the result of deep-seated biases about gender and are frequently resistant to questioning these preconceptions (Barker and Ricardo 2005). Efforts to question the sexual behavior of men often run into resistance by men—including national leaders—who perceive that they are being bashed, maligned, or even worse, portrayed as weak and dysfunctional (which is considered unmanly).

Examples of Men-Streaming Gender in Development[3]

While limited progress has been made on the policy front, a growing array of program and research initiatives have sought to engage men in promoting gender equality in developing and developed countries. These include clinic-based efforts to engage men in primary health care or in specialized reproductive and sexual health clinics, fatherhood (for example, educational sessions, group discussions, or support groups for adult and adolescent fathers), media campaigns to promote positive images of men's involvement in the lives of their children, HIV/AIDS programs to engage men in preventing mother-to-child transmission, and support groups for HIV-positive fathers (Barker and Ricardo 2005). UNAIDS focused its 2000–2001 World AIDS Campaign on men and boys with the slogan, "Men Make a Difference" (UNAIDS 2000 as cited in Barker and Ricardo 2005).

In South Asia, men and women activists are working together to fight violence against girls and women. In North America and Western Europe, where there is more accumulated experience on men and gender, the majority of programs aiming to reduce violence against women attempt to include men in some way.

Perhaps the most successful male violence intervention program worldwide is the White Ribbon Campaign, which, while founded in Canada, has been successfully launched in more than a dozen countries, including Cambodia, China, Denmark, Norway, Sweden, the United States, and Vietnam. However, very little impact analysis has been carried out on gender programs aimed at men.

Programs for men generally target discrete risk groups, largely focusing on unidirectional communication of information or service delivery. Regrettably, few programs address the underlying impact of gender socialization and norms on men's behaviors. In addition, most of the research and programs on male involvement focus on adult men, while work with young men has been mainly limited to small-scale projects that often work in isolation. Moreover, a gender perspective has not been applied to men and young men in postconflict settings. This is understandable to a certain extent. The chaos following a conflict and the limited institutional capacity hinder conflict countries from dealing with a whole range of development issues, including the complexities of gender and masculinities. However, as Richards (this volume) points out, postwar reconstruction, especially programs targeting the reintegration of ex-combatants, should include reflection on gender roles in relation to peace, security, and social reconstruction.

Moving to Men-Streaming: Policy Directions and Recommendations

Addressing gender issues ultimately will require liberating men and women from the straightjackets of gender norms, constructs, and pressures. Although this process has begun for women, efforts for men are incipient. Changing traditional gender behaviors, which are rooted in deeply held beliefs and societal constructs, will obviously take time—but it will take even longer if there is continued resistance in the gender community to recognizing that men have gendered issues and let men in. The challenge is made more difficult because most men have never had the opportunity to reflect on their struggles and problems in a gender-specific way. Barker (2005) points out that for most of the young men he has interviewed around the world, it is the first time someone was asking them about their experiences *as men.* The difficulty is exacerbated because according to prevailing norms of manhood, men are not supposed to express feelings, emotions, and pain, or to grumble and complain—to do so is to demonstrate weakness, to be unmanly.

As Barker and Ricardo (2005) point out, change is happening even without program interventions and policy initiatives to promote it. Increased education for girls and women around the world is clearly challenging gender norms. Structural changes mean that economic advantages of men compared to women have eroded. Men in diverse settings throughout the world confirm the importance of women's education and income and perceive that these are good for families. And many men and boys are changing how they view women. Nonetheless, this change goes hand in hand with traditional gender hierarchies. Men—particularly young men—are accepting change but at the same time hanging on to traditional views. Thus, the time has clearly come to apply a gender perspective in development that includes and engages men and addresses the deep-rooted social constructs of gender inequity that affect both women and men.

Throughout this volume, specific recommendations and programming examples are provided, to varying extents, by all authors. The section that follows attempts to provide an overview of these and proposes general directions.

Awareness on Male Gender Issues

The international development community needs to understand the importance of gender issues as they pertain to men. Thirty years of gender discourse and practice on women has increased the visibility of women's equity issues among state agencies and development organizations. However, awareness of men and gender is limited to narrow academic and gender circles. It is now necessary for policy makers and development practitioners to understand that gender matters for boys and men, to understand how boys and men are socialized, and to recognize the costs or stresses from male socialization and identities on men, their families, and society as a whole. This is not to convert young men into victims or to downplay the many ways that women face serious and pervasive disadvantages in the current gender order. Rather, it is about understanding that men have gendered identities and pressures, and that these, in turn, are linked to some of the most problematic and intractable development issues of the day, such as HIV/AIDS and armed conflict.

Data and Research on Men and Gender

Despite the belated recognition that gender is also about men, an understanding of the complexities of the issues and how these play out in developing countries in different cultural contexts remains extremely limited. One problem is that data disaggregated by sex, age, and ethnicity are extremely limited, as noted in different chapters by Jacobsen, Barker, and others. There is also a need to collect new types of disaggregated data on issues such as crime and violence in order to better understand gender dimensions. Areas that would benefit from additional research include: deconstructing gender identities in different cultural contexts using a life cycle perspective; identifying the influence of different socialization agents, such as education systems, the workplace, communities, and the armed forces, on male gender identities and relations; understanding changes in interhousehold dynamics resulting from changing economies and globalization; and identifying factors that protect men and boys from destructive behaviors related to gender.

Additional research also needs to be done to understand the effectiveness of initiatives on men and gender issues. Limited formal and anecdotal evidence from existing programs and experiences suggests that working with boys and young men can be effective in ensuring more equitable and responsible behaviors through adolescence and adulthood. Much of the work, however, has been project-based and short-term, with relatively little systematic documentation and evaluation of these various efforts (Barker and Ricardo, this volume). Questions thus remain on how to best engage men in diverse cultural and socioeconomic settings.

Addressing Men and Manhood through a Gender Lens

Policies, programs, and initiatives to address male gender issues must consistently take into account the relational element of gender. In the same way that it is short sighted to try to empower women without engaging men, it is similarly inadequate to try to change male gender roles and the construction of manhood without engaging women. Gender roles are constructed and reconstructed and must be questioned by both men and women (Barker 2005). We must thus learn from the mistakes of WID and GAD and apply a truly gender—i.e., relational—perspective.

Men and Fatherhood

For men, the gender role that perhaps holds the most promise but has received relatively limited attention is that of fatherhood. The benefits of fatherhood that accrue to families are numerous, including increased income for the household, the provision of role models for children, enhanced security for the family, and higher educational achievement of children. But men themselves are likely to be the greatest beneficiaries of their greater involvement as fathers. According to Barker's chapter on fatherhood, men report that "fatherhood and their relationships with their children give their lives meaning, give them a sense of purpose and are among the most meaningful social roles and relationships they experience in their lives." But there are other benefits as well. Qualitative studies of men from low-income settings describe having a child and being meaningfully engaged in fathering as the reason for leaving gangs and ceasing to be involved in different forms of delinquency (Barker, this volume). In the Caribbean, men attached existential meaning to fatherhood, equating not having children with "birds without wings, trees without leaves, frustration and death" (Chevannes 2001, p. 225). Programs to enhance fathers' roles have been incorporated into sexual and reproductive health initiatives and school-based and youth-specific programs; fatherhood has also been promoted through group education and support groups for men, mass media and community-based education, and job and vocational training (Barker, this volume). Nurturing this kind of positive social energy is the essence of development.

Activities to Engage Men (and Women) on Male Gender Issues

Ultimately, supporting innovative approaches that address men and gender issues—as well as the parallel action research to identify the effectiveness of such programs—will be central for moving the male gender agenda forward. One suggestion is to establish "gender mainstreaming funds" that target men, as have

been established for women in the past. As noted by Jacobsen and Barker and
Ricardo (this volume), innovative programs have mostly been in the fields of
HIV/AIDS, reproductive health and family planning, parenting, and domestic vio-
lence; explicit activities to engage men on masculinity issues have also occurred.
Barker and Ricardo (2005) identified the following creative programs that target
men and gender issues in Sub-Saharan Africa:

- *Climbing into Manhood Program (Kenya),* a pilot health education initiative for
  young men, has been incorporated into the traditional male circumcision ritual;
- *Conscientizing Male Adolescents (Nigeria)* engages young men on issues related to
  gender-based oppression through a long-term group education and reflection
  process;
- *The Fatherhood Project (South Africa)* promotes positive images and expectations
  of men as fathers and works to create a programmatic and policy environment
  for supporting men's greater involvement with children;
- *Men as Partners (South Africa)* engages young and adult men and women in the
  promotion of gender equity through small group educational workshops, com-
  munity-level mobilization, and national advocacy;
- *Men Sector (Botswana),* a national alliance of governmental and nongovernmental organizations, seeks to reduce HIV/AIDS by engaging men in
  prevention and caregiving;
- *Soul City (South Africa)* uses diverse media strategies, including television, radio,
  and newspaper, to disseminate information and promote reflection on pressing health and social issues;
- *Stepping Stones (Africa Region)* engages entire communities of young and adult
  men and women in workshops and critical reflections on gender roles, communication, and relationships;
- *Targeted AIDS Intervention (South Africa)* uses peer education and sport to engage
  young men in discussions about women's rights, sexuality, HIV/AIDS, and
  caregiving; and
- *Positive Men's Union (TASO-Uganda)* encourages HIV-positive men to be
  involved in prevention efforts and in providing care for themselves, their families, and their communities.

In analyzing these innovative programs, Barker and Ricardo identify a number
of common operating principles: (a) nearly all programs include some discussion
about masculinity and gender norms in their group activities to allow men to
reflect on how prevailing gender norms affect them and others; (b) in addition to
engaging men themselves, most programs seek to change the social environment
in which men operate, thus applying an ecological approach to engage peer groups,
social groups, or entire communities to promote changes in social norms related
to gender; (c) most programs seek to build broad-based alliances at the local and
sometimes national level to contribute to changing discourses about men and
manhood (for example, credible national organizations such as the armed forces,

the police, trade unions, and others), and to increase reach and influence; and (d) most programs recognize the multiple needs of low-income men and try to assist men in this regard (for example, by assisting men in seeking work or developing social networks that assist in the search for work).

A Final Word

The study of men and masculinity is not new. Going back as far as 1977, British writer Andrew Tolson published *The Limitations of Masculinity*, an in-depth analysis of how gender identities, as conventionally defined, condemn a great many men to a quest of societal ideals that they cannot hope to realize, thereby leading to their frustration and discontent, and broader societal ills. Over the last decade, interest and discussion over the topic of men *as men* has been growing in academic, political, and media settings, with the primary thrust being on how boys are losing ground to girls in education and how men's underemployment and unemployment are leading to a "crisis of masculinity."

In the context of the developing world, however, attention to men and masculinity is belated and tentative—the latter in sharp contrast to the outrage displayed over the inequities faced by women, and likely reflecting caution about encroaching on feminist territory. Indeed, the inclusion of men in gender and development discourse appears only grudgingly, and with the emphasis continuing to be on how boys and men can contribute to women's gender agenda and ensure that women continue to be firmly in control.

The impetus to address men's gender issues in development is unlikely to come from the gender community. The political capital invested in gender in terms of women and the levels of mistrust and fear over male dominance will likely be too much to overcome. And while interest in men's issues will continue in specialized areas such as HIV/AIDS and reproductive health, actions are likely to remain marginal and tentative. Rather, the interest, drive, and energy to address men *as men* will likely come from the broader-based social development community with its focus on social exclusion and conflict and violence prevention—or even the security sector in its quest to understand the root causes of conflict, violence, and terrorism.

The time for men-streaming development, however, has come, whether it happens directly within the gender and development model or through more indirect channels. Unrealistic, unattainable, and rigid norms of conduct and expectations placed on men contribute not only to disparities and inequities on women, but to men's discontent—and when these expectations are combined with factors such as racism, adultism, and weak states—to the underdevelopment and destruction of nations and regions, and even to terrorism. Since men and women collude in the reproduction of these gender norms, both are implicated in their deconstruction and liberation. Almost three decades after Tolson, the full implications—and the urgency—of the "limits of masculinity" are finally beginning to be understood in the context of both developing and developed countries.

Notes

1. According to Kimmel (2002b), the following features have been associated with inter-personal and intersocial violence: (a) the manhood ideal is the fierce and handsome warrior; (b) public leadership is associated with male dominance, both of men over other men and of men over women; (c) women are prohibited from public and political par-ticipation, and most public interaction is between men rather than between men and women or among women; (d) boys and girls are systematically separated from an early age; (e) initiation rites for boys focus on lengthy spatial separation of boys, during which time they are separated from women, taught male solidarity, bellicosity, and endurance, and are trained to accept the dominance of older groups of men; (f) emotional displays of male virility, ferocity, and sexuality are highly elaborated; (g) the ritual celebration of fertility focuses on male generative ability, not female ones; and (h) male economic activ-ities and the products of their labor are prized over those of females.

2. According to Braudy, in a world of polarized masculinity and femininity, an individual woman is considered to be a woman unless proven otherwise. Although men may hold social power as men, an individual man has to continuously strive and be tested (Braudy 2003, p. 552).

3. These examples are quoted from Barker and Ricardo (2005), on which the Barker and Ricardo chapter of this volume are based.

Bibliography

Abdool, K. Q., E. Preston-Whyte, and K. S. S. Abdool. 1992. "Teenagers Seeking Condoms at Family Planning Services: A Providers' Perspective." *South African Medical Journal* 82 (5): 356–59.

Abdullah, I. 1997. "Bush Path to Destruction: The Origin and Character of the Revolutionary United Front (RUF/SL)." *Africa Development* 22 (3/4): 45–76. [Special Issue: *Lumpen Culture and Political Violence: the Sierra Leone Civil War.*]

———. 1998. "Bush Path to Destruction: The Origin and Character of the Revolutionary United Front/Sierra Leone." *Journal of Modern African Studies* 36 (2): 203–34.

Achatz, M., and C. A. MacCallum. 1994. *Young Unwed Fathers: Report from the Field.* Philadelphia: Public/Private Ventures.

ACORD. 2000. Northern Uganda Planning Workshop Report, Gulu, Uganda, April 25–May 3.

Action Aid. 2000. "Involving Men for Gender Equity: Stepping Stones Experiences in Reproductive and Sexual Health (RSH) and HIV/AIDS Intervention." Paper presented at the Oxfam Gender and Men Workshop, Oxford, U.K., June 10–12.

Adams, Marie Jeanne, ed. 1980. *Special Issue on Men's and Women's Societies in Sierra Leone and Liberia, with Special Attention to Masking.* Zürich: Ethnologische Zeitschrift Zürich.

African Rights. 1995. *Rwanda: Death, Despair and Defiance.* London: African Rights.

Agadjanian, V. 2002. "Men Doing Women's Work: Masculinity and Gender Relations among Street Vendors in Maputo, Mozambique." *The Journal of Men's Studies* 10 (3): 329.

Alatorre, J. 2001. "Iniciativa para la paternidad responsable en el Istmo Centroamericano." Unpublished manuscript.

————. 2002. *Paternidad responsable en el Istmo Centroamericano.* Mexico City: United Nations Economic Commission for Latin America and the Caribbean (CEPAL).

Almeras, D. 1997. "Compartir las responsabilidades familiares: Una tarea para el desarrollo." Background document for participants of the conference "Séptima Conferencia Regional sobre la Integración de la Mujer en el Desarrollo Económico y Social de América Latina y el Caribe," CEPAL, Santiago, Chile, November, 19–21.

Alsina, Cristina, and Laura Borràs Castanyer. 2000. "Masculinidad y violencia." In *Nuevas masculinidades,* ed. Marta Segarra and Angels Carabi, 83–101. Barcelona: Icaria.

Alsop, Bronwen. 2001. "Fatherhood and Masculinity Programs in Mexico: Identification and Analysis," Latin America and the Caribbean Region, Gender Sector Unit Working Paper, World Bank, Washington, DC.

Amuyunzu, M., T. Allen, H. Mwenesi, K. Johnson, O. Egesah, M. Parker, and J. Fox-Rushby. 1995. "The Resonance of Language: Health Terms in Kenya." *Quality of Life Research* 4 (5): 388–89.

Anderson, E. 1990. *Streetwise: Race, Class and Change in an Urban Community.* Chicago: University of Chicago Press.

Ankerl, Guy. 1986. *Urbanization Overspeed in Tropical Africa, 1970–2000: Facts, Social Problems, and Policy.* Geneva: INU Press, Interuniversity Institute.

Ansell, N. 2002. "'Of Course We Must Be Equal but...': Imagining Rural Futures in Two Southern African Secondary Schools." *Geoforum* 33 (2): 179–94.

Aponte, Mauricio, and Carlos Iván García. 2002. *Explotación sexual infantil en Bogotá.* Bogotá: Departamento Administrativo de Bienestar Social.

Archer, J. 1984. "Gender Roles as Developmental Pathways." *British Journal of Social Psychology* 23: 245–56.

Archibald, Steve, and Paul Richards. 2002. "Conversion to Human Rights? Popular Debate about War and Justice in Sierra Leone." *Africa* 72 (3): 339–67.

————. 1994. "Violence between Men." In *Male Violence,* ed., J. Archer, 121–43. London: Routledge.

Argenti, N. 2002. "Youth in Africa: A Major Resource for Change." In *Young Africa: Realising the Rights of Children and Youth,* ed. A. De Waal and N. Argenti. Trenton, NJ: Africa World Press.

Arias, Omar. 2000. "Male Economic Marginalization in Argentina, Brazil, and Costa Rica." Latin America and the Caribbean Region, Gender Sector Unit Working Paper, World Bank, Washington, DC.

————. 2001. "Are Men Benefiting from the New Economy? Male Economic Marginalization in Argentina, Brazil, and Costa Rica." World Bank Policy Research Working Paper 2743, World Bank, Washington, DC.

Arriagada, Irma. 2001. *Familias latinoamericanas. Diagnóstico y políticas públicas en los inicios del nuevo siglo.* Santiago, Chile: ECLAC.

Ashwin, Sarah, ed. 2000. *Gender, State and Society in Soviet and post-Soviet Russia.* London: Routledge.

Assis, S. 1999. *Traçando caminhos em uma sociedade violenta: A vida de jovens infratores e de seus irmãos não-infratores*. Rio de Janeiro: Editora Fiocruz.

Atieno, R. 2001. "Formal and Informal Institutions' Lending Policies and Access to Credit by Small-Scale Enterprises in Kenya: An Empirical Assessment." AERC Research Paper III, Nairobi, Kenya.

Atkin, L., and J. Alatorre. 1991. "The Psychological Meaning of Pregnancy among Adolescents in Mexico City." Paper presented at the Biennial Meeting of the Society for Research in Child Development, Seattle, April 18–20.

AVSC International, and IPPF. 1999a. "Male Participation in Sexual and Reproductive Health: New Paradigms." *Symposium Report*. New York: AVSC/IPPF Western Hemisphere Region.

———. 1999b. *Five Case Studies for the Symposium on Male Participation in Sexual and Reproductive Health: New Paradigms*. New York: AVSC/IPPF Western Hemisphere Region.

Badinter, Elisabeth. 1993. *XY, la identidad masculina*. Bogotá: Norma.

Bailey, Barbara. 1997. "Sexist Patterns of Formal and Non-Formal Education Programmes: The Case of Jamaica." In *Gender: A Caribbean Multi-Disciplinary Perspective*, ed. Barbara Bailey and Christine Barrow. Kingston, Jamaica: Ian Randle Publishers.

Bailey, Barbara. 2002. "Gendered Education, Fact or Fiction: The Realities in a Secondary-Level Classroom." In *Gendered Realities: Essays in Caribbean Feminist Thought*, ed. Patricia Mohammed. Mona, Jamaica: University of the West Indies Press.

Bailey, Wilma, Clement Branche, Gail McGarrity, and Sheila Stewart. 1996. *Family and the Quality of Gender Relations in the Caribbean*. Institute of Social and Economic Research, Mona, Jamaica, University of the West Indies.

Balabanovaa, Dina, Martin Bobak, and Martin McKeea. 1998. "Patterns of Smoking in Bulgaria." *Tobacco Control* 7: 383–85.

Bangoura, D., with S. Minard, and C. Perret. 2005. *Review of Retrospective and Prospective Studies on West Africa*. Paris: Sahel and West Africa Club.

Bankole, A., S. Singh, V. Woog, and D. Wulf. 2004. *Risk and Protection: Youth and HIV/AIDS in Sub-Saharan Africa*. New York: Alan Guttmacher Institute.

Barker, Gary. 1998a. "Salud y Género (Mexico): Participatory Workshops on Masculinity and Male Involvement." Draft Report, July 14.

———. 1998b. "Non-violent Males in Violent Settings: An Exploratory Qualitative Study of Pro-social Low Income Adolescent Males in Two Chicago (USA) Neighborhoods." *Childhood: A Global Journal of Child Research* 5 (4): 437–61.

———. 2000a. "Gender Equitable Boys in a Gender Inequitable World: Reflections from Qualitative Research and Programme Development in Rio de Janeiro." *Sexual and Relationship Therapy* 15 (3): 263–82.

———. 2000b. *What about Boys? A Literature Review on the Health and Development of Adolescent Boys*. Geneva: World Health Organization.

————. 2001. "Peace Boys in a War Zone: Identity and Coping among Adolescent Men in a Favela in Rio de Janeiro, Brazil." Doctoral dissertation, Erikson Institute, Loyola University, Chicago.

————. 2002. "Engaging Boys in Sexual and Reproductive Health: Lessons, Dilemmas and Recommendations for Action." Background paper by the Population Council for the "UNFPA Workshop on Adolescent and Youth Sexual and Reproductive Health," New York, May 1–3.

————. 2005. *Dying to be Men: Youth and Masculinity and Social Exclusion.* Oxford, U.K.: Routledge.

Barker, G., and I. Loewenstein. 1997. "Where the Boys Are: Attitudes Related to Masculinity, Fatherhood and Violence toward Women among Low Income Adolescent and Young Adult Males in Rio de Janeiro." *Youth and Society* 29 (2): 166–96.

Barker, G., and C. Ricardo. "Young Men and the Construction of Masculinity in Sub-Saharan Africa." Social Development Papers, Conflict Prevention & Reconstruction 26, World Bank, Washington, DC.

Barraclough, Simon. 1999. "Women and Tobacco in Indonesia." *Tobacco Control* 8: 327–32.

Barriteau, V. 2000. "Examining the Issues of Men, Male Marginalisation and Masculinity in the Caribbean: Policy Implications." Centre for Gender and Development Studies Working Paper 4, University of the West Indies, Cave Hill, Jamaica.

Barrow, C. 1998. "Caribbean Masculinity and Family: Revisiting Marginality and 'Reputation'" In *Gender Portraits: Essays on Gender Ideologies and Identities,* ed., C. Barrow, 339–58. Kingston, Jamaica: Ian Randel Publishers in Association with the Centre for Gender and Development Studies, University of West Indies.

————. 2001. "Children Rights and Caribbean Family Life: Contesting the Rhetoric of Male Marginality, Female-headed Households and Extended Family Breakdown." *Children's Rights* 3: 189–213.

Batliwala, S. 1994. "The Meaning of Women's Empowerment: New Concepts from Action." In *Population Policies Reconsidered: Health, Empowerment and Rights,* ed. S. Gita, A. Germain and L. Chen. Cambridge, MA: Harvard University Press.

BBC (British Broadcasting Corporation). 2004. "Aids: Killing Africa's Soldiers." June 21.

Becker, H. 2000. "'Becoming Men.' Masculine Identities among Young Men in Two Namibian Locations." *Development Update* 3 (2): 54–70.

Bennett, T. 1998. "Using Children in Armed Conflict: A Legitimate African Tradition. Criminalizing the Recruitment of Child Soldiers." Institute of Security Studies Monograph Series 32, Pretoria, South Africa.

Berdal, M., and D. Malone. eds. 2001. *Greed and Grievance: Economic Agendas in Civil Wars.* Boulder, CO: Lynne Rienner.

Bernard van Leer Foundation. 1996. "The Role of Fathers in Child Development." Discussion Paper, Bernard van Leer Foundation.

———. 2000. "The Role of Fathers in Child Development: A Discussion Paper." Unpublished manuscript. Bernard van Leer Foundation.

———. 2001. "Fathers Matter Too." *Early Childhood Matters: The Bulletin of the Bernard van Leer Foundation* 97 (February).

Bhasin, Kamla. 2001. "Gender Training with Men: Experiences and Reflections from South Asia." In *Men's Involvement in Gender and Development Policy and Practice: Beyond Rhetoric*, ed. Caroline Sweetman, 20–34. Oxford, U.K.: Oxfam.

Bjornson, Wendy, Cynthia Rand, and John E. Connett. 1995. "Gender Differences in Smoking Cessation after 3 Years in the Lung Health Study." *American Journal of Public Health* 85: 223–30.

Blake, Judith. 1961. *Family Structure in Jamaica: The Social Context of Reproduction*. Glencoe, IL: The Free Press.

Blanc, A., B. Wolff, A. Gage, A. Ezeh, S. Neema, and J. Ssekamatte-Ssebuliba. 1996. *Negotiating Reproductive Outcomes in Uganda*. Calverton, MD: Macro International.

Bledsoe, C. 1980. *Women and Marriage in Kpelle Society*. Stanford, CA: Stanford University Press.

———. 1984. "The Political Use of Sande Ideology and Symbolism." *American Ethnologist* 11 (3): 455–72.

Boulay, M., and T. Valente. 1999. "The Relationship of Social Affiliation and Interpersonal Discussion to Family Planning Knowledge, Attitudes and Practice. *Family Planning Perspectives* 25 (3): 112–18.

Bourdieu, P. 1998. *La domination masculine*. Paris: Editions du Seuil.

Bouta, T., G. Frerks, and I. Bannon. 2005. *Gender, Conflict and Development*. Washington, DC: World Bank.

Braudy, Leo. 2003. *From Chivalry to Terrorism: War and the Changing Nature of Masculinity*. New York: Vintage Books.

Breines, Ingeborg, Robert Connell, and Ingrid Eide, eds. 2000. *Male Roles, Masculinities and Violence: A Culture of Peace Perspective*. Paris: UNESCO Publishing.

Brody, Eugene B. 1981. *Sex, Contraception and Motherhood in Jamaica*. Cambridge, Mass. and London, U.K.: Harvard University Press.

Bronfenbrenner, U. 1986. "Ecology of the Family as a Context for Human Development: Research Perspectives." *Developmental Psychology* 22 (6): 723–42.

Brown, Janet, Patricia Anderson, and Barry Chevannes. 1993. "The Contribution of Caribbean Men to the Family." Unpublished manuscript. Caribbean Child Development Centre, University of the West Indies.

Brown, J., and B. Chevannes. 1998. *'Why Man Stay So': An Examination of Gender Socialization in the Caribbean*. Kingston, Jamaica: University of the West Indies.

————. 2001. "Redefining Fatherhood: A Report from the Caribbean." *Early Childhood Matters*, 25–37. Bernard Van Leer Foundation.

Brown, J., A. Newland, P. Anderson, and B. Chevannes. 1995. "Caribbean Fatherhood: Underresearched, Misunderstood." Caribbean Child Development Centre and Department of Sociology and Social Work, University of the West Indies, Kingston, Jamaica.

Bruce, Judith, Cynthia Lloyd, and Ann Leonard, with Patrice Engle, and Niev Duffy. 1995. *Families in Focus: New Perspectives on Mothers, Fathers and Children*. New York: Population Council.

Bujra, J. 2000. "Targeting Men for a Change: AIDS Discourse and Activism in Africa." In *Masculinities Matter: Men, Gender and Development*, ed. F. Cleaver. Durban, South Africa: Zed Books.

Burazeri, G., E. Roshi, R. Jewkes, S. Jordan, V. Bjegovic, and U. Laaser. 2005. "Factors Associated with Spousal Physical Violence in Albania: Cross-Sectional Study." *British Medical Journal* 331: 197–201.

Burgess, T. 2003. "Imagined Generations: Constructing Youth in Revolutionary Zanzibar." African Studies Centre, Leiden, The Netherlands.

Burín, Mabel. 2000. "La hostilidad: Modalidades de procesamiento propias de la masculinidad." In *Varones. Género y subjetividad masculina*, ed. Mabel Burín and Isabel Meler, 199–221. Buenos Aires: Paidós.

Bursik, R., and H. Grasmick 1995. "Defining Gangs and Gang Behavior." In *The Modern Gang Reader*, ed. M. Klein, C. Maxson, and J. Miller. Los Angeles, CA: Roxbury Publishing Company.

Buvinic, Mayra, Andrew Morrison, and Michael Shifter. 1999. "Violence in Latin America and the Caribbean: A Framework for Action." Sustainable Development Department, Technical Study, Inter-American Development Bank, Washington, DC.

Çagatay, Nilüfer. 1998. "Gender and Poverty." Social Development and Poverty Elimination Division, Working Paper 5, United Nations Development Programme (UNDP), New York.

Caiazza, Amy, and Heidi Hartmann. 2001. "Measuring Women as if Women Mattered: Final Report from IWPR's Working Group on Social Indicators of Women's Status." Institute for Women's Policy Research, Washington, DC.

Calvo, Fabiola 1987. *Colombia: EPL, una historia armada*. Madrid: Vosa.

Camacho, Álvaro, and Álvaro Guzmán. 1997. "La violencia urbana en Colombia: Teorías, modalidades, perspectivas." In *Nuevas visiones sobre la violencia en Colombia*. Bogotá: Iepri-Fescol.

Campbell, C. 2001. "Going Underground and Going after Women: Masculinity and HIV Transmission amongst Black Workers on the Gold Mines" In *Changing Men in Southern Africa*, ed. R. Morrell. Natal: University of Natal Press/Zed Books.

Carovano, Kathryn. 1995. "HIV and the Challenges Facing Men." UNDP, HIV and Development Programme, Issues Paper 15, UNDP, New York.

Carrigan, T., R. Connell, and J. Lee. 1985. "Towards a New Sociology of Masculinity." *Theory and Society* 15 (5).

Carton, B. 2001. "Locusts Fall form the Sky: Manhood and Migrancy in Kwazulu." In *Changing Men in Southern Africa*, ed. R. Morrell. Natal, South Africa: University of Natal Press/Zed Books.

Carvalho, Maria Luiza Mello de. 2001. *A Participação do Pai no Nascimento da Criança: as famílias e os desafios institucionais.* Mestrado. EICOS/Instituto de Psicologia/UFRJ.

Centers for Disease Control and Prevention. 1992. *Physical Fighting among High School Students—United States, 1990.* Atlanta, GA: Centers for Disease Control and Prevention.

CBS (Central Bureau of Statistics), and GOK (Government of Kenya). 2001. *1999 Population and Housing Census, Volume 1.* Nairobi: GOK.

CBS, Ministry of Health, and ORC Macro. 2004. *Kenya Demographic and Health Survey 2003.* Calverton, MD: CBS, MOH, and ORC Macro.

CESPI/USU, and Instituto Promundo. 2001. *Children, Youth and their Developmental Supports: Strengthening Family and Community Supports for Children and Youth in Rio de Janeiro. Initial Results 2000–2001.* Rio de Janeiro: CESPI/USU and Instituto Promundo.

Chang, Leslie. 1997. "Juice Makes Taiwanese See Red in More than Saliva." *Wall Street Journal*, August 22, 1.

Chanock, M. 1991. "A Peculiar Sharpness: An Essay on Property in the History of Customary Law in Colonial Africa." *Journal of African History* 32 (1): 65–88.

Chant, Sylvia, and Matthew C. Gutmann. 1999. "Men-Streaming' Gender? Questioning New Currents in Gender and Development Policy." Draft Report for the World Bank, Washington, DC.

———. 2002. "'Men-streaming' Gender? Questions for Gender and Development Policy in the Twenty-first Century." *Progress in Development Studies* 2 (4): 269–82.

Chauveau, J.-P. 2005. "Rapports intergenerationnels, frontiere agraire et gouvernmentalite locale en pays gban (Centre-Ouest ivorien): une mise en perspective historique." Unpublished manuscript.

———. 2006. "How Does an Institution Evolve? Land, Politics, Intra-Household Relations and the Institution of the 'Tutorat': Between Autochthons and Migrant Farmers in the Gban Region (Côte d'Ivoire)." In *Land Rights and the Politics of Belonging in West Africa*, ed. R. Kuba and C. Lentz. Athens, OH: Ohio University Press.

Chen, J. W., and J. H. Shaw. 1996. "A Study on Betel Quid Chewing Behavior among Kaohsiung Residents Aged 15 Years and Above." *Journal of Oral Pathology & Medicine* 25 (3): 140–43.

Chevannes, Barry. 1985. Jamaica Men: Sexual Attitudes and Beliefs. Unpublished manuscript. Kingston, Jamaica: National Family Planning Board.

———. 2001a. "Fatherhood in the African-Caribbean Landscape: An Exploration of Meaning in Context." *Children's Rights*: 214–26.

————. 2001b. *Learning to Be a Man: Culture, Socialization and Gender Identity in Some Caribbean Communities.* Kingston, Jamaica: University of the West Indies Press.

Christensen, K., M. Kristiansen, H. Hagen-Larsen, A. Skytthe, L. Bathum, B. Jeune, K. Andersen-Ranberg, J. W. Vaupel, and K. H. Ørstavik. 2000. "X-linked Genetic Factors Regulate Hematopoietic Stem-Cell Kinetics in Females." *Blood* 95 (7): 2449–451.

CIA (Central Intelligence Agency). 2002. *CIA Answers to Questions for the Record: Worldwide Threat Briefing 2002.* http://www.fas.org/irp/congress/2002_hr/020602cia.html

Cincotta, R., R. Engelman, and D. Anastasion 2003. *The Security Demographic: Population and Civil Conflict after the Cold War.* Washington, DC: Population Action International.

Clarke, Anthony. 2002. *Hombres. La masculinidad en crisis.* Madrid: Taurus.

Clarke, Edith. 1966. *My Mother who Fathered Me: A Study of the Family in Three Selected Communities in Jamaica.* London: George Allen and Unwin.

Clay, Daniel C., Theobald Kampayana, and Jean Kayitsinga. 1997. "Inequality and the Emergence of Nonfarm Employment in Rwanda." In *Changing Rural Social Systems: Adaptation and Survival,* ed. Nan E. Johnson and Ching-li Wang. East Lansing, MI: Michigan State University Press.

Clay, Daniel C., Jean Kayitsinga, Theobald Kampayana, I. Ngenzi, and J. Olson. 1989. *Strategies Non-Agricole au Rwanda: Rapport Preliminaire.* SESA Document de Travail, Service des Enquetes et des Statistiques Agricoles, Kigali, Rwanda.

Cleaver, F. 2000. "Do Men Matter? New Horizons in Gender and Development." *Development Research Insights* 35. http://www.id21.org/insights/insights35/.

————. ed. 2003. *Masculinities Matter! Men, Gender and Development.* London: Zed Books.

Coale, Ansley J. 1991. "Excess Female Mortality and the Balance of the Sexes in the Population: An Estimate of the Number of 'Missing Females.'" *Population and Development Review* 17 (3): 517–23.

Cock, J. 2001. "Gun Violence and Masculinity in Contemporary South Africa." In *Changing Men in Southern Africa,* ed. R. Morrell. Natal, South Africa: University of Natal Press/Zed Books.

Cockburn, C. 1999. "Gender, Armed Conflict and Political Violence." Background paper for the conference "Gender, Armed Conflict and Political Violence," World Bank, Washington, DC.

Cohen, David. 2000. "FatherWork in Europe. Phase One." Unpublished manuscript, Report to the Bernard Van Leer Foundation.

Collier, P. 2000. *Economic Causes of Civil Conflict and their Implications for Policy.* Washington, DC: World Bank.

Commeyras, M., and M. Montsi. 2000. "What if I Woke Up as the Other Sex? Botswana Youth Perspective on Gender." *Gender and Education* 12 (3): 327–46.

Commission for Africa. 2005. *Our Common Interest. Report of the Commission for Africa.* http://www.commissionforafrica.org.

Connell, R. W. 1995. *Masculinities.* Berkeley, CA: University of California Press.

———. 2003. "Masculinities, Change, and Conflict in Global Society: Thinking about the Future of Men's Studies." *Journal of Men's Studies* 11 (3): 249–70.

Cooper, Christopher. 2000. "In Yemen, Some Try this Antidrug Message: Just Say No—to Qat." *New York Times,* December 28, 1.

Cornwall, Andrea. 1997. "Men, Masculinity and Gender in Development." In *Men and Masculinity,* ed. Caroline Sweetman, 8–13. Oxford, U.K.: Oxfam.

———. 2000. "Missing Men? Reflections on Men, Masculinities and Gender in GAD." *IDS Bulletin* 3 (2).

———. 2003. "To Be a Man Is More than a Day's Work: Shifting Ideals of Masculnity in Ado-Odo, Southwestern Nigeria." In *Men and Masculinites in Modern Africa,* ed. L. A. Lindsay and S. F. Miescher. Portsmouth, NH: Heinemann.

Cornwall, A., and N. Lindisfarne. 1994. "Dislocating Masculinity: Gender, Power and Anthropology." In *Dislocating Masculinity. Comparative Ethnographies,* ed. A. Cornwall and N. Lindisfarne, 11–47. London and New York: Routledge.

Correia, M. 2003. "Gender." In *Colombia: The Economic Foundation of Peace,* ed. M. Giugale, O. Lafourcade, and C. Luff, 767–85. Washington, DC: World Bank.

Courtney, D. 1998. "Better to Die than Cry?: A Longitudinal and Constructionist Study of Masculinity and the Health Risk Behavior of Young American Men." Doctoral dissertation, University of California at Berkeley, Dissertation Abstracts International Publication No. 9902042.

Cowan, C. 1988. "Working with Men Becoming Fathers: The Impact of a Couples Group Intervention." In *Fatherhood Today: Men's Changing Role in the Family,* ed. P. Bronstein and C. Cowan, 276–98. New York: John Wiley and Sons.

Crossette, Barbara. 2001. "Living in a World without Women." *New York Times,* November 4.

CSVR (Centre for the Study of Violence and Reconciliation). 1998. "Into the Heart of Darkness: Journeys of the Agents in Crime, Violence and Death," CSVR, Johannesburg, South Africa.

Cunningham, Wendy. 2001. "Breadwinner or Caregiver? How Household Role Affects Labor Choices in Mexico." Latin America and the Caribbean Region Policy Research, Gender Sector Unit Working Paper 2743, World Bank, Washington, DC.

Currens, G. E. 1972. "The Loma Avunculate: An Exercise in the Utility of Two Models." *Ethnology* 11 (2): 111–21.

DABS (Departamento Administrativo de Bienestar Social). 2003. *Conversatorios entre hombres* (2nd. edition). Bogotá: DABS-Humanizar.

Dallaire, Lieutenant-General Roméo (with Major Brent Beadsley). 2004. *Shake Hands with the Devil: The Failure of Humanity in Rwanda.* New York: Carroll and Graf Publishers.

Dann, Graham. 1987. *The Barbadian Male: Sexual Attitudes and Practices.* London: Macmillan Caribbean.

Day, R. D. 1998. *Social Fatherhood: Conceptualizations, Compelling Research, and Future Direction.* National Center on Fathers and Families. Philadelphia: University of Pennsylvania.

Davis, J. E., and W. E. Perkins. 1995. *Fathers' Care: A Review of the Literature.* Philadelphia: NCOFF, University of Pennsylvania.

Davison, J. ed. 1988. *Agriculture, Women and Land: The African Experience.* Boulder, CO: Lynn Rienner.

D'Azevedo, W. 1962. "Some Historical Problems in the Delineation of a Central West Atlantic Region." *Annals, New York Academy of Sciences* 96 (2): 512–38.

———. 1969–1971. "A Tribal Reaction to Nationalism, Parts 1–4." *Liberian Studies Journal* 1(2) [1969], 2(1): 1–21 [1969/1970], 2(1): 43–63 [1970], 3(1): 99–115, [1971]: 1–19.

de Keijzer, B. 1995. "Masculinity as a Risk Factor." Paper presented at the Coloquio Latinoamericano sobre Varones, Sexualidad y Reproducción. Zacatecas, Mexico, November 17–18.

———. 1998. "Paternidad y transición de género." In *Familias y relaciones de género en transformación*, ed. B. Schmuckler. Mexico City: Population Council and Edamex.

———. "La salud y la muerte de los hombres." Unpublished manuscript.

Des Forges, Alison. 1999. *Leave None to Tell the Story: Genocide in Rwanda.* New York, Washington, London, Brussels, and Paris: Human Rights Watch, International Federation of Human Rights.

Deyo, Frederic C. 1989. *Beneath the Miracle: Labor Subordination in the New Asian Industrialism.* Berkeley, CA: University of California Press.

Díaz, Ximena, and Julia Medel. 2002. "Familia y trabajo: distribución del tiempo y relaciones de género." In *Trabajo y familia: Conciliación? Perspectivas de género*, ed., J. Olavarría and C. Céspedes Santiago de Chile: FLACSO-Chile, SERBAM and Centro de Estudios de la Mujer.

Dissel, A. 1997. "Youth, Street Gangs and Violence in South Africa." Centre for the Study of Violence and Reconciliation, Johannesburg.

DNP (Departamento Nacional de Planeación). 2000. "Indicadores de coyuntura social." *Newsletter* 24. Bogotá: DNP-SISD.

———. 2001. "¿Nos parecemos al resto del mundo? El conflicto Colombiano en el contexto internacional." *Archivos de Macroeconomía*, Documento 143. Bogotá: DNP.

———. 2003. "Cifras de violencia 1996–2002." Dirección de Justicia y Seguridad, *Electronic Newsletter.* http://www.dnp.gov.co

Dolan, C. 2000. "What Do You Remember? A Rough Guide to the War in Northern Uganda 1986–2000." COPE Working Paper 33.

———. 2003a. "Does War Reinforce a Dominant Notion of Masculinity?" http://www.id21.org/society/s10bcd1g1.html

———. 2003b. "Collapsing Masculinities and Weak States—A Case Study of Northern Uganda." In *Masculinities Matter! Men, Gender and Development,* ed. F. Cleaver. Durban: Zed Books.

Donzelot, Jacques. ed. 1979. *La policía de las familias.* Valencia, Spain: Pre-textos.

Douglas, M., and S. Ney. 1998. *Missing Persons: A Critique of Personhood in the Social Sciences.* Berkeley, CA: University of California Press.

Drennan, M. 1998. "Reproductive Health: New Perspectives on Men's Participation." *Population Reports, Series J,* 46, Johns Hopkins University School of Public Health, Population Information Program, Baltimore.

Durkheim, E. 1964 [1893]. *The Division of Labor in Society,* (trans. G. Simpson). New York: Free Press.

Ebata, Michi, Valeria Izzi, Alexandra Lendon, Eno Ngjela, Peter Sampson, and Jane Lowicki-Zucca. 2005. *Youth and Violent Conflict: Society and Development in Crisis? A Strategic Review with a Special Focus on West Africa.* New York: Bureau for Crisis Prevention, UNDP.

The Economist. 1996a. "The Trouble with Men." September 28, 19–20.

———. 1996b. "Tomorrow's Second Sex." September 28, 23–26.

Economist Intelligence Unit. 2005a. *Rwanda: Country Profile 2005.* London: Economist Intelligence Unit.

———. 2005b. *Rwanda: Country Report: August 2005.* London: Economist Intelligence Unit.

Elbe, S. 2002. "HIV/AIDS and the Changing Landscape of War in Africa." *International Security* 27: 159–77.

Ellis, S. 1997. "Young Soldiers and the Significance of Initiation: Some Notes from Liberia." Afrika-Studiecentrum, Leiden, The Netherlands. http:/www.asc.leidenuniv.nl/pdf.

———. 1999. *The Mask of Anarchy: The Destruction of Liberia and the Religious Dimension of an African Civil War.* London: Christopher Hurst.

Emler, N., and S. Reicher. 1995. *Adolescence and Delinquency: The Collective Management of Reputation.* Oxford, U.K.: Blackwell Publishers.

Endeley, J., and S. Happi. 2002. "The Conceptualization of Masculinity in an African Society in a New Era (Post-Beijing Decade): Case Study of Men in Cameroon." Paper presented at a meeting on Gendered Identities/Construction of Gender, Makerere, Uganda. http://www. makerere.ac.ug/womenstudies/congress/abstract/ gender%20identities.htm.

EngenderHealth. 2001a. "Working with Men."
   http://www.engenderhealth.org/ia/wwm/index.html.
———. 2001b. "Salud y Género: Case Study: Participatory Workshops on
   Masculinity and Male Involvement."
   http://www.engenderhealth.org/ia/wwm/emcase4.html.
Engle, P. 1995. "Men in Families: Report of a Consultation on the Role of Males
   and Fathers in Achieving Gender Equality." UNICEF.
   http://www.unicef.org/reseval/malesr.html.
———. 1997. 'The Role of Men in Families: Achieving Gender Equity and
   Supporting Children." In *Men and Masculinity*, ed. Caroline Sweetman,
   8–13. Oxford, U.K.: Oxfam.
Engle, P., and C. Breaux. 1998. "Fathers' Involvement with Children: Perspectives
   from Developing Countries." *Social Policy Report* 12: 1–21.
Engle, P., and A. Leonard. 1995. "Fathers as Parenting Partners." In *Families in
   Focus: New Perspectives on Mothers, Fathers, and Children*, ed. J. Bruce,
   C. Lloyd, and A. Leonard, with P. Engle, and N. Duffy, 49–69. New York:
   Population Council.
Erulkar, A. 1998. *Adolescent Experiences and Lifestyles in Central Province
   Kenya*. Nairobi: Population Council and Family Planning Association
   of Kenya.
Etienne, M. 1997 "Women and Men, Cloth and Colonization: The
   Transformation of Production-Distribution Relations among the
   Baule (Ivory Coast)." In *Perspectives on Africa: A Reader in Culture, History
   and Representation*, ed. R. Grinker and C. Steiner. Oxford, U.K.:
   Blackwell.
Evans, Hyacinth. 2001. *Gender and Achievement in Secondary Education in Jamaica:
   Social Policy Analysis and Research Project*. Kingston, Jamaica: The Planning
   Institute of Jamaica.
Evans, J. 1997. "Both Halves of the Sky: Gender Socialization in the Early Years."
   *Coordinator's Notebook: An International Resource for Early Childhood
   Development* 20: 1–27.
Everatt, D. 2000. "From Urban Warrior to Market Segment? Youth in South
   Africa 1990–2000." *Development Update* 3 (2).
Faludi, Susan. 1999. *Stiffed: The Betrayal of the American Man*. New York: W.
   Morrow and Co.
FAO (Food and Agriculture Organization). 2004. "Leasing Agricultural Land."
   Land Tenure Notes 1. Rome: FAO.
Fenoaltea, S. 1984. "Slavery and Supervision in Comparative Perspective: A
   Model." *Journal of Economic History* 44 (3): 635–68.
Fenton, J. 1948. *Outline of Native Law in Sierra Leone*. Revised Edition. Freetown:
   Government Printer.
Fernandes, R. C. 2002. "Educação de jovens em situação de risco: Dados do
   problema e ações da sociedade. Apresentação para *O Globo*." Viva Rio, Rio
   de Janeiro.

Figueroa, M. 1997a. "Gender Privileging and Socio-Economic Outcomes: The Case of Health and Education in Jamaica." Paper presented to the Ford Foundation Workshop on Family and the Quality of Gender Relations, Mona, Jamaica, March 5–6.

————. 1997b. "Male Privileging and Male Academic Underperformance in Jamaica." Paper presented at the Symposium on the Construction of Caribbean Masculinity, University of the West Indies, St. Augustine, Trinidad and Tobago.

Finger, W. 1998. "Condom Use Increasing," *Network* 18 (3).

Fithen, C., and P. Richards. 2005. "Making War, Crafting Peace: Militia Solidarities in Sierra Leone." In *No Peace, No War: An Anthropology of Contemporary Armed Conflicts*, ed. P. Richards. Oxford, U.K.: James Currey.

Fleshman, M. 2001. "Small Arms in Africa: Counting the Cost of Gun Violence." *Africa Recovery* 15 (4): 1.

Flood, Michael. 2004. "Men, Gender, and Development." *Development Bulletin* 64: 26–30.

Focus. 1998. *Sexual Abuse and Young Adult Reproductive Health.* http://www.pathfind.org/pf/pubs/focus/IN%20FOCUS/sexabuseinfocus.html

Ford, M. 1989. "Pacification under Pressure: The Political Economy of Liberian Intervention in Nimba 1912–1918." *Liberian Studies Journal* 14 (2): 44–63.

Ford-Smith, Honor. 1986. *Lionheart Gal: Life Stories of Jamaican Women.* London: The Women's Press.

Foreman, M., ed. 1999. *AIDS and Men: Taking Risks or Taking Responsibility?* London: PANOS/ZED Books.

Fortes, Meyer. 1949. "Time and Social Structure: An Ashanti Case Study." In *Social Structure: Studies Presented to A. R. Radcliffe-Brown*, ed. Meyer Fortes. Oxford, U.K.: Oxford University Press.

Fox, G. L., and M. Benson. 2001. "Violent Men, Bad Dads? Fathering Profiles of Men Involved in Intimate Partner Violence." Paper prepared for the Workshop on Measuring Father Involvement National Institutes of Health, Bethesda, MD, February 8–9.

Franco, Saúl. 1999. *El quinto: no matar. Contextos explicativos de la violencia en Colombia.* Bogotá: TM Editores-Iepri-Universidad Nacional.

Frazier, E. Franklin. 1951. *The Negro Family in the United States.* New York: Dreyden Press.

Frederiksen, B. 2000. "Popular Culture, Gender Relations and the Democratization of Everyday Life in Kenya." *Journal of Southern African Studies, Special Issue: Popular Culture and Democracy* 26 (2): 209–22.

Fuller, Norma. 1997. *Identidades masculinas. Varones de clase media en el Perú.* Lima: Pontíficia Universidad Católica del Perú.

————. 2000. "Significados y prácticas de la paternidad entre varones urbanos del Perú: Lima, Cuzco e Iquitos." In *Paternidades en América Latina*, ed. Norma Fuller. Lima, Perú: Pontíficia Universidad Católica del Perú.

————. 2001. *Masculinidades. Cambios y permanencias. Varones de Cuzco, Iquitos y Lima.* Lima: Pontíficia Universidad Católica del Perú.

Furstenberg, F. 1991. "Daddies and Fathers: Men Who Do for their Children and Men Who Don't." Draft for the Manpower Demonstration Research Corporation.

Furstenberg, F., and K. Mullan Harris. 1991. "When Fathers Matter/Why Fathers Matter? The Impact of Patternal Involvement on the Offspring of Adolescent Mothers." Unpublished manuscript, Temple University, Temple.

Gadsen, V., and M. Hall. 1995. *Intergenerational Learning: A Review of the Literature.* Philadelphia NCOFF, University of Pennsylvania.

Gage, A. 1998. "Sexual Activity and Contraceptive Use: The Components of the Decision Making Process." *Studies in Family Planning* 29 (2): 154–66.

Ganju, D., S. Jejeebhoy, V. Nidadavolu, K. G. Santhya, W. Finger, S. Thapa, I. Shah, and I. Warriner. 2004. "Sexual Coercion: Young Men's Experiences as Victims and Perpetrators." Population Council. New Delhi: Population Council.

García, Brígida. ed. 2000. *Women, Poverty, and Demographic Change.* Oxford, U.K.: Oxford University Press.

García, S. Carlos Iván. 1998 *'En algún lugar parcharemos:' Normas de interacción y valores de los parches de la Localidad 11 de Santa Fe de Bogotá, Bogotá.* Bogotá: Observatorio de Cultura Urbana-TM Editores.

————. 2002. *Edugénero. Aportes investigativos para el cambio de las relaciones de género en la institución escolar (2nd edition).* Bogotá: DIUC-Universidad Central.

García-Hjarles, G. 2001. *Estudio aplicado de paternidad andina.* Lima, Perú: PMS Allin Tayta, Ministerio de Promoción de la Mujer y el Desarrollo Humano (PROMUDEH), Instituto Nacional de Bienestar Familiar (INABIF) y Ministerio de Educación (MINEDU).

Garfield, E., and J. Arboleda. 2003. "Violence, Sustainable Peace, and Development." In *Colombia: The Economic Foundation of Peace*, ed. M. Giugale, O. Lafourcade and C. Luff, 35–58. Washington, DC: World Bank.

Gasibirege, S., and S. Babalola. 2001. *Perceptions about the Gacaca Law in Rwanda: Evidence from a Multi-Method Study.* Special Publication 19, Center for Communication Programs, Johns Hopkins University School of Public Health, Baltimore.

Gear, S. 2001. "Sex, Sexual Violence and Coercion in Men's Prisons." Paper presented at the "AIDS in Context International Conference," University of Witwatersrand, South Africa, April 4–7.

Gerstein, D., J. Hoffmann, C. Larison, L. Engelman, S. Murphy, A. Palmer, L. Chuchro, M. Toce, R. Johnson, T. Buie, M. A. Hill, R. Volberg, H. Harwood, A. Tucker, E. Christiansen, W. Cummings, and S. Sinclair 1999. "Gambling Impact and Behavior Study." Report to the National

Gambling Impact Study Commission, National Opinion Research Center, Chicago.

Getz, Trevor. 2004. *Slavery and Reform in West Africa: Toward Emancipation in 19th Century Senegal and the Gold Coast.* Athens, OH: Ohio University Press.

Ghee, L. T. 2002. "Youth and Employment in the Asia-Pacific Region: Prospects and Challenges." Paper presented at the "Youth Employment Summit," Alexandria, Egypt, September 7–11.

Ghoussoub, Mai, and Emma Sinclair-Webb, eds. 2000. *Imagined Masculinities: Male Identity and Culture in the Modern Middle East.* London: Saqi Books.

Gibbs, J. 1985. "The Kpelle of Liberia." In *Peoples of Africa*, ed. James Gibbs Jr. New York: Holt, Rinehart & Winston.

Giddens, Anthony. 1992. *La transformación de la intimidad. Sexualidad, amor y erotismo en las sociedades modernas.* Madrid: Cátedra.

———. 1997. *La modernidad e identidad del yo. El yo y la sociedad en la época contemporánea.* Barcelona: Ediciones Península.

Gilmore, D. 1990. *Manhood in the Making: Cultural Concepts of Masculinity.* New Haven, CT: Yale University Press.

Girard, F. 2003. *'My Father Didn't Think This Way': Nigerian Boys Contemplate Gender Equality.* New York: Population Council.

Giugale, M., O. Lafourcade, and Connie Luff, eds. 2003. *Colombia: The Economic Foundation of Peace.* Washington, DC: World Bank.

Global Fund for Children. 2002. *The Dangers of Neglecting Education for Boys.* New York: GFC.

Global Health Council. 2005. *Rwanda: Urban Growth Rate.* http://atlas. globalhealth.org/indicator_detail.cfm?IndicatorID=136&Country=RW

Goldstein, R. B., S. I. Powers, J. McCusker, K. A. Mundt, B. F. Lewis, and C. Bigelow. 1996. "Gender Differences in Manifestations of Antisocial Personality Disorder among Residential Drug Abuse Treatment Clients." *Drug and Alcohol Dependence* 41 (1): 35–45.

Gómez Alcaraz, Fredy Hernán. 2000. *Las masculinidades y los varones. Construcciones históricas diversas, masculinidades en Colombia. Reflexiones y perspectivas.* Foro Memorias (July 25). Bogotá: AVSC International-UNFPA-UN Gender, Women and Development Program-Haz Paz.

Gómez Alcaraz, Fredy Hernán, Margarita Bernal, and Carlos Iván García. 2001. *Las masculinidades y la violencia intrafamiliar* (Volume 5). Bogotá: Haz Paz Policy of the Office of the Presidential Counsel for Social Policy, and UNDP.

Gordon, G., and A. Welbourn. 2003. *Three Case Studies: Involving Men to Address Gender Inequities.* Washington, DC: Interagency Gender Working Group (IGWG).

Gordon, R. 1998. "Girls Cannot Think as Boys Do: Socializing Children through the Zimbabwean School System." *Gender and Development* 6 (2): 53–58.

Gorgen, R., M.Yansane, M. Marx, and D. Millimounou. 1998. "Sexual Behavior and Attitudes among Unmarried Urban Youths in Guinea." *International Family Planning Perspectives* 24 (2): 65–71.

Government of Sierra Leone. n.d. [c. 2004] *Sierra Leone: National Youth Policy.*

Grace, J. 1977. "Slavery and Emancipation among the Mende in Sierra Leone." In *Slavery in Africa: Historical and Anthropological Perspectives*, ed. Suzanne Miers and Igor Kopytoff. Madison, WI: University of Wisconsin Press.

Grant, E., A. Grant, J. Brown, E. Manuthu, K. Michenik, and J. Njeru. n.d. "Seizing the Day: Right Time, Right Place, and Right Message for Adolescent Male Reproductive Sexual Health. Lessons from the Meru of Eastern Province, Kenya." Unpublished manuscript.

Green, C. 1997. "Young Men: The Forgotten Factor in Reproductive Health." FOCUS on Young Adults, Occasional Paper 1, FOCUS, Washington, DC.

Greenfield, Sidney. 1966. *English Rustics in Black Skin: A Study of Modern Family Forms in a Pre-Industrialised Society.* New Haven, CT: College and University Press.

Gregson, S., C. A. Nyamukapa, G. P. Garnett, P. R. Mason, T. Zhuwau, M. Caraël, S. K. Chandiwana, and R. M. Anderson. 2002. "Sexual Mixing Patterns and Sex-Differentials in Teenage Exposure to HIV Infection in Rural Zimbabwe." *The Lancet* 359 (9321): 1896–903.

Greig, Alan, Michael Kimmel, and James Lang. 2000. "Men, Masculinities and Development: Broadening our Work towards Gender Equality." UNDP Gender in Development Monograph Series 10, UNDP, New York.

Grout, E. 2002. "Keep Awake: AIDS in the World." A Series of Essays Toward a General Convention. http://www.rci.rutgers.edu/~lcrew/dojustice/j025.html

The Guardian. 2001. "South Africa; Out of School, Out of Work". *Africa News*, April 20.

Gupta, N., and M. Mahy. 2003. "Sexual Initiation among Adolescent Girls and Boys: Trends and Differentials in Sub-Saharan Africa." *Archives of Sexual Behavior* 32 (1): 41–53.

Gustafsson-Wright, E., and J. van der Gaag. 2003. "Children and Youth at Risk: A Life-cycle Approach with an Illustration from Guatemala." Human Development Network, World Bank, Washington, DC.

Gutiérrez, Gabriel. 1993. *Inseguridad y delito en Santafé de Bogotá.* Bogotá: Editorial.

Gutmann, Matthew C. 1996. *The Meanings of Macho: Being a Man in Mexico City.* Berkeley, CA: University of California Press.

———. 2000. *Ser hombre de verdad en la ciudad de México.* México: El Colegio de México.

Guzmán, L. J. 2001. "La reproducción de los varones en México: El entorno sexual de la misma. Estudios de casos." Unpublished PhD dissertation, Universidad Nacional Autónoma de México (UNAM), Mexico.

Gysling, Jacqueline, and Cristina Benavente. 1996. *Trabajo, sexualidad y poder. Mujeres de Santiago.* Santiago de Chile: FLACSO-Chile.

Hall, S. 2002. "Daubing the Drudges of Fury: Men, Violence and the Piety of the Hegemonic Masculinity Thesis." *Theoretical Criminology* 6 (1): 35–61.

Halperin, Tulio. 1997. *Historia contemporánea de América Latina.* Buenos Aires: Alianza Editorial.

Hamermesh, Daniel S. 1986. "The Demand for Labor in the Long Run." In *Handbook of Labor Economics,* ed. Orley Ashenfelter and Richard Layard, 429–71. Amsterdam: North-Holland.

Harriott, A. 2000. *Police and Crime Control in Jamaica: Problems of Reforming Ex-Colonial Constabularies.* Kingston, Jamaica: University of the West Indies Press.

Harrison, A., N. Xaba, and P. Kunene. 2001. "Understanding Safe Sex: Gender Narratives of HIV and Pregnancy Prevention by Rural South African School-Going Youth." *Reproductive Health Matters* 17: 63–71.

Hawkes, S. 2001. "Evidence for STI/HIV Interventions with Heterosexual Men: Results from a Systematic Review." Unpublished manuscript, Population Council, New York.

Hazzard, William R. 1985. "Atherogenesis: Why Women Live Longer than Men." *Geriatrics* 40: 42–48.

Hearn, Jeff. 1992. *Men in the Public Eye: The Construction and Deconstruction of Public Men and Public Patriarchies.* London and New York: Routledge.

Heise, L. 1994. "Gender-based Abuse: The Global Epidemic." *Caderno de Saúde Pública* 10 (1): 135–45.

Helgerson, John L. 2002. "The National Security Implications of Global Demographic Change" (April). http://www.au.af.mil/au/awc/awcgate/cia/helgerson2.htm

Helzner, Judith Frye. 1996. "Men's Involvement in Family Planning." *Reproductive Health Matters* (7): 146–54.

Hendrixson, Anne. 2003. "The Youth Bulge: Defining the Next Generation of Young Men as a Threat to the Future." *Different Takes* 19, Population and Development Program at Hampshire College.

———. 2004. "Angry Young Men, Veiled Young Women: Constructing a New Population Threat." Corner House Briefing 34 (December), Dorset, U.K. http://www.thecornerhouse.org.uk/pdf/briefing/34veiled.pdf

Henriques, Fernando. 1953. *Family and Colour in Jamaica.* London: Eyre and Spottiswoode.

Hernández, D. 1996. "Género y roles familiares: La voz de los hombres." Tesis de maestría en antropología social. Mexico: CIEAS.

Herskovits, Melville. 1941. *The Myth of the Negro Past.* New York: Harpers.

Herskovits, Melville, and Frances Herskovits. 1976. *Trinidad Village.* New York: Octagon Books.

Higman, Barry. 1975. "Slave family and Household in the British West Indies, 1800–1834." *Journal of Interdisciplinary History* 6 (2).

Hoben, Susan J. 1989. "School, Work and Equity: Educational Reform in Rwanda." African Research Studies 16, African Studies Center, Boston University, Boston, MA.

Hoffman, J., L. Huang, D. Gerstein, A. Brittingham, C. Larison, and M. Toce. 1999. "Analysis of the Casino Survey: Report to the National Gambling Impact Study Commission." Chicago: National Opinion Research Center.

Holden, Constance. 1987. "Why Do Women Live Longer than Men?" *Science* 238: 158–60.

Holland, J., C. Ramazanoglu, S. Sharpe, and R. Thomson. 1994. "Achieving Masculine Sexuality: Young Men's Strategies for Managing Vulnerability." In *AIDS: Setting a Feminist Agenda*, ed. L. Doyal, J. Naidoo, and T. Wilton, 122–48. Philadelphia: Taylor and Francis.

Holmes, C. B., H. Hausler, and P. Nunn. 1998. "A Review of Sex Differences in the Epidemiology of Tuberculosis." *International Journal of Tuberculosis and Lung Disease* 2 (2): 96–104.

Holsoe, S. 1977. "Slavery and Economic Response among the Vai (Liberia and Sierra Leone)." In *Slavery in Africa: Historical and Anthropological Perspectives*, ed. Suzanne Miers and Igor Kopytoff. Madison, WI: University of Wisconsin Press.

Holter, Øystein Gullvåg. 2000. "Masculinities in Context: On Peace Issues and Patriarchal Orders." In *Male Roles, Masculinities and Violence: A Culture of Peace Perspective*, ed. Ingeborg Breines, Robert Connell and Ingrid Eide, 61–83. Paris: UNESCO.

Hope, Kempe Ronald. 1998. "Urbanization and Urban Growth in Africa." *Journal of Asian and African Studies* 33 (4): 345–58.

Hopenhayn, M. 2002. "Youth and Employment in Latin America and the Caribbean: Problems, Prospects, and Options." Paper presented at the Youth Employment Summit, Alexandria, Egypt, September 7–11.

Hser, Y. I., M. D. Anglin, and Y. Liu. 1991. "A Survival Analysis of Gender and Ethnic-Differences in Responsiveness to Methadone-Maintenance Treatment." *International Journal of the Addictions* 25 (11a): 1295–315.

Human Rights Watch. 2001. *Uprooting the Rural Poor in Rwanda*. New York, Washington, London, and Brussels: Human Rights Watch.

———. 2003a. *Rwanda Lasting Wounds: Consequences of Genocide and War for Rwanda's Children*. New York: Human Rights Watch. http://www.hrw.org/reports/2003/rwanda0403/rwanda0403.htm

———. 2003b. "Just Die Quietly: Domestic Violence and Women's Vulnerability to HIV in Uganda." Human Rights Watch, New York.

Human Rights Watch and CLEEN. 2002. "Nigeria: The Bakassi Boys: The Legitimization of Murder and Torture." Human Rights Watch 14 (5A), New York.

Humphreys, M., and P. Richards. 2005. "Prospects and Opportunities for Achieving the MDGs in Post-Conflict Countries: A Case-Study of Sierra

Leone and Liberia." CGSD Working Paper 27, Columbia University, New York.

Humphreys, M., and J. Weinstein. 2004. "What the Fighters Say: A Survey of Ex-combatants in Sierra Leone, June–August 2003." CGSD Working Paper 20, Columbia University, New York.

Huntington, Samuel P. 1996. *The Clash of Civilizations and the Remaking of the World Order*. New York: Simon & Shuster.

Hutchison, Elizabeth. 1995. "La defensa de las 'Hijas del Pueblo'. Género y política obrera en Santiago a principios de siglo." In *Disciplina y desacato. Construcción de la identidad en Chile. Siglos IXX y XX*, ed. L. Godoy. Santiago, Chile: SUR/CEDEM.

Instituto Brasileiro de Geografia e Estatística (IBGE). 1998. *Demographic Census of 1980, 1991/PNAD 1996*. Rio de Janeiro: IBGE.

Interagency Gender Working Group (IGWG). 2003. *Three Case Studies: Involving Men to Address Gender Inequities*. New York: IGWG.

International Labour Organization (ILO). 2005. *Facts on Youth Employment*. Geneva: ILO.

International Organisation for Migration (IOM), and ANEC (National Association of Colombian Nurses). 2002. *Lecturas de silencios: Propuesta de atención integral para mujeres violadas sexualmente por razones del conflicto armado colombiano*. Bogotá: IOM-ANEC.

International Planned Parenthood Foundation (IPPF), Western Hemisphere Region. 2001a. "Brothers for Change: Working with Male Perpetrators of Violence in Jamaica." *Forum* 15 (1): 2–3.

———. 2001b. "Rock and Male Roles: Using Technology and Music to Teach Young Men about Gender Roles and Sexual and Reproductive Health." *Forum* 15 (1): 4–5.

InterWorld Radio. 2003. "Boys' Talk: Young Men and HIV."

IRIN (UN Office for the Coordination of Humanitarian Affairs). 2003. "Rwanda: US Official Pledges to Mobilise Resources in Fight against HIV/AIDS, December 3." http://www.plusnews.org/AIDSreport.asp? ReportID=2807&SelectRegion=Great_Lakes&SelectCountry=RWANDA

Irvin, A. 2000. "Taking Steps of Courage: Teaching Adolescents about Sexuality and Gender in Nigeria and Cameroon." International Women's Health Coalition, New York.

Islas, Francisco Cervantes. 1999. "Helping Men Overcome Violent Behavior toward Women." In *Too Close to Home: Domestic Violence in the Americas*, ed. Andrew R. Morrison and María Loreto Biehl, 143–47. Washington, DC: Inter-American Development Bank.

Jacobsen, Joyce P. 1991. "Earnings and Employment Differences by Race and Sex, by Economic Sector." PhD dissertation, Stanford University, Stanford, CA.

Jacobson-Widding, A. 1983. *Identity: Personal and Socio-cultural*. Stockholm: Almquist & Wiksell.

Jejeebhoy, S. 2000. "Women's Autonomy in Rural India: Its Dimensions, Determinants and the Influence of the Context." In *Women's Empowerment and Demographic Processes*, ed. Harriet B. Presser and Gita Sen. Oxford, U.K.: Oxford University Press.

Jelin, Elizabeth. 1994. "Las familias en América Latina." In *Familias siglo XXI*, ed. ISIS. Santiago, Chile: ISIS.

———. 1998. *The Economics of Gender, Second Edition*. Malden, MA: Blackwell.

Jewkes, R. 1998. "Promoting Adolescent Sexual and Reproductive Health." Keynote address to the "Fifth Reproductive Health Priorities Conference," Vanderbijlpark, South Africa, August.

Jewkes, R., J. B. Levin, and L. A. Penn-Kekana. 2003. "Gender Inequalities: Intimate Partner Violence and HIV Preventive Practices: Findings of a South African Cross-Sectional Study." *Social Science and Medicine* 56: 125–34.

Joekes, Susan. 1987. *Women in the World Economy: An INSTRAW Study*. Oxford, U.K.: Oxford University Press.

Johansson, Sten, and Ola Nygren. 1991. "The Missing Girls of China: A New Demographic Analysis." *Population and Development Review* 17 (1): 35–51.

Johnson, D. 1995. "Father Presence Matters." NCOFF, University of Pennsylvania, Philadelphia, PA.

Jones, A. 1983. *From Slaves to Palm Kernels: A History of the Galinhas Country (West Africa) 1730–1890*. Wiesbaden, Germany: Steiner Verlag.

Jordan, W. 1995. *Role Transitions: A Review of the Literature*. Philadelphia, PA: NCOFF, University of Pennsylvania.

Joshua, Milton Obote. 2001. "Gender Training with Men: Experiences and Reflections from East Africa." In *Men's Involvement in Gender and Development Policy and Practice: Beyond Rhetoric*, ed. Caroline Sweetman, 35–43. Oxford, U.K.: Oxfam.

Kaler, A. 2003. "My Girlfriends Could Fill a Yanu-Yanu Bus." *Demographic Research* (Special Collection) 1 (11).

Kandeh, J. 2001. "Subaltern Terror in Sierra Leone." In *Africa in Crisis: New Challenges and Possibilities*, ed. A. T. Zack-Williams, D. Frost, and A. Thomson, 179–95. London: Pluto Press.

Kanyenze, G., G. Mhone, and T. Sparreboom. 2000. "Strategies to Combat Youth Unemployment and Marginalisation in Anglophone Africa." ILO/SAMAT Discussion Paper 14, ILO, Geneva.

Kaplan, Robert D. 1994. "The Coming Anarchy." *Atlantic Monthly* (February), 44–76.

———. 1996. *The Ends of the Earth: A Journey at the Dawn of the 21st Century*. New York: Random House.

Kaplan, Suzanne. 2005. *Children in Africa with Experiences of Massive Trauma: A Research Review*. Department for Research Cooperation, SIDA. http://www.multietn.uu.se/staff/pers-homepages/Kaplan_SIDA4629en_Children_in_Africa_w.pdf

Kariuki, C. 2004. "Masculinity and Adolescent Male Violence: A Case Study of Three Secondary Schools in Kenya." University of Cape Town, Cape Town, South Africa.

Katz, Jorge. 2000. *Reformas estructurales, productividad y conducta tecnológica en América Latina*. Santiago, Chile: Fondo de Cultura Económica/ECLAC.

Kaufman, C., S. Clark, N. Manzini, and J. May. 2002. "How Community Structures of Time and Opportunity Shape Adolescent Sexual Behavior in South Africa." Policy Research Division Working Paper 159, Population Council, New York.

Kaufman, M. 1997. "Las experiencias contradictories del poder entre los hombres." In *Masculinidades, poder y crisis*, ed. Teresa Valdés and José Olavaria, 63–81. Santiago, Chile: Isis Internacional-FLACSO.

Keijzer, B. 1995. "Masculinity as a Risk Factor." Paper presented at the "Coloquio Latinoamericano sobre Varones, Sexualidad y Reproducción." Zacatecas, Mexico, November 17–18.

Kemper, Yvonne. 2005. *Youth in War-to-Peace Transitions: Approaches of International Organizations*. Berlin: Berghof Research Center for Constructive Conflict Management.

Kerrigan, D. 2000. *Peer Education and HIV/AIDS: Past Experience, Future Directions*. Washington, DC: Horizons/Population Council.

Kiama, W. 1999. "Men who Have Sex with Men in Kenya." In *AIDS and Men Taking Risks or Taking Responsibility?*, ed. M. Foreman. London: PANOS/ZED Books.

Kibwana, K., and L. M. Mute. 2000. *The Law and the Quest for Gender Equality in Kenya*. Nairobi: Claripress.

Kimmel, Michael. 1996. *Manhood in America: A Cultural History*. New York: Free Press.

———. 2002a. "Men Masculinities and Development." Unpublished manuscript prepared for the World Bank.

———. 2002b. "Gender, Class and Terror." *The Chronicle of Higher Education: The Chronicle Review* (February 8). http://chronicle.com/free/v48/i22/22b01101.htm.

Kingree, J. B. 1995. "Understanding Gender Differences in Psychosocial Functioning and Treatment Retention." *American Journal of Drug and Alcohol Abuse* 21: 267–81.

Klippenberg, Juliane. 2004. *Rwanda Still in Our Human Rights Blind Spot*. Human Rights Watch. http://hrw.org/english/docs/2004/07/25/rwanda9189.htm

Klubock, Thomas. 1995. "Hombres y mujeres en El Teniente. La construcción de género y clase en la minería chilena del cobre, 1904–1951." In *Disciplina y desacato. Construcción de la identidad en Chile. Siglos IXX y XX*, ed. L. Godoy. Santiago, Chile: SUR/CEDEM.

Kornblit, A., A. Mendes Diz, and M. Petracci. 1998. "Being a Man, Being a Father: A Study on the Social Representations of Fatherhood." Paper

presented at the "Men, Family Formation and Reproduction Seminar,"
Organized by the International Union for the Scientific Study of
Population (IUSSP) and the Centro de Estudios de la Población
(CENEP), Buenos Aires, May 13–15.

Kraemer, Sebastian. 2000. "The Fragile Male." *British Medical Journal* 321: 23–30.

Kuperman, Alan J. 2001. *The Limits of Humanitarian Intervention: Genocide in
Rwanda.* Washington, DC: Brookings Institution Press.

Kurtz, J. Roger. 1998. *Urban Obsessions Urban Fears: The Postcolonial Kenyan Novel.*
Trenton, NJ, and Asmara, Eritrea: Africa World Press.

Lang, E., K. Arnold, and P. Kupfer. 1994. "Frauen Werden Alter." *Zeitschrift fur
Gerontologie* 27 (1): 10–15.

Large, Judith. 1997. "Disintegration Conflicts and the Restructuring of
Masculinity." In *Men and Masculinity*, ed. Caroline Sweetman, 23–30.
Oxford, U.K.: Oxfam.

Leach, F. 2003. "Learning to Be Violent: The Role of the School in Developing
Adolescent Gendered Behaviour." *Compare* 33 (3): 385–400.

Leñero, L. 1994. "Los varones ante la planificación familiar." In *Maternidad sin
riesgos en Mexico*, ed. M. Elu and A. Langer. Mexico: Instituto Mexicano de
Estudios Sociales (IMES).

Leopold, R. 1991. "Prescriptive Alliance and Ritual Collaboration in Loma
Society." PhD dissertation, Indiana University, Indiana.

Leo-Rhynie, Elsa. 1987. "Academic Performance of Boys and Girls in Jamaican
Schools." Paper prepared for the First Interdisciplinary Seminar on
Women and Development Studies, "Gender, Culture and Caribbean
Development," University of the West Indies, Mona, Jamaica.

Levine, J. A. 1993. "Involving Fathers in Head Start: A Framework for Public
Policy and Program Development." *Families in Society: The Journal of
Contemporary Human Services* 74 (1): 4–19.

Lindsay, Keisha. 2002. "Caribbean Male: Endangered Species?" Center for
Gender and Development Working Paper 1, University of the West Indies,
Mona, Jamaica.

Lindsay, L. A., and S. F. Miescher, eds. 2003. *Men and Masculinites in Modern Africa.*
Portsmouth, NH: Heinemann.

Little, K. 1965. "The Political Function of the Poro." Parts 1 and 2. *Africa* 35 (4):
349–65; and 36 (1): 69–71.

Llorente, María Victoria, Rodolfo Escobedo, Camilo Echandía, and Mauricio
Rubio. 2001. "Violencia homicida en Bogotá: Más que intolerancia."
CEDE Document, 2001(04), CEDE, Bogotá.

Lockwood, D. 1992. "Solidarity and Schism: 'The Problem of Disorder.'" In
Durkheimian and Marxist Sociology. Oxford, U.K.: Clarendon Press.

López, Humberto, Quentin Wodon, and Ian Bannon. 2004. "Rwanda: The Impact
of Conflict on Growth and Poverty." Social Development Notes, Conflict
Prevention and Reconstruction 18, World Bank, Washington, DC.

Louw, Ronald. 2001. "Mkhumbane and New Traditions of (Un) African Same-Sex Weddings." In *Changing Men in Southern Africa*, ed. R. Morrell. Natal, South Africa: University of Natal Press/Zed Books.

Lovgren, Stefan. 2001. "All That Glitters." *US News & World Report,* August 13, Page 5.

Lowicki, Jane, and Allison Pillsbury. 2000. *Untapped Potential: Adolescents Affected by Armed Conflict. A Review of Programs and Policies.* New York: Women's Commission for Refugee Women and Children. http://www.asylumsupport.info/publications/womenscommssion/potential.pdf

Luke, N., and K. Kurz. 2002. *Cross-Generational and Transactional Sexual Relations in sub-Saharan Africa: Prevalence of Behavior and Implications for Negotiating Safer Sexual Practices.* Washington, DC: International Center for Research on Women (ICRW).

Lundgren, R. 1999. *Research Protocols to Study Sexual and Reproductive Health of Male Adolescents and Young Adults in Latin America.* Washington, DC: Pan American Health Organization.

Luyt, R. 2005. Masculinity and Aggression in South Africa: Research Notes." *Sexuality in Africa Magazine* 2 (1): 11–14.

Lyra, J. 1998. "Paternidade adolescente: Da investigacao a intervencao." In *Homens e masculinidades: Outras palavras*, ed. M. Arilha, S. Ridenti, and B. Medrado. São Paulo, Brazil: ECOS and Editora 34.

Mac an Ghaill, Maírtín. 1996. *Understanding Masculinities, Social Relations and Cultural Arenas.* Buckingham, U.K.: Open University Press.

Mackey, W., and R. Day. 1979. "Some Indicators of Fathering in the United States: A Crosscultural Examination of Adult Male-Child Interactions." *Journal of Marriage and Family* 41 (3): 287–99.

MacPhail, C., and C. Campbell. 2001. "'I Think Condoms Are Good, but, aai, I Hate Those Things': Condom Use among Adolescents and Young People in a Southern African Township." *Social Science & Medicine* 52: 1613–27.

Macrae, Callum. 2004. "Uganda's Fallen Child Rebels". *BBC News,* April 8.

Maitse Teboho. 1998. "Political Change, Rape, and Pornography in Post-Apartheid South Africa." *Gender and Development* 6 (3): 55–59.

Majors, R., and J. M. Billson. 1992. *Cool Pose: The Dilemmas of Black Manhood in America.* New York: Simon & Schuster.

Makimoto, K., H. Oda, and S. Higuchi. 2000. "Alcohol Effects on the Fetus, Brain, Liver, and Other Organ Systems—Is Heavy Alcohol Consumption an Attributable Risk Factor for Cancer-Related Deaths among Japanese Men?" *Alcoholism: Clinical and Experimental Research* 24 (3): 382–85.

Malaza-Debose, M. 2001. "Gender Based Experiences in Preventing and Coping with HIV/AIDS in Post-Conflict Sub-Saharan Africa." Paper presented at the "Preventing and Coping with HIV/AIDS in Postconflict Societies: Gender Based Lessons from Sub-Saharan Africa Conference," Durban, South Africa, March 26–28.

Mamdani, Mahmood. 2001. *When Victims Become Killers: Colonialism, Nativism, and the Genocide in Rwanda.* Princeton, NJ: Princeton University Press.

Marks, M. 1992. "Youth and Political Violence: The Problem of Anomie and the Role of Youth Organizations." Centre for the Study of Violence and Reconciliation, Seminar 5, Johannesburg, South Africa.

Marsiglio, W. 1998. "Adolescent Male Sexuality and Heterosexual Masculinity: A Conceptual Model and Review" *Journal of Adolescent Research* 3 (3–4): 285–303.

Marsiglio, W., S. Hutchinson, and M. Cohan. 1999. "Young Men's Procreative Identity: Becoming Aware, Being Aware and Being Responsible." Unpublished manuscript, University of Florida, Gainesville, FL.

Masanja, P., and E. J. Urassa. 1993. *The Marginalisation of Men.* Paper prepared for the conference "Population Reconsidered," Swedish Development Agency (SIDA), Harare, Zimbabwe.

Maslen, S. 1997. *The Reintegration of War-Affected Youth: The Experience of Mozambique.* Geneva: ILO.

Massing, A. 1980. *The Economic Anthropology of the Kru (West Africa).* Wiesbaden, Germany: Franz Steiner Verlag.

Mataure, P., T. Scalway, S. Ray, and M. Foreman. 2000. *Men and HIV in Swaziland.* PANOS/SAfAIDS/UNAIDS.

Mataure P., W. McFarland, K. Fritz, A. Kim, G. Woelk, S. Ray, and G. Rutherford. 2002. "Alcohol Use and High Risk Sexual Behaviour among Adolescents and Young Adults in Harare, Zimbabwe." *AIDS and Behavior* 6: 211–19.

Mauro, A., K. Araujo, and L. Godoy. 2001. "Trayectorias laborales masculinas y cambios en el mercado de trabajo." In *Hombres: Identidad/es y Violencia*, ed. J. Olavarría. Santiago, Chile: FLACSO, UAHC y Red de Masculinidades.

Mazurana, Dyan E., Susan A. McKay, Kristopher C. Carlson, and Janet C. Kasper. 2002. "Girls Fighting Forces and Groups: Their Recruitment, Participation, Demobilization, and Reintegration." *Peace and Conflict: Journal of Peace Psychology* 8 (2): 97–123.

McAdoo, J. L. 1988. "Changing Perspectives on the Role of the Black Father," In *Fatherhood Today: Men's Changing Role in the Family*, ed. P. Bronstein and C. Cowan. New York: John Wiley and Sons.

McBride, B. 1991. "Parent Education and Support Programs for Fathers: Outcome Effects on Paternal Involvement." *Early Child Development and Care* 67: 73–85.

McKay, Susan A., and Dyan Mazurana. 2004. *Where Are the Girls? Girls in Fighting Forces in Northern Uganda, Sierra Leone and Mozambique: Their Lives During and After War.* Montreal: Rights and Democracy.

Meertens, Donny. 2000. *Ensayos sobre tierra, violencia y género. Hombres y mujeres en la historia rural de Colombia 1930–1990.* Bogotá: Universidad Nacional-Centro de Estudios Sociales.

Meirelles, Z., and C. Minayo Gomez. 1999. "Quando o futuro é a morte: Adolescentes no narcotrafico." Unpublished manuscript, State University of Rio de Janeiro, Nucleo de Estudos em Saúde do Adolescente, and the Escola Nacional de Saude Publica.

Melvern, Linda. 2004. *Conspiracy to Murder: The Rwandan Genocide.* London and New York: Verso.

Mesquida, Christian G., and Niel I. Wiener. 1996. "Human Collective Aggression: A Behavioural Ecology Perspective." Research Report 55 (July), LaMarsh Centre for Research on Violence and Conflict Resolution, York University, Toronto, Canada.

———. 1999. "Male Age Composition and Severity of Conflicts." *Politics and the Life Sciences* 18 (2): 181–89.

Michailof, S., M. Kostner, and X. Devictor. 2002. "Post-Conflict Recovery in Africa: An Agenda for the Africa Region." Africa Region Working Paper Series 30, World Bank, Washington, DC.

Micheli, A., A. Mariotto, A. Rossi, G. Gatta, and P. Muti. 1998. "The Prognostic Role of Gender in Survival of Adult Cancer Patients." *European Journal of Cancer* 34 (14): 2271–278.

Miller, Errol. 1986. *Marginalization of the Black Male: Insights from the Development of the Teaching Profession.* Mona, Jamaica: Institute of Social and Economic Research, University of the West Indies.

———. 1991. *Men at Risk.* Kingston, Jamaica: Jamaica Publishing House.

Misser, Francois. 2004. "Rwanda: From Doomsday to Boom Time." London: *The Sunday Independent/Independent Online.* http://www.int.iol.co.za/general/news/newsprint.php?art_id=qw1077 44400461S530&sf=

Mkandawire, T. 2002. "The Terrible Toll of Post-Colonial Rebel Movements in Africa: Towards an Explanation of Violence against the Peasantry." *Journal of Modern African Studies* 40 (2): 181–215.

Momsen, Janet Henshall. 1991. *Women and Development in the Third World.* London: Routledge.

Moodie, T. D. 2001. "Black Migrant Mine Labourers and the Vicissitudes of male Desire." In *Changing Men in Southern Africa,* ed. R. Morrell. Natal, South Africa: University of Natal Press/Zed Books.

Moore, S., and D. Rosenthal. 1993. *Sexuality in Adolescence.* Oxford, U.K.: Routledge.

Morales, P. C. 1995. "Qué motiva a los hombres a limitar su fecundidad?" Paper presented at the "Coloquio Latinoamericano sobre Varones, Sexualidad y Reproducción," Zacatecas, Mexico, November 17–18.

Morrell, R. 1998 "Of Boys and Men: Masculinity and Gender in Southern African Studies," *Journal of Southern African Studies* 24 (18).

———. 2001. *Changing Men in Southern Africa.* Natal: University of Natal Press/Zed Books.

————. 2002. "Men, Movements, and Gender Transformation in South Africa." *The Journal of Men's Studies* 10 (3): 309.

Moser, Caroline. 1993. *Gender Planning and Development: Theory, Practice and Training.* London and New York: Routledge.

Moser, Caroline, and B. van Bronkhorst. 1999. "Youth Violence in Latin America and the Caribbean: Costs, Causes, and Interventions." Urban Peace Program Series, LCR Sustainable Development Working Paper 4, World Bank, Washington, DC.

Moser, Caroline, and F. Clark, eds. 2001. *Victims, Perpetrators or Actors: Gender, Armed Conflict and Political Violence.* London: Zed Books.

Mosher, D., and S. Tomkins. 1988. "Scripting the Macho Man: Hypermasculine Socialization and Enculturation." *The Journal of Sex Research* 25 (1): 60–84.

Mulrine, Anna. 2001. "Are Boys the Weaker Sex?" *U. S. News & World Report* July 30, 40–47.

Murison, Katharine, ed. 2003. *Africa South of the Sahara.* London and New York: Europa Publications.

Murphy, Kim. 1992. "Yemen Ritual Gives You Something to Chew On." *Los Angeles Times,* June 23, 6.

Murphy, W. 1980. "Secret Knowledge as Property and Power in Kpelle Society: Elders Versus Youth." *Africa* 50: 193–207.

Murphy, W., and C. Bledsoe. 1998. "Kinship and Territory in the History of a Kpelle Chiefdom (Liberia)." In *The African Frontier: The Reproduction of Traditional African Societies,* ed. Igor Kopytoff. Bloomington, IN: Indiana University Press.

Murray, Christopher, and Allan D. Lopez. 1996. *The Global Burden of Disease.* Cambridge, MA: Harvard University Press for WHO and the World Bank.

Mwenzwa, E. M. 2004. "Gender Relations and their Implication for Rural Development: The Case of Mwingi Central Division, Kenya." Unpublished MA thesis, Department of Sociology, University of Nairobi.

National Center on Fathers and Families (NCOFF). 2002. *The Fathering Indicators Framework: A Tool for Quantitative and Qualitative Analysis.* Philadelphia: NCOFF.

National Institute of Legal Medicine and Forensic Sciences (INML y CF). 2002. Forensis. Datos para la vida, 2001. Bogotá: INML y CF-GTZ.

National Office of the General Public Prosecutor (NOGPP). 1993. *Mortalidad en Santafé de Bogotá.* Bogotá: NOGPP.

National Poverty Reduction Programme and Ministry of Local Government and Social Affairs, Republic of Rwanda. n.d. *Ubudehe mu Kurwanya Ubukene: Ubudehe to Fight Poverty.* http://www.worldbank.org/wbi/attackingpoverty/programs/rwanda-nprp.pdf.

Nationmaster. 2005a. *Map & Graph: People: Urbanization.* http://www.nationmaster.com/graph-B/peo_urb

————. 2005b. *Map & Graph: Education: Pupils reaching grade 5.*
http://www.nationmaster.com/graph-B/ edu_pup_rea_gra_5.

————. 2005c. *Map & Graph: Military: Armed forces growth.* http://www.
nationmaster.com/graph-T/mil_arm_for_gro.

Nava, R. 1995. "Los hombres como padres en el DF a principios de los noventa."
Unpublished Master's thesis, UNAM, Mexico.

Newby, Margaret, and Ann E. Biddlecom. 1997. "Absent and Problematic Men:
Demographic Accounts of Male Reproductive Roles." Population
Council Policy Research Division Working Paper 103, Population
Council, New York.

Newman, Jesse. 2005. "Protection through Participation: Young People Affected
by Forced Migration and Political Crisis." Refugee Studies Centre
Working Paper 20, Refugee Studies Center, University of Oxford, Oxford,
U.K.

Niang, C., M. Diagne, Y. Niang, A. Moreau, D. Gomis, M. Diouf, K. Seck,
A. Wade, P. Tapsoba, and C. Castle. 2002. "Meeting the Sexual Health
Needs of Men who Have Sex with Men in Senegal." *Horizons, Washington,
DC.*

Nisbett, Richard E., and Dov Cohen. 1999. "Men, Honor and Murder." *Scientific
American* (Special Issue on Men's Health).

Nock, Steven L. 1998. *Marriage in Men's Lives.* New York and Oxford, U.K.:
Oxford University Press.

Nolasco, S. 1993. *O Mito da Masculinidade.* Rio de Janeiro: Rocco.

Nordstrom, Carolyn. 1999. "Girls and War Zones: Troubling Questions." In
Engendering Forced Migration: Theory and Practice, ed. Doreen Indra. New
York and Oxford, U.K.: Berghahn Books.

Nzioka, C. 2001. "Perspectives of Adolescent Boys on the Risks of Unwanted
Pregnancy and Sexually Transmitted Infections: Kenya." *Reproductive Health
Matters* (9): 108–17.

Obura, Anna. 2003. *Never Again: Educational Reconstruction in Rwanda.* Paris:
International Institute for Educational Planning, UNESCO.

O Globo. 2002a. "Jovens longe da escola ficam mais perto do trafico." September
29.

————. 2002b. "O primeiro e ultimo emprego: Trafico oferece mais trabalho a
jovens de 15 a 17 anos do que o mercado formal." December 8. "

————. 2002c. "UNICEF: educação dos jovens no país é alarmante." December
12.

Ofcansky, Thomas. 2003. "Rwanda: Recent History." In *Africa South of the Sahara
2003*, ed. Katharine Murison. London and New York: Europa
Publications.

Office of Conflict Management and Mitigation. 2005. *Youth and Conflict: A
Toolkit for Intervention.* Washington, DC: Office of Conflict Management
and Mitigation (USAID).

Office of Transition Initiatives (OTI). 2000. "Diamonds and Armed Conflict in
    Sierra Leone: Proposal for Implementation of a New Diamond Policy and
    Operations." USAID OTI Working Paper.
Ogbu, Osita, and Gerrishon Ikiara. 1995. "The Crisis of Urbanisation in Sub-
    Saharan Africa." *Courier* 149 (January–February): 52–59.
Okojie, C. 2003. "Employment Creation for Youth in Africa: The Gender
    Dimension." Paper presented at "Jobs for Youth: National Strategies for
    Employment Promotion," Geneva, June 15–16.
Olavarría, J. 2000. "Ser padre en Santiago de Chile." In *Paternidades en América
    Latina*, ed. Norma Fuller. Lima, Perú: Pontíficia Universidad Católica
    del Perú.
———. 2001a. *¿Hombres a la deriva? Poder, trabajo y sexo.* Santiago, Chile:
    FLACSO-Chile.
———. 2001b. *Y todos querían ser (buenos) padres. Varones de Santiago de Chile en
    conflicto.* Santiago, Chile: FLACSO-Chile.
Olavarría, José, Cristina Benavente, and Patricio Mellado. 1998. *Masculinidades popu-
    lares. Varones adultos jóvenes de Santiago.* Santiago, Chile: FLACSO-Chile.
Olavarría, José, and C. Céspedes. 2002. *Trabajo y familia: ¿Conciliación? Perspectivas
    de género.* Santiago, Chile: FLACSO-Chile, SERBAM y Centro de Estudios
    de la Mujer CEM.
Olavarría, José, and Enrique Moletto. 2002. Hombres: Identidad/es y sexuali-
    dad/es. Tercer Encuentro de Estudios de Masculinidad/es. Santiago de
    Chile: Red Masculinidad-UAHC-FLACSO.
Olavarría, José, and R. Parrini. 1999. *Los padres adolescentes. Hombres adolescentes y
    jóvenes frente al embarazo y nacimiento de un/a hijo/a. Antecedentes para la formu-
    lación y diseño de políticas públicas en Chile.* Santiago, Chile: UNICEF-FLACSO.
———. eds. 2000. *Masculinidad/es. Identidad, sexualidad y familia. Primer Encuentro
    de Estudios de Masculinidad.* Santiago, Chile: Red Masculinidad Chile-
    UAHC-FLACSO.
Omari, C. K. 1980. "Development." Proceedings of the Workshop held at
    YMCA, National Council of Social Welfare and Service, Moshi, Tanzania,
    September 20–27.
Ortiz Pérez, Isabel. 2000. "Atención educativa-terapéutica a hombres agresores."
    In: *Masculinidades en Colombia. Reflexiones y perspectivas*, Foro Memorias
    (July 25), 129–37. Bogotá: AVSC International-UNFPA-UN's Gender,
    Women and Development Program-Haz Paz. http://www.
    usaid.gov/ hum_response/oti/country/sleone/diamonds.html.
Ould-Abdallah, Ahmedou. 2000. *Burundi on the Brink 1993–95: A UN Special
    Envoy Reflects on Preventive Diplomacy.* Washington, DC: United States
    Institute of Peace Press.
Ouzgane, Lahoucine, and Robert Morrell, eds. 2005. *African Masculinities. Men in
    the Late Nineteenth Century to the Present.* Scottsdale, South Africa:
    University of KwaZulu-Natal Press.

Palacio Valencia, María Cristina, and Ana Judith Valencia Hoyos. 2001. *La identi-dad masculina: Un mundo de inclusiones y exclusiones.* Manizales, Colombia: Universidad de Caldas.
Palmary, I., and C. Moat. 2002. *Preventing Criminality among Young People.* Johannesburg: Centre for the Study of Violence and Reconciliation.
PANOS Institute. 1998. "AIDS and Men: Old Problem, New Angle." PANOS HIV/AIDS Briefing 6, December, PANOS Institute, London.
Parke, R. 1981. *Fathers.* Cambridge, MA: Harvard University Press.
Parker, Susan Wendy, and Carla Pederzini. 1999. Gender Differences in Education in Mexico." Working Paper, World Bank, Washington, DC.
Parry, Odette. 2000. *Male Underachievement in High School Education in Jamaica, Barbados, and St. Vincent and the Grenadines.* Kingston, Jamaica: Canoe Press.
Perls, Thomas T., and Ruth C. Fretts. 1998. "Why Women Live Longer Than Men." *Scientific American*, Special Issue on Women's Health: 100–103.
Peters, K., and P. Richards. 1998. 'Why We Fight: Voices of Youth Ex-Combatants in Sierra Leone." *Africa* 68 (1): 183–210.
Peters, K., P. Richards, and K. Vlassenroot. 2003. "What Happens to Youth During and After Wars? A Preliminary Review of Literature on Africa and an Assessment of the Debate." RAWOO Working Paper.
Peterson, Scott. 2000. *Me Against My Brother: At War in Somalia, Sudan, and Rwanda: A Journalist Reports from the Battlefields of Africa.* New York and London: Routledge.
Pettifor, A. E., H. V. Rees, A. Steffenson, L. Hlongwa-Madikizela, C. MacPhail, K. Vermaak, and I. Kleinschmidt. 2004. "HIV and Sexual Behavior among Young South Africans: A National Survey of 15–24 Year Olds." Reproductive Health Research Unit, University of the Witwatersrand, Johannesburg.
Pickwell, S. M., S. Schimelpfening, and L. A. Palinkas. 1994. "Betelmania—Betel Quid Chewing by Cambodian Women in the United States and its Potential Health Effects." *Western Journal of Medicine* 160 (4): 326–30.
Pinker, Steven. 2002. *The Blank Slate.* London: Penguin.
Polgreen, Lydia. 2005. "In First for Africa, Woman Wins Election as President of Liberia." *New York Times* November 12, A1.
Pollack, William S. 1998. *Real Boys: Rescuing our Sons from the Myths of Boyhood.* New York: Random House.
Pool, R., J. Hart, G. Green, S. Harrison, S. Nyanzi, and J. A. G Whitworth. 2000. "Men's Attitudes to Condoms and Female Controlled Means of Protection against HIV and STDs in South-Western Uganda." *Culture, Health and Sexuality* 2 (1): 197–212.
Population Council. 1998. "Getting Men Involved in Family Planning: Experiences from an Innovative Program." Final Report, Washington, DC.
———. 2001. "The Unfinished Transition: Gender Equity: Sharing the Responsibilities of Parenthood." Population Council Issues Paper,

Washington, DC. http://www.popcouncil.org/publications/ issues_papers/transition_4.html

Pottier, Johan. 2002. *Re-imagining Rwanda: Conflict, Survival and Disinformation in the Late Twentieth Century.* Cambridge, U.K.: Cambridge University Press.

Powell, Dorian. 1985. "Caribbean Women and their Responses to Familial Experience." *Social and Economic Studies* 35 (2).

Power, Samantha. 2002. *"A Problem from Hell": America in the Age of Genocide.* New York: Basic Books.

Presidential Program for Human Rights and Humanitarian International Law of the Presidency of the Republic. 2002. *Niñez y conflicto armado en Colombia,* Bogotá.

Preston-Whyte, E. M., and M. Zondi. 1991. "Adolescent Sexuality and its Implications for Teenage Pregnancy and AIDS." *Continuing Medical Education* 9 (11): 1389–397.

Promundo/Ecos/PAPAI. 2002. "Salud y genero." *Working with Young Men Series.* Sao Paulo: Promundo/Ecos/PAPAI.

Promundo and NOOS. 1998. Pesquisa nacional por amostra de domicilios 1997 [CD-ROM]. Microdados. Rio de Janeiro: IBGE.

———. 2002. *Gender Violence and Sexual and Reproductive Health: A Qualitative and Quantitative Study with Men Ages 15–60 in Two Neighborhoods in Rio de Janeiro.* Rio de Janeiro: Instituto Promundo and Instituto NOOS.

———. 2003. *Men, Gender-based Violence and Sexual Reproductive Health: A Study with Men in Rio de Janeiro, Brazil.* Rio de Janeiro: Instituto Promundo and Instituto NOOS.

Pruett, K. 1993. "The Paternal Presence." *Families in Society: The Journal of Contemporary Human Services* (January): 46–50.

Prunier, Gérard. 1995. *The Rwanda Crisis: History of a Genocide.* New York: Columbia University Press.

PSI (Population Services International). 2003. "Misconceptions, Folk Beliefs, and Denial: Young Men's Risk for STIs and HIV/AIDS in Zambia." Working Paper 53, PSI.

Pulerwitz, J., G. Barker, and M. Segundo. 2004. "Promoting Healthy Relationships and HIV/STI Prevention for Young Men: Positive Findings from an Intervention Study in Brazil." *Horizons Research Update,* Population Council, Washington, DC.

Putnam, Robert. 2000. *Bowling Alone: The Collapse and Revival of American Community.* New York: Simon & Schuster.

Pyne, Hnin Hnin, Mariam Claeson, and Maria Correia. 2002. "Gender Dimensions of Alcohol Consumption and Alcohol-Related Problems in Latin America and the Caribbean." World Bank Discussion Paper 433, World Bank, Washington, DC.

Rakodi, Carole. 1997. "Introduction." In *The Urban Challenge in Africa: Growth and Management of its Large Cities,* ed. C. Rakod. Tokyo, New York and Paris: United Nations University Press.

Ramjee G., E. Gouws, and A. Andrews. 2001. "The Acceptability of a Vaginal Microbicide among South African Men." *International Family Planning Perspectives* 27 (4): 64–70.

Ramkisson, M. 2001. "Implications of Father Absence and Father Presence in the Lives of Children." Unpublished thesis, University of the West Indies, Mona, Jamaica.

Ranger, T. 1993. "The Communal Areas of Zimbabwe." In *Land in African Agrarian Systems*, ed. T. J. Bassett and D. Crummey. Madison, WI: University of Wisconsin Press.

Rapport du Seminaire sur le Processus "Ubudehe mu Kurwanya Ubukene" [Ubudehe to Fight Poverty]. 2002. Unpublished manuscript.

Rau, B. 2002. "Combating Child Labour and HIV/AIDS in sub-Saharan Africa: A Review of Policies, Programmes, and Projects in South Africa, United Republic of Tanzania, and Zambia to Identify Good Practices." Geneva: ILO and International Programme on the Elimination of Child Labour.

Rawls, A. 2003. "Conflict as a Foundation for Consensus: Contradictions of Industrial Capitalism in Book III of Durkheim's Division of Labor." *Critical Sociology* 29 (3): 295–335.

Rendon, M. 2000. "Trabajo de hombres y trabajo de mujeres en México durante el siglo XX." PhD dissertation, Facultad de Economía, UNAM, Mexico.

Republic of Liberia. 2003. *Act to Govern the Devolution of Estates and Establish the Rights of Inheritance for Spouses of Both Statutory and Customary Marriages*, approved by the House of Representatives October 7, 2003, Monrovia, Ministry of Foreign Affairs, Interim Government of National Unity, Republic of Liberia.

Restrepo, Luis Carlos. 2003. *Más allá del terror. Abordaje cultural de la violencia en Colombia.* Bogotá: Aguilar.

Reyntjens, Filip. 2004. "Rwanda, Ten Years On: From Genocide to Dictatorship." *African Affairs* 103 (April): 177–210.

Richards, P. 1995. "Rebellion in Liberia and Sierra Leone: A Crisis of Youth?" In *Conflict in Africa*, ed. O. W. Furley. London: Tauris.

———. 1996. *Fighting for the Rain Forest: War, Youth and Resources in Sierra Leone.* Oxford, U.K.: James Currey (reprinted with additional material 1998).

———. 2000. "Chimpanzees as Political Animals in Sierra Leone." In *Natural Enemies: People-Wildlife Conflicts in an Anthropological Perspective*, ed. J. Knight. London: Routledge.

———. 2003. "Mining and the Messiah: The Masterless Classes in Sierra Leone." Paper presented at the Workshop "Mining Frontiers: Social Conflicts, Property Relations and Cultural Change in Emerging Boom Regions," Max Planck Institute for Social Anthropology, Halle/Saale, Germany, June 16–18.

———. 2004. "New War: An Ethnographic Approach." In *No Peace, No War: An Anthropology of Contemporary Armed Conflicts*, ed. P. Richards. Oxford, U.K.: James Currey.

Richards, P., S. Archibald, K. Bah, and J. Vincent, J. 2003. "Where Have All the Young People Gone? Transitioning Ex-combatants Towards Community Reconstruction after the War in Sierra Leone." Unpublished report submitted to the National Commission for Disarmament, Demobilization and Reintegration, Government of Sierra Leone.

Richards, P., K. Bah, and J. Vincent. 2004. "Social Capital and Survival: Prospects for Community-Driven Development in Post-Conflict Sierra Leone." Social Development Papers: Community Driven Development, Conflict Prevention & Reconstruction 12, World Bank, Washington, DC.

Richards, P., S. Archibald, W. Modad, E. Mulbah, T. Varpilah, and J. Vincent. 2005. "Community Cohesion in Liberia: A Post-War Rapid Rural Assessment." Social Development Papers: Conflict Prevention & Reconstruction 21, World Bank, Washington, DC.

Rivers, K., and P. Aggleton. 1998. *Gender and the HIV Epidemic: Men and the HIV Epidemic*. New York: HIV and Development Programme, UNDP.

―――. 1999. *Gender and the HIV Epidemic: Adolescent Sexuality.* New York: HIV and Development Programme, UNDP.

Roberts, George. 1955. "Some Aspects of Mating and Fertility in the West Indies." *Population Studies* 8 (3).

Roberts, George, and Sonja Sinclair. 1978. *Women in Jamaica.* New York: KTO Press.

Robertson, A. F. 1987. *The Dynamics of Productive Relationships: African Share Contracts in Comparative Perspective.* Cambridge, U.K.: Cambridge University Press.

Rodgers, D. 1999. "Youth Gangs and Violence in Latin America and the Caribbean: A Literature Survey." World Bank Urban Peace Program Series, LCR Sustainable Development Working Paper 4, World Bank, Washington, DC.

Rodman, Hyman. 1971. *Lower-class Families: The Culture of Poverty in Negro Trinidad.* New York: Oxford University Press.

Rojas, O. 1999. "Paternidad y vida familiar en la Ciudad de México: Un acercamiento al papel desempeñado por los varones en el proceso reproductivo." Presentación al Seminario General de la Red de Estudios de Población, ALFAPOP, Celaterra, February 8–12.

Rosenblatt, Karin. 1995. "Masculinidad y trabajo: El salario familiar y el estado de compromiso, 1930–1950." *Proposiciones* 26, SUR, Santiago, Chile.

Rosenthal, Elisabeth. 1999. "Women's Suicides Reveal Rural China's Bitter Roots." *New York Times* January 24, 12.

Rowe, Richard, Barbara Maughan, Carol M. Worthman, E. Jane Costello, and Adrian Angold. 2004. "Testosterone, Antisocial Behavior, and Social Dominance in Boys: Pubertal Development and Biosocial Interaction." *Biological Psychiatry* 55: 546–52.

Ruiz, Marta. 2002. *Esta ciudad que no me quiere. Relatos de jóvenes de Bogotá.* Bogotá: Fescol-Cerec.

Ruddick, S. 1998. (As cited in C. Cockburn, C. [1999].) "Gender, Armed
Conflict and Political Violence." Background Paper for the World Bank
Conference "Gender, Armed Conflict and Political Violence," World Bank,
Washington, DC.

Rushby, Kevin. 1995. "The High Life." *Geographical Magazine* 67 (January):
14–17.

Russell, G. and M. Radojevic. 1992. "The Changing Role of Fathers? Current
Understandings and Future Directions for Research and Practice." *Infant
Mental Health Journal* 13 (4): 296–311.

Rutenberg, N., C. E. Kaufman, K. Macintyre, L. Brown, and A. Karim. 2002.
"Pregnant or Positive: Adolescent Childbearing and HIV Risk in South
Africa." Policy Research Division Working Paper 162, Population Council,
New York.

Sampath, Niels. 1997. "'Crabs in a Bucket': Reforming Male Identities in
Trinidad." In *Men and Masculinity*, ed. Caroline Sweetman, 47–54. Oxford,
U.K.: Oxfam.

Sampson, R. J., and J. H. Laub. 1993. "Crime in the Making: Pathways and
Turning Points through Life." Cambridge, MA: Harvard University Press.

Sánchez, Gonzalo, and Donny Meertens. 2002. *Bandoleros, gamonales y campesinos.
El caso de la violencia en Colombia.* Bogotá: El Áncora Editores.

Sánchez-Sosa, J., and L. Hernández-Guzmán 1992. "La relación con el padre
como factor de riesgo psicológico en México." *Revista Mexicana de
Psicología* 9 (1): 27–34.

Scalway, Thomas. 2001. *Young Men and HIV: Culture, Poverty and Sexual Risk.*
Geneva: UNAIDS/PANOS Institute.

Schafer, J. 2001. "Guerillas and Violence in the War in Mozambique: De-
Socialization or Re-Socialization?" *African Affairs* 100: 214–37.

Schmittroth, Linda, ed. 1995. *Statistical Record of Women Worldwide.* New York:
Gale Research.

Schwartz, G. 1987. *Beyond Conformity or Rebellion: Youth and Authority in America.*
Chicago: University of Chicago Press.

Segovia Mora, Guillermo. 1994. *La violencia en Santafé de Bogotá.* Bogotá: Ecoe
Ediciones.

Seidler, Víctor J. 2000. *La sinrazón masculina, masculinidad y teoría social.* University
Program on Gender Studies, Higher Research and Study Center in
Social Anthropology, Universidad Nacional Autónoma de México,
Editorial Paidós.

Sen, Amartya. 1989. *Development as Freedom.* New York: Knopf.

Sen, G., and S. Batliwala. 2000. "Empowering Women for Reproductive Rights."
In *Women's Empowerment and Demographic Processes*, ed. Harriet B. Presser
and Gita Sen, Oxford, U.K.: Oxford University Press.

Senderowitz, J. 2000. "A Review of Program Approaches to Adolescent
Reproductive Health." *USAID Poptech Assignment* 2000: 176.

Servicio Nacional de la Mujer (Sernam). 1996. "Transformaciones en la familia con motivo de la incorporación de la mujer en el trabajo." Working Paper 49, Sernam, Santiago, Chile.

———. 1998. "Familia y reparto de responsabilidades." Documento 58, Sernam, Santiago, Chile.

Shaw, M., and L. Tschiwula. 2002. "Developing Citizenship among Urban Youth in Conflict with the Law." Paper commissioned by the Safer Cities Program of UN-HABITAT. *Environment and Urbanization* 14 (2): 59–69.

Shaw, M., J. van Dijk, and W. Rhomberg. 2003. *Determining Trends in Global Crime and Justice: An Overview of Results from the United Nations Surveys of Crime Trends and Operations of Criminal Justice Systems.* Vienna: UN Office on Drugs and Crime.

Shkolnikov, V. M., M. G. Field, and E. M. Andreev. 2001. "Russia: Socioeconomic Dimensions of the Gender Gap in Mortality." In *Challenging Inequities in Health: From Ethics to Action,* ed. T. Evans, M. Whitehead, F. Diderichsen, A. Bhuiya, and M. Wirth, 139–55. Oxford, U.K.: Oxford University Press.

Shoumatoff, Alex. 1988. *African Madness.* New York: Alfred A. Knopf.

Shrader, Elizabeth. 2001. "Methodologies to Measure the Gender Dimensions of Crime and Violence." World Bank Policy Research Working Paper 2648, World Bank, Washington, DC.

Silberschmidt, M. 2001. "Disempowerment of Men in Rural and Urban East Africa: Implications for Male Identity, Sexuality and Sexual Behaviour." *World Development* 29 (4): 657–71.

Silberschmidt, M. 2005. "Poverty, Male Disempowerment, and Male Sexuality: Rethinking Men and Masculinities in Rural and Urban East Africa." In *African Maculinities. Men in the Late Nineteenth Century to the Present,* ed. Ouzgane, Lahoucine, and Robert Morrell. Scottsdale, South Africa: University of KwaZulu-Natal Press.

Silberschmidt, M., and V. Rasch. 2001. "Adolescent Girls, Illegal Abortions and 'Sugar Daddies.'" *Social Science and Medicine* 52: 1815–826.

Simey, T. S. 1946. *Welfare and Planning in the West Indies.* London: Oxford University Press.

Singh, Susheela, Deirdre Wulf, Renee Samara, and Yvette P. Cuca. 2000. "Gender Differences in the Timing of First Intercourse: Data from 14 Countries." *International Family Planning Perspectives* 26 (1): 21–28.

Single, Eric, Lynda Robson, and Jurgen Rehm. 1999. "Morbidity and Mortality Attributable to Alcohol, Tobacco, and Illicit Drug Use in Canada." *American Journal of Public Health* 89 (3): 385–90.

Smith, Raymond. 1956. *The Negro Family in British Guiana.* London: Routledge and Kegan Paul.

Smith, Sue. 2001. "Tackling Male Exclusion in Post-Industrialized Settings: Lessons from the UK." In *Men's Involvement in Gender and Development Policy and Practice: Beyond Rhetoric,* ed. Caroline Sweetman, 56–58. Oxford, U.K.: Oxfam.

Social Science and Reproductive Health Research Network. 2001. "Gender Socialization and Male Responsibility in the Family: A Comparative Analysis of Three Socio-Cultural Groups in Nigeria." *Annals of the Social Science Academy of Nigeria* (13): 99–108.

Sommers, Marc. 1995. "A New African World: Rwandan and Other African Youths." *Global Justice* 1 (3): 69–74.

———. 1998. "A Child's Nightmare: Burundian Children at Risk," Women's Commission for Refugee Women and Children, New York.

———. 2001a. *Fear in Bongoland: Burundi Refugees in Urban Tanzania.* New York and Oxford: Berghahn Books.

———. 2001b. "Peace Education and Refugee Youth." EPAU Working Paper, UNHCR, Geneva.

———. 2001c. "Young, Male and Pentecostal: Urban Refugees in Dar Es Salaam, Tanzania." *Journal of Refugee Studies* 14 (4): 347–70.

———. 2001d *Youth: Care and Protection of Children in Emergencies: A Field Guide.* Save the Children USA. http://www.ineesite.org/assess/field_guide_sommers.pdf

———. 2002. *Youth: Care & Protection of Children in Emergencies: A Field Guide.* Washington, DC: Children in Crisis Unit, Save the Children.

———. 2003. *Urbanization, War, and Africa's Youth at Risk: Towards Understanding and Addressing Future Challenges.* Washington, DC: Basic Education and Policy Support (BEPS) Activity and Creative Associates International. http://www.beps.net/publications/BEPS-UrbanizationWarYouthat Risk-.pdf

———. 2005. "It Always Rains in the Same Place First: Geographic Favoritism in Rural Burundi." Africa Program Issue Briefing 1 (July). Washington, DC: Woodrow Wilson International Center for Scholars. http://www.wilsoncenter. org/topics/docs/IB001.pdf

———. 2006. "In the Shadow of Genocide: Rwanda's Youth Challenge." In *Troublemakers or Peacemakers? Youth and Post-Accord Peacebuilding*, ed. Siobhán McEvoy-Levy. South Bend, IN: University of Notre Dame Press.

Sommers, Marc, and Liz McClintock. 2003. "On Hidden Ground: One Coexistence Strategy in Central Africa." In *Imagine Coexistence: Restoring Humanity after Violent Ethnic Conflict*, ed. Antonia Chayes and Martha Minow. San Francisco, CA: Jossey-Bass.

Souza e Silva, J., and A. Urani. 2002. "Situation of Children in Drug Trafficking: A Rapid Assessment." *Investigating the Worst Forms of Child Labor* 20 (Brazil), International Programme on the Elimination of Child Labour (IPEC) and ILO, Geneva.

Sonenstein, F., K. Leighton, L. L. Duberstein, C. F. Turner, and J. H. Pleck. 1998. "Changes in Sexual Behavior and Condom Use Among Teenaged Males: 1998 to 1995." *American Journal of Public Health* 88 (6): 959–69.

South Africa Police Service Department for Safety and Security. 2004. *Crime Statistics per Category.* http://www.saps.gov.za/statistics/reports/crimestats/2004/_pdf/crimes/Rape.pdf

Stavrou, S., R. Stewart, and A. Stavrou. 2000. *The Reintegration of Child Soldiers and Abducted Children: A Case Study of Palaro and Pabbo, Gulu District, Northern Uganda.* In *ACT Against Child Soldiers in Africa: A Reader,* ed. E. Bennett, V. Gamba, and D. van der Merwe. Pretoria: Institute of Security Studies.

Sternberg, Peter. 2001. "Challenging *Machismo* to Promote Sexual and Reproductive Health: Working with Nicaraguan Men." In *Men's Involvement in Gender and Development Policy and Practice: Beyond Rhetoric,* ed. Caroline Sweetman, 59–67. Oxford, U.K.: Oxfam.

Stycos, J. M., and K. W. Back. 1964. *The Control of Human Fertility in Jamaica.* Ithaca, NY: Cornell University Press.

Swart-Kruger, J., and L. Richter. 1997. "AIDS-Related Knowledge, Attitudes and Behavior among South African Street Youth: Reflections on Power, Sexuality and the Autonomous Self." *Social Science and Medicine* 45 (6): 957–66.

Sweetman, Caroline, ed. 1997. *Men and Masculinity.* Oxford, U.K.: Oxfam.

———. 2001a. "'Sitting on a Rock': Men, Socio-economic Change, and Development Policy in Lesotho." In *Men's Involvement in Gender and Development Policy and Practice: Beyond Rhetoric,* ed. Caroline Sweetman, 71–79. Oxford, U.K.: Oxfam.

———, ed. 2001b. *Men's Involvement in Gender and Development Policy and Practice: Beyond Rhetoric.* Oxford, U.K.: Oxfam.

Takahashi, Miki, and Caroline Cederlof. 2000. "Street Children in Central America: An Overview." Latin America and the Caribbean Region, World Bank, Washington, DC. http://wbln0018.worldbank.org/external/lac/lac.nsf/6dd54801ceee52f2852567d6006ca780/19e661ab7bbb25de852568cf006ad8a8.

Tauchen, H., A. D. Witte, and S. K. Long. 1991. "Domestic Violence: A Nonrandom Affair." *International Economic Review* 32: 491–511.

Taylor, Christopher C. 1999. *Sacrifice as Terror: The Rwandan Genocide of 1994.* New York and Oxford, U.K.: Berg.

Taylor, R. 1991. "Poverty and Adolescent Black Males: The Subculture of Disengagement." In *Adolescence and Poverty: Challenge for the 1990s,* ed. P. Edelman and J. Ladner, 139–63. Washington, DC: Center for National Policy Press.

Tenet, George J. 2002. "Remarks by the Director of Central Intelligence George J. Tenant at the Nixon Center Distinguished Service Award Banquet, December 11, 2002." http://www.usembassy.it/file2002_12/alia/A2121606.htm

Thorup, Cathryn L., and Sheila Kinkade. 2005. *What Works in Youth Engagement in the Balkans.* Baltimore: International Youth Foundation; Skopje: Balkan Children and Youth Foundation.

Tierney, Joseph P., and Jean Baldwin Grossman. 2000. "Making a Difference: An Impact Study of Big Brothers Big Sisters." Philadelphia, PA: Public/Private Ventures. http://www.ppv.org/indexfiles/pubsindex.html.

Tolson, Andrew. 1977. *The Limits of Masculinity*. London: Tavistock Publications.

Tomori, Martina, Bojan Zalar, and Blanka Kores Plesnicar. 2000. "Gender Differences in Psychosocial Risk Factors among Slovenian Adolescents." *Adolescence* 35 (139): 431–43.

Torrey, Barbara Boyle. 1998. "We Need More Research on the Impact of Rapid Urban Growth." *Chronicle of Higher Education* October 23, B6.

Toulis, N. 1990. "The Relationship between Women and Development in Kenya." *Cambridge Anthropology* 14 (2): 69–86.

Townsend, N. 1997. "Men, Migration, and Households in Botswana: An Exploration of Connections Over Time and Space." *Journal of Southern African Studies* 23 (3): 405–20.

Turner, S. 1999. "Angry Young Men in Camps: Gender, Age and Class Relations among Burundian Refugees in Tanzania." Working Paper 9, UNHCR, Geneva.

Ukeje, C. 2001. "Youths, Violence and the Collapse of Public Order in the Niger Delta of Nigeria." *Africa Development* 26 (1&2): 338–66.

UNAIDS. 1999a. "Gender and HIV/AIDS: Taking Stock of Research and Programmes." UNAIDS/99.16E. http://www.unaids.org/publications/documents/human/gender/una99e16.pdf

———. 1999b. *Report on the Global HIV/AIDS Epidemic*. Geneva: UNAIDS. http://www.unaids.org

———. 2000a. *Report on the Global HIV/AIDS Epidemic*. Geneva: UNAIDS. http://www.unaids.org

———. 2000b. *Men and AIDS—A Gendered Approach. World AIDS Campaign*. Geneva: UNAIDS.

———. 2003. *AIDS Epidemic Update*. Geneva: UNAIDS.

———. 2004. *Report on the Global AIDS Epidemic*. Geneva: UNAIDS.

UNDP. 2001. *Human Development Report 2001: Making New Technologies Work for Human Development*. New York and Oxford, U.K.: Oxford University Press.

———. 2002. *Human Development Indicators 2002*. New York: UNDP. http://hdr.undp.org/reports/global/2002/en/indicator

———. 2004. *Human Development Report*. New York: UNDP.

———. 2005a. *Youth and Violent Conflict: Society and Development in Crisis? A Strategic Review with a Special Focus on West Africa*. New York: Bureau of Crisis Prevention and Recovery, UNDP.

———. 2005b. *Linking Industrialisation with Human Development. Fourth Kenya Human Development Report*. Nairobi: UNDP.

UNDP and International Council on National Youth Policy. 2003. Government of Rwanda National Youth Policy: Youth Policy in Rwanda. http://www.ceasurf.org/icnyp/rwanda.doc.

UNESCO. 2002. "Education for All Global Monitoring Report: Is the World on Track?" Montreal: UNESCO Institute for Statistics.

———. 2004. *Global Education Digest*. Paris: UNESCO.

UN-Habitat. 2004. *Strategy Paper on Urban Youth in Africa: A Focus on the Most Vulnerable Groups: A Safer Cities Perspective.* Safer Cities Programme, United Nations Human Settlements Programme.

UNICEF. 1997. *The Role of Men in the Lives of Children: A Study of How Improving Knowledge About Men in Families Helps Strengthen Programming for Children and Women.* New York: UNICEF.

———. 1998. "Avances hacia las metas para las niñas, las adolescentes y las mujeres. Seguimiento de las metas del Acuerdo de Santiago." Bogotá: UNICEF.

———. 2000. "Ending Gender Violence and Reaching Other Goals: What Do Men and Violence Have To Do with It?" UNICEF Workshop Report, UNICEF, New York, March 23–24.

———. 2002a. *Adolescence: A Time that Matters.* New York: UNICEF.

———. 2002b. February 2002. *Working for and with Adolescents—Some UNICEF Examples (Selected Case Studies).* New York: Adolescent Development and Participation Unit. http://www. unicef.org/adolescence/ working_with_and_for_adolescents.pdf

———. 2004. *The State of the World's Children.* New York: UNICEF.

United Nations Population Division. 2000. *World Marriage Patterns.* New York: United Nations.

———. 2002. *World Urbanization Prospects: The 2001 Revision.* New York: United Nations Department of Economic and Social Affairs, Population Division.

United States Conference of Mayors. 2000. "A Status Report on Hunger and Homelessness in America's Cities 2000." Washington, DC.

United States Department of Commerce. 2001. "Total Population in Households and Group Quarters by Sex and Selected Age Groups, for the United States: 2000." Bureau of the Census. http://www.census.gov/ population/www/cen2000/grpqtr.html

United States Department of Education. 2000. *Digest of Education Statistics, 2000.* Washington, DC: National Center for Education Statistics.

United States Department of Health and Human Services (USDHHS). 2001. "Deaths for 358 Selected Causes, by 5-year Age Groups, Race, and Sex: United States." Washington, DC: USDHHS. http://www.cdc.gov/nchs/data/ vs00199table292.pdf

———. 2000. *Health United States—2000.* Washington, DC: USDHHS and National Center for Health Statistics.

United States Department of Justice. 1997. "The Prevalence and Consequences of Child Victimization." In *NIJ Research Preview.* Washington, DC: National Institutes of Justice.

Unsworth, Sue, and Peter Uvin. 2002. "A New Look at Civil Society Support in Rwanda?" Unpublished manuscript.

Urdal, H. 2004. "The Devil in the Demographics: The Effect of Youth Bulges on Domestic Armed Conflict, 1950–2000." Social Development Papers: Conflict Prevention & Reconstruction 14, World Bank, Washington, DC.

Uribe, María Victoria. 1996. *Matar, rematar y contramatar. Las Masacres de la Violencia en el Tolima 1948–1964*. Bogotá: Cinep.

Utas, M. 2005. "Building a Future? The Reintegration and Remarginalization of Youth in Liberia." In *No Peace, No War: An Anthropology of Contemporary Armed Conflicts*, ed. P. Richards. Oxford, U.K.: James Currey.

Uvin, Peter. 1998. *Aiding Violence: The Development Enterprise in Rwanda*. West Hartford: Kumarian Press.

Valdés, T., and E. Gomáriz. 1992. *Mujeres latinoamericanas en cifras*. Santiago, Chile: Instituto de la Mujer España-FLACSO-Chile.

———. 1995. *Mujeres latinoamericanas en cifras. Tomo comparativo*. Santiago, Chile: Instituto de la Mujer España-FLACSO-Chile.

Valdés, T., C. Benavente, and J. Gysling. 2000. *El poder en la pareja, la sexualidad y la reproducción. Mujeres de Santiago*. Santiago de Chile: FLACSO-Chile.

Valdés, Teresa, and José Olavarría. 1998. "Los estudios sobre masculinidades en América Latina: Cuestiones en torno a la agenda internacional." Paper presented at "Participación Masculina en la Salud Sexual y Reproductiva: Nuevos Paradigmas," Oaxaca, Mexico.

Valkonen, T., and F. VanPoppel. 1997. "The Contribution of Smoking to Sex Differences in Life Expectancy—Four Nordic Countries and the Netherlands 1970–1989." *European Journal of Public Health* 7 (3): 302–10.

Van Allen, J. 1997. "'Sitting On a Man': Colonialism and the Lost Political Institutions of Igbo Women." In *Perspectives on Africa: A Reader in Culture, History and Representation*, ed. R. Grinker and C. Steiner. Oxford, U.K.: Blackwell.

Van Rossem J., and D. Meekers. 2000. "An Evaluation of the Effectiveness of Targeted Social Marketing to Promote Adolescent and Young Adult Reproductive Health in Cameroon." *AIDS Education and Prevention* 12 (5): 383–404.

Varga, C. A. 2001. "The Forgotten Fifty Per Cent: A Review of Sexual and Reproductive Health Research and Programs Focused on Boys and Young Men in Sub-Saharan Africa." *African Journal of Reproductive Health* 5 (2): 175–95.

Veale, Angela, and Giorgia Donà. 2003. "Street Children and Political Violence: A Socio-Demographic Analysis of Street Children in Rwanda." *Child Abuse and Neglect* 27: 253–69.

Verhey, B. 2001. "Child Soldiers: Preventing, Demobilizing and Reintegrating." World Bank Africa Region Working Paper 23, World Bank, Washington, DC.

Vernon, R. 1995. "Algunos hallazgos básicos de la investigación operativa sobre vasectomía en América Latina." Paper presented at the "Coloquio

Latinoamericano sobre Varones, Sexualidad y Reproducción," Zacatecas, Mexico, November 17–18.

Vetten, L. 2000. "Invisible Girls and Violent Boys: Gender and Gangs in South Africa." *Development Update* 3 (2).

Vivas, M. 1993. "Del lado de los hombres: Algunas reflexiones en torno a la masculinidad." Tesis licenciatura en etnología, Instituto Nacional de Antropología e Historia (ENAH), Mexico.

Viveros, Mara. 2000. "Paternidades y masculinidades en el contexto colombiano contemporáneo." In *Paternidades en América Latina*, ed. Norma Fuller. Lima: Pontíficia Universidad Católica del Perú.

———. 2002. *De quebradores y cumplidores. Sobre hombres, masculinidades y relaciones de género en Colombia.* Bogotá: Universidad Nacional de Colombia.

Viveros, Mara, José Olavaria, and Norma Fuller. 2001. *Hombres e identidades de género. Investigaciones desde América Latina.* Bogotá: Universidad Nacional de Colombia.

Voyame, Joseph, Richard Friedli, Jean-Pierre Gern, and Anton Keller. 1996. *La Coopération Suisse au Rwanda.* Bern, Switzerland: Département Fédéral des Affaires Etrangères.

Waite, Linda J., and Maggie Gallagher. 2000. *The Case for Marriage: Why Married People are Happier, Healthier, and Better Off Financially.* New York: Doubleday.

Waller, David. 1996. *Rwanda: Which Way Now?* Oxford, U.K.: Oxfam.

Wanjira, K. 1999. "Men Who Have Sex With Men in Kenya." In *Aids and Men Taking Risks or Taking Responsibility?*, ed. M. Foreman. London: PANOS/ZED Books.

Ward, Kathryn. ed. 1990. *Women Workers and Global Restructuring.* Ithaca, NY: ILR.

Watson, B. 1992. *Young Unwed Fathers Pilot Project: Initial Implementation Report.* Philadelphia: Public Private Ventures.

Weiss, R. D., J. Martínez-Raga, M. L. Griffin, S. F. Greenfield, and C. Hufford. 1997. "Gender Differences in Cocaine Dependent Patients: A 6 Month Follow-Up Study." *Drug and Alcohol Dependence* 44 (1): 35–40.

Welzer-Lang, Daniel, ed. 2000. *Nouvelles Approches des Hommes et du Masculin.* Toulouse: Presses Universitaires du Mirail.

Westermeyer, Joseph, and Amy E. Boedicker. 2000. "Course, Severity, and Treatment of Substance Abuse among Women versus Men." *American Journal of Drug and Alcohol Abuse* 26 (4): 523–35.

White, Sarah C. 1997. "Men, Masculinities, and the Politics of Development." In *Men and Masculinity*, ed. Caroline Sweetman, 14–22. Oxford, U.K.: Oxfam.

WHO (World Health Organization). 1998. "Gender and Health." WHO Technical Paper WHO/FRH/WHD/98.16., WHO, Geneva.

———. 2000a. "Working with Adolescent Boys: Programme Experiences." WHO/FCH/CAH/00.10, WHO, Geneva.

———. 2000b. *What About Boys? A Literature Review on the Health and Development of Adolescent Boys.* Geneva: WHO.

————. 2000c. "Consultation of Program Experiences Working with Adolescent Boys in Health Promotion." Unpublished manuscript, WHO, Geneva.

————. 2003. "Integrating Gender into HIV/AIDS Programmes." Review Paper, WHO, Geneva.

————. 2004. *World Health Report*. Geneva: WHO.

WHO/UNAIDS. 2001. *The Health and Development of African Male Adolescents and Young Men*. Geneva: WHO.

Wilkinson, Clive. 1987. "Women, Migration and Work in Lesotho." In *Geography of Gender in the Third World*, ed. Janet Henshall Momsen and Janet G. Townsend, 225–39. Albany, NY: State University of New York.

Wilson, Peter. 1973. *Crab Antics: The Social Anthropology of English—Speaking Negro Societies of the Caribbean*. New Haven, CT: Yale University Press.

Wilson, W. J. 1996. *When Work Disappears: The World of the New Urban Poor*. New York: Vintage Books.

Women's Commission for Refugee Women and Children. 2001. *Against all Odds: Surviving the War on Adolescents. Promoting the Protection and Capacity of Ugandan and Sudanese Adolescents in Northern Uganda*. New York: Women's Commission for Refugee Women and Children.

Wood, K., and R. Jewkes. 1997. "Violence, Rape, and Sexual Coercion: Everyday Love in a South African Township." *Gender and Development* 5 (2): 41–46.

————. 2001. "Dangerous Love: Reflections on Violence among Xhosa Township Youth." In *Changing Men in Southern Africa*, ed. R. Morrell. Natal, South Africa: University of Natal Press/Zed Books.

World Bank. 1996. *Report on Human Development in Brazil*. Washington, DC: World Bank.

————. 1997. "Crime and Violence as Development Issues in Latin America and the Caribbean." Paper prepared for the conference on "Urban Crime and Violence," Rio de Janeiro, March 2–4.

————. 2000a. "Exploring the Implications of the HIV/AIDS Epidemic for Educational Planning in Selected African Countries: The Demographic Question." World Bank, Washington, DC.

————. 2000b. *Can Africa Claim the 21st Century?* Washington, DC: World Bank.

————. 2001a. *Engendering Development: Through Gender Equality in Rights, Resources, and Voice*. Washington, DC: World Bank and Oxford University Press.

————. 2001b. *World Development Indicators*. Washington, DC: World Bank.

————. 2002a. *Integrating Gender into the World Bank's Work: A Strategy for Action*. Washington, DC: World Bank.

————. 2002b. *Estudio del Tema de Genero en Colombia*. Bogotá: World Bank.

————. 2003. *Desafíos y oportunidades para la equidad de género en América Latina y el Caribe*. Washington, DC: World Bank.

————. 2005a. *World Development Indicators*. Washington, DC: World Bank.

————. 2005b. *Empowering People by Transforming Institutions: Social Development in World Bank Operations.* Washington, DC: World Bank.

————. 2005c. "Children & Youth: A Framework for Action 2005." HDNCY 1, World Bank, Washington, DC.

World Bank. 2005d. *Evaluating a Decade of World Bank Gender Policy: 1990–99.* Washington, DC: World Bank.

World Economic Forum. 2005. *Women's Empowerment: Measuring the Global Gender Gap.* Geneva: World Economic Forum.

World Organization Against Torture. 1992. *El Terrorismo de Estado en Colombia.* Brussels: NCOS Editions.

Wyss, B. 1995. "Gender and Economic Support of Jamaican Households: Implications for Children's Living Standards." PhD dissertation, University of Massachusetts, Amherst.

Xaba, T. 2001. "Masculinity and its Malcontents: the Confrontation between Struggle Masculinity and Post-struggle Masculinity." In *Changing Men in Southern Africa*, ed. R. Morrell. Natal, South Africa: University of Natal Press/Zed Books.

Yang, M. S., I. H. Su, J. K. Wen, and Y. C. Ko. 1996. "Prevalence and Related Risk Factors of Betel Quid Chewing by Adolescent Students in Southern Taiwan." *Journal of Oral Pathology & Medicine* 25 (2): 69–71.

Yon, C., O. Jiménez, and R. Valverde. 1998. "Representations of Sexual and Preventive Practices in Relation to STDs and HIV/AIDS among Adolescents in Two Poor Neighborhoods in Lima (Peru): Relationships between Sexual Partners and Gender Representations." Paper presented at the "Seminar on Men, Family Formation and Reproduction," Buenos Aires, May 13–15.

Youth at the United Nations. 2002. "Country Profiles on the Situation of Youth: Rwanda: Statistics on Youth Educational Indicators." http://esa.un.org/socdev/unyin/country3b.asp?countrycode=rw

Zack-Williams, A. B. 1995. *Tributors, Supporters and Merchant Capital: Mining and Under-Development in Sierra Leone.* Aldershot, U.K.: Avebury Press.

Zaluar, A. 1994. "Gangsters and Remote-Control Juvenile Delinquents: Youth and Crime." In *Children in Brazil Today: A Challenge for the Third Millennium,* ed. I. Rizzini, 195–217. Rio de Janeiro: Editora Universitaria Santa Ursula.

Zvetina, Daria. 2000. "Father Care: Redefining Fatherhood in Low-Income Communities." *The Heer Research Center at Erikson Institute* 2 (Fall): 1–16.

Index

informal sector, 90, 126
initiatives. *See* programs
injuries, 110*n*.3
intergenerational tension, 249
    Kenya, 221, 237-238, 243-244*n*.1
    Sub-Saharan Africa, 164-165, 176,
        192*n*.4
    West Africa, 207, 208-209
    women, 192*n*.4
internally displaced persons (IDPs),
    Sub-Saharan Africa, 161
International Youth Foundation, 158*n*.11
intravenous drug users, Sub-Saharan
    Africa, 187
Islamic terrorism, 252

Jamaica
    children, 49-50
    men's role, 91*n*.3
jobs. *See* employment

Kenya
    analytical framework and methodology,
        222-224
    economic growth, 219-220
    livelihood and masculinity, xxiv, 219-244
    study sites, 223
killers, contract, Colombia, 101

labor force, 31, 33-34
    exploitation, 207-209
    female, 19
    flexible arrangements, 34
    participation, 19
    reconfiguration, 18-19
    rural Rwanda, 145
    West Africa, 202-203, 207-209
    women, 34-35, 48, 202-203
labor movements, 31-32
labor structure, 33
    family type and, 31
land. *See* property rights
Latin America
    fatherhood, xxi, 43-72
    gender relations, identity, and
        work-family balance, xx-xxi, 29-42
legislation, 30
    labor laws, 33-34

Liberia, war and postwar reconstruction,
    xxiii-xiv, 195-218
life cycle approach, 65
life expectancy, 7-8
    disability-adjusted, 10
    gender differences, 7-8, 11-15
    quality-adjusted, 9-11
    Rwanda, 147
literacy
    Kenya, 229-230
    Rwanda, 148
    women, 229-230
literature, 2-3
litigation, West Africa, 216, 217*n*.7
livelihood, masculinity and, Kenya, xxiv,
    219-244
losing men, 5

manhood, 252-253, 257
    achieving, 247-248
    discussions, 189
    sexuality and, 168-170
    Sub-Saharan Africa, 160, 168-170
    see also masculinity
marginalization of men, 5, 82, 220, 245
    Caribbean, 86-87
    conflict and, 251
    Kenya, 240-241
    low-income, 124
    Sub-Saharan Africa, 156-157, 190
    youth, 156-157
marriage, 21-22, 75, 247
    Kenya, 226-227
    Sub-Saharan Africa, 176-177
    wealth and, 203-204
    West Africa, 202-204, 206-207, 213-214,
        216, 217*n*.6
    see also bride wealth
masculinity, 5-6, 38, 45-46, 131
    Caribbean, 89-90
    Colombia, xxi-xxii, 93-110
    development and, 253
    discussion, 26, 189
    hegemonic, 245-248
    initiatives, 106-108, 109, 110*n*.6
    Kenya, xxiv, 219-244
    refugee camps, 177
    research, 191

www.ingramcontent.com/pod-product-compliance
Lightning Source LLC
Chambersburg PA
CBHW071835270326
41929CB00013B/2002